KEYWORDS IN REMIX STUDIES

Keywords in Remix Studies consists of 24 chapters authored by researchers who share interests in remix studies and remix culture throughout the arts and humanities. The essays reflect on the critical, historical and theoretical lineage of remix to the technological production that makes contemporary forms of communication and creativity possible. Remix enjoys international attention as it continues to become a paradigm of reference across many disciplines, due in part to its interdisciplinary nature as an unexpectedly fragmented approach and method useful in various fields to expand specific research interests. The focus on a specific keyword for each essay enables contributors to expose culture and society's inconclusive relation with the creative process, and questions assumptions about authorship, plagiarism and originality. *Keywords in Remix Studies* is a resource for scholars, including researchers, practitioners, lecturers and students, interested in some or all aspects of remix studies. It can be a reference manual and introductory resource, as well as a teaching tool across the humanities and social sciences.

Contributors: Janneke Adema, Patricia Aufderheide, Thomas J Billard, Dahlia Borsche, xtine burrough, Samantha Close, Francesca Coppa, Frank Dufour, Yomna Elsayed, Pau Figueres, Michele C. Forelle, Owen Gallagher, David J. Gunkel, Nate Harrison, T Storm Heter, Henry Jenkins, Akane Kanai, Karen Keifer-Boyd, Christine Liao, Rogelio Lopez, Annette N. Markham, Paul D. Miller aka DJ Spooky, Eduardo Navas, Mark Nunes, Richard Rinehart, Aram Sinnreich, Rebecca Tushnet, John Vallier, Joshua Wille, Emilia Yang

Eduardo Navas is the author of *Remix Theory: The Aesthetics of Sampling* (2012) and *Spate: A Navigational Theory of Networks* (2016). He is co-editor of *The Routledge*

Companion to Remix Studies (2015). He currently researches and teaches principles of cultural analytics and digital humanities in the School of Visual Arts at Pennsylvania State University. He is Research Faculty in the College of Arts and Architecture's Arts & Design Research Incubator (ADRI), and a Center for Humanities and Information Research Fellow (CHI) also at Pennsylvania State University.

Owen Gallagher is a lecturer of Web Media at Bahrain Polytechnic, specializing in graphic design, filmmaking, animation and interactive media. He received his Ph.D. in Visual Culture from the National College of Art and Design (NCAD) and has published a number of book chapters and journal articles on remix culture, intellectual property and visual semiotics, as well as presenting his research internationally. Gallagher is co-editor of *The Routledge Companion to Remix Studies* (2015) and maintains a number of websites including totalrecut.com, an online community archive of remix videos, and criticalremix.com, an outlet for ongoing remix-related research.

xtine burrough makes participatory projects for networked publics. burrough is co-editor of *The Routledge Companion to Remix Studies* (2015), author of *Foundations of Digital Art and Design* (2013) and editor of *Net Works: Case Studies in Web Art and Design* (2011). She is editor of *The Visual Communication Quarterly*. An associate professor in the School of Arts, Technology, and Emerging Communication at the University of Texas at Dallas, burrough co-directs the Social Practice & Community Engagement (SP&CE) Media Lab and LabSynthE, a laboratory for the creative investigation of synthetic and electronic poetry.

KEYWORDS IN REMIX STUDIES

Edited by
Eduardo Navas, Owen Gallagher
and xtine burrough

NEW YORK AND LONDON

First published 2018
by Routledge
711 Third Avenue, New York, NY 10017

and by Routledge
2 Park Square, Milton Park, Abingdon, Oxon OX14 4RN

Routledge is an imprint of the Taylor & Francis Group, an informa business

© 2018 Taylor & Francis

The rights of Eduardo Navas, Owen Gallagher and xtine burrough to be identified as the authors of the editorial material, and of the authors for their individual chapters, has been asserted in accordance with sections 77 and 78 of the Copyright, Designs and Patents Act 1988.

All rights reserved. No part of this book may be reprinted or reproduced or utilised in any form or by any electronic, mechanical, or other means, now known or hereafter invented, including photocopying and recording, or in any information storage or retrieval system, without permission in writing from the publishers.

Trademark notice: Product or corporate names may be trademarks or registered trademarks, and are used only for identification and explanation without intent to infringe.

Library of Congress Cataloging-in-Publication Data
Names: Navas, Eduardo, editor. | Gallagher, Owen, editor. | burrough, xtine, editor.
Title: Keywords in remix studies / edited by Eduardo Navas, Owen Gallagher, and xtine burrough.
Description: New York : Routledge, 2018. | Includes bibliographical references and index.
Identifiers: LCCN 2017021980| ISBN 9781138699632 (hardcover) | ISBN 9781138699649 (softcover) | ISBN 9781315516417 (ebook)
Subjects: LCSH: Appropriation (Arts) | Appropriation (Arts)—Terminology. | Remix—History and criticism. | Remix—Terminology.
Classification: LCC NX197 .K49 2018 | DDC 700—dc23
LC record available at https://lccn.loc.gov/2017021980

ISBN: 978-1-138-69963-2 (hbk)
ISBN: 978-1-138-69964-9 (pbk)
ISBN: 978-1-315-51641-7 (ebk)

Typeset in Bembo
by Florence Production Ltd, Stoodleigh, Devon, UK

 Printed in the United Kingdom by Henry Ling Limited

CONTENTS

Acknowledgements viii
List of Figures x
Notes on Contributors xiii

   Introduction 1
   Eduardo Navas, Owen Gallagher and xtine burrough

1 Appropriation 14
   Authored in Collaboration with Contributors

2 Archive 23
   Richard Rinehart

3 Authorship 33
   John Vallier

4 Bricolage 43
   Annette N. Markham

5 Collaborative 56
   Aram Sinnreich

6 Consumerism 67
   Pau Figueres

7	Copyright/Fair Use Patricia Aufderheide	83
8	Creativity xtine burrough and Frank Dufour	92
9	Cut-up Janneke Adema	104
10	Deconstruction David J. Gunkel	115
11	DIY Culture Akane Kanai	125
12	Fan Culture Joshua Wille	135
13	Feminism Karen Keifer-Boyd and Christine Liao	147
14	Intellectual Property Nate Harrison	158
15	Jazz T Storm Heter	168
16	Location Dahlia Borsche, translated by Jill Denton	178
17	Mashup Nate Harrison and Eduardo Navas	188
18	Memes Authored in Collaboration with Contributors	202
19	Parody Mark Nunes	217
20	Participatory Politics Henry Jenkins and Thomas J Billard, with Samantha Close, Yomna Elsayed, Michelle C. Forelle, Rogelio Lopez, and Emilia Yang	230

21	Remix *Eduardo Navas*	246
22	Sampling *Owen Gallagher*	259
23	Transformative *Francesca Coppa and Rebecca Tushnet*	273
24	Versioning *Paul D. Miller aka DJ Spooky*	283

Index *293*

ACKNOWLEDGEMENTS

This book would not have been possible without the support of many individuals who unselfishly collaborated with us. First, we would like to thank all of the contributors who accepted our invitation to write essays on selected keywords. Their willingness to go through a long editing process makes more than evident their commitment to each of their respective fields of research. We also thank our editor at Routledge, Erica Wetter, for considering our proposal for a *Keywords* text, and the editorial board at Routledge for finding potential in a second anthology on Remix Studies. We also thank Mia Moran, Assistant Editor at Routledge, who oversaw the book's process during its early stages, reviewed it and prepared it for its final production. We thank the remix community, who, as before, generously participated in a survey, which we distributed during the proposal stage of this project, asking about particular terms they found were relevant in remix studies. Their responses were vital in our selections of keywords for this publication.

Eduardo Navas, Owen Gallagher and xtine burrough

I would not have been able to complete this project without the support of colleagues, friends, and family. First, I must thank xtine and Owen for being great colleagues. I have truly enjoyed our continued collaborations and look forward to more. I thank Graeme Sullivan, Director of the School of Visual Arts at Pennsylvania State University, for his ongoing support in all aspects of my teaching and research. I especially thank him for supporting my application for a Spring 2017 Fellowship at the Center for Humanities and Information (CHI) in the College of Liberal Arts, which provided me with the needed time to finish this and other projects. I thank Eric Hayot, CHI Director, and John Russell, CHI Co-Director, who supported my fellowship and created a vibrant environment for fellows to discuss work in progress. I thank Andrew Belser, Director of the Arts & Design Research Incubator (ADRI) for supporting my ongoing research, and creating a strong interdisciplinary community. I also thank Andrew Schulz, Associate Dean for Research, and Barbara Korner, Dean of the College of Arts and Architecture for supporting all of my activities in the School of Visual Arts. I thank my family, especially my wife and partner, Annie Mendoza, who is always unselfish and supportive of all that I do. And I thank my two sons Oscar Eduardo and Oliver Antonio who continue to amaze me, and successfully remind me about what is ultimately important in life.

Eduardo Navas

I would like to thank my co-editors and long-time collaborators, Eduardo and xtine, for their ongoing diligence and high standards and for always being a pleasure to work with. I would also like to express my appreciation to our growing community of colleagues, from this book and the last, who responded to our vision with enthusiasm and gratitude. I look forward to our future collaborations. I thank my parents, Brendan and Frances, for their love and unwavering encouragement in all of my endeavors. I am very grateful to my colleague and friend, Brendan Muller, for supporting my extracurricular activities and my mentor Paul O'Brien for his ongoing guidance and direction. Finally, and most importantly, I want to thank my daughters, Jennifer and Rebecca, and my partner Angela for their understanding, support, love and encouragement during the many times I had to spend away from them working to make this book a reality.

Owen Gallagher

To my husband and partner, Paul Martin Lester, our two sons Parker and Martin, and to my parents Viola and Bill: "thank you" barely captures the essence of my gratitude. Your support, encouragement, wisdom, and silliness sustained me in this project, as it always does. I would also like to fondly acknowledge my peers at The University of Texas at Dallas, as well as my life-long mentors, Christopher James, Steven Kurtz and Humberto Ramirez for their ongoing support . . . and silliness. Eduardo Navas and Owen Gallagher are delightful to work with—in this book and our previous collection—I hope we continue to have opportunities to be grateful together.

xtine burrough

FIGURES

5.1	Prevalence of terms according to Google Ngram, 1870–2008.	61
6.1	Times Square, New York, February 1, 2015. Courtesy of the author.	68
6.2	Shoe store, Bilbao downtown. Courtesy of the author.	73
6.3	Pau Figueres. *Sleeping with the Fish*. Courtesy of the author.	74
6.4	Helmut Smits. *The Real Thing*. Photograph by Ronald Smits. Courtesy of the author.	76
6.5	Superflex. *Flooded McDonald's*. Courtesy of the author.	77
6.6	Cellular screenshot of the Palmer Museum's Nike Swoosh and an Instagram reaction to it. Courtesy of the author.	79
7.1	*Let's Go Crazy* was a YouTube video response project xtine burrough created with students at California State University, Fullerton from 2007 to 2013. For more information, see http://letsgocrazy.info/.	89
8.1	Cory Arcangel, *Drei Klavierstücke op. 11*, 2009. Three YouTube videos, www.coryarcangel.com/things-i-made/2009-003-dreiklavierstucke-op-11.	96
8.2	Norman Bates in front of the Bates Mansion as seen during the *Psycho* section of the Universal Studios Studio Tour in Hollywood. Source: Alfred A. Si on Wikipedia.	97
8.3	Jonathan McIntosh, "Donald Duck Meets Glenn Beck in Right Wing Radio Duck," 2010. Political remix on YouTube, http://popculturedetective.agency/2010/right-wing-radio-duck-donald-discovers-glenn-beck.	99
8.4	Megan MacKay, "Ray Rice Inspired Makeup Tutorial," 2014. YouTube makeup tutorial, https://youtube/zyNa9kqq8mk.	100

11.1	Screenshot of Candice Breitz's work on Vimeo.	127
12.1	Screenshot of "*Man of Tomorrow*—Trailer 2" by YouTube user JobWillins.	135
12.2	Screenshot of *The Phantom Edit*, a recut of *Star Wars Episode I: The Phantom Menace* by Mike J. Nichols on YouTube.	138
13.1	Screenshot of Regender.com.	152
17.1	nGrams showing the words "mashup" and "mash up" in print. Note that some of the material found online in the 1960s are actually scans of publications from previous years.	189
17.2	"Mash Down" by the Roots, 1977.	190
17.3	Negativland, "U2," EP released in 1991.	191
17.4	Danger Mouse, *The Grey Album*, released in 2004.	192
17.5	Eclectic Method, screen shot from "Eclectic Method—A Brief History of Sampling."	195
18.1	Princess Leia as an icon of the Women's Marches, 2017.	203
18.2	Karen Treat Keifer-Boyd wearing the pussyhat at the Women's March in 2017.	204
18.3	The Koi Dance (Love Dance) as an online video meme.	205
18.4	"Smoking in the boys' room" becomes "Vaping in the gender neutral bathroom" in this meme critical of the status quo.	205
18.5	La Paz Dancing Zebra Meme, available on green screen for global remix opportunities.	206
18.6	The *Civil War* meme provides fans a platform for generating new arguments between characters.	207
18.7	Postcard from the cover of Jacques Derrida's *La Carta Postale*.	208
18.8	Mandy Patinkin as Inigo Montoya from *The Princess Bride* reimagined as a meme for his often cited quote, "You keep using that word. I do not think it means what you think it means."	209
18.9	Original film still from *Øystein og jeg* on Norwegian Broadcasting (NRK) in 2001, with Øystein Backe (helper) and Rune Gokstad (desperate monk). Written by Knut Nærum.	210
18.10	A parody meme created with footage from *Downfall*.	211
18.11	*Dumb and Dumber*.	211
18.12	*You on Kazoo* meme screenshots from the YouTube video.	212
18.13	"Never Gonna Give You Up" YouTube video for Rick Astley's 1987 pop-single.	213
18.14	René Magritte's *The Treachery of Images* is appropriated into a meme.	213
18.15	Jennifer Lawrence meme as representation of identity.	214
18.16	Imminent Ned meme used as an announcement for an upcoming fan edit.	215

xii Figures

19.1	Robert Ryang's remix of clips from *The Shining* transforms the horror/thriller film into a father/son buddy pic: "I'm your new foster father . . . I'd do *anything* for you."	219
19.2	Phil de Vellis's "Vote Different" replaces Big Brother with Hillary Clinton, creating political parody through dialogic recontextualization.	221
19.3	"I love doing the raping." Bombs Away documents its ambiguously political remix of a pre-existing parody remix, transforming parodic commentary into a lyrical refrain.	224
19.4	Simpsonwave and other pastiche remixes maintain an ambivalent relation to sampled sources, making it difficult to distinguish parodic and authentic citations.	226
20.1	Screenshot from "Winter is Trumping."	231
20.2	Screenshot from "Drunk Trump 1: Your Drunk Neighbor: Donald Trump."	234
20.3	No-nosed Trump meme.	235
20.4	Screenshot of "Donald Trump in *Mean Girls*."	236
20.5	Sample Bernie vs. Trump meme.	237
20.6	Screenshot of the title image from "Sanders (Bernie Sanders + Hamilton)."	239
20.7	Birdman slaps Trump.	240
20.8	Censored Trump and Pence logo.	241
20.9	Trump/Putin logo.	242
22.1	Screenshot of "Be in the moment" scene from *The Get Down* (2016) featuring Grandmaster Flash teaching the fundamentals of turntablism to his followers (www.youtube.com/watch?v=fo2Hqz0vamU).	264
22.2	Screenshot from *A Glorious Dawn* (2009), with Carl Sagan "singing" about science (www.youtube.com/watch?v=zSgiXGELjbc).	267
22.3	Screenshot from "How Sampling Transformed Music" (2014), depicting Mark Ronson remixing previous TED talks live in front of an audience.	269

NOTES ON CONTRIBUTORS

Janneke Adema is a Research Fellow at the Centre for Disruptive Media at Coventry University (UK). She is the co-editor of two books, *Really, We're Helping to Build This . . . Business: The Academia.edu Files* (Open Humanities Press, 2016) co-edited with Gary Hall and *Symbiosis* (Open Humanities Press, 2011) co-edited with Pete Woodbridge. She has co-edited special issues of *The Journal of Electronic Publishing* and *The Journal of Media Practice* and has published in *New Formations, The International Journal of Cultural Studies, New Media & Society, The Journal of Media Practice, New Review of Academic Librarianship, The Journal of Electronic Publishing, Krisis: Journal for Contemporary Philosophy*, and *LOGOS: The Journal of the World Book Community*. Her research focuses on experimental publishing, the material-discursive practices of scholarly research and communication, book history, media studies, critical theory, remix and radical open access. She blogs at https://openreflections.wordpress.com.

Patricia Aufderheide is University Professor in the School of Communication at American University, and the author of, among others, *Documentary Film: A Very Short Introduction*, and the co-author, with Peter Jaszi, of *Reclaiming Fair Use: How to Put Balance Back in Copyright*. The founder of the Center for Media & Social Impact at American University, she runs the Fair Use and Free Speech program there. Aufderheide has received Fulbright and Guggenheim awards. She has received numerous journalism and scholarly awards, including the Preservation and Scholarship award in 2006 from the International Documentary Association, a career achievement award in 2008 from the International Digital Media and Arts Association, the Woman of Vision Award from Women in Film and Video (DC) in 2010, and the George S. Stoney Documentary award from the University Film and Video Association in 2015. Aufderheide serves on the board of directors of the Independent Television Service, which produces innovative television programming for underserved audiences under the umbrella of the Corporation for Public Broadcasting.

Thomas J Billard conducts research on transgender coverage in political media, transgender representations in mass media, graphic design in brand culture, and processes of production and encoding in graphic design. He holds a BA in political communication from the George Washington University and is currently a doctoral student in the Annenberg School for Communication and Journalism at the University of Southern California.

Dahlia Borsche is research associate at Humboldt-University's Trans-Cultural Musicology department in Berlin. Before this she worked and lectured at the universities in Cologne and Klagenfurt (Austria) as well as at Free University Berlin. Besides her academic career, she is co-curator of CTM-Festival's discourse program (Berlin) and was active as a curator, promoter and DJane for many years. Her main research interests concern questions of contemporary popular and transcultural music processes and practices, thereby expanding traditional discipline boundaries to the fields of sound, media and cultural studies.

xtine burrough makes participatory projects for networked publics. Her recent work recovers feminist texts through mediation and reimagines virtual crowd workers as bodies with agency. Using social platforms, databases, search engines, blogs and applications in combination with popular sites like Facebook, YouTube or Mechanical Turk, she creates web communities promoting interpretation and autonomy. burrough is passionate about using digital tools to translate common experiences into personal arenas for discovery. Emergent themes in her work include culture jamming, remix, appropriation and translation. burrough has written, edited and co-edited several books including *The Routledge Companion to Remix Studies* (2015), *Foundations of Digital Art and Design* (2013) and *Net Works: Case Studies in Web Art and Design* (2011). She is Editor of *The Visual Communication Quarterly*. An associate professor in the School of Arts, Technology, and Emerging Communication at the University of Texas at Dallas, burrough co-directs the Social Practice & Community Engagement (SP&CE) Media Lab with Drs. Olivia Banner and Kim Knight. She co-organizes LabSynthE, a laboratory for the creative investigation of synthetic and electronic poetry with Dr. Frank Dufour, and she is an Advisory Board Member of the Feminist Research Collective.

Samantha Close, Yomna Elsayed, Michele C. Forelle, Rogelio Lopez and Emilia Yang are Ph.D. Students at the University of Southern California and members of the Civic Paths Research Group, which explores continuities between online participatory culture and civic engagement through outreach, creative work and academic inquiry. The team is currently working on *Popular Culture and the Civic Imagination: A Casebook*.

Francesca Coppa is a professor of English at Muhlenberg College and a founding member of the Organization for Transformative Works, a non-profit established by fans to provide access to and to preserve the history of fanworks and culture. Her collection of transformative tales, *The Fanfiction Reader: Folk Tales for the Digital Age* (2017) was just published by the University of Michigan Press and she is currently writing a book about fan vidding.

Frank Dufour is a professor in the school of Arts, Technology, and Emerging Communication at the University of Texas at Dallas where he teaches sound design and aesthetics of interactive arts. His research is primarily dedicated to the perception of sound and music from a phenomenological perspective. Frank Dufour is a member of the laboratory Musique et Informatique de Marseille (MIM) in which he works on the use of the system of the Temporal Semiotic Units to develop visualizations of music and create inter-semiotic translations. In the school of ATEC, Frank Dufour is one of the founders of LabSynthE (Laboratory of Synthetic and Electronic Poetry), dedicated to the study and practice of poetry in the context of digital technologies. As an artist, he works with the independent art laboratory, Agence5970 on interactive audiovisual installations. http://agence5970.com/frank-dufour and www.utdallas.edu/atec/artstechnology/dufour.

Pau Figueres is a visual artist and researcher. The main concern in his work deals with the effects of late capitalism, hyper-consumerism and commercial brand remix issues. He completed a BBA with a major in Marketing at Coventry Business School, UK (1998) and a BFA and a MFA at EHU/UPV University of the Basque Country Art School (2012), where he is a PHD candidate. He worked as a graphic designer for Siemens in Genova, Italy previous to his career as an artist. He has exhibited his work internationally and his most important exhibitions include group exhibitions at Guggenheim Bilbao and Artium Vitoria. He was a Visiting Scholar at Penn State Sova (2015) where he developed his work entitled *Aesthetics of Hyper-Consumerism: Commercial Brands as Resource in Contemporary Art* and *The Revolution Will Be Sponsored* (https://larevolucionserapatrocinada.wordpress.com). He has worked as lecturer and researcher at the department of sculpture of EHU/UPV University of the Basque Country Art School. More at www.paufigueres.es.

Owen Gallagher is a lecturer of Web Media at Bahrain Polytechnic, specializing in graphic and web design, filmmaking and sound design, 2D and 3D animation, VFX, game design and interactive media. He received his Ph.D. in Visual Culture from the National College of Art and Design (NCAD), a Master's in Design Communication from the University of Ulster and a Bachelor of Design in Digital Media from LYIT. He is a co-editor of the *Routledge Companion to*

Remix Studies (2015) and has published a number of book chapters and journal articles on remix culture, intellectual property and visual semiotics, as well as presenting his research at numerous international conferences. He has published a number of widely circulated remix videos online and is particularly concerned with the role of copyright in the digital age and its effect on remix creativity. Gallagher is a musician and songwriter and has played in a variety of bands over the past two decades, as well as producing and publishing both original and remixed music. He maintains a number of websites including totalrecut.com, an online community archive of remix videos; remixstudies.org, an archive of remix theory and praxis seminars; and criticalremix.com, a blog and resource for his ongoing remix-related research.

David J. Gunkel is an award-winning educator and scholar, specializing in the philosophy of technology with a particular focus on information and communication technology. He is the author of more than 50 scholarly articles published in journals of communication, philosophy, interdisciplinary humanities and computer science. He has published seven books—*Hacking Cyberspace* (Westview Press, 2001), *Thinking Otherwise: Philosophy, Communication, Technology* (Purdue University Press, 2007), *Transgression 2.0: Media, Culture and the Politics of a Digital Age* (Continuum, 2011), *The Machine Question: Critical Perspectives on AI, Robots, and Ethics* (MIT Press, 2012), *Heidegger and Media* (Polity, 2014), *Of Remixology: Ethics and Aesthetics After Remix* (MIT Press, 2016) and *The Changing Face of Alterity: Communication, Technology and Other Subjects* (Rowman & Littlefield, 2016). He has lectured and delivered award-winning papers throughout North and South America and Europe and is the founding co-editor of the *International Journal of Žižek Studies* and the Indiana University Press book series Digital Game Studies. Dr. Gunkel currently holds the position of Presidential Teaching Professor in the Department of Communication at Northern Illinois University. His teaching has been recognized with numerous awards, including NIU's Excellence in Undergraduate Teaching Award in 2006 and the Presidential Teaching Professorship in 2009.

Nate Harrison is an artist and writer working at the intersection of intellectual property, cultural production and the formation of creative processes in modern media. His work has been exhibited at the American Museum of Natural History, the Whitney Museum of American Art, the Centre Pompidou, the Los Angeles County Museum of Art, and the Kunstverein in Hamburg, among others. Harrison has several publications current and forthcoming, and has also lectured at a variety of institutions, including Experience Music Project, Seattle; the Art and Law Program, New York; and SOMA Summer, Mexico City. From 2004 to 2008 he co-directed the Los Angeles project space Esthetics as a Second Language. Harrison is the recipient of the Videonale Prize as well as the Hannah Arendt Prize in Critical Theory and Creative Research. Harrison earned his doctorate from the University of California, San Diego's Art and Media History, Theory and Practice Program. He also received a Bachelor of Fine Arts from the University of Michigan and a Master of Fine Arts from California Institute of the Arts. Harrison serves on the faculty at the School of the Museum of Fine Arts at Tufts University, and lives in Brooklyn, New York.

T Storm Heter teaches philosophy at East Stroudsburg University, where he also directs the Frederick Douglass Institute for Intercultural Studies and the Diversity Dialogue Project. He writes primarily about existentialism and race, and is the author of *Sartre's Ethics of Engagement: Authenticity and Civic Virtue* (Continuum, 2006). His current work focuses on jazz, race and critical listening practices. He is currently completing a manuscript titled *Clogged Up Ears: Jazz and Creolized Listening* that explores discourses of racial authenticity in American jazz cultures. Heter is also a jazz drummer, who currently performs with the East Stroudsburg University Jazz Big Band Ensemble, under the direction of Matt Vashlishan.

Henry Jenkins is the Provost's Professor of Communication, Journalism, Cinematic Arts and Education at the University of Southern California and the founder and former co-director of the MIT Comparative Media Studies Program. His books include *Textual Poachers: Television Fans and Participatory Culture*, *Convergence Culture: Where Old and New Media Collide*, *Participatory Culture in a Networked Era* and *By Any Media Necessary: The New Youth Activism*.

Akane Kanai is an early career researcher and lecturer in Sociology and Anthropology at the University of Newcastle, Australia, with research interests spanning gender, race and affect in visual, popular and digital cultures. Her recent Ph.D. research has been published in journals such as *Celebrity Studies*, *Social Media and Society*, *Feminist Media Studies*, and the *Journal of Gender Studies*. She is currently working on a monograph for Palgrave Macmillan on youthful femininity, affect and identity in digital spaces.

Karen Keifer-Boyd is Professor of Art Education and Women's, Gender, and Sexuality Studies at Pennsylvania State University, and 2012 Fulbright Distinguished Chair in Gender Studies at Alpen-Adria-Universität Klagenfurt, Austria. Her writings on feminist pedagogy, visual culture, inclusion, cyberart activism, transcultural dialogues, action research and social justice arts-based research are in more than 50 peer-reviewed research publications and have been translated into several languages. She co-authored three books: *Including Difference* (NAEA, 2013). *InCITE, InSIGHT, InSITE* (NAEA, 2008) and *Engaging Visual Culture* (Davis, 2007); and co-edited *Real-World Readings in Art Education: Things Your Professors Never Told You* (Falmer, 2000). Keifer-Boyd is co-founder and editor of the international journal *Visual Culture & Gender*.

Christine Liao is an Assistant Professor at the University of North Carolina Wilmington. She teaches arts integration to undergraduates and graduates in the Elementary Education program. Her research areas include media arts, digital performance, theorizing virtual body and identity, exploring interactions between virtual and real, STEAM, technology integration in art education and community art. She has presented in national and international conferences including the National Art Education Association (NAEA), the American Educational Research Association (AERA) and the International Society of Education through Arts (InSEA) and has published in the *Journal of Art Education*, *Visual Culture and Gender*, *Journal of Virtual Worlds Research* and *Visual Arts Research*. She has also authored and co-authored several book chapters published by NAEA, Springer and IGI Global. She is the Managing Editor of *International Journal of Education and the Arts*, Chair of the NAEA Art Education Technology Issues Group from 2013 to 2016, and Web Coordinator of NAEA Women's Caucus. Christine received her Ph.D. in Art Education and minor in Science, Technology, and Society from Penn State University.

Annette N. Markham is MSO Professor of Information Studies at Aarhus University in Denmark, where she directs a Digital Living MA program and is founding director of the international Future Making Research Consortium, focused on innovative methods and ethics for social research in the digital age. Her ethnographic work studying lived experience of Internet users is well represented in her first book, *Life Online* (Sage, 1998). She has written numerous texts around methodologies that use remix and bricolage as fundamental concepts. Annette earned a doctorate in Communication Studies focusing on organizational culture at Purdue University. More at annettemarkham.com

Paul D. Miller aka DJ Spooky is a composer, multimedia artist and writer. His written work has appeared in *The Village Voice*, *The Source* and *Artforum* among other publications. Miller's work as a media artist has appeared in the Whitney Biennial; the Venice Biennial for Architecture (2000); the Ludwig Museum in Cologne, Germany; Kunsthalle, Vienna; the Andy Warhol Museum in Pittsburgh and many other museums and galleries. His video installation "New York Is Now" was exhibited in the Africa Pavilion of the 52 Venice Biennial 2007, and the Miami/Art Basel fair of 2007. Miller's award-winning book *Rhythm Science* was published by MIT Press in 2004, and was followed by *Sound Unbound*, an anthology of writings on electronic music and digital media, published in 2008. Miller's latest book is *The Book of Ice* (Mark Batty Publisher). Over the course of his career, Miller has collaborated with a vast array of recording artists, ranging from Metallica to Chuck D; from Steve Reich to Yoko Ono. Miller's large-scale, multimedia performance pieces include "Rebirth of a Nation" (now on DVD), and "Terra Nova: Sinfonia Antarctica," which was commissioned by the Brooklyn Academy of Music for the Next Wave Festival 2009.

Eduardo Navas produces art and media projects, critical texts and occasional curatorial projects. He has been a juror for various art organizations including Turbulence.org, Rhizome.org and Terminal Awards. Navas was consultant for Creative Capital (NYC), 2008–2009, and for The Herb Alpert Award in the Arts (LA), 2014–2015. He currently researches and teaches principles of cultural analytics and digital humanities in the School of Visual Arts at Pennsylvania State University. He is an embedded researcher in the College of Arts and Architecture's Art & Design Research Incubator (ADRI), and a 2016–2017 Center for Humanities and Information Research Fellow (CHI) at Penn State. He was a 2010–2012 Postdoctoral Fellow in the Department of Information Science and Media Studies at the University of Bergen, Norway. He is an affiliated researcher at the Software Studies Lab, CUNY (2010-present). Navas is the author of *Remix Theory: The Aesthetics of Sampling* (Springer, 2012) and *Spate: A Navigational Theory of Networks* (INC, 2016). He is co-editor of *The Routledge Companion to Remix Studies* (Routledge, 2015).

Mark Nunes is Professor of Interdisciplinary Studies and Chair for the Department of Cultural, Gender and Global Studies at Appalachian State University. He is author of *Cyberspaces of Everyday Life* (University of Minnesota Press, 2006) and an edited volume entitled *Error: Glitch, Noise, and Jam in New Media Cultures* (Bloomsbury, 2010). His current work explores how social media platforms operate as a context for challenging visual frames of reference for the personal, the political, and the historical. Recent publications include "Selfies, Self-Witnessing and the 'Out-of-Place' Digital Citizen," in *Selfie Citizenship* (ed. Adi Kuntsman, Palgrave, 2017), "Engaging Appalachia: Digital Literacies, Mobile Media, and a Sense of Place" in *Carolinas Communication Annual 31* (2015), and "Ecstatic Updates: Facebook, Identity, and the Fractal Subject" in *New Visualities, New Technologies: The New Ecstasy of Communication* (ed. Hille Koskela and J. Macgregor Wise, Ashgate, 2013).

Richard Rinehart is Director and Chief Curator of the Samek Art Museum at Bucknell University. He has served as Digital Media Director and Adjunct Curator at the UC Berkeley Art Museum and as curator at New Langton Arts and for the San Jose Arts Commission. He juried for the Rockefeller Foundation, Rhizome.org and others. Rinehart has taught courses on art and new media at UC Berkeley, UC Santa Cruz, the San Francisco Art Institute and elsewhere. He served on the boards of the Berkeley Center for New Media, New Langton Arts and the Museum Computer Network. He has lead NEA- and NEH-funded national research projects on new media, art, preservation and museums. He has recently published a book with MIT Press on preserving digital culture, co-authored with Jon Ippolito entitled *Re-Collection: Art, New Media, & Social Memory* (http://re-collection.net).

Aram Sinnreich is an Associate Professor at American University's School of Communication, in the Communication Studies division. Sinnreich's work focuses on the intersection of culture, law and technology, with an emphasis on subjects such as emerging media and music. He is the author of two books, *Mashed Up* (2010), and *The Piracy Crusade* (2013), and has written for publications including the *New York Times*, *Billboard* and *Wired*. Prior to arriving at AU, Sinnreich served as Assistant Professor at Rutgers University's School of Communication and Information, Director at media innovation lab OMD Ignition Factory, Managing Partner of media/tech consultancy Radar Research, Visiting Professor at NYU Steinhardt and Senior Analyst at Jupiter Research. He is also a bassist and composer, and has played with groups and artists including progressive soul collective Brave New Girl, dub-and-bass band Dubistry, and Ari-Up, lead singer of the Slits. Along with co-authors Dunia Best and Todd Nocera, Sinnreich was a finalist in the 2014 John Lennon Songwriting Contest, in the jazz category. Sinnreich holds a Ph.D. in Communication from the University of Southern California, and a Master's in Journalism from Columbia University.

Rebecca Tushnet is a Professor of Law at Harvard. She previously clerked for Associate Justice David H. Souter and taught at NYU and Georgetown. Her work focuses on copyright, trademark and advertising law. With Eric Goldman, she publishes a casebook on advertising and marketing law. She helped found the Organization for Transformative Works, a nonprofit dedicated to supporting and promoting fanworks. Her blog, tushnet.blogspot.com, is one of the top intellectual property blogs, and her writings may be found at tushnet.com. She is also an expert on the law of engagement rings.

John Vallier has been Head of Distributed Media in the University of Washington Libraries since 2006. In this role he collects, preserves and ensures access to a wide range of audio/video/film, including a large collection of Seattle area music. He has taught on a range of topics at UW, such as remix for Cinema and Media Studies, PNW music for the Honors Program, and collection development for the Information School. With Laurel Sercombe he co-taught courses about sound archiving in the School of Music. Vallier has published articles for All Music Guide, European Meetings in Ethnomusicology, Oxford University Press, the Music Library Association, the International Association of Sound and Audiovisual Archives, and others. Before coming to UW, Vallier was the archivist at the UCLA Ethnomusicology Archive, 2002-2006. At UCLA he conceived of community outreach projects—Archiving Filipino American Music in LA (AFAMILA) and Gospel Archiving in LA (GALA)—as well as other grant-funded projects that focused on the preservation and repatriation of ethnographic sound recording collections. At UCLA Vallier also co-taught courses on sound archiving with Anthony Seeger and worked with Lorraine Sakata on the preservation of Central Asian sound archives. As a drummer and percussionist, John has toured with indie-rock bands and performed/recorded original music for records, video games and movie soundtracks.

Joshua Wille is a Ph.D. candidate in Film and Media Studies at the University of Kansas, where his research is focused on fan edits and film revisionism. His writing on the history, theory and practice of fan editing has been published in *Transformative Works and Cultures* and in books such as *Fan Phenomena: James Bond* (Intellect, 2015) and *Fan Phenomena: The Lord of the Rings* (Intellect, 2015). As a fan editor himself, Wille created *Watchmen: Midnight*, which is an alternative version of the film *Watchmen* (2009) that more closely reflects the narrative structure, characterizations and spirit of the original comics by Alan Moore and Dave Gibbons. Wille has delivered research-oriented presentations along with screenings of *Watchmen: Midnight* at fan conventions and academic events in the United States, Germany and the Netherlands.

INTRODUCTION

Eduardo Navas, Owen Gallagher and xtine burrough

Keywords in Remix Studies contributes to research on remixing as a creative form of expression across media and culture. The book's focus on keywords is meant to support the relation of the critical, historical and theoretical lineage of remix to the technological production that makes contemporary forms of communication and creativity possible. Remix, as an activity as well as a scholarly pursuit, enjoys international attention as it continues to become a paradigm of reference across many disciplines. This is in part due to its interdisciplinary nature as an unexpectedly fragmented approach and method, useful in various fields to expand specific research interests. In this sense, *Keywords in Remix Studies* can be considered a follow-up as well as a complementary volume to continue the discussion on themes covered in *The Routledge Companion to Remix Studies* (2015),[1] which we previously edited to develop a cohesive understanding of remix as a cultural and social activity.

In our use of keywords for a publication on remix studies we acknowledge a foundational reference to Raymond Williams's *Keywords: A Vocabulary of Culture and Society*.[2] Williams's book foresaw issues relevant in contemporary fields of research, including the need to organize specialized terms that go beyond basic dictionary definitions for a better understanding of a particular subject of study—in his seminal book, the study was a broad semi-indexical evaluation of the relation of culture to society. Consequently, Williams developed a new interdisciplinary method that could be used by any field of research, whether new or well-established. He makes evident his awareness of such a contribution in the introduction to his *Keywords*. Williams deliberately organized his selection of words with interdisciplinarity in mind, thus creating a book relevant to anyone studying culture and society in any field, from the arts to the social sciences. It is with this interdisciplinary, critical position in mind that we, as editors of *Keywords in*

Remix Studies, considered the selection of keywords for this publication. *Keywords in Remix Studies* offers a specific and intimate focus on remix by placing an emphasis on particular terms that play an important role in the shaping of remix as a practice, as well as a field of study. The book's implementation of keywords connects it with the growing set of anthologies that focus on terms considered important across different fields of research. When developing our approach to the contextualization of material throughout our book we evaluated other keyword publications, such as *Key Words in Religion, Media and Culture* (Routledge, 2008), *Keywords in Sound* (Duke University Press, 2015), and *Keywords for American Cultural Studies* (NYU Press, 2014), among others.[3]

The critical position of *Keywords in Remix Studies*, similarly to our previous publication, is informed by various schools of thought. The chapters are authored by practicing researchers who share constant interests in remix studies and remix culture in direct relation to various fields of research in the humanities. *Keywords in Remix Studies* is relevant to scholars across a range of academic disciplines, including new media studies, visual culture, musicology, art history and theory, design, media, art and technology, art education, cultural studies, communication studies, critical theory, digital humanities and composition studies, among others.

Remix studies is preceded by, and related in terms of practice and production to remix culture, an international movement that began in the late 1990s, which is closely linked to open-source and do-it-yourself (DIY) activities. As an activity, remix derives from the act of remixing music, which hip hop and disco DJs started to perform in the 1970s, initially in New York City. The creative activity of remixing music became a staple of electronic dance music (EDM) through the organization of raves in major cities across the globe. The popularization of remixing in all genres of electronic music sparked a general awareness of the ways people repurpose and recycle all things in life. Remix studies emerged as the reflective paradigm that has grown with the aim to better understand how people have been and continue to be exposed to the effects of remixing and remix culture as more and more individuals participate. Many are not deliberate remixers; however, they share content based on principles of remixing to participate in social media and networked communication. The level of interest in remix therefore is stable and continues to grow over time, as evidenced by the dramatic increase in remix-related content, whether it be texts, videos or music. In academia this is evident in the number of academic conferences, symposia and seminars exploring remix from different disciplinary angles and the widespread adoption of the term to describe everything from music composition to fashion.[4]

At the time of writing, it is generally argued that positive attitudes relating to musical remixes changed how people understand their creative output and its relationship to intellectual property. But, as it happens with all things that reshape people's understanding of the world, the act of remixing inevitably experienced and continues to encounter major legal conflicts between the private sector and growing online social media communities that tend to repurpose and recycle material; sometimes for a simple exchange of ideas, and at others times with an interest in expressing a creative idea or work. Due to its deliberate reliance on repurposing material to develop new work, remix, as a basic act of creation, often confronts ethical questions under the paradigm of fair use in terms of intellectual property. In effect, the act of remixing often exposes our inconclusive relation with the creative process, and questions assumptions about authorship, plagiarism and originality, to name just a few cultural variables.

One assumption about remix is that by default it implies that whatever is produced under the paradigm must be free (as in free beer). This is not necessarily the case. Remix arguably carries the assumption of remixed content's need to be free due to the influence of remix culture generally understood as free culture— that is the free exchange of ideas, as popularized by Lawrence Lessig, and other organizers of Creative Commons. Lessig wrote a series of influential books to advocate for a fair adjustment of established copyright law in order to do justice to the way creative production is taking place as more and more people share work and communicate across the Internet. A recurring result of this strong connotation in the general understanding of the word *remix* by practitioners and researchers who feel strongly about the free sharing of ideas is to decide to work only within the ideal premise of the complete, open sharing of all things. This is certainly a valid position, and one that is slowly helping shape the way research is being published by commercial, academic, and university presses, but such a position is not the predominant form today. We hope it will be in the future.

Keywords in Remix Studies is not published as a free publication—in this sense it does not live up to the ideals of remix culture. It is published within a model that asks contributors to let the publisher have copyright privilege for a period of two years before the authors can share the content or reuse it as they freely please. It is important to note that the contributors are also able to share their essays with colleagues and other researchers through academic repositories so that their ideas may become part of ongoing debates as they find it necessary and fair to their academic goals. In this sense, the material may not be fully open on the Internet for anyone to take but it is shareable through compromises that are, in our view, transitional steps towards more open ways to produce research of the highest quality possible. We hope that readers who may hold ideal positions on the open sharing of information will see *Keywords in Remix Studies* as a step towards new forms of publication that are sensitive to the professional realities of cultural production and communication.

As editors of two anthologies on remix studies, we have certainly developed ideal forms of cultural exchanges of our own. And for this reason when we edited *The Routledge Companion to Remix Studies*, we also launched the website companion, remixstudies.com. In the introduction of the *Companion* we contextualized our online presence as one that would be continually active, but admittedly this was not the case, due to the limitations we faced as we tried to remain committed to our various obligations at our respective educational institutions while being active in our research and practices related to remix. For this reason, we take the opportunity in this introduction to express our intent to offer remixstudies.com as a resource that is not necessarily updated on a daily basis, but should be considered a repository where we can note the changes that are taking place in remix studies and remix culture after this publication is released. We plan to make the website a significant resource with a cohesive bibliography relevant to remix as well as occasional announcements on important developments in remix studies and remix culture. We also plan to include brief entries on keywords that were not included in this publication, and we are considering new ways that the website can be used to share research about remix. We hope that remix scholars and practitioners find this more modest approach reasonable to the realities we face as individuals who are invested in remix as a creative act as well as our subject of long-term research.

Keywords in Remix Studies is primarily aimed at scholars (including researchers, practitioners, lecturers and students) interested in some or all aspects of remix studies; however, we believe that it should also be of interest to media professionals, amateur remix practitioners and members of the general public with an interest in remix. We hope that our readers find multiple uses for the publication as a reference manual and introductory resource, as well as a teaching tool across the humanities and social sciences. We edited the volume for individuals who are both familiar and unfamiliar with remix studies or remix culture, and for this reason it should be appropriate for graduate and undergraduate-level students, depending on their acquaintance with remix. It is with all of this in mind that we asked contributors to share their views on the keywords that form part of this publication.

Contributions

Keywords in Remix Studies consists of 24 chapters dedicated to specific words that have defined and played a relevant role in remix studies as an area of research and practice. We invited contributors who are influential in their respective fields with the purpose of making the text relevant to diverse groups of scholars. We began the process of word selection by sending a survey to members of our community to ask which words are most relevant for them in remix studies. We used these results to evaluate which words could be included in the book. The selection of keywords was based on the number of times certain words were mentioned in relation to the apparent influence such words played or continue to play in remix studies, based on our own research. We then considered contributors who had written about the selected terms or a related focus and asked for their possible contribution. Sometimes, a contributor would suggest the variation of a term that was still related to our initial suggestion or even a different term; we often decided to go along with the suggestions if we considered that the change remained relevant to the overall organization of the volume. We went through this process understanding that the result of the selected words is but a mere fragment of the growing lexicon related to remix as a field of study. For this reason, as with our previous edited project, *The Routledge Companion to Remix Studies*, we hope that *Keywords in Remix Studies* will be considered a node to a larger ongoing discussion about remixing as a powerful cultural action.

The chapters are organized alphabetically, but there are three worth noting upfront that actually put directly into practice the principles behind the words included in this volume. The chapters on "Appropriation," "Memes" and "Versioning" are discussed along with others in the actual description of all of the contributions, which follows below. These three chapters function as exemplary snapshots of where remix theory meets practice.

Various chapters are written by two or more people. This, for us as editors, is evidence of one of the basic principles of remix—to create through constant collaboration. In this way, each and every chapter in its own way not only historicizes and theorizes remix, but also demonstrates it in action.

We must also make a brief note about the range of approaches that all of the chapters offer. The basic principle in each chapter is to offer an understanding of a keyword with a critical appreciation respective to the contributors' interests. This means that sometimes the definition is loosely presented, while in other cases, authors unpack how such denotations may have developed and how they appear to be understood at the time of publication, by starting with a dictionary definition. The approaches range from formal historical exegesis to hermeneutics, combined with a more personal voice. Some include analytics, while others rely on close examination of the word's development within a social structure. Others are specific to a period in which the contributor considers that the term played an important role, while some try to cover the general spectrum of the term's evolution. In short, the methods and approaches to the keywords included in this volume are as varied as the approaches to remixing itself, and in this sense an overview of all of the chapters would function as a collage of methods that demonstrates the interdisciplinary tendencies used to research remix.

The book opens with the keyword "Appropriation." This chapter is a collection of brief statements contributed by most of the authors and remixed by us, the editors. The goal of the chapter is to put into practice appropriation in the process of defining the word itself. The chapter reads quite similarly to other chapters, and each contributor is credited for his or her fragment of the chapter in the endnotes. A certain tension may be sensed if one tries to isolate each contribution as an individualized critical view. The issue at play in this textual megamix is to understand how ideas are shared and repetitively redefined through constant appropriation.

Richard Rinehart writes in Chapter 2, "Archive," about remix's relation to the archive in terms of the cultural imaginary that is informed by a romantic notion. He proposes to slip behind the façade of the romanticized archive in order to examine its historical and theoretical underpinnings, and to move past the archive's apparent romantic image by defining it in historical and professional terms. He repositions the archive as a remix of cultural heritage.

In Chapter 3, "Authorship," John Vallier defines the many variables that historically inform the concept of the author by highlighting how remix and its preceding forms have continually disrupted the concept of the individual creator. He revisits the theories of Roland Barthes, Michel Foucault and Walter Benjamin along with those of contemporary literary and remix theorists in order to argue that accepting the general understanding of the author in effect limits our potential for producing new works. Vallier optimistically proposes remix as a means to reconfigure contemporary approaches to creative production that may well move beyond the current constrictive understanding of a single author for a more open process already evident in remix culture.

Annette N. Markham argues in Chapter 4, "Bricolage," that the term's relation to remix, upon a close examination functions differently, even though both terms may at times be used synonymously. Markham takes us on a historical journey to prove this point. She discusses the role of the bricoleur as tinkerer and handyman, initially introduced by Lévi-Strauss in French anthropology, by unpacking bricolage in terms of epistemology and ontology. Markham repositions bricolage in relation to object and action to end with a clear position on how and why bricolage and remix are actually different, as the former can be viewed with a sense of finality while the latter with a sense of incompleteness and constant flow. She argues that we should be clear when to use the terms while also continuing the debate on how the terms inform each other.

Aram Sinnreich writes about the word "Collaborative" in Chapter 5. He offers a detailed sociocultural analysis of the word in order to define it and explore the apparent tension at play between collective and individualistic production. Sinnreich discusses the assumptions of expression in terms of cultural history that legitimate collaboration as part of institutions, and goes on to argue that the word collaborative took a major shift with the rise of a "digital culture" that began to develop in the 1990s. Sinnreich consequently argues that remix practices not only appear to problematize labor and capital but also make apparent the limitations of optimistic views on collaboration as an answer to current constrictions on collective creativity itself.

Pau Figueres, in Chapter 6, considers "Consumerism" in a hyper-state of late capitalism. He evaluates how remix plays a role in relation to art practice in a time when global markets have opened up new ways to distribute goods and consume them. Figueres argues that the relationship between consumerism and art is well established and that a new stage has emerged in which remix plays an occasionally conflictive role (being used for and against) in the questioning of the ongoing normalization of what he refers to as hyper-consumerism.

In Chapter 7, "Copyright/Fair Use," Patricia Aufderheide discusses how intellectual property law reshapes our understanding of remixing ranging from citations in texts to media mashups. She argues that uncertainty and the possibility of lawsuits, even when a person is exercising fair use, come to play major roles in creative decisions by artists and cultural producers. Such uncertainty is difficult to surmount due to the fact that international copyright laws vary, and this places even more stress on creative individuals who want to share work internationally. Education emerges as the means of empowerment, but Aufderheide argues that the challenge remains in finding a balance in user rights and copyright.

In Chapter 8, "Creativity," xtine burrough and Frank Dufour consider how homogeneous and heterogeneous sampling play a major role in the creative process. Instead of striving to provide a general understanding of creativity, the authors focus on creativity in relation to questions that appear to recur in terms of primultimacy: problems that remain unresolved and that make evident that all things in life recur to constantly become new. Transformation is then linked to creativity and framed in terms of sampling by offering case studies in which projects are considered as methodology for a new consciousness defined by remixing.

Janneke Adema, in Chapter 9, discusses the "Cut-up," a term she relates to cut/copy and paste in terms of transferring all forms of data that may take the form of image, sound or text. She relates the cut-up to writing techniques as well as theories of intertextuality. Adema introduces her own views on what she calls "the digital cut-up" to consider how basic principles explored previously take on new dematerialized forms with digital technology in terms of remix practice. She proposes the cut-up in post-human terms, and suggests ways in which to cut well can open up ways to dynamic states of becoming.

David J. Gunkel, in Chapter 10, examines how "Deconstruction" is a remix in its own right due to the fact that Derrida appropriated elements from previous philosophers, particularly Heidegger, in order to develop his own theories on how new things may emerge in-between the binary position of construction and destruction. He explains how the term has often been misused in remix studies. To demonstrate this, he discusses Derrida's own definition to show how many individuals who are active as both theorists and practitioners actually use the term to imply "decomposition" or "taking apart." Ultimately, Gunkel does not necessarily dismiss the misuse of deconstruction, but rather argues that its misinterpretation has become part of the way deconstruction operates in remix practice as well as culture at large.

In Chapter 11, Akane Kanai discusses "DIY Culture" as a term that gains global relevance based on the intertwined relation of mass media and Western ideas. She points out the importance of not accepting simplistic definitions of DIY as part of remix discourse because both are part of an advanced form of capitalism, in which innovation has taken over what otherwise could be considered derivative production. Kanai argues for an awareness of misplaced emphasis on creativity as original over repetitive reproduction to keep in place comfortable definitions of active and passive gender roles. She offers a strong case for a better understanding of DIY culture by presenting many examples of women who have developed works that put into question conventionalized definitions of gender.

Joshua Wille offers a close analysis of the term "Fan Culture" in Chapter 12, by focusing on fan edits of films such as *Superman vs. Batman*, *The Hobbit* and the *Star Wars* series. Wille considers the creative role of appropriation and transformation in terms of remixing among fan communities to argue that participation is an important cultural binder for the sharing and viewing of fan edits. Wille argues that the ongoing flow of remixed edits is evolving into new forms of movie making and viewing that are in turn becoming a body of permanent works-in-progress for fans who know how to produce derivative works as well as for general audiences.

Karen Keifer-Boyd and Christine Liao consider "Feminism" in relation to remix in Chapter 13. They propose "feminist remix" as a critical term that enables them to discuss the multiple layers at play in the ways women are portrayed across media. The authors provide an extensive list of examples that demonstrate how women have deployed remix as an important critical feminist method with the aim to reposition gender roles. Their examples include *Project Everyone*, a remix of girls dancing to the Spice Girls' song "Wannabe," and remixes by Elisa Kreisinger such as *Mad Men: Set Me Free*. Keifer-Boyd and Liao consider feminist remix at its core as a creative form that confronts patriarchal ideology head-on.

In Chapter 14, "Intellectual Property," Nate Harrison articulates the many challenges that IP has placed on new creative forms. He argues that we are so immersed in IP that we cannot notice it when we encounter it, for example, in end-user licenses such as the common "I agree" button online users regularly click every time they install new software or apps. Harrison reviews a history of IP leading to the term's current definition. He provides historical information with concrete examples of intellectual property conflicts in order to ask us to reconsider the challenges that creativity and fair forms of communication are faced with if we are not willing to rethink what intellectual property is and, most importantly, should be.

T Storm Heter, in Chapter 15, discusses "Jazz" as a musical art form that explored principles later found in remix. Heter specifically goes over the history of the turntable as a pivotal tool that proved to be essential for many musicians in jazz improvisation. He explains how they learned to play by listening to innovators such as Miles Davis, and he explains in detail how basic techniques such as bringing the needle back to the beginning of a riff repeatedly to study the chords and melodies was a predecessor to the turntable evolving into an instrument in its own right. He also discusses how the turntable itself became remixed when software was designed to emulate how it was previously used for contemporary jazz musicians.

Dahlia Borsche, in Chapter 16, discusses "Location" as an unacknowledged variable that nevertheless plays a major role in remix practice. She evaluates how the idea of location has become subsumed by the possibility of being constantly connected, and the ability to produce and share content with ever-increasing efficiency. Borsche argues for an awareness of the location of culture by updating post-colonial theory, thereby repositioning remix as a practice that can only be concretely understood when we take the time to look into the actual physical context in which remixes are produced. For Borsche this can lead to a resistance against hegemony; doing so can expose the multiple contexts in which remix takes place in order to contest what Borsche refers to as deterministic concepts of space.

Nate Harrison and Eduardo Navas, in Chapter 17, discuss how the meaning of the word "Mashup" evolved from its basic understanding of mashing food together, to destroying things, to a common euphemism for the recombination of music and code across media and culture. They discuss how the word historically is understood in terms of plunderphonics, memes and software mashups to argue that while the word mashup may often be used interchangeably with the word remix, there are some differences that, upon closer examination, make evident that the mashup opens the way for a third meaning. Harrison and Navas advocate that the mashup, in effect, reconfigures the possibilities to engage with remixed source material by showing how such material remains recognizable within a new form of expression.

For Chapter 18, "Memes," most of the authors in *Keywords to Remix Studies* contributed brief descriptions of memes of cultural interest, along with corresponding images. The motivation behind this collective effort is to put into practice the intertextual relation among contributors by considering their selections in relation to the other chapter contributions. The chapter can be considered a heterogeneous node in which diverging interests come together as a mashed up entity: a megamix of critical voices.

Mark Nunes, in Chapter 19, defines "Parody" as a dialogic form that repositions what it literally appropriates in order to undermine or question what may be taken at face value of the originating form. Nunes discusses parody in dialogic terms to show how through ever-evolving forms of citation and sampling, parody can point towards pastiche. He applies theories by Bakhtin as well as other structuralists and post-structuralists to discuss specific media mashups as part of an ecology of remix that attains meaning only when a cultural awareness is at play. This drives parody remixes into the realm of political commentary, and in effect Nunes presents a clear picture of how parody functioning as pastiche results as a reflection of specific moments in history, given that much of the material produced is meant to be considered in relation to ongoing debates of current events.

Chapter 20 is a collective contribution on "Participatory Politics" by Henry Jenkins and Thomas J Billard, with Samantha Close, Yomna Elsayed, Michelle C. Forelle, Rogelio Lopez and Emilia Yang. They consider remix as a form of participation and perform a close analysis of various political remixes and memes that are critical comments on the presidential elections of 2016. Jenkins's theory of convergence functions as a backdrop to explain how participatory culture can be a transitional cultural platform to move to participatory politics. To demonstrate the complexity of this process, they discuss how political remixes since Obama's first election have become fair game for any political position on the left, right or middle of the spectrum. This, in effect, makes evident the fact that remix can be repurposed for diverging agendas. However, the key argument in their case is that thanks to participatory politics and remix, a new generation of young activists have found a voice by way of moving from participatory culture to participatory politics.

In Chapter 21, "Remix," Eduardo Navas discusses various stages of remix, from a basic creative concept in music production to its role as a cultural binder that gained relevance in remix culture, and eventually remix studies. Navas explains that the various stages of remix consist of new ways to understand how and why we produce new things with the recycling or repurposing of pre-existing material, whether they be ideas or material production. He provides an overview of diverging positions on how remix is defined according to binary definitions of original and copies, and proposes that remixers and remix scholars remain ever-aware of the potential of becoming homogenized or formulaic. The remix community must stay critically engaged by way of repurposing the very material that defines it.

Owen Gallagher discusses the keyword "Sampling" in Chapter 22. Gallagher considers definitions that have shaped sampling in remix culture and remix studies to argue that there is certain incoherence and contradiction in how sampling is discussed, understood and debated; consequently, this has direct repercussions on the way that sampling is theorized. A major issue for Gallagher is that some of the definitions of sampling are over-expansive and in turn do not match the reality in which remix actually takes place. For this reason, Gallagher argues that our definition of sampling needs to be more concrete and have an intimate sensitivity to the context in which it actually occurs.

In Chapter 23, Francesca Coppa and Rebecca Tushnet discuss the keyword "Transformative" in direct relation to copyright law. They discuss how transformativeness became part of the mainstream, then use case studies to show how new meaning is created in fan fiction and fanvids. The authors relate their analysis to fan culture at large. They boldly confront issues such as: What makes a remixed work truly transformative? What factors make it so different from the source material that it is considered a new work in its own right? These are crucial questions for copyright law when defining a work in terms of fair use. They ultimately position their argument for transformative works in terms of social justice that can bring about a revolution of the self.

The last keyword is "Versioning" and, appropriately, the final chapter—written in two parts—bears versions within it. In this sense, our last contribution puts into action the very meaning of the term. The chapter is a critical reflection on remix's relation to music culture and the politics of class, race and ethnicity. The first part of the chapter is a versioned reflection by Paul D. Miller (DJ Spooky, that Subliminal Kid) in which he discusses Melania Trump's 2016 plagiarism of

Michelle Obama's 2008 speech for the Democratic convention alongside a court ruling against Kraftwerk, who sued for unauthorized sampling of one their compositions. The second part is the transcript of a conversation between Paul D. Miller and Eduardo Navas in which they discuss the social, technological and cultural dimensions of remix in terms of versioning and the real political implications of media representations and repurposing of material that gains massive popular value.

The brief descriptions of the 24 chapters above provide a general sense of what they offer as a whole. What will become evident to readers as they engage with respective contributions is that each is a clear reflection of the political times in which *Keywords for Remix Studies* was published. Many of the examples discussed, such as video mashups and memes are quite critical of the politics of the time, and engage with the uncertain future that the world is facing with the rise of particularly extremist views in governments, not only in the United States but throughout the globe. What may become evident when considering the range of interests and points of view at play across the keywords and their respective contributors is that remix studies is quite literally everywhere. Remix has its roots in marginal collective experiences by groups who struggled to gain a voice and agency against racism and class difference, while creating viable spaces and forms to express the importance of diversity in terms of gender and sexual orientation. Hip hop and disco are the two music cultures that are often mentioned in terms of such struggles, but remix's roots go back to the Jamaican struggle of decolonization as well as other forms of resistance that continue to take place in diverse places throughout the world. The favelas of Belém, in the north of Brazil, are an example—where tecno brega has proven to be a major creative musical force. Remix is a vehicle of cultural change for anyone who holds a minoritarian position in relation to a majoritarian paradigm. For it is the minor that redefines the major; it is through the minor that real change happens, and the major in turn is constantly redefined through the questioning and interventions that the minor performs within the major in a never-ending process that, in this case, can be understood within the realm of remix. Mainstream's fallacy is in its blindness to this process of constant change, which at times may appear to move in a constructive direction and at others diverts to states that appear detrimental to the health of minoritarian production within, through and even against majoritarian production.[5] The range of contributors, and their views, is evidence that remix belongs to no one: not one gender, nor one ethnicity or social background. Remix thrives on its possibility to be put into action by anyone— to be operationalized wherever possible. Nobody owns it; nobody can claim it as only theirs. No one can demand that it speaks only for a particular culture, or for one particular struggle. A territorializing move on remix only exposes the inability of a person or group to see remix for what it really is: the possibility of recursively becoming what one reimagines, and to be able to connect with others by way of the constant sharing of ideas.

Notes

1 Eduardo Navas, Owen Gallagher and xtine burrough, eds., *The Routledge Companion to Remix Studies* (Routledge, 2015).
2 Williams first organized his list of keywords to complement his publication *Culture and Society: 1780–1950* (Columbia University Press, 1958). Given the length of his first major book, editors advised him not to include the list. It would be 20 years later that his keywords would become a proper publication.
3 See Bibliography for a selected list of keyword books and related publications.
4 "Athleisure" is perhaps the most obvious example in popular fashion—an actual trend of athletic wear designed for all forms of social engagements.
5 This is a position based on the theory of minoritarian language by Deleuze and Guatarri. See Gilles Deleuze and Felix Guatarri "Postulates of Linguistics" in *A Thousand Plateaus: Capitalism and Schizophrenia*, trans. Brian Massumi (Minnesota Press, 1998), pp. 102–110.

Bibliography

Keywords

Adams, Rachel et al. *Keywords for Disability Studies*. NYU Press, 2015.
Burgett, Bruce and Hendler, Glenn. *Keywords for American Cultural Studies*, 2nd edition. NYU Press, 2014.
Carter, Ronald. *Keywords in Language and Literacy*. Routledge, 1995.
Franco, Susanne. *Dance Discourses: Keywords in Dance Research*. Routledge, 2007.
Cary, Watt and Nelson, Stephen. *Academic Keywords: A Devil's Dictionary for Higher Education*. Routledge, 2002.
Heilker, Paul and Vandenberg, Peter. *Keywords in Writing Studies*. Utah State University Press, 2015.
———. *Keywords in Composition Studies*. Heinemann, 1996.
Lesko, Nancy. *Keywords in Youth Studies: Tracing Affects, Movements, Knowledges*. Routledge, 2011.
Morgan, David, ed. *Key Words in Religion, Media and Culture*. Routledge, 2008.
Nel, Philip and Paul, Lissa. *Keywords for Children's Literature*. NYU Press, 2011.
Novak, David and Sakakeeny, Matt. *Keywords in Sound*. Duke University Press, 2015.
Rajagopalan, Rajesh and Mishra, Atu. *Nuclear South Asia: Keywords and Concepts*. Routledge, 2014.
Schlund-Vials, Cathy, Trinh Võ, Linda and Wong, K. Scott. *Keywords for Asian American Studies*. NYU Press, 2015.
Williams, Raymond. *Keywords: A Vocabulary of Culture and Society New Edition*. Oxford University Press, 2014.

Remix Studies

Amerika, Mark. *remixthebook*. Duke Press, 2011.
Evans, David. *Appropriation: Documents of Contemporary Art*. MIT Press, 2009.
Gunkel, David J. *Of Remixology*. MIT Press, 2016.
Jenkins, Henry et al. *Spreadable Media: Creating Value and Meaning in a Networked Culture*. NYU Press, 2013.

Laderman, David and Westrup, Laurel. *Sampling Media*. Oxford University Press, 2014.
Lessig, Lawrence. *Remix: Making Art and Commerce Thrive in the Hybrid Economy*. Penguin Press, 2008.
Miller, Paul D. *Sound Unbound*. MIT Press, 2008.
———. *Rhythm Science*. MIT Press, 2004.
Morales, Aaron. *American Mashup: A Popular Culture Reader*. Longman, 2011.
Navas, Eduardo. *Remix Theory: The Aesthetics of Sampling*. Springer, 2012.
Navas, Eduardo, Gallagher, Owen and burrough, xtine, eds., *The Routledge Companion to Remix Studies*. Routledge, 2015.
Sinnreich, Aram. *Mashed Up: Music, Technology and the Rise of Configurable Culture*. University of Massachusetts Press, 2010.
———. *The Piracy Crusade*. University of Massachusetts Press, 2014.
Sonvilla-Weiss, Stefan. *Mashup Cultures*. Springer, 2010.

1
APPROPRIATION

Authored in Collaboration with Contributors

This chapter is an act of appropriation. Authors included in *Keywords in Remix Studies* shared brief thoughts about appropriation, which were then compiled and remixed by the editors. Each author's contribution is acknowledged in bold type in the endnotes. The chapter is written with the aim of letting the authors' voices come through as much as possible while the essay as a whole forms a critical reflection on the act of appropriation by putting into practice the act, itself. A tension may well develop in which the authors' voices may be on the threshold of moving past what each originally meant. This may happen even if not much was adjusted in each contribution in order to fit into a specific narrative due to the fact that each reflection has been reframed into a pluralized view on appropriation that at times may deliberately contradict itself. If anything, such tension is part of the reflections on appropriation in direct relation to authorship and the possibilities of plagiarism and stealing.

> Good artists copy
> great artists steal
> Bad artists imitate
> great artists steal
> Good artists steal
> [anti]capitalists [dis]appropriate[1]

Appropriation in art is a method for creative expression that can be empowering. It is the practice of owning something and giving it new meaning. Informed by Isabelle Graw's essay, "Dedication Replacing Appropriation," noting that appropriation is subversion and criticism, it can also be framed in terms of empowerment. Taking a piece from existing images, objects, text, art or ideas and providing new interpretations to the piece gives artists extended language to communicate and speak truth to power. To give a cultural example, appropriation has long existed as a strategy for art-making that can be found in traditional Chinese painting instruction dating back thousands of years. Modern and contemporary appropriation has diverse meanings, functions and representations. Critical intention is the common denominator. The intention of criticism or providing alternative perspectives is what makes appropriation a powerful means for activism. Appropriation not only empowers artists, but also empowers viewers to think actively and engage in a dialogue with the work by conflicting a viewer's prior understanding of the appropriated and the new interpretation.[2]

Defining Appropriation

Let's get literal. "Appropriation" is the nominal version of the late Middle English verb "appropriate," which was originally appropriated from the Latin *appropriatus* which is the past participle (a kind of verbal remix) of *appropriare*, meaning "to make one's own." This Latin verb was initially fabricated by mashing up the words *ad* and *proprius*, which is a word that had been originally used to designate whatever is peculiar to a person or thing or to identify what is characteristic of a person or thing. As such, the word *proprius* is properly speaking the opposite of both *communis* and *alienus*. Following this line of linguistic appropriation, whereby one language has taken over and made its own something that was originally derived from another, "appropriation" can be properly characterized as precisely this act of taking something over and making it one's own. The word, therefore, means what it does and does what it means.[3]

In recent times, appropriation as a concept appears to be undergoing renewed popularity due to its relevance in explaining not simply the emergence of new forms of cultural remix, but in addition, its ability to describe the racialized dimensions of making things into "property." As Lisa Nakamura notes, affordances of digital platforms allow users to treat images as resources, whose value is derived from moving them from the context in which they were created, to another. In her own case study of "racialized showspace," Western users turn African men, featured wearing bras, hitting each other in the face with fish, and pouring milk on each other's heads, into trophy photos for circulation in meme traffic. The value from these sexualized, humiliated bodies does not accrue to the people themselves but to the person who distributes their circulation. In what is often termed "cultural" appropriation in popular discourse, we find a useful way to understand continuing practices that reinforce racialized relations of dominance.[4]

Authorship and Appropriation

The word "appropriation" contains within it the dialectic of authorship. As the OED tells us, to appropriate is to "Take (something) for one's own use, typically without the owner's permission." In the case of remix culture, video collages, mashups, and the like, all reflect an assertion of new modes of authorship at the expense of traditional practices based on authorial originality and private property. The "death of the author" simultaneously breathes new life into authorship writ large. Creativity necessarily requires destruction. Appropriation is the politics of authorship.[5]

Remix artists, due to their ongoing reevaluation of authorship in relation to creativity, are usually explicit about their borrowing, whereas the majority of "original" authors borrow heavily from others without acknowledging their contribution in the new work. The image of the original author popularized by the eighteenth-century publishing industry is a myth—everyone borrows from and builds on the work of those who came before them; however, remix artists tend to borrow more directly through the act of sampling. The individual artist is always dependent upon external sources. The artist and author are merely secondary facilitators of cultural texts, weaving together tapestries of citations, intertextual artworks built upon explicit and implicit references to previous works, codified and connected to all other artworks that came before. Culture may be conceptualized as consisting of bricolage, remediation, and implicit participation. A writer never begins with a blank page no more than an artist starts with a blank canvas. Each begins their respective process at the end of a long tradition of creative practice that came before them, outside of which it is impossible to operate.[6]

Appropriation as Practice

In Paul D. Miller's chapter, "Versioning," he explains that appropriation "is as old as language itself. It does not ask permission and it never gives permission. It is basically creativity as a verb—not as an adjective."[7] This idea may resonate with some people when considering appropriation as a creative strategy. So, how does one appropriate well? What makes an appropriation successful? In considering this, let us borrow from a master painter, color theorist, and design educator, Josef Albers.

In an interview, Albers said, "one plus one equals three." If you are unfamiliar with Albers' concept, put up two fingers like a peace sign and then notice how whatever you frame between your fingers creates a third element. This third element has the potential to transform the message of the peace sign. It is especially noticeable when that third element is brought to the foreground through contrast in its formal properties, whether aesthetic (shape, size, hue, value, rotation, and so on) or linguistic (its semantic role).

Successful appropriations are like Albers' riddle—the borrowed work in addition to its context or juxtapositions creates a third meaning. Measuring the success of a work of appropriation must be related to the degree to which the foreground (the new meaning) and backgrounds (borrowed context) are at once separated and understood. The system in which one plus one equals three is based on Miller's idea that creativity is a verb and appropriation is its strategy.[8]

Taking a step back, it can be argued that there is nothing special about remix appropriation. If we start from the assumption that all art begs, borrows, and steals from other works, then remix is no different than any other creative practice. But, of course, there is a difference, namely that what remix appropriates it incorporates as a sampled excerpt stitched directly into the newly created work. Remix *materializes* its intertextuality, foregrounding what it borrows, for all to see. Remix appropriation comes closest to the creative strategy of collage, in that sampled source materials are always visible as such, even as they come together to create a new work. Remix lets us see the borrowing at the same time that it provides the basis for novel, creative production. In this regard, remix appropriation is never fully *appropriation* in its etymological sense of making-one's-own.[9]

Playing with Appropriation

It is undeniable, regardless of how much remix may or may not rely on appropriation to create new works, that appropriation is play, and at the core of creating. Without it there is no making, no production, no art, no science. Let's take the experience of a drummer as an example:

> in entering a musical tradition such as a jazz or punk, I attempt to learn sonic styles by way of imitating and appropriating those that resonate. As John Coltrane said, "I've found you've got to look back at the old things and see them in a new light" (Coltrane 1960). By entering into and imitating/appropriating traditions I open myself up to its structures and codes. I am played by, while playing and creating in, tradition. "Whoever plays is also played: the rules of the game impose themselves upon the player, prescribing the to and fro (hin und her) and delimiting the field where everything 'is played'" (Ricœur, 1981: 186). The gift of ethically (not necessarily legally) grounded appropriation is that it goes both ways.

When we appropriate, create and play, we are appropriated and played by the tradition. It is not static or unidirectional. Appropriation is cyclical, until artificially curtailed by instrumentalist motives, such as economic agendas or political ideologies.[10]

The unidirectional form in which appropriation appears to function can be useful to understand its creative potential in art as the recontextualization of a referent to change its meaning. The referent's meaning is transformed because its visual or linguistic sign is read differently in a new context. For example, in "After Walker Evans" (1981) artist Sherrie Levine exhibited Walker Evans's photographs as her art, and 20 years later, Michael Mandiberg offered the work online in "After Sherie Levine" with certificates of authenticity to create an object with cultural value but no economic value. Does the meaning and its value change when the same work is interpreted as produced by a woman then a man again? The meaning of a sign is not fixed; it varies over time, in different contexts, and by the intent of the speaker/writer/artist/reader/viewer.[11]

Ownership and Authenticity

What does it mean to own a sign? Is it the same as owning the referent? Artist Sophia Wallace's "Cliteracy" six-foot neon sign and "100 Laws of Cliteracy" street art about the organ drew attention with physical signs to a referent that women own within their body but is little understood and more often shamed. Do we deliberately and inadvertently steal signs as well as their referent throughout the process of annihilation? Hock E Aye VI Edgar Heap of Birds, an internationally recognized Cheyenne Arapaho artist, highlights the atrocities committed against native people in the United States with "Native Hosts," a series of signs with the name of the local area printed backward followed by the words "Today your host is," and the name of a local Native American tribe that has been displaced or are victims of genocide in the United States. Maya Lin's "What's Missing" science-based artwork maps the disappearance of species habitat degradation and loss with markers of places named for the species that once thrived at the location but no longer exists. These examples of appropriation in art bring to light erased, absent, concealed, and socially taboo referents.[12]

Appropriation in performance studies can help us negotiate the following contradiction: that, to quote Augusto Boal's epigraph to Richard Schechner's *Performance Studies*, in theatre, "a truly artistic show will always be unique, impossible to be repeated," where "in life, we never really do anything for the first time, always repeating past experiences, habits, rituals and conventions." Our art, though it may be repeated word for word on the stage, is every time unique; our lives, although experienced moment to moment in time, is made of behaviors that we learn, train for, rehearse. Performance studies helps us reimagine new and complex relationships between originality, citation, and repetition: what a performer brings to the moment versus what is in the script or direction. Reflecting on this in broad terms, there appears to be a related contradiction in appropriation art: one could argue that an "authentic" culture is just one where we cannot recognize the sampled, mashed up, or quoted parts anymore, where "appropriation art" is what we call it when we can recognize the pieces the artist has used. This means that, ironically, it's appropriation art that implicitly or explicitly credits the work of others in its creation, while it is the supposedly authentic that erases its collaborators and its history. This is not to say that we do not need to attend to issues of power, fairness, and equity in culture and culture-making (theatre included)—it is never right to exploit or dehumanize people who have less power than yourself—but to be against appropriation in art is to subscribe to ideas of originality that many consider inherently false and notions of art-making that go against practical experience.[13]

An alternative understanding of appropriation traces its roots back to the Birmingham School of Cultural Studies—particularly writers like Dick Hebdige and Stuart Hall who were attempting to understand how youth subcultures defined themselves in opposition to their parent cultures through the active appropriation and reinscription of signs. For example, they described the ways that the punk movement tapped the Swastika not specifically to denote Nazism but to express their rejection of the values of the previous generation. Under this model, appropriation often involves a struggle over meanings—as signs shed their old associations against their will—and as new groups lay claim to older cultural resources as a means of expressing their identities, affiliations, and politics. Appropriation may be understood as a process that involves both analysis and commentary. Sampling intelligently from the existing cultural reservoir requires a close analysis of the existing structures and uses of this material; remixing requires an appreciation of emerging structures and latent potential meanings. Read in these terms, appropriation has social, aesthetic, and political implications. Today's digital tools and networks make appropriation and remixing a more pervasive practice, but cultural studies still offers some useful tools for understanding its stakes.[14]

Appropriation may be perceived as being more about the act of the taking—the assertion that the power one has asserted by copying is appropriate—than about the specifics of what has been taken. For instance, within fan culture, even though we don't always know why some texts inspire creativity, there's generally something specific about them that attracts us, as opposed to appropriation artist Jeff Koons's devil-may-care dismissal of the specificity of the works he copies. In one fair use case that he ultimately won, Koons explained that to him, the legs of the model in one photo he copied were "not anyone's legs in particular." But without a "why" for the specific material appropriated, the discourse of appropriation art may be more about artistic power and art world credibility.[15]

In contrast, emergent and controversial forms of remix such as fan edits illustrate that appropriation is a vital component of contemporary media. Appropriation involves diving into the dynamic and occasionally windswept sandbox of human culture and building something of one's own. Sometimes this means doing so in defiance of society or the law, but as Lawrence Lessig observes:

> We, as a society, can't kill this new form of creativity. We can only criminalize it. We can't stop our kids from using the technologies we give them to remix the culture around them. We can only drive that remix underground.[16]

Implicit Contradictions in Appropriation

Appropriation can be used in one's own creative output as a convenient shorthand for a range of cultural practices that use pieces of one work as elements in another, from fan fiction to collage to mashup. It's simple and convenient; even non-scholars are likely to be familiar with the term, and therefore to need little explanation or background when it's invoked.

The problem is, some people hate the word. To suggest that culture can be "appropriated" is to accept *prima facie* that (1) culture may be a form of "property," and (2) the owner of the cultural property suffers a loss when it's "appropriated" by someone else. Neither of these is necessarily the case. As artists, critics, and philosophers have noted for millennia, the cultural production of meaning is an inherently collective process, and creation *ex nihilo* is not only mythical but illogical. Nobody can create a meaningful cultural artifact or engage in meaningful cultural practice without using the codes, tools and materials established by those who came before. Therefore, the practice of establishing ownership over one moment in this timeless and contiguous chain of communication is a more or less arbitrary act that only serves the purpose of establishing a basis for economic and power relations, a social mechanism jury-rigged onto a cultural one.

The premise that culture is a subcategory of property, therefore, is not merely a *consequence* of the dominance of industrial capitalism in contemporary society, but an *instrument* of that dominance. It normalizes mercantile relations as the basis of all social relations, even as it normalizes cultural expression as a mere instrument of social organization. Of course, there is some truth in these claims—as members of a hierarchical, industrial capitalist society, we can't help but understand our cultural practices through this lens, and the expectation of property leaves its imprint on the codes and practices that creators choose and deploy in the course of cultural production. Furthermore, this was likely always the case; it is difficult to believe that some prelapsarian past existed in which culture was "pure" from the contagion of power.

However, if we are to fight effectively against the mechanisms of power in our own society, a good place to start is by engaging critically in the process of understanding how those mechanisms are encoded into our cultural behaviors and institutions. And one of the first steps in that process is unpacking, and changing, the language we use to define those behaviors and institutions. A good start would be to stop calling cultural expression "appropriation."[17]

Conclusion

At the most basic level of action, the act of taking something pre-existing and acknowledging the source is appropriation, but when such taking is unacknowledged and the work is presented as one's own it becomes plagiarism. The latter is the case when what one takes is legitimated as a work credited to a proper author. But let's step back a bit and consider the reuse or repurposing of words—that is the appropriation of basic forms of communication, as is the case with this and all other sentences that form this chapter; in such acts of appropriation there is no need for acknowledgement. Basic words can be used as one's own without proper accreditation to an author. Words are shared source material for everyone to use. One could coin a term and expect not to be credited every time it is used in public space, or even in writing, especially if the word becomes common knowledge. One could only hope that all things produced could function this way; that would create an ideal situation for the exchange of ideas and all things. When considering this, appropriation has the potential to show the friction of authorship in relation to stealing, making evident the possibilities for what could happen if we were able to look beyond ideological principles of intellectual property. As a subversive act, in order to make this possibility evident to those who don't notice it, one could even argue that stealing is fair game for artists, and in fact, as the epigraph at the top of this chapter shows, a few artists, in their own way, repeatedly have reflected on stealing as part of the creative process. In the end, what is exposed when debating such details, regardless of whether the act is unethical or not is the fact that we all take something from others in order to repurpose it, and in this sense appropriation exposes the limitations of authorship. It makes transparent the fact that nothing is original, just unique to the moment it is experienced.[18]

It can be argued, then, that these practices of extending what would perhaps previously be seen as plagiarism in an appropriation discourse go beyond what is commonly seen as appropriation or remix practices. They clearly intend to actively disturb or undermine the system of authorship, and the notions of originality and authority that come with it by "hollowing" out or putting those notions to the test. In this respect, we can see the above examples as illustrations of how practices and concepts of appropriation and plagiarism exist on a spectrum, where appropriation practices in an art context will most likely be judged as plagiarism practices within academia. This might have to do with the fact that the difference between plagiarism and appropriation remains so unclear. Therefore any appropriation that takes place within an academic context that does not adhere to a citation or referencing context will run the risk of being condemned. In this respect, Kenneth Goldsmith's strategy in terms of uncreative writing can be seen as more subversive when he argues for extending forms of appropriation that are accepted within the artistic field, but which are still seen as plagiarism within a literary or academic context, into scholarship.[19]

A lot of things have changed in the past two decades. A lot of things have remained the same. We have moved from the tyranny of physical media to the seemingly unlimited possibilities of total digital immersion. We have moved from a top down, mega-corporate dominated media, to a hyper-fragmented multiverse where any kind of information is accessible within reason (and sometimes without!). The fundamental issue is that "memory" and how it responds to the digital etherealization of all aspects of the information economy we inhabit conditions everything we do in this twenty-first-century culture of post-modern, post-digital, post-everything contemporary America. Whether it's the legions of people who walk the streets with Bluetooth-enabled earbuds that allow them to ignore the physical reality of the world around them, or the Pokémon Go hordes playing the world's largest video game as it's overlaid on stuff that happens "IRL" (In Real Life) that layer digital role-playing over the world: diagnosis is pending. But the fundamental fact is clear: digital archives are more important than ever and how we engage and access the archival material of the past, shapes and molds the way we experience the present and future. Playing with the archive is a kind of digital analytics of the subconscious impulse to collage: to appropriate.[20]

Notes

1 The prefixes in the brackets are included to point to the conflictive ambiguity of appropriation as a creative form in relation to capitalism. A remixed poem based on **Pau Figueres**'s contribution: "After Banksy's after Picasso sentence, I thought of my own way of saying it after both of them."
2 **Christine Liao**. References: Isabelle Graw, "Dedication Replacing Appropriation: Fascination, Subversion and Dispossession in Appropriation Art." In Philipp Kaiser, ed., *Louise Lawler and Others*, pp. 45–67, Hatje Cantz Publishers, 2004.
3 **David Gunkel**.
4 **Akane Kanai**. References: Lisa Nakamura, "'I WILL DO EVERYthing That Am Asked': Scambaiting, Digital Show-Space, and the Racial Violence of Social Media," *Journal of Visual Culture* (2014) 13(3): 257–274.
5 **Nate Harrison**. References: www.oxforddictionaries.com/definition/english/appropriate.
6 **Owen Gallagher**.
7 **Paul D. Miller**.
8 **xtine burrough**. References: John H. Holloway, John A. Weil and Josef Albers, "A Conversation with Josef Albers," *Leonardo* (1970) 3(4): 459–464, p. 462.
9 **Mark Nunes**.
10 The quote is **John Vallier**'s personal experience as a drummer. References: John Coltrane, "Coltrane on Coltrane," *Down Beat*, September 29, 1960; Paul Ricœur, "Appropriation," in Joel B. Thompson, ed. and trans., *Hermeneutics and the Human Sciences*, Cambridge University Press, 1981.
11 **Karen Keifer-Boyd**.
12 Ibid.
13 **Francesca Coppa**. References: Richard Schechner, *Performance Studies: An Introduction*, Routledge, 2002, vi.
14 **Henry Jenkins et al.** References: Dick Hebdige, *Subculture: The Meaning of Style*, Routledge, 1979; Stuart Hall and Tony Jefferson, *Resistance Through Rituals: Youth Subcultures in Post-War Britain*, Routledge, 1993.
15 **Rebecca Tushnet**. References: Amy Adler, "Fair Use and the Future of Art," *New York University Law Review* (2016) 91: 559–626; Rebecca Tushnet, "My Fair Ladies: Sex, Gender, and Fair Use in Copyright, American University Journal of Gender," *Social Policy and the Law* (2007) 15: 273–304.
16 **Joshua Wille**. References: Lawrence Lessig, *Remix: Making Art and Commerce Thrive in the Hybrid Economy* (New York: The Penguin Press, 2008), 109.
17 **Aram Sinnreich**.
18 **Eduardo Navas**. References: The last sentence is taken from the essay "Regenerative Knowledge," http://remixtheory.net/?p=1337. It also is a digital composite available online: http://navasse.net/RegenCultProj/index.html.
19 **Janneke Adema**. References: Kenneth Goldsmith, *Uncreative Writing*, Columbia University Press, 2011.
20 **DJ Spooky**, Introduction to "The New Memory Palace" http://djspooky.com/the-new-memory-palace.

2
ARCHIVE

Richard Rinehart

The archive is a romantic notion. In the academic imagination, it conjures the spirits of Derrida, Foucault, and Borges. It evokes Casaubon from Umberto Eco's novel *Foucault's Pendulum*, evading secret societies in a global quest to solve an ancient mystery.[1] As an academic trope, it has been electrified in scholarly texts,[2] disrupted in conference panels,[3] and cruised in queer art exhibitions.[4] In the public eye, the archive is the chamber of secrets. The archive exhibits just the right combination of imagined characteristics—historic, nerdy, and arcane—that make it the academic equivalent of sea shanties or steampunk. I don't mean to trivialize the archive—in fact the goal of this chapter is to expand our understanding of it. The archive is a rich cultural imaginary that should continue to be theorized, as I will do below in relation to the equally rich imaginary of remix. I want to trace the façade of the archive so that we can slip behind it momentarily for two reasons. The first is that the realities of the archive can be messy, slow, and intricate. The praxis offers detail and resolution that serve to make ideation around the archive more textured and nuanced. Second, considering the historic and operational conditions in relation to theories of the archive allows us to create meaningful connections between the two. These connections should not be conceived of as a mesh gear that constantly engages, continuously regulating the movements of theory and practice. Instead, consider theory as a clutch that can disconnect to let the engine of the imaginary rev fast on subversive or utopian fantasies and then reconnect in order for those fantasies to drive the practical realities of the archive. The best way to move past the romantic image of the archive is to do something unromantic—to define the subject of this discussion in historic, institutional, and professional terms.

The Archive (Unromantically Theorized)

What is "the archive" as theorized in academic venues and invoked in popular imagery? The answer requires looking back at its historic origins and development in the context of other contemporaneous institutions such as the library and museum. I have neither space nor need here to repeat the exhaustive and well-documented history of the archive; rather I will include only details relevant to its history in the context of remix. First, all archives serve a basic function. An archive is an instrument of social memory—our long-term collective memory. Social memory is a requisite and defining characteristic of any civilization in that it provides for the continuity of a civilization year after year and, in some cases, century after century.[5] Social memory takes many forms that can be seen as situated along a continuum of informal and formal memory. Informal or folk memory has taken the forms of popular stories and songs, jokes, lullabies, crafts—and today, memes, tweets, and posts. Informal memories originate in a culture organically and are highly mutable. To the extent that they are generated and transmitted according to a set of rules, those rules are implicit, also mutable, and their creators and stewards are largely unaware of them.

Formal memory is society's canonical memory. It is usually selected and stewarded by organized castes or credentialed professionals who often work within social institutions such as governments and religions. Formal memory tends to be more stable than informal and it is managed according to explicit rules that are passed on during the training of its stewards. Formal memories often take the shape of government records, laws, religious texts, and so on. Naturally, there is overlap between informal and formal memory; a cultural meme may be initially generated and transmitted informally and then collected and organized formally. Formal memory is distinguished in part by its institutional form of stewardship. Within society's institutional structures of government, religion, education, commerce, and so on, its function is performed by "cultural heritage organizations," whose primary purpose is social memory. Such types of organizations known today originated in ancient times and, since the advent of Modernism, with its penchant for specialization and consistency, have been distilled to three prime models: libraries, museums, and archives.

Despite the distinctions between libraries, museums, and archives, there is considerable overlap and mixing among them. Archives might hold a collection of paintings that one would expect to see in a museum; they may describe those paintings in an archival manner, detailing provenance and original order. Museums often include libraries, typically research and reference libraries for internal use. And libraries often incorporate archives, as is the case with many academic libraries. Professionals often collaborate across these types of organizations on shared vocabularies or preservation strategies, the latter especially in response to the onslaught of new born-digital material that presents these organizations with common technological challenges. Libraries, museums, and archives are even combined into one agency at the federal funding level in the U.S.: the Institute of Museum and Library Services. It is the amalgamation of these professional practices, their institutional setting, and their common memory function, more than any specific type of cultural heritage organization that is invoked in "the archive."

The archive is a mashup; a remix designed to embody canonical social memory. My subject, then, is the archive as a representation of formal social memory and its relationship to remix practices. The archive as a trope, for our purposes here, does not denote only professional archival organizations per se. It may incorporate practices and examples from any specific type of cultural heritage organization. "Archive" lends itself to this semantic slippage. As I mentioned earlier, the elastic term "archive" may refer to a building, a collection, and/or an organization. Additionally, archive is the only one of the aforementioned institutional terms that functions as both noun and verb. In the context of the archive and remix, "archiving" means socially remembering, but it does not necessarily denote professional archival emphases on provenance or original order. Archiving may incorporate a library-like access model in which users "take the object home," rather than indicating archival white glove treatment. That's all fine. The archive has been loosened from strict professional definition, but it has not become a nebulous term that refers to any kind of memory or index. It indicates formal social memory and is thus informed, if not constrained, by the real world practices of cultural heritage organizations. For instance, the equation of the archive with society's canonical and institutional memory means that discussions around remixing the archive are inherently political.

The theoretical possibilities for remixing the archive are stronger when considered in relation to operational realities. For instance, the archive is not merely an abstract entity; it has a body. Most libraries, museums, and archives are physical sites, each of which offers numerous opportunities for creative intervention. There are about 35,000 museums[6] and 120,000 libraries[7] in the United States today. To put that in context, there are roughly 11,000 Starbucks stores and 14,000 McDonald's franchises in the U.S.[8] Of course, the latter usually sit on much more visible real estate, leading to the illusion that access points for fast food vastly outnumber those for cultural heritage. Taken together, the archive is a treasury of shared cultural heritage that has more than 155,000 doors. We might enter these doors with a sense of wonder, interrogation, or suspicion.

Wonder

The precursor to the modern museum in Europe was the studiolo, kunstkammer, wunderkammer, or cabinet of wonders.[9] These were usually rooms within the home of a wealthy person set aside for displaying trophies of exploration and conquest. The objects in these collections were often plundered from lands outside Europe: a body of a crocodile from Africa; a netsuke from Japan; a nautilus shell from the South Pacific. As such, these wunderkammern were shrines to Europe's colonial mania and spaces where the world was symbolically brought under the dominion of the Euclidean European gaze. But they served another purpose that became equally influential on the modern museum and that speaks to its capacity for remix. In the wunderkammer, each object was not isolated by its geographic origin, its historicity, or its location in a hierarchical taxonomy. Rather, each artifact revealed its deeper symbolic meaning in relation to the others. As these collections were arranged by their collectors into a physical cosmology, the cabinet-room became the world-in-a-bottle, the world remixed. It was important that the objects comprising this bottle world were physical and that they were (largely) real. These facts indexically connected the symbolic cosmology to the real world, conferring not proof perhaps, but a certain gravitas. The modern museum proceeded to split these collections into disciplinary channels—art, anthropology, and natural history—and further ordered them into sub-sets organized by style, typology, era, culture, and so on. This organization modeled the modern cosmology: history. Modern museological methods are more accurate and sensitive to the original context and meaning of objects. This is not to say that the modern museum is a better way of knowing the world. In the wunderkammer, collections were remixed, often with cavalier disinterest in historical accuracy and original context, toward creating meaning larger than the sum of their parts. The goal here was not accuracy or even understanding. The wunderkammer was an instrument for wondering.

Modern museums eventually eased up on presenting fixed taxonomical arrangements of their collections in favor of changing exhibitions. Exhibitions recapture a bit of the wunderkammer's strategy of reshuffling artifacts in order to see new meanings emerge from their interrelationships. New technologies allow us to go even further toward remixing these two collection modalities. Modern museological methods created a host of contextual data about objects that was taxonomical and structured and thus lent itself to the logic of the database. Now, we can easily pick any node of that data—author, originating region, creation date—and spin a galaxy of artifacts on that pivot point. The spirit of the original wunderkammer is kept lovingly alive in the Museum of Jurassic Technology in Culver City, California. This museum presents the visitor with beautifully presented exhibits that appear to be exhaustively researched. However, the arcane exhibits, such as "Athanasius Kircher: The World Is Bound with Secret Knots," are half real and half fabrication. You might call it a speculative museum. Every time I enter the museum, my mind becomes suspended in the space between fact, fiction, and fantasy and I leave in a state of epistemological dissonance that can only be described as wonder.

Interrogation

So far, I've written about remixing the archive from within; as part of the development of the institution or due to changes in the practice of the professionals sheltered in its vaults. Now, I'd like to cite some examples of those remixing the archive from slightly further outside the center of power though still as invited guests. In 1969, the Museum of Art at the Rhode Island School of Design invited Andy Warhol to guest-curate an exhibition drawn from their collection.[10] The resulting presentation was a hybrid museum collection exhibition and artist installation. The exhibition title, "Raid the Icebox I," revealed some of the mischievous tenor of the project. To the dismay of museum staff, Warhol piled shoes from the collection into a corner and stacked museum files on a desk in the gallery. He hung Windsor chairs from the walls and casually leaned fake (copies of) famous paintings along the walls. His remixing of the physical arrangement of artifacts shifted our focus from the taxonomical to the sociological and suggested that the museum may be less an intellectual temple of art history and perhaps more of an historic bounty chest of the rich.

After Warhol's assault on the classism of the archive, artist Fred Wilson exposed the aforementioned Eurocentric and colonial origins that had been and continue to linger not too far under its surface. In 1992, Wilson was invited to guest curate an exhibition at the Maryland Historical Society.[11] His remix of the collection, entitled "Mining the Museum," was telling. In one display, he juxtaposed filigreed silverware with slave shackles to suggest that one could not be made without the other. This display's pithy title, "metalwork," showed, in one word, how the taxonomies of Modernist collections tended to atomize objects so that the damning histories revealed in their interrelationships are papered over by seemingly neutral, objective, and naturalized systems of organization.

Warhol, Wilson, and numerous other agents have remixed the archive over the years, but their remixes have largely been limited to redescribing or rearranging objects from the collection. They have not been able to remix individual objects—until now. Artistic homage and appropriation has been around since art was born. Remix, though, is different from appropriation in one significant way. Appropriation most often entails an artist using an image or process created by another artist, whereas remix allows an artist to reuse the actual materials used in the original; that's usually impossible with traditional art forms. Who wants to cut up their original painting just so another artist can use it? Remix, however, is endemic in new media art. When artists remix the digital source material from another artist, they gain access to more than the public connotations in the work; they gain access to the hand and the craftsmanship (or coding skill) of the first artist. They gain access to the work's "material subconscious"—the ways in which the interaction between the source artist and medium influenced the outcome of the work. This can be played out in new remixed works not just as a rote outward effect, but also as an underlying condition. Remix opens up a broad new space for the remix artist and creates a new type of relationship between them, the source artist, and the public.

"Level of Confidence" is an artwork by Rafael Lozano-Hemmer that commemorates 43 students from the Ayotzinapa normalista school in Iguala,

Guerrero, Mexico.[12] In 2014, these students were victims of a mass political kidnapping and were most likely killed. "Level of Confidence" consists of a screen displaying the faces of the 43 students and a database of their facial recognition data. A camera scans the face of each visitor to the artwork and compares it to this database, constantly looking for the disappeared students in the faces of viewers and expressing the match as a percentage, a level of confidence that will never be 100%. Lozano-Hemmer open-sourced the source code for this digital artwork on the code-sharing site GitHub. To date, this free code has been used by two other groups to develop versions of the work that spotlight missing populations in Canada and Argentina.[13] The work is also for sale through commercial galleries as a limited edition of 12. Neither of these distribution strategies on its own is particularly notable. Other artists have created open-source digital art and yet more have sold their digital works in the art market. But few artists have done both simultaneously for the same work. Lozano-Hemmer's strategy defies the logic of the false dilemma that if an artwork is available for free that there is no reason to buy it. The artist is calling out art museums who purport to support artists, the creation of new work, and the preservation of important pieces, but who, in practice, collect only unique artifacts that will add to the exclusive prestige of their collection. Lozano-Hemmer has leveraged the unique properties of new media to rally both formal and informal social memory and, in so doing, he has remixed the logic of the archive.

Records and data about cultural heritage materials are valuable in addition to the materials themselves. Data about cultural collections comprise the index of formal social memory and the contents of such records—how each record frames its referred object—speak volumes about what we choose to remember and what we choose to forget. The popularity of the web brought not only new tools, but also a new consciousness around information access. Libraries responded first, readily taking their open access policies and structured digital information from their card catalog and LAN to the Internet. In contrast, museums went from providing essentially no comprehensive public access to collection records to providing online databases of records and images of their collections. Online access to records has provided qualitative shifts in the function of formal social memory as, for instance, it provides rural populations and remote researchers with unprecedented access to cultural information. Even visitors physically accessing the archive are often only scratching the surface. For instance, museums typically exhibit less than 10 percent of their collections at any given time.[14] Comprehensive access to collection records and other metadata unearths the other 90 percent and reveals the true extent of the archive. Such progress is important, but these online databases are designed around the atomization of each object, offering each record as a discrete unit that makes it easy to access but difficult to reuse or remix.

Going a step beyond providing online users with tools for searching individual records, several museums and libraries now provide access to their collection records as a comprehensive dataset, along with new permissions encouraging broad reuse. This encourages remixers to think about collections holistically and to forge new meanings from the interrelationships between objects. The Museum of Modern Art has open-sourced their collection records as one file via GitHub[15] and the Cooper Hewitt Museum of Design even provides an API that facilitates using their open source records on the same site.[16] Because much of their collection is older and free from copyright concerns, the Met Museum released more than 400,000 high-resolution images of their collection into the public domain.[17] The Smithsonian Library (a library within a museum) provides not only records about the books in their collections, but digital versions of the books themselves, as do an increasing number of libraries. All of these examples describe using new technologies to provide records of or enhanced access to physical cultural collections. However, as I mentioned earlier, many new objects entering the collections of museums, libraries, and archives are, themselves, born-digital artifacts. These new collections offer new and unique opportunities for remixing the archive.

I have written in the past about remixing the archive under the concept of the "open museum."[18] In the open museum, replicable and open digital objects are not artificially constrained with legal contracts to mimic the unique physicality and economic value of physical objects like paintings. Instead, artifacts such as "Level of Confidence" are collected by collaborative groups of institutions, directing more resources toward the artist and ensuring the distributed longevity of the digital object. In the open museum, institutions encourage cultural remixing of collections by open sourcing not only their records, but also the digital artifacts themselves. I was able to put some of these ideas into practice in my previous post at the UC Berkeley Art Museum and Pacific Film Archive in a curatorial project called NetArtchive.[19] NetArtchive presented one Internet artwork per month. Each artist allowed their finished work to be presented during an online exhibition and then, after the exhibition closed, they allowed the public to download the source files behind each finished work. A Creative Commons license encouraged ways in which each collection of images, video, and source code could be used in research and teaching or remixed into new works. NetArtchive was only as long-lived as my tenure at Berkeley and I learned a valuable lesson about optimistically permanent-sounding project names. Happily, the online contemporary art organization Rhizome developed an ongoing program called, "The Download,"[20] in which viewers can download source files for Internet artworks that Rhizome exhibits including some of the most innovative artists working in the medium. Finally, you can take the artwork home with you.

Suspicion

It's easy, for me at least, to get excited about seeing what happens to culture when previously hidden or entirely new genres of collections are increasingly made available for remixing. But insomuch as remix can be a critical strategy, it also behooves us to be critical of it. One potential danger of uncritically applying ideas of remix to the archive is the ideological chain in which open-source culture is linked to the sharing economy, which in turn affects neo-liberal social and economic policies. Wired, for instance, champions the point of view that open systems = open markets.[21] The chain seems to form invisibly. Since new technologies are so much a part of the discourse of remix, this ideology can become an unspoken *a priori* condition to remix. In turn, remix practices become symptomatic if not complicit in neo-liberalism. Others have written about this linkage, arguing either for or against it.[22] Remix as a critical practice must disclose, if not adjudicate, implicit ideologies rather than silently reify them. We've already seen a generation of cultural producers whose day job consists of slaving away at menial jobs for micro-payments in online sweatshops like Mechanical Turk. At night, they produce the artworks, music, and code that is later remixed by others; a privilege for which they are dismally compensated. Like Uber drivers or Airbnb providers, these artists are employed by apps whose investors profit from the artist's creativity without encumbering the responsibilities of providing benefits, retirement, or the option of collective bargaining. Neo-liberal capital atomizes laborers just as modern museums atomized the objects in the wunderkammer. This Dickensian remix dystopia is not especially new to artists. It is eerily similar to the art market under which artists have been struggling since . . . well, Dickens.

The ideological chain outlined above is insidious, but not unbreakable and this is where formal social memory comes in. For instance, the chain is forged on the premise that open systems = open markets. However, that equation can be rewritten to propose that open systems = open government. Opening up formal social memory to remix is a form of open government. Additionally, the institutions that perform formal social memory—the archive—collectively command vast resources. As these institutions develop new funding opportunities and new projects like The Download or the open museum that encourage open source culture, it is also our responsibility to build them on just social and economic models. This is one arena in which connecting the theories and practices of the archive is a necessary critical practice because an imaginary without ethics is a terrible thing.

History

The materials held in the archive comprise the evidence of history. The artworks, letters, fossils, machines, and manuscripts in the world's museums, libraries, and archives are "primary sources"[23] on which historic facts and arguments are based. This evidence is used to guide rigorous scholarship and to protect against political lies that rely on distorting history. The latter social memory function is so important that destruction of cultural heritage has been tried as a crime against humanity in world courts.[24] Historiography provides methods for using primary evidence to construct histories, but it provides no guarantee of total truth. For instance, the existence of this historic chain of evidence in the archive might suggest that there is one true objective history against which we can compare falsehoods. Of course, this is not the case. As Warhol's and Wilson's projects highlight, we choose what to remember and what to leave out. This is true not only in how we interpret a given artifact, but in its *a priori* selection and the taxonomy used to classify it. Even preservation is half science and half a host of socially charged choices. Most good history may be traced back to a primary source, but a primary source may spawn multiple valid histories. This cultural fecundity, this remixed imaginary, protects against power as much as the archive's potential to fix the truth against a lie.

The archive is a remix of cultural heritage. It also incorporates remix in the form of exhibitions and artist interventions that rearrange artifacts to conjure new meanings. Its structured metadata lends itself to the logic of remix. And the introduction of born-digital artifacts offers us the means of remixing the internal materiality of its objects. All of these, but especially the latter, demand that the archive develop new methods for preservation, hermeneutics, and historiography. These methods should be built not as bulwarks against the entropy of remix (because remix is not entropy) but as dynamic activities that incorporate the robust flexibility of remix. In this way, remix keeps the archive from becoming a brittle index and, instead, makes it a tool for wondering. In return, the archive contributes to the formulation of remix as a mature method. This is the dance; the clockwork of our romantic imaginary.

Notes

1 Umberto Eco, *Foucault's Pendulum* (London: Vintage, 2001).
2 Louis Cabri, "Discursive Events in the Electronic Archive of Postmodern and Contemporary Poetry," *English Studies in Canada* 30, no. 1 (2004): 51–72.
3 Angela Segal, "Disrupting the Archive," February 1, 2015, accessed August 31, 2016, https://materialpiers.wordpress.com/2015/02/01/disrupting-the-archive/.
4 "Cruising the Archive: Queer Art and Culture in Los Angeles, 1945–1980," July 13, 2012, accessed August 31, 2016, https://cruisingthearchive.org/.
5 Maria G. Cattel, *Social Memory and History: Anthropological Perspectives*, ed. Jacob J. Climo and Maria G. Cattell, 2nd ed. (New York: AltaMira Press, 2002).
6 "Museum Universe Data File," January 23, 2016, accessed August 31, 2016, www.imls.gov/research-evaluation/data-collection/museum-universe-data-file.
7 "Number of Libraries in the United States," September 4, 2015, accessed August 31, 2016, www.ala.org/tools/libfactsheets/alalibraryfactsheet01.
8 "The United States Has More Than 35,000 Museums," June 24, 2014, accessed August 31, 2016, http://hyperallergic.com/134152/the-united-states-has-more-than-35000-museums/.
9 Oliver Impey and A.C. MacGregor, eds., *The Origins of Museums: The Cabinet of Curiosities in Sixteenth and Seventeenth-Century Europe* (London: House of Stratus, 2001).
10 Deborah Bright, "Shopping the Leftovers: Warhol's Collecting Strategies in Raid the Icebox I," *Art History* 24, no. 2 (April 2001).
11 "Mining the Museum," accessed August 31, 2016, http://beautifultrouble.org/case/mining-the-museum/.

12 Rafael Lozano-Hemmer, "Project 'Level of Confidence,'" 2015, accessed August 31, 2016, www.lozano-hemmer.com/level_of_confidence.php.
13 "An Artwork Forces Us to Face Mexico's Disappeared Students," August 7, 2015, accessed August 31, 2016, http://hyperallergic.com/228317/an-artwork-forces-us-to-face-mexicos-disappeared-students/.
14 Geraldine Fabrikant, "Showcasing Archives, Museums Bring out the Good Stuff," *The New York Times*, November 15, 2014, accessed August 31, 2016, http://www.nytimes.com/2009/03/19/arts/artsspecial/19TROVE.html?_r=0.
15 "Museum of Modern Art Collection," GitHub, accessed August 31, 2016. https://github.com/MuseumofModernArt/collection.
16 "Cooper Hewitt Collection," GitHub, accessed August 31, 2016. https://github.com/cooperhewitt/collection.
17 "Metropolitan Museum Initiative Provides Free Access to 400,000 Digital Images," accessed August 31, 2016, http://metmuseum.org/press/news/2014/oasc-access.
18 Rinehart, Richard, and Jon Ippolito. *Re-collection: Art, New Media, and Social Memory* (Cambridge, MA: MIT Press, 2014), p. 106.
19 Richard Rinehart, "BAM/PFA NetArtchive," Archive.is, 2009, accessed August 31, 2016, http://archive.is/g09Pc.
20 "The Download: Sorry to Dump on You like This.zip," Rhizome, accessed August 31, 2016, http://rhizome.org/editorial/2015/nov/12/the-download/.
21 "WIRED Endorses Optimism," Wired.com, accessed August 31, 2016, www.wired.com/2016/08/wired-endorses-hillary-clinton/.
22 "A Wave of Disruption Is Sweeping in to Challenge Neoliberalism," *The Guardian*, March 12, 2015, accessed August 31, 2016, www.theguardian.com/sustainable-business/2015/mar/12/disruption-challenge-neoliberalism-commons-political-system.
23 "Primary Sources: A Guide for Historians—LibGuides at Princeton University," Princeton University, accessed August 31, 2016, http://libguides.princeton.edu/history/primarysources.
24 Lily Kuo, "Destroying History Is Now Being Charged as a War Crime," Huffington Post, accessed August 31, 2016, Document1www.huffingtonpost.com/entry/cultural-war-crime_us_57bb2058e4b0b51733a4a34b.

3
AUTHORSHIP

John Vallier

At first glance, the concept of authorship appears self-evident: it denotes an individual's act of having written, composed, or more generally created an original work. Part and parcel of this understanding is a view that the author is afforded a legally sanctioned claim of ownership over their innovative efforts, be it a book, an article, a musical composition, video, or perhaps a chapter about *authorship*. In short, an author *authors*—and owns—what s/he creates.

While commonplace, such an understanding is, like all concepts, rooted in historical, political, and cultural arcs of knowing that are far from predetermined. Remix, "the creative and efficient exchange of information made possible by digital technologies that is supported by the practice of cut/copy and paste"[1] has, in particular, called this prosaic understanding of authorship into question. Through such generative practices as dub, DJing, plunderphonics, fan-vidding, music video mashups, and a host of other remix-infused movements, traditional notions of individual creation, originality, and ownership have been disrupted and supplanted with ideas of anonymity, hacking, appropriation, communal creation, alteration, and sharing.

Throughout this essay I highlight the historical underpinnings of authorship, showing how it has evolved through key eras and movements. I describe how the disruptive and productive power of remix and its predecessors are evolving our understanding of authorship. I stress the way such practices, as well as alternative understandings of the term, provide counternarratives to commonly ascribed interpretations. With this I aim to give remix scholars, fans, and practitioners a nuanced insight into what we mean by *authorship*. Accepting a prosaic understanding of this term may, after all, place unnecessary limitations on our efforts to create new, productive works.

Authorship Defined

Dictionary definitions offer a grounded start for the exploration of any term. According to The Oxford English Dictionary, *author* is variously defined as "The writer of a book or other work; a person whose occupation is writing books,"[2] "an inventor, founder, or constructor (of something); a creator,"[3] and "the creator of an artistic work; a painter, photographer, film-maker, etc."[4] The OED goes on to describe an author as an individual with "authority," that is a "person on whose authority a statement is made; an authority, an informant."[5]

The historical vestiges of the term are unveiled via its etymological traces. *Author*, we are told, is preceded by the Anglo-Norman *auctor* and the Middle French *aucteur*:

> [W]riter of a book or other work . . . , creator, originator, source, person or thing which gives rise to something (second half of the 12th cent., originally and frequently with specific reference to God as the creator of the universe), the writings of an author collectively (first half of the 13th cent.), authority, informant (c1235 or earlier in Anglo-Norman in an apparently isolated attestation, 1546 in continental French), ancestor, parent (14th cent.).[6]

Stretching back further, the OED disinters the keyword's authoritarian roots by identifying its Greek forbearer, "αὐθεντικός . . . the author of a document being viewed as the guarantor of its authenticity."[7]

Authorship's Historical Mashup

The OED's definition and accompanying etymology begins to illustrate how our understanding of authorship developed into what it is today. To expand our awareness, I present a review of key historical moments for the term, knowing full well that that such an effort will be relatively general given the 2,000 or more years of history that inform the development of the term.

In the West, the origins of authorship are often traced back to Homer, the earliest of the epic Greek poets. While it is commonly accepted that Homer did not literally write down the *Iliad* or the *Odyssey*, he is nonetheless credited with authorship of these works. Andrew Bennett demonstrates how this modern understanding of Homer as author involves "anachronistic ways of thinking about the 'authorship' of the Iliad and the Odyssey."[8] Bennett reminds us of Albert Lord and his *The Singer of Tales*, a work that demands a recontextualization of our perception of authorship when applying it to poets of the Homeric age:

> Our real difficulty arises from the fact that, unlike the oral poet, we are not accustomed to thinking in terms of fluidity . . . It seems to us necessary

to construct an ideal text or to seek an original, and we remain dissatisfied with an ever-changing phenomenon. I believe that once we know the facts of oral composition we must cease trying to find an original of any traditional song. From one point of view each performance is an original. From another point of view it is impossible to retrace the work of generations of singers to that moment when some singer first sang a particular song.[9]

Given Lord's analysis, the Homeric notion of authorship should be appreciated as a communal one, where songs, poems, forms, and linguistic structures are handed down, remade anew with each performance, and reinserted back into the *to and fro* of tradition. This is not to deny, as Bennett writes, "that Homer may in fact have been an individual who brought the poems now known as the Iliad and the Odyssey to a level of perfection that transcends every other oral epic poem that has come down to us."[10] Whatever his poetic prowess, the point here is that authorship of the Homeric era is "fundamentally different from that of later, literate and especially print-based cultures, cultures which rely on a specific relationship between text and original writer, poet or 'author.'"[11]

Moving forward, we arrive at Plato, an author with a truly antagonistic attitude towards the craft. While Plato is credited with having scribed and subsequently claimed authorship over Socrates and other orators' expressions, he was ethically and politically dead set against the act of writing as, for example, is expressed in his portrayal of Socrates in the *Phaedrus*:

> Then anyone who leaves behind him a written manual, and likewise anyone who takes it over from him, on the supposition that such writing will provide something reliable and permanent, must be exceedingly simple-minded; he must really be ignorant of Ammon's utterance, if he imagines that written words can do anything more than remind one who knows that which the writing is concerned with.[12]

Plato's "writing against writing,"[13] and by extension, his overall distrust of authorship, is rooted in his conceptualization of *mimesis*. Often translated as imitation or a copy of the real, *mimesis* is a term that mimetic expert Matthew Potolsky describes as being much more nuanced and complex. Yes, mimesis "describes the relationship between artistic images and reality: art is a copy of the real. But this definition hardly accounts for the scope and significance of the idea. Mimesis can be said to imitate a dizzying array of originals: nature, truth, beauty, mannerisms, actions, situations, examples, ideas."[14] Plato's formative understanding of the term was imbued with suspicion. "Plato's theory of mimesis is very much a theory of political life," notes Potolsky.[15] "The imitator is not just a bad craftsman but a danger to the health of the republic; mimesis is not just a matter of stories and pictures but a problem for the nature of humanity itself."[16] Writing was for

Plato a compromised second-hand imitation of genuine testimony. Writing was merely a semblance of what was said and known, a particular copy of a universal form and, therefore, inherently imperfect.

Aristotle had a more productive understanding of mimesis and, by association, of authorship. He appropriated Plato's depreciated notion of the term and flipped its meaning into a constructive, creative, and uniquely human phenomena worthy of reasoned investigation.[17] For Aristotle, in the hands of competent artists—be they poets, authors, or what have you—mimesis had the creative potential to generate something new and enduring. "Rather than being mere imitator, the artist is a maker, a craftsperson."[18] Mimesis was not something alien to be distrusted. Aristotle's mimesis was innate in humans and critical to the process of learning and developing reason, that which Aristotle celebrated most of all.

In medieval times, the *auctor* practiced their craft without promise of individual recognition. This sense of authorship stands out against our own. "By contrast with the 'modern' sense of the author as a personalized individual expressing intentions and a particular subjectivity, the medieval *auctor* is seen as effectively, even if not always in practice, anonymous."[19] In this sense, the medieval author greatly parallels that of the Hellenistic as it involved "submission to the tradition."[20] However, with the adoption and wide distribution of the printing press in the fifteenth and sixteenth centuries, a substantive change in the author's role began to take shape. This technology of reproduction gave authors the capability of distributing their works widely and, therefore, the possibility of accruing acclaim beyond their locale. "At the same time," writes Hadi Nicholas Deeb, "those technologies ironically facilitated copying by other people. This tension began to imbue the author with attributes of ownership. For example, Dürer's colophon to a 1511 edition of his woodcut prints sharply warned would-be 'thieves.'"[21] The shift from author as anonymous craftsperson rooted in tradition, to author as an individual authority that created reproducible works, was underway.

Further buttressing the connection between authorship and ownership, were emerging Enlightenment-era revelations about possession and private property. In *Book II* of his *The Limits of Human Understanding*, John Locke argued that when an individual detaches something from its natural state, that person has "mixed his labour with it and joined it to something that is his own, and thereby makes it his property."[22] For Locke, a person had a natural right to own the products of their labor. "For this 'labour' being the unquestionable property of the labourer, no man but he can have a right to what that is once joined to."[23] When extended to the notion of authorship, the result is clear: what an author authors is theirs to own. This Lockean ideal—further buoyed by "the indubitable *cogito ergo sum* of Cartesian rationalism, the immediate individualized faith instituted by the Protestant Reformation, and the concept of personal property as articulated in the work of Thomas Hobbes"[24]—was legally sanctioned in 1710 when the Parliament of Great Britain passed the Statute of Anne. This statute marks the birth of copyright law in which judicial and governmental bodies, not private entities, began to regulate copyright.

The Romantic era had a profound and long-lasting impact on our contemporary notion of authorship. As Martha Woodmansee writes, the Romantic author was an adulated individual, "blessed with unique insight" who would "bring forth new and original works of art in the world."[25] Notions of "genius" and "originality" exemplify the Romantic author. By way of example, Woodmansee points to Wordsworth, who in 1815 claimed that "the genius is someone who does something utterly new, unprecedented, or in the radical formulation that he prefers, produces something that never existed before."[26]

Wordsworth's ideas reiterate those of Edward Young, as expressed in his *Conjectures on Original Composition*. Laura Lenhart describes how Young's "work would be influential on many German philosophers during the eighteenth century, who adopted his thoughts on original composition in their own work on the nature of authorship and literary property."[27] Lenhart shows how his thoughts came to shape the two primary features that we identify with Romantic authorship: "First, it is notable that the source of originality lies in the mind of the writer. Secondly, while the genius produces both works that are imitations and works that are original, original works are to be valued more than imitations."[28] In this way, the author-genius is understood as being wholly innovative in their output—free from the bonds of history, culture, and tradition.

The Death and Specter of the Author

This notion of the lone author, as one who creates works intrinsically imbued with a sacrosanct aura of originality, forms the basis for much of our modern understanding of the term. However, as we have seen from the distilled history above, this prevailing sense only began to emerge with the invention of the printing press. In "The Death of the Author," Roland Barthes traces this growth, describing the author as "a modern figure, a product of our society insofar as, emerging from the Middle Ages with English empiricism, French rationalism and the personal faith of the Reformation, it discovered the prestige of the individual."[29] Barthes's modern author is forged through these eras and stands in the twentieth century as a solitary and original authority. According to Barthes, it had become a popular assumption to grant the author ultimate authority, even to the point of controlling the interpretation of their work:

> The explanation of a work is always sought in the man or woman who produced it, as if it were always in the end, through the more or less transparent allegory of the fiction, the voice of a single person, the author 'confiding' in us.[30]

With his essay, Barthes confronts and ultimately attempts to extinguish the omnipotence and omniscience of the author. As Bennett writes, Barthes disrupts "the power-structures embedded within the promotion of such a figure, within conventional accounts of authorship, textuality and the literary institution."[31] Barthes does this by reconfiguring the "message of the Author-God ..." as a "multi-dimensional space in which a variety of writings, none of them original, blend and clash."[32] When presented with this "tissue of quotations drawn from innumerable centres of culture,"[33] it is the reader, not the author, who ultimately generates its meaning(s). With the intentional fallacy exposed, Barthes declares:

> there is one place where this multiplicity is focused and that place is the reader, not, as was hitherto said, the author. The reader is the space on which all the quotations that make up a writing are inscribed without any of them being lost.[34]

By upending the author's authority and legitimizing the interpretative power of the reader, Barthes in essence exchanges the former with the latter. Barthes, Bennett contends, replaces "the controlling, limiting subjectivity of the author with the controlling, limiting subjectivity of the ... anonymous reader."[35]

In his "What is an Author?" (1969), Michel Foucault extends Barthes's critique. While agreeing with Barthes that the author is a construct—one that came into being during a "privileged moment of *individualization* in the history of ideas, knowledge, literature, philosophy, and the sciences"[36]—he moves beyond authorial mortality to ask us what functions continue to linger:

> [I]t is not enough to declare that we should do without the writer (the author) and study the work itself ... It is not enough ... to repeat the empty affirmation that the author has disappeared. For the same reason, it is not enough to keep repeating (after Nietzsche) that God and man have died a common death. Instead, we must locate the space left empty by the author's disappearance, follow the distribution of gaps and breaches, and watch for the openings that this disappearance uncovers.[37]

Using this fissure as a deconstructive foil, Foucault compels us, as Ron Moy observes, to "use the metaphorical disappearance of the author ... revealing and exploiting inconsistencies in order to advance our understanding of the discourses at play with the authorship debate."[38] In so doing, Foucault uncovers the persistence of functions that live beyond the author, such as legal and disciplinary systems that delineate and control discourse on the topic. When comparing these two essays, Bennett contends that "Barthes is concerned only with a certain absence, a 'negative' space of writing. Foucault is concerned with the social and historical construction of a 'writing subject' and posits writing as a space in which this disappearing is endlessly enacted."[39] In the end, and with the author's passing, Foucault declares:

given the historical modifications that are taking place, it does not seem necessary that the author function remain constant in form, complexity, and even in existence. I think that, as our society changes, at the very moment when it is in the process of changing, the author function will disappear.[40]

Has this moment arrived?

Authorship Remixed, Re-Envisioned

The "cut/copy and paste" practice of remix is, like authorship, forged from tradition. While remix today uses software to generate digital samples, it first grew from such analog era movements as photomontage, détournement, collage, and eventually—in the realms of music and sounds—dub and plunderphonics. Remix, along with these twentieth-century precedents, embodies the post-authorial worldviews envisioned by Barthes and Foucault. As Navas writes:

> Remix's dependency on sampling questioned the role of the individual as genius and sole creator, who would "express himself." Sampling . . . allows for the death of the author; therefore, it is no coincidence that around the time when remixes began to be produced, during the sixties and seventies, authorship—as discourse—was entertained by Roland Barthes and Michel Foucault, respectively.[41]

Gunkel echoes Navas's observations on remix's role in the authorial turn, underscoring the part it played and continues to play in signaling the emergence of a new form of post-individualistic authorship. "The mashup and remix are widely recognized as an artifact (if not the principal illustration) of this alternative configuration. In reworking the recorded material of others, remix challenges the usual assumption of authorship and moves away from the Romantic notion of artistic genius.[42] Remix is emblematic of a postmodern form of production, where sampling, collaboration, reuse, and recontextualization are embraced, encouraged, and valued. It stands in opposition to the author-god and its claim to spontaneously release original works of genius.[43] It affords us a critically grounded and communally oriented means of creation, where participation is maximized and room for alternative modes of understanding (e.g., indigenous notions of ownership) and action (e.g., digital détournement) can be realized.[44] In this way it resonates with Walter Benjamin's call to commandeer production from the ruling class for the purpose of cultural critique and resistance. While the legacy of the author-function continues to pervade legal structures (e.g., increased corporate ownership) and disciplinary expectations (e.g., the expectancy of original scholarship in the academy), such constrictive understandings will undoubtedly wither as remix culture expands.

Notes

1 Eduardo Navas, "The Author Function in Remix," *Remix Theory*, accessed September 15, 2016, http://remixtheory.net/?p=309.
2 "author, n.1a," OED Online, Oxford University Press, accessed September 15, 2016, www.oed.com/viewdictionaryentry/Entry/13329.
3 "author, n.2b," OED Online, Oxford University Press, accessed September 15, 2016, www.oed.com/viewdictionaryentry/Entry/13329.
4 "author, n.2e," OED Online, Oxford University Press, accessed September 15, 2016, www.oed.com/viewdictionaryentry/Entry/13329.
5 "author, n.5," OED Online, Oxford University Press, accessed September 15, 2016, www.oed.com/viewdictionaryentry/Entry/13329.
6 "author, etymology," OED Online, Oxford University Press, accessed September 15, 2016, www.oed.com/viewdictionaryentry/Entry/13329.
7 Ibid.
8 Andrew Bennett, *The Author* (New York: Routledge, 2005), 32.
9 Albert B. Lord, *The Singer of Tales* (Cambridge, MA: Harvard University, 1960), 100.
10 Andrew Bennett, *The Author* (New York: Routledge, 2005), 32.
11 Ibid., 35.
12 Reginald Hackforth, *Phaedrus* (Cambridge: Cambridge University Press, 1952), 158.
13 Seán Burke, *The Ethics of Writing Authorship and Legacy in Plato and Nietzsche* (Edinburgh: Edinburgh University Press, 2007), 56.
14 Matthew Potolsky, *Mimesis* (New York: Routledge, 2006), 1.
15 Ibid., 29.
16 Ibid.
17 Ibid., 33.
18 Ibid., 35.
19 Andrew Bennett, *The Author* (New York: Routledge, 2005), 40.
20 Ibid., 41.
21 Hadi Nicholas Deeb, *Remixing Authorship Copyright and Capital in Hollywood's New Media Age* (PhD dissertation, UCLA, 2014), 20.
22 John Locke, *Second Treatise of Government* (New York: Barnes & Noble Books, 2004), 17.
23 Ibid.
24 David J. Gunkel, *Of Remixology: Ethics and Aesthetics after Remix* (Cambridge, MA: MIT Press, 2016), 117.
25 Martha Woodmansee, "The Genius and the Copyright: Economic and Legal Conditions of the Emergence of the Author," *Eighteenth Century Studies* 17 (1984): 425–448.
26 Ibid., 430.
27 Laura. R. Lenhart, "Normative Notions of Authorship and Participation in the iSociety," accessed on September 15, 2016, www.ideals.illinois.edu/bitstream/handle/2142/15228/Notions_of_Authorship1.pdf?sequence=2.
28 Ibid.
29 Roland Barthes, "The Death of the Author," in *Authorship: From Plato to the Postmodern: A Reader*, ed. Seán Burke (Edinburgh: Edinburgh University Press, 1995), 221.
30 Ibid.
31 Andrew Bennett, *The Author* (New York: Routledge, 2005), 15.
32 Roland Barthes, "The Death of the Author," in *Authorship: From Plato to the Postmodern: A Reader*, ed. Seán Burke (Edinburgh: Edinburgh University Press, 1995), 223.
33 Ibid.
34 Ibid., 224.
35 Andrew Bennett, *The Author* (New York: Routledge, 2005), 129.

36 Michel Foucault, "What is an Author?" in *Authorship: From Plato to the Postmodern: A Reader*, ed. Seán Burke (Edinburgh: Edinburgh University Press, 1995), 225, emphasis in original.
37 Ibid., 226–227.
38 Ron Moy, *Authorship Roles in Popular Music: Issues and Debates* (New York: Routledge, 2015), xii.
39 Andrew Bennett, *The Author* (New York: Routledge, 2005), 20.
40 Michel Foucault, "What is an Author?" in *Authorship: From Plato to the Postmodern: A Reader*, ed. Seán Burke (Edinburgh: Edinburgh University Press, 1995), 230.
41 Eduardo Navas, "The Author Function in Remix," *Remix Theory*, accessed September 15, 2016, http://remixtheory.net/?p=309.
42 David J. Gunkel, *Of Remixology: Ethics and Aesthetics after Remix* (Cambridge, MA: MIT Press, 2016), 129.
43 As John Logie writes, "Mashup and remix composition are in a notion of play with respect to the concept of authorship. These compositions celebrate curation, connection, collaboration, and critique (whether conscious or not). As such they are at odds with US copyright law's foundational organization around an author/work model." John Logie, "Peeling the Layers of the Onion: Authorship in Mashup and Remix Cultures," in *The Routledge Companion to Remix Studies*, ed. Eduardo Navas, Owen Gallagher and xtine burrough (New York: Routledge, 2015), 552.
44 Authorship's pre-Enlightenment roots are in tune with this understanding as we have seen with the Homer's own recitation of tradition bearing epic poems.

Bibliography

Barthes, Roland. "The Death of the Author." In *Authorship: From Plato to the Postmodern: a Reader*, ed. Seán Burke. Edinburgh: Edinburgh University Press, 1995.
Bennett, Andrew. *The Author*. London: New York: Routledge, 2005.
Burke, Seán. *The Ethics of Writing Authorship and Legacy in Plato and Nietzsche*. Edinburgh: Edinburgh University Press, 2007.
Deeb, Hadi Nicholas. *Remixing Authorship Copyright and Capital in Hollywood's New Media Age*. PhD dissertation, UCLA, 2014.
Foucault, Michel. "What is an Author?" In *The Book History Reader*, eds. David Finkelstein and Alistair McCleery, pp. 225–230. New York: Routledge, 2002.
Gunkel, David J. *Of Remixology: Ethics and Aesthetics after Remix*. Cambridge, MA: MIT Press, 2016.
Hackforth, R. *Phaedrus*. Cambridge: Cambridge University Press, 1952.
Lenhart, Laura. R. "Normative Notions of Authorship and Participation in the iSociety." Accessed on September 15, 2016: www.ideals.illinois.edu/bitstream/handle/2142/15228/Notions_of_Authorship1.pdf?sequence=2
Locke, John. *Second Treatise of Government*. New York: Barnes & Noble Books, 2004.
Logie, John. "Peeling the Layers of the Onion: Authorship in Mashup and Remix Cultures." In *The Routledge Companion to Remix Studies*, eds. Eduardo Navas, Owen Gallagher and xtine burrough, pp 190–200. New York: Routledge, 2015.
Lord, Albert B. *The Singer of Tales*. Cambridge, MA: Harvard University, 1960.
Moy, Ron. *Authorship Roles in Popular Music: Issues and Debates*. New York: Routledge, 2015.
Navas, Eduardo. "The Author Function in Remix." *Remix Theory*. Accessed September 15,2016: http://remixtheory.net/?p=309.

OED Online. Oxford University Press, accessed September 15, 2016: www.oed.com/viewdictionaryentry/Entry/13329.

Potolsky, Matthew. *Mimesis*. New York: Routledge, 2006.

Woodmansee, Martha. "The Genius and the Copyright: Economic and Legal Conditions of the Emergence of the Author." *Eighteenth Century Studies* 17 (1984): 429.

4
BRICOLAGE

Annette N. Markham

Bricolage can be characterized as *an action* one takes (as a bricoleur), *an attitude* (or epistemology), and the resulting *product* or outcome of both. It is also an approach built (and/or well-suited) for political resistance. Associated concepts include pastiche, collage, remix. Bricolage is used mostly in art, organizational studies, and interpretive sociology to describe a particular type of knowledge and artistic production.[1] Remix and bricolage are often used synonymously, but a close look at the concept of bricolage reveals interesting etymological distinctions, which can usefully add nuance to the concepts that underlie various practices and products associated with remix culture.

Origin

Bricolage is a French term that roughly translates to *tinkerer* or *handyman*. Its contemporary usage is traced to French anthropologist Claude Lévi-Strauss, who used the term in *The Savage Mind:*

> In its old sense the verb "bricoler" applied to ball games and billiards, to hunting, shooting and riding. It was however always used with reference to some extraneous movement: a ball rebounding, a dog straying or a horse swerving from its direct course to avoid an obstacle. And in our own time the 'bricoleur' is still someone who works with his hands and uses devious means compared to those of a craftsman.[2]

When considered as a keyword in remix studies, it is the use of any available means or whatever is at hand that makes bricolage relevant. Even more specifically, according to Louridas,[3] the key element in the above conceptualization by Lévi-

Strauss is that the available materials for thought or action are finite, heterogeneous, and limited to those which are incidental or *un mouvement incident* ("extraneous" in the English translation above). The following passage from Lévi-Strauss clarifies that:

> The bricoleur is adept at performing a large number of diverse tasks; but, unlike the engineer, he does not subordinate each of them to the availability of raw materials and tools conceived and procured for the purpose of the project. His universe of instruments is closed and the rules of his game are always to always make do with 'whatever is at hand', that is to say with a set of tools and materials which is always finite and is also heterogeneous because what it contains bears no relation to the current project, or indeed to any particular project, but is the contingent result of all the occasions there have been to renew or enrich the stock or to maintain it with the remains of previous constructions or destructions.[4]

Lévi-Strauss uses bricolage analogically to compare mythological or magical ways of knowing to scientific methods. The difference, he articulates at one point, is that science "uses structures, in the form of its underlying theories and hypotheses, to arrive at its results, which take the form of events. Bricolage works the opposite way: it creates structures, in the form of its artefacts, by means of contingent events." Bricolage, then, is the process and product of using what is ready at hand to get the job done, whether that job is philosophy, art, architecture, design, management, or video mashups.

After Lévi-Strauss brings the word to anthropologists in the 1960s, it gets taken up by many others to discuss knowledge production more generally within the radicalization of the sciences of the epoch. Derrida, for example, discusses the concept at length in a 1966 lecture, both praising and critiquing Lévi-Strauss's concept, saying: "If one calls bricolage the necessity of borrowing one's concepts from the text of a heritage which is more or less coherent or ruined, it must be said that every discourse is bricoleur."[5]

In the 1970s, cultural theorists associated with the Birmingham Center for Contemporary Cultural Studies (CCCS) "used the concept to describe the aesthetic practices of working-class subcultures of the 1960s and 1970s," focusing on the ways these "subcultural practitioners challenge the hegemony of the dominant (read bourgeois) culture not through explicit acts of resistance, but 'obliquely' through style."[6]

Bricolage emerges in qualitative sociology and communication studies during the interpretive turn of the 1990s to encapsulate various processes of interpretive methods. The concept of bricolage now relates closely to artistic practice during the 2000s, as cut/copy/paste practices associated with digital media get easier, bricolage joins many other concepts as ways to describe various practices and products associated with remix culture.

Below, I discuss bricolage as epistemology, action, and product. This is a deliberate choice—to tie the concept of bricolage closely to the academic process of sensemaking, whereby scholars shift from thinking about what we have come to know to telling the world what we know. More precisely, this entry emerges from my own use of bricolage, pastiche, fragmented narrative, and remix as inspirations for experimenting with tools and techniques that resonate with the complexity of twenty-first-century cultural formations.[7]

Bricolage as an Epistemology

Bricolage both reflects and reifies a way of knowing that many of us in the early twenty-first century take for granted. I'm by no means the first to notice that

> we comprehend the world in moments, fragments, glimpses. I might see something one way one day and completely revise my understanding of it another day based on any number of things that happen: conversations I have that spark new ideas, scents on the wind that provoke particular memories, movies I watch, parks I meander through to collect thoughts and leaves.[8]

McCoy provides a list of approaches that have long challenged "simplistic realist ontology, the rational knowing subject, and the transparency of language."[9] Her tip-of-the-iceberg list includes such terms as deconstruction, Foucauldian genealogy, rhizomatics, diffraction, troubling, praxiography, method assemblage, and post-humanist performativity.

We could add many to this list, but the key point is that there is now a long legacy of scholarship built from what Kincheloe calls "an epistemology of complexity."[10] There is a widespread and still growing acknowledgment that objective or "god's eye" approaches to understanding and representing the social are deeply flawed in that they are, for the most part, reductionist. While abstraction may be inevitable for humans, as Mol and Law note,[11] there are ways to go about it without simplification. However, this requires a significant shift in one's stance or attitude. Since the 1960s, bricolage has been a primary term to facilitate and articulate this theoretical reorientation.

Bricolage brings serendipity to the foreground. Serendipity, in this sense, is not accidental but incidental. In distinguishing accident from serendipity, Meyers notes that accident implies mindlessness, whereas "accidental discoveries would be nothing without keen, creative minds knowing what to do with them."[12] In his book *Happy Accidents*, Meyers argues that scientific and specifically medical discoveries come through recognition of, rather than stumbling across. This implies a state of readiness for shifting one's perception so as to see what is already there in a different or new way.

In the field of qualitative inquiry, Kincheloe,[13] following Denzin and Lincoln,[14] links this state of readiness to the development of a critical consciousness that allows researchers to acknowledge and work within situations and relations of complexity. As Kincheloe refines his argument over time, we can note a shift from an emphasis on serendipity that comes from multidisciplinarity[15] to one that actively resists monological knowledge. In his later argument, Kincheloe describes:

> In its hard labours in the domain of complexity the bricolage views research methods actively rather than passively, meaning that we actively construct our research methods from the tools at hand rather than passively receiving the 'correct', universally applicable methodologies.[16]

Tinkering, in the Lévi-Straussian sense, then, is not just about using whatever is at hand, but involves a critically oriented, multiperspectival, and reflexive cognition.

Kincheloe goes further to develop "the bricolage" as not only an epistemological but also an ontological shift toward a relational understanding of the world, noting "bricoleurs act on the concept that theory is not an explanation of nature—it is more an explanation of our relation to nature."[17] With attention on both complexity and relationality, the basic foundations of knowledge production necessarily change. Here, it is worth quoting Kincheloe at length:

> What the bricolage is dealing with in this context is a double ontology of complexity: first, the complexity of objects of inquiry and their being-in-the-world; second, the nature of the social construction of human subjectivity, the production of human "being." Such understanding opens a new era of social research where the process of becoming human agents is appreciated with a new level of sophistication. The complex feedback loop between an unstable social structure and the individual can be charted in a way that grants human beings insight into the means by which power operates and the democratic process is subverted. In this complex ontological view, bricoleurs understand that social structures do not determine individual subjectivity but constrain it in remarkably intricate ways. The bricolage is acutely interested in developing and employing a variety of strategies to help specify these ways subjectivity is shaped.[18]

Bricolage situates well as an epistemology of how we come to know the world. It also fits well and has been used within most if not all the "post" stances emerging in and after the 1960s. Yet as I run across this term in the vernacular setting, as it is used in hundreds of texts to discuss art, fashion, leadership, literature, music, poetic forms, remix, research methods, subcultural movements, and so forth, I don't get a sense that most usage is epistemological. In a more everyday sense, it is a description or even a justification for a particular patchwork approach that involves assembling materials together, pasting and layering to find meaning, and reusing what we've used before in new ways, all terms that fit well with remix. There is a persistent notion that bricolage also involves using what is ready at hand, which we might associate with but is not limited to practices of DIY. Referring again to Derrida, if we accept how culture and knowledge is enacted, understood, or made sense of, everything could be considered bricolage.[19] Let us look more closely at the idea of bricolage as action.

See Chapter 11, "DIY Culture."

Bricolage as an Action

As organizational theorist Karl Weick wrote in 1993, "the defining characteristic of a bricoleur is that this person makes do with whatever tools and materials are at hand." Drawing from Lévi-Strauss, Weick adds:

> these resources are always heterogeneous because, unlike the materials available to the engineer, the bricoleur's materials have no relation to any particular project. Elements are collected and retained on the principle that they may come in handy.[20]

This "making do" has remained a persistent characteristic of bricolage since the 1960s, no matter where and how the term is used. Importantly, this "making do" is neither random nor unskilled. Rather, it is the power to use what is immediately or perhaps even incidentally at hand to make sense of a situation or solve a problem. Thayer[21] uses bricolage to describe the fundamental actions of strong leaders to "make things work by ingeniously using whatever is at hand" or "fixing things on the spot through a creative vision of what is available and what might be done with it."[22]

If we follow this interpretation, bricolage is similar but different from closely associated actions of remix and improvisation. Weick[23] explains: "If there is a key to success as a bricoleur it is buried in Lévi-Strauss's statement that objects "are not known as a result of their usefulness; they are deemed to be useful or interesting because they are first of all known."[24] In other words, bricolage depends at least in part on the accidental, incidental, and contingent. When materials are at hand, we will tend to use these as a form of action. Thus bricolage is also about limits. There is an intriguing notion that the materials are situated proximally—whether physically or psychologically—to the problem at hand.

In this interpretation, knowledge-making is less about seeing everything as a nail because we only have a hammer and more about using a hammer as a steering wheel since it's both available and it works. In this way, the action of the bricoleur may be distinct from other types of creative sensemaking actions, such as remix or improvisation.

This element of limitations leads us to consider where these limitations come from, or who is more likely to engage in what we might call bricolage. Johnson's[25] work emphasizes the importance of considering the ideological situation within which the term arose in anthropology, as a term to describe the savage, the non-engineer, the "Other" of the so-called rational (read, colonialist) world. In my reading of post-colonialist theorist Maria Belen Martin Lucas,[26] there is a strong connection between the activities common to bricolage and the limitations of being a woman in traditional patriarchal societies. She begins with Virginia Woolf's writing in 1929, which is worth repeating here:

> Who shall say that even now "the novel" . . . this most pliable of all forms is rightly shaped for her use? No doubt we shall find her knocking that into shape for herself when she has the free use of her limbs; and providing some new vehicle, not necessarily in verse, for the poetry in her . . . The book has somehow to be adapted to the body, and at a venture one would say that women's books should be shorter, more concentrated, than those of men, and framed so that they do not need long hours of steady and uninterrupted work. For interruptions there will always be.[27]

This adaptation of the book to the body gives us, Martin Lucas argues, a "new concept of narrative which we currently nominate 'body writing.'"[28] The "short story cycle" is one variation on this, emerging among communities of Canadian writers:

> The distinctive characteristics of this genre are the recurrence of characters, settings, events, and or symbols; interdependence between the stories in the cycle; sequential development of the events by a process of accumulation of details; re-construction of the narrative in each new story; and fragmentation of the chronological line.[29]

The action of bricolage is not only within, but across stories as imagined and enacted by others in the community.

In the case of short story cycles as a particular instance or type of activity, one can notice how the bricoleur doesn't simply use external objects at hand but includes embodied time and space, her situation, her interruptions, her multiple roles, as material knowing. This enables us to blur and strengthen the connection between the method or action and the active and critical consciousness, or epistemology.[30]

I use this example from postcolonial scholar María Belén Martín Lucas deliberately, to point to the longer history of the bricoleur as an actor, or the action of bricolage as "cultural counter-practice."[31] We need not look far to find many crafts particular to or emerging from women's social experiences, such as quilting, which provide a slightly different historical trajectory for bricolage than

Lévi-Strauss's definitions. In the lives of the so-called savage, we can see the bodies of those who are most likely to engage in bricolage. These "Others" are presumed to have a special way of knowing (mythical or magical), and act accordingly. As Johnson suggests, our Lévi-Straussian bricoleur "may be a marginal figure, and bricolage a 'survival' of older practices which are now tolerated only as hobbies or pastimes in modern industrial societies."[32]

By looking at bricolage as action in its historical and everyday practice, especially in this example by women in traditional patriarchal societies, we can notice those elements of bricolage that resist linearity, universality, monologic, and reductionism by reclaiming fragmentation, multiplicity, fluidity, and complexity.

Bricolage has become a model and perhaps a metonym for how resistance (cultural, structural, political, etc.) is built into certain ways of knowing and not others. The concept might broadly include any attempt to make meaning by "drawing on available material, cognitive, affective, and social resources."[33]

Bricolage as Product

Bricolage encompasses a potentially endless array of activities, only some of which end up being bricolage in form or even visibly bricolage. The outcome of quilting or mashing up Internet memes would be clearly noticed as bricolage. The outcome of fragmented or deconstructionist analysis might be less visible as bricolage, since it may or may not exhibit the characteristic patchwork or assemblage we associate with bricolage. If we zoom in on social research and methodologies that use or refer to bricolage, we can see a strong emphasis on multiplicity and non-linearity. The product, therefore, is not so easily separated from the process or epistemology.

The bricoleur, if we look back to Lévi-Strauss's conceptualizations and borrow from Johnson's excellent in-depth history, works in a constrained space whereby the tools and knowledge are limited to the immediate past/present. Lévi-Strauss's depiction contrasts the bricoleur to the engineer. Whereas the rationale for the latter is to go beyond what is available, the former stays within the limits of what is already there. But when it comes to the actual product of bricolage, this is less obviously developed in Lévi-Strauss's description. Since the 1960s, we see many uses of the term that simply state that the outcome of the bricoleur's action is bricolage, which we can say is a combination of elements chosen because they are readily at hand—whatever that might look like.

Weick's later development of the concept helps us see that a bricoleur's materials and tools are chosen by their proximity to the thinker, the situation, or the problem. As one example, Weick uses Harper's detailed study of a craftsman in upper New York state who makes tractors out of various parts of other things. This is not because the bricoleur is seeking to make art but because, within a limited access model, he is able to creatively combine existing elements into a structure that later, others and perhaps he himself, take to be novel. Martin Lucas[34] uses the example of story cycles to illustrate how bricolage emerges as a mosaic from different fragments of stories, over time, created recursively and reflexively by Canadian female writers.

The product of academic work differs from other types of bricolage. Although Kincheloe discusses bricolage as a characteristic element of interpretive qualitative research,[35] most of what we recognize as bricolage is only visible as genre or format of presenting research to others. In this sense, bricolage as product is the unique collage, montage, composite, fragmented, or layered account that comes out of the process of interpretive or postmodern inquiry. Otherwise, bricolage becomes an explanation, whereby it is not bricolage in itself. This is an important distinction.

As exemplary transformation of academic texts in the Internet era, we can look to hypertext. Michael Joyce,[36] Shelley Jackson,[37] Jill Walker Rettberg,[38] and other hypertext scholars in the 1980s and 1990s experimented with texts that highlight how our cognitive processing functions by association. It worked well in experimental formats—hypertext as experienced on the web reflects this associative thinking very well. In peer-reviewed journals or books it was very difficult to replicate this in writing. John December built a strong model for hypertext articles in *CMC Magazine*, which was, for a time, adopted by the *Journal of Computer Mediated Communication*, but this quickly fell out of fashion. Many of us felt it was just too disconcerting. This aligns well with Fisher's notion[39] that as homo-narrans, or storytelling animals, we are somewhat locked into our linear narrative ways.

In my own scholarly practice, I have been working to find a vocabulary that effectively disrupts the predominance of traditional textbook models for social research methods, to find visual tools for unlearning linearity and an orientation toward individuals and objects. In my academic ethnographic writing, I have produced fragmented narratives, used multiple fonts to highlight different voices, presented alternate endings, and presented texts in nonlinear format. This is actually a common practice in interpretive qualitative inquiry circles. Still, I'm struck by how, even now, "linear arguments constructed in traditional forms give us a false sense of security about the solidity or unity of our interpretations as well as the ways we arrive at those interpretations."[40] The Internet provides the capacity to enact bricolage in ways that were not possible before. I, and perhaps others, have been more likely to call this remix rather than bricolage, although this is not universal. However, it is an interesting ending point to conclude with, as there might be a reason to more fully compare these terms conceptually to parse out their singularities and overlaps.

Bricolage and/vs Remix

As noted above, bricolage is often conflated with other similar terms. In this discussion, we can see many connections between concepts of bricolage and remix, especially if we think of the basic processes of using pre-existing materials, combining disparate elements, and making something new. I found it useful, in being challenged to distinguish between bricolage and remix,[41] to focus on the purpose of doing either.

In examining more closely the apparent rationale, we can get a sense of the underlying epistemological and ontological frameworks that direct, guide, or prompt one's decisions or habits. Here, we can begin to see some interesting distinctions, if perhaps only theoretically: bricolage is a label more often granted than chosen, whereas remix tends to be the opposite. There is also an ideological distinction when we look at where the term appears. Following Lévi-Strauss, the term bricolage was taken up in organizational theory, sociology, and, surprisingly, in the medical and hard sciences, whereas remix grew out of marginalized practices and has only recently gained momentum as a viable academic practice or product.[42] Of course, remix is also a newer term, so the distinctions are only now being made.

The difference may be in the output of one's efforts, which is a direct connection to one's purpose. The bricoleur, if we take the strict sense of Lévi-Strauss, is making something—a product or a thing, such as a quilt or a painting or a tractor. Following and extending from his work, organizational theorists such as Thayer[43] and Weick[44] talk about leaders as bricoleurs, whereby the product is not object but subject, intangible and social. Whether in initial or later usage, bricolage as a concept seems to value most highly the outcome or product of the bricoleur. We can conceptualize and use bricolage as an attitude and process, of course, but the outcome is where the value and impact of bricolage lies.

I see this more clearly when I compare bricolage to remix, where the focus is on the ongoing and inherently unfinished process of remixing. If we look to the work of contemporary remix theorists, the attention on products and outcomes notwithstanding, there is a temporary quality that renders remix powerful. A meme is not a meme unless it morphs into something else and travels beyond its original conception. "Remix focuses our attention on the way temporally situated arguments are assembled and reassembled as they traverse various audiences."[45]

If we see remix as extending or enacting bricolage, we can envision the product as it lives, in motion. The social life of, say, a mashup video, as experienced, passed along, voted "up" or "down," and remixed by others, provides a form that illustrates complexity but resists encapsulation as a final story; Each subsequent rendering has meaning for someone. The purpose is not to come to a conclusion or solve a problem, but to provoke, raise questions, and by doing so, start a conversation.[46]

Bricolage, on the other hand, is not a term associated with synonyms such as incomplete, unfinished, or partial. It is an assemblage that emerges from the combination of serendipity, proximity, and contingency. This distinguishes it from the science of engineering. To engage in bricolage, one must have both a willingness to be open to different ways of perceiving and a readiness to put that willingness into action. In the end, if we look to the more classic notions of bricolage, something is finished and the project has a sense of finality, as when we can knot the last thread and lay the quilt out for inspection and use.

I end this keyword with a quote and some questions. In my work "Remix Culture, Remix Methods," I write:

> Remix is not something we do in addition to our everyday lives, it is the way we make sense of our world, by transforming the bombardment of stimuli into a seamless experience. If we take seriously the idea that everything we take to be "real" is a constant negotiation of relationships between people and things, and that culture is "habit writ large," remix as a form of sensemaking embraces this framework.[47]

Could bricolage be substituted for remix throughout this quotation? Is bricolage a synonym to remix? A smaller concept? An umbrella concept? A parallel development? Although I suggest some distinctions in this chapter, these questions signal that the concepts are not set in stone, inviting further reflection and conversation about how they might be cultivated in tandem, distinguished further, or otherwise developed. Remix and bricolage refer to actions, attitudes, and outcomes, depending on their usage. They invite open-ended outcomes and value a state of readiness, which makes them useful concepts to open up new possibilities for both the practice and products of research.

Notes

1 I write this entry in first person as an academic scholar who has used bricolage and other terms to teach qualitative research methods and to describe my own ethnographic work in digital culture contexts. It is written for other scholars, but the examples can be shifted away from using bricolage in contemporary humanities and social sciences inquiry to other arenas where the term seems appropriate to describe what is happening.
2 Claude Lévi-Strauss, *The Savage Mind*, trans. George Weidenfeld (London: Weidenfeld and Nicolson Ltd, 1966), 11.
3 Panagiotis Louridas, "Design as Bricolage: Anthropology Meets Design Thinking," *Design Studies* 20, no. 6 (1999): 517–535.
4 Lévi-Strauss, *The Savage Mind*, 17.
5 Jacques Derrida, *Writing and Difference* (Chicago: University of Chicago Press, 1978), 285.
6 See, for example, Brent Luvaas, *DIY Culture: Fashion, Music, and Global Digital Culture* (London: Bloomsbury, 2012), 110–111. Drawing on Dick Hebdige, *Subculture: The Meaning of Style* (London: Routledge, 1979), 17.
7 One might notice my tendency to use interpretive research methods as a way of working through the concept, which is a direct result of my own bricolage of my educational background and consequent ready-at-hand resources. For a different breakdown of the bricoleur as agent and bricolage as action, I refer readers to Johnson's excellent *Bricoleur and Bricolage: From Metaphor to Universal Concept* from 2012.
8 Annette Markham, "'Go Ugly Early': Fragmented Narrative and Bricolage as Interpretive Method," *Qualitative Inquiry* 11, no. 6 (2005): 17.

9 Kate McCoy, "Toward a Methodology of Encounter: Opening to Complexity in Qualitative Research," *Qualitative Inquiry* 18, no. 9 (2012): 763.
10 Joe L. Kincheloe, "On to the Next Level: Continuing the Conceptualization of the Bricolage," *Qualitative Inquiry* 11, no. 3 (2005): 324.
11 Annemarie Mol and John Law, "Complexities: An Introduction," In *Complexities: Social Studies of Knowledge Practices*, eds. John Law and Annemarie Mol (Durham: Duke University Press, 2002), 6.
12 Morton Meyers, *Happy Accidents: Serendipity in Modern Medical Breakthroughs* (New York: Arcade Publishing, 2007), 6.
13 Specifically, Joe L. Kincheloe, "Describing the Bricolage: Conceptualizing a New Rigor in Qualitative Research," *Qualitative Inquiry* 7, no. 6 (2001): 679–692; and also Kincheloe, "On to the Next Level,"
14 Norman Denzin and Yvonna Lincoln, "The Discipline and Practice of Qualitative Research," In *Handbook of Qualitative Research*, 2nd edition, ed. Norman Denzin and Yvonna Lincoln (Thousand Oaks, CA: Sage, 2000), 1–36.
15 Kincheloe, "Describing the Bricolage," 679–692.
16 Kincheloe, "On to the Next Level," 324.
17 Ibid.
18 Ibid.
19 Derrida, *Writing and Difference*, 365.
20 Karl Weick, "Organizational Redesign as Improvisation," in *Organizational Change and Redesign: Ideas and Insights for Improving Performance*, ed. George P. Huber, and William H. Glick (Oxford: Oxford University Press, 1993), 346–379.
21 Lee Thayer, "Leadership/Communication: A Critical Review and a Modest Proposal," in *Handbook of Organizational Communication*, ed. Gerald M. Goldhaber, and George A. Barnett (Norwood, NJ: Ablex, 1988), 231–264.
22 Ibid., 239.
23 Weick, "Organizational Redesign," 352.
24 Ibid., 353. (citing Lévi-Strauss, *The Savage Mind*, 9)
25 Christopher Johnson, "Bricoleur and Bricolage: From Metaphor to Universal Concept," *Paragraph* 35, no. 3 (2012): 355–372.
26 Maria B. Martin Lucas, "Weaving, Patchwork and Bricolage: Women's Crafts/Women's Texts," in *Many Sundry Wits Gathered Together. I Congreso de Filologia Inglesa*, ed. Gonzalez Fernández Corugedo (Coruña: Servicio de Publicacións da Universidade da Coruña, 1996), 239–246.
27 Virginia Woolf, *A Room of One's Own* (San Diego: Harcourt Brace Jovanovich, 1929), 80–81.
28 Martin Lucas, "Weaving, Patchwork and Bricolage," 239.
29 Ibid., 240.
30 Kincheloe, "On to the Next Level," 324; Denzin and Lincoln, "The Discipline and Practice of Qualitative Research," 1–36.
31 Hal Foster, *Postmodern Culture* (London: Pluto Press, 1985), 200.
32 Johnson, "Bricoleur and Bricolage," 367.
33 Miguel P. Cunha, Joao V. Cunha, and Ken N. Kamoche, "Organizational Improvisation: What, When, How, and Why," in *Organizational Improvisation*, ed. Ken N. Kamoche, Miguel P. Cunha, and Joao V. Cunha (London: Routledge, 2002), 103.
34 Martin Lucas, "Weaving, Patchwork and Bricolage," 239.
35 Kincheloe, "Describing the Bricolage," 679; Kincheloe, "Next Level Conceptualization," 324.
36 Michael Joyce, "Notes Toward an Unwritten Nonlinear Electronic Text: 'The Ends of Print Culture,'" *Postmodern Culture* 2, no. 1 (1991).
37 Shelley Jackson, *Patchwork Girl* (Eastgate Systems, 1995).

38 Jill Walker Rettberg, "Piecing Together and Tearing Apart: Finding the Story in Afternoon," in HYPERTEXT '99 Proceedings of the Tenth ACM Conference on Hypertext and Hypermedia: Returning to Our Diverse Roots, Darmstadt, Germany, February 22–25 1991 (New York: ACM, 1991), 111–117.
39 Walter Fisher, "The Narrative Paradigm: In the Beginning," *Journal of Communication* 35, no. 4 (1985): 74–89.
40 Markham, "Go Ugly Early," 17.
41 See the entry *Remix Method or Bricolage?* in Aske Kammer's blog from 2011, available from www.askekammer.dk/2011/12/05/remix-method-or-bricolage/.
42 As represented well by the edited collection by Eduardo Navas, Owen Gallagher, and xtine burrough, eds. *The Routledge Companion to Remix Studies* (New York: Routledge, 2015).
43 Thayer, "Leadership/Communication."
44 Weick, "Organizational Redesign"
45 Markham, Annette. "Remix Culture, Remix Methods: Reframing Qualitative Inquiry for Social Media Contexts." In *Global Dimensions of Qualitative Inquiry*, edited by Norman K. Denzin, and Michael D. Giardina, 63–81. Walnut Creek, CA: Left Coast Press, 2013, 71–72.
46 Ibid.
47 Ibid.

Bibliography

Cunha, Miguel P., Cunha, Joao V., and Kamoche, Ken N. "Organizational Improvisation: What, When, How, and Why." In *Organizational Improvisation*, edited by Ken N. Kamoche, Miguel P. Cunha, and Joao V. Cunha, 93–134. London: Routledge, 2002.

Denzin, Norman, and Lincoln, Yvonna. "The Discipline and Practice of Qualitative Research." In *Handbook of Qualitative Research*, 2nd edition, edited by Norman Denzin and Yvonna Lincoln, 1–36. Thousand Oaks, CA: Sage, 2000.

Derrida, Jacques. *Writing and Difference.* Chicago: University of Chicago Press, 1978.

Fisher, Walter. "The Narrative Paradigm: In the Beginning." *Journal of Communication* 35, no. 4 (1985): 74–89.

Foster, Hal. *Postmodern Culture.* London: Pluto Press, 1985.

Hebdige, Dick. *Subculture: The Meaning of Style.* London: Routledge, 1979.

Jackson, Shelley. *Patchwork Girl.* Eastgate Systems, 1995.

Johnson, Christopher. "Bricoleur and Bricolage: From Metaphor to Universal Concept." *Paragraph* 35, no. 3 (2012): 355–372.

Joyce, Michael. "Notes Toward an Unwritten Nonlinear Electronic Text: 'The Ends of Print Culture.'" *Postmodern Culture* 2, no. 1 (1991).

Kincheloe, Joe L. "Describing the Bricolage: Conceptualizing a New Rigor in Qualitative Research." *Qualitative Inquiry* 7, no. 6 (2001): 679–692.

Kincheloe, Joe L. "On to the Next Level: Continuing the Conceptualization of the Bricolage." *Qualitative Inquiry* 11, no. 3 (2005): 323–350.

Lévi-Strauss, Claude. *The Savage Mind.* Translated by George Weidenfeld. London: Weidenfeld and Nicolson Ltd, 1966.

Louridas, Panagiotis. "Design as Bricolage: Anthropology Meets Design Thinking." *Design Studies* 20, no. 6 (1999): 517–535.

Luvaas, Brent. *DIY Culture: Fashion, Music, and Global Digital Culture.* London: Bloomsbury, 2012.

Martin Lucas, Maria B. "Weaving, Patchwork and Bricolage: Women's Crafts/Women's Texts." In *Many Sundry Wits Gathered Together. I Congreso de Filologia Inglesa*, edited by Gonzalez Fernández Corugedo, 239–246. Coruña: Servicio de Publicacións da Universidade da Coruña, 1996.

Markham, Annette. "'Go Ugly Early': Fragmented Narrative and Bricolage as Interpretive Method." *Qualitative Inquiry* 11, no. 6 (2005): 813–839.

Markham, Annette. "Remix Culture, Remix Methods: Reframing Qualitative Inquiry for Social Media Contexts." In *Global Dimensions of Qualitative Inquiry*, edited by Norman K. Denzin, and Michael D. Giardina, 63–81. Walnut Creek, CA: Left Coast Press, 2013.

McCoy, Kate. "Toward a Methodology of Encounter: Opening to Complexity in Qualitative Research." *Qualitative Inquiry* 18, no. 9 (2012): 762–772.

Meyers, Morton A. *Happy Accidents: Serendipity in Modern Medical Breakthroughs.* New York: Arcade Publishing, 2007.

Mol, Annemarie and Law, John. "Complexities: An Introduction." In *Complexities: Social Studies of Knowledge Practices*, edited by John Law and Annemarie Mol, 1–23. Durham: Duke University Press, 2002.

Navas, Eduardo, Owen Gallagher, and xtine burrough, eds. *The Routledge Companion to Remix Studies.* New York: Routledge, 2015.

Thayer, Lee. "Leadership/Communication: A Critical Review and a Modest Proposal." In *Handbook of Organizational Communication*, edited by Gerald M. Goldhaber and George A. Barnett, 231–264. Norwood, NJ: Ablex, 1988.

Walker Rettberg, Jill. 1999. "Piecing Together and Tearing Apart: Finding the Story in *Afternoon.*" In *HYPERTEXT '99 Proceedings of the Tenth ACM Conference on Hypertext and Hypermedia: Returning to Our Diverse Roots, Darmstadt, Germany, February 22–25 1991,* 111–117. New York: ACM.

Weick, Karl. "Organizational Redesign as Improvisation." In *Organizational Change and Redesign: Ideas and Insights for Improving Performance*, edited by George P. Huber, and William H. Glick, 346–379. Oxford: Oxford University Press, 1993.

Weick, Karl E. *Sensemaking in Organizations.* Thousand Oaks, CA: Sage, 1995.

Woolf, Virginia. *A Room of One's Own.* San Diego: Harcourt Brace Jovanovich, 1929.

5
COLLABORATIVE

Aram Sinnreich

The word "collaborative" has, in its linguistic roots, a lot to tell us about our cultural history, and about the expectations and institutions we've developed around the process of creative expression. Yet, like all expectations and institutions, our conceptualization of the creative process also serves as a mask for power, legitimizing some modes of social activity and organization while precluding or delegitimizing others. In the first half of this chapter, I will pull apart some of these threads, examining what we understand as "collaborative" on a syllable-by-syllable basis, beginning with the word's root, followed by its prefix and suffix. In the second half, I will try to weave them back together, into something new.

Creative Expression as Labor

The root of the word "collaborative" is "labor." When we use this term in the context of art and culture, we are accepting, *prima facie*, the premise that creative expression is a form of *work*, and that those who produce it are *workers*. This premise, in turn, suggests the existence of a creative economy, and of a social organization that not only entails the division of labor but also the commodification of creative expression. In other words, the concept of creative collaboration presumes the existence of professional artists.

The categorical definition of creative expression as a form of labor, and the professionalization and industrialization of the creative process, are relatively new phenomena. For most of human history, in most cultures around the world, art was not separate from any other aspect of the lived experience, let alone something that could be bought or sold. Music was an activity that families and communities used to facilitate social interaction, mark identity, and coordinate physical activity (in fact, some musicologists and anthropologists now believe that music's organizational capacities are responsible for the emergence of human consciousness and organized society).¹ Similarly, painting and other visual arts were decorative, illustrative, documentary, and/or functionary in nature, rather than "Artworks" produced for a specialized economy. As Walter Benjamin famously observed, the "aura" of these artifacts was intimately tied to their institutional, geographical and temporal circumstances, and their power was indistinguishable from the power of the social institutions within which they were produced, viewed, and interpreted.²

By the same token, the people who produced these visual and musical artifacts were not *artists*, or creative professionals, as we would now understand them. While skilled individuals were certainly celebrated for their ability to play an instrument, paint a portrait, or recite an epic poem, such activities were not understood as a discrete vocation, but rather as an aspect of that person's broader role in religion, politics, medicine, education, or even physical labor (as in the case of field hollers).

The first glimmers of our modern notions of "art" and "artistry" were born in the Italian Renaissance, when creative expression began to emerge as a professional category separate from its (other) social and institutional functions. This process was integral to the broader social changes of the centuries that followed, including the increasing stratification of society, the rise of a powerful bourgeoisie, European colonial expansion, the internationalization of markets, the adoption of the printing press, and, ultimately, industrialization. The evolving philosophy of art wasn't merely a *reflection* of these social organizational shifts, but rather an *instrument* of them; the professionalization and commodification of creative expression served to naturalize the existence of industries and markets themselves, and the division of creative labor served as a map for the division of industrial labor.³

In the modern era, these categories became so naturalized, they were practically invisible. The emergence of multibillion-dollar international markets for literature, music, visual art, and newer creative forms such as photography, cinema, and software lent institutional momentum to the reification of art, and created an economic foundation for the rise of creative professions, ultimately comprising what Richard Florida has dubbed the "super-creative core"⁴ at the heart of all information-based economies.

While this "core" of professional creators is large, it does not include the majority of people who engage in some form of creative expression. Those who do not garner a significant portion of their income or reputation from such professions—such as most "garage band" members, quilters, or "underground" cartoonists, to name a few examples—are relegated to the status of "amateurs," and are not only understood to be creatively and socially inferior, but are actively ridiculed in popular television and film narratives, and are institutionally excluded from unions, guilds, collection societies, and other platforms for accreditation, remuneration and employment.

Thus, in the modern era, only professional and celebrated creators are considered "real" artists, and only professionally produced creative expression is considered to be "real" art. This erasure of what James Carey[5] termed the "ritual" function of communication, and the commensurate elevation of the marketplace as the arbiter of creative authenticity, is one of the chief mechanisms by which the ideology of industrial capitalism has been successfully normalized throughout what is commonly referred to as the "developed world."

Why Is There a "Co-" in "Collaborative"?

The prefix of the world "collaborative" (namely "co-") is another seemingly simple element that carries a lot of semiotic baggage. Of course, the prefix means "together," and its Latin roots (in the preposition *com*) run through a wide swath of the English language, from "compassion" to "comprehension" to "confusion," helping to shape our social and cultural imagination, and, in turn, our societies and cultures.

What do we mean when we add "co-" to "labor"? At a literal level, it means working together. According to the *Oxford English Dictionary*, this compound word refers especially to shared labor "in a literary or artistic production, or the like." Yet consider the tacit implications of the term. If the concept of shared labor requires a special prefix, it logically follows that labor itself, without the prefix, is *the work of a single individual*—especially in the case of literary or artistic production, or the like. Thus, the concept of collaboration involves some clever semiotic sleight-of-hand: in its very coinage, which ostensibly gives a name to the act of shared cultural production, it normalizes the premise of solo creation by treating it as the linguistic default.

Like the concepts of art and artistry, the concept of solo creation is itself a recent invention, and anything but the default for most cultural production, throughout most of human history. In the ancient world, poets and artists invoked the gods and muses as the sources of their work, and represented themselves as mere vessels for divine inspiration. During the Middle Ages and the Renaissance, it was widely understood, and commonly accepted, that all creative expression was rooted in the act of copying, taking themes and motifs from previous work and adapting them to the circumstances of the new work. As the painter and art historian Mark Rothko pointed out, "the Renaissance artist appropriated everything from everywhere, making no distinction between the innovations of his next-door neighbor and those from across the continent."[6] Similarly, in the baroque and classical eras, most of the "great" Western musical composers routinely copied entire musical passages from other works into their own. Handel was particularly notorious for this practice, though it was even common for later composers like Mozart and Beethoven.

In addition to this widespread copying by one creator from another, a significant portion of cultural expression has actually been produced in a collective context. To begin with, many of the works that we conceive of as "authored" by individuals are actually produced by groups of people. From Rembrandt's workshop to Andy Warhol's factory to Thomas Kinkade's "semi-industrial"[7] production process, for instance, countless paintings bearing the signatures of celebrated artists were physically produced by their employees and/or colleagues with limited input or merely oversight by the "artist" himself.

Second, there are many cultural forms, such as cinema, that are virtually impossible to create in a solo context. The typical Hollywood film has hundreds or even thousands of names in its closing credits, and a great many of them are people who played what most would think of as a "creative" role, from wardrobe design to set design to lighting design (to say nothing of the actors themselves). The premise that a film's director is its one true author was only pioneered with the rise of "auteur theory" in the 1940s and 1950s, although, tellingly, the director neither owns the copyright in most cases, nor collects the award for "Best Picture" when a film wins an Oscar.

Finally, there is a great deal of cultural production that makes no claims whatsoever to solo authorship or individual vision. From "indigenous art" to "folklore" to "street culture" to "undergrounds," the diverse range of aesthetic systems and artworks developed within communities external to the marketplace share little in common other than the fact that they frequently lack claims of ownership and originality by discrete individuals. The reason for this is obvious: cultural production *never* happens in a vacuum, creation is *never* completely the work of a lone individual, and anyone who claims otherwise does so for economic reasons (or for reputational reasons with economic benefits).

If our cultural history and milieu are so clearly the result of group efforts and collective processes, why do we even have the notion of solo creation—and its logical corollary, "collaboration?" Much ink has been spilled on the history and ideology of what is often referred to as "Romantic" authorship in recent decades, and to review even a fraction of it here would be beyond the scope of this chapter's aim (although John Vallier's chapter in this book no doubt gives it ample treatment). Suffice it to say that a range of thinkers, from social theorists like Michel Foucault[8] and Roland Barthes[9] to legal scholars like Martha Woodmansee[10] and Peter Jaszi,[11] identify the ideology of solo creation as (1) instrumental to the organization of liberal society around the individual, at the expense of collectivism and communities, and (2) integral to our system of cultural ownership, rooted in intellectual property law, which hinges on the premise of incentivizing individual authors through granting them monopoly rights over the expression of "their" ideas.

See Chapter 3, "Authorship."

Indeed, a brief review of the history of the term's usage demonstrates that the concept of collaboration became widespread only *after* the ideology of copyright in America had shifted from its Enlightenment origins as an instrument of the public good to a post-Romantic vision of the law as an enforcer of an artist's individual rights. When it was first enacted in 1790, American copyright law limited monopolies to 14-year periods, and covered only books, maps, and charts. This limited scope and term was deliberate. As the law's architects made clear, its function was to encourage a rich and diverse public sphere, and a robust public domain, by allowing authors to charge for access to their work for a limited duration before ceding ownership to the public at large. Over the next century, however, as Romantic notions of authorship took hold, the shifting ideologies of cultural production led to changes in the law. Terms became much longer in duration, and the scope of copyright widened to include prints, musical compositions, dramatic compositions, photographs, and, in 1870, "works of art" such as paintings. Additionally, in this same year, copyright's power was extended to the creation and authorization of "derivative works." In other words, now authors and artists would not merely control the rights to their own creations, but would also own creations by other people if they were sufficiently *influenced* by their own work. This was a definitive victory for Romantic notions of original authorship, and a repudiation of the age-old premise that cultural expression is inherently collective.

This is the cultural moment in which the concept of "collaboration" was born. According to a search of Google Books, the term appeared in only one-millionth of a percent of all books in 1850. By 1880, its prevalence had grown by an order of magnitude, and by 1900 it had grown a hundredfold. The use of the term continued to climb during the rise of "modernity" in the first half of the twentieth century, and by 1941, the term was *1,000 times more prevalent* than it had been a mere three generations earlier.[12]

To summarize: The "co " in "collaborative" is linked directly to the rise of Romantic notions of solo authorship, and, conversely, to the ideological and legal erasure of shared creation as the default condition for cultural expression. By prefixing the term with a syllable signaling collaborative effort, the concept paradoxically reifies the premise that creativity is, by default, the product of an individual rather than a community or a collective.

Adjectiving Collaboration

I will not spend as much time addressing the suffix of the word "collaborative" as I did on its linguistic root and prefix, but it does bear some scrutiny in the context of creative expression and remix studies. As discussed above, the term "collaboration"—a noun describing both the act and the product of shared creative labor—emerged from obscurity in the late nineteenth century and grew precipitously through the mid-twentieth century. The verb form of the word, "collaborate," emerged a little bit later, around the turn of the century, and its use has remained fairly flat since World War II, with a slight rise during the age of digital media. However, the adjective form of the word, "collaborative," which is the subject of this chapter, emerged far later. It was first adopted in the

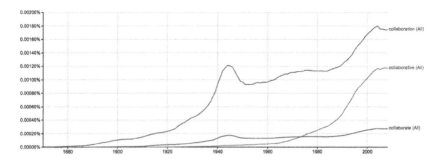

FIGURE 5.1 Prevalence of terms according to Google Ngram, 1870–2008

post-war period, then eclipsed the verb form in the mid-1970s and climbed precipitously from the mid-1980s through the mid-2000s, its curve nearly identical to the rise of the noun form 60 years earlier (Figure 5.1).

What is the significance of the rise of the adjectival form "collaborative" in the late twentieth and early twenty-first centuries? If the noun form was a hallmark of the modern era, I believe the adjectival form marks the emergence of postmodernism, and correlates with the "death of the author," as chronicled by Barthes[13] and Foucault.[14]

The notion of "collaboration" is all about authorship. It describes a mode of cultural production, privileging one model of social organization (solo creation) over another (collective production) through a form of linguistic primacy. Yet for all of its hegemonic weight, the term is still grounded in the actions of human beings; the word "collaboration" identifies *something that people do*, or the product of shared labor.

By contrast, the adjective "collaborative" describes *things themselves*, shifting the focus away from human action and towards the commodity. This is one of the defining attributes of postmodernism: the erasure of the circumstances of production and the relegation of the author to the role of a data point describing the artifact, rather than the genesis of the artifact. Yet the postmodern rejection of authorship is, in this case, hardly a victory for those communities and collectives that were effaced through the Romantic and modernist embrace of "collaboration." To the contrary, the word "collaborative" serves as a double-effacement. Not only have the circumstances of production been reduced to a descriptive afterthought attached to the commodity artifact, but those circumstances are themselves presumed to entail solo creation, unless specifically described otherwise.

In short, the word "collaborative," when applied to a cultural artifact, tacitly suggests that: (1) cultural production acquires meaning and legitimacy solely through industrial organization and exploitation of labor and through the commodification of the artifact in the marketplace; (2) cultural production is presumed to be the work of discrete individuals, while collective expression is the notable exception rather than the rule; and (3) the shared ideation and labor that goes into producing a "collaborative" cultural artifact is merely one of countless possible descriptors, a flavoring like "vanilla-scented," "single origin," or "new and improved," whose role is to distinguish one commodity from another in the eyes of discriminating consumers, rather than to illuminate the circumstances of its production.

Remixing "Collaborative"

As Figure 5.1 demonstrates, the prevalence of terms such as "collaboration" and "collaborative" has grown drastically since the 1990s. No doubt, this has much to do with the widespread adoption of networked computing and communication platforms, to the emergence of a "digital culture" (or, more accurately, cultures) transacted via those platforms, and to the ballooning wealth and power of Silicon Valley and the hypertrophic commodification of digital culture over the past decade or two. Indeed, countless advertisements for computers, portable devices, software and Internet service providers lure us with promises that their goods and services will make us feel more connected and bring us closer together, while simultaneously boosting our productivity and protecting our individuality— perfectly mirroring the ideological contours of the term "collaborative."

Yet, in practice, digital culture has turned out to be singularly resistant to the logic of modernity, the delineations of copyright law, and the ideology of authorship that underpin the word "collaborative." To begin with, the concept of cultural "labor" that has been enshrined in our social and economic institutions since the birth of copyright and elevated to the level of moral imperative since the rise of Romanticism has now been revealed for the fiction it always was.

From Axel Bruns's discussion of "produsage"[15] to George Ritzer and Nathan Jurgenson's use of the term "prosumption,"[16] a great many media scholars and cultural theorists have spent the years since the turn of the twenty-first century documenting and analyzing the ways in which emerging digital media practices like mashups, remixes, and memes inhabit the gray area between the traditional polarities of production and consumption. It's not merely that a mashup creator or a meme sharer is difficult to classify. Rather, the very act of copying and pasting pieces of pre-existing media into a "new" work, and then sharing it on a platform where its meaning is constructed hermeneutically through waves of collective interpretation, reconfiguration, and redistribution, is a process that shatters the ontological foundations of production and consumption as categories of action in cultural expression.

To use James Carey's analytical framework,[17] remix culture represents the reinscription of *ritual* communication onto a medium built to reflect and extend the premise of *transmissive* communication (the packet-switching architecture undergirding all Internet communications exists explicitly for the purpose of preserving the fidelity of messages as they travel from sender to receiver). The implications of this ontological crisis extend far beyond the cultural realm; as I argue elsewhere, by destabilizing the producer/consumer dichotomy, the cultural logic of the remix destabilizes the logical foundations of industrial capitalism itself.[18]

To make matters even more complicated, remix practices don't merely undermine the categorical architecture of cultural production, they also problematize the relationship of labor to capital in a cultural context. To be sure, these relationships have always been problematic, and the entire Marxist canon is built on problematizing them. In the 1990s, Maurizio Lazzarato proposed that "immaterial labor," the *shared* work of giving a commodity its "informational and cultural content,"[19] is central to the production of value in a media environment, yet remains unrecognized, uncompensated, and therefore fundamentally exploited. Following on this, Michael Hardt and Antonio Negri proposed "affective labor," or the regulation of mood, emotion and attitude, as a category of immaterial labor whose value is of vital importance and growing economic value to hegemonic power in the "age of empire."[20] For the past decade or so, scholars of digital media such as Mark Andrejevic,[21] Tiziana Terranova,[22] and Gina Neff[23] have sought to apply these terms to the activities of remixers, Wikipedia contributors, social media users, and to the billions of other Internet users whose affective and other immaterial contributions to digital culture are exploited for profit and power by corporate and state actors.

As to the prefix and suffix of "collaborative" in a digital media context, they are just as difficult to reconcile as the word's linguistic root. The crisis of authorship engendered by the breakdown of the consumer/producer dichotomy, and the obvious redundancy of cultural ideation, laid bare by search engines and social media feeds, lays to rest any illusions we may once have entertained about the originality or singularity of cultural expression. It's virtually impossible to conceive of an image, phrase, or motif that has not already been posted somewhere by someone, and then subject to endless revision, reinterpretation, and ridicule on the servers of 4chan, Reddit, or some other digital hall of mirrors. This evident fact renders the "co-" in "collaborative" superfluous at best.

The adjectival suffix of "collaborative" has become equally superfluous, as the Internet in its current form doesn't merely obscure the mode of production, but actively reduces labor itself to the status of a commodity. Just as Internet protocols assign discrete, equivalent IP addresses to each node on the network, regardless of its shape, function or centrality, the harvesting of data and metadata from every user by both state and corporate actors reduces each of us to the sum of our measurable parts. In the era of "big data," we are all made small, although none of us is smaller than any other. With this collapsing of labor and commodity, and the functional equivalence between all the network's nodes, the distinction between noun and adjective is also blurred. Nothing is more—or less—than what it is described to be, and therefore the distinction between "collaboration" and "collaborative" loses any functional meaning.

Post-Script: Post-Collaborative?

There are two recent developments that suggest possible post-scripts to this story. As Figure 5.1 shows, the rapid discursive ascent of both the noun "collaboration" and the adjective "collaborative" level off abruptly beginning around the mid-2000s (at the time of writing, data are only available through 2008). This period corresponds with the emergence of a cultural moment that was for a time referred to as "Web 2.0," and is now historically recast as the birth of social media. If there is, indeed, a correspondence between this leveling-off and the emergence of a new paradigm in digital communications, what is its significance?

An optimistic interpretation would be that, with the rise of Myspace, Facebook, and Twitter, the Romantic author finally met his death, and the term "collaborative" accordingly lost its frisson. In this moment, creative expression was freed of its shackles, and human culture began to turn back to its pluralistic prelapsarian origins in which every voice contains all voices, and no idea can be claimed as property. I would like to believe that.

A less optimistic interpretation would hold that, once social media became the dominant platform for digital expression, both individual authorship *and* collective ideation became moot ideas. Cultural expression remained propertized, but the entire marketplace of ideas was cornered by a handful of immense corporations whose authority exceeded either law or economics, rooted as it was in their total command over the architecture of communication and in the completely unidirectional, hierarchical flow of information *from* users *into* corporate-controlled databases. In this context, "collaborative" has no meaning because Facebook is in fact the sole author of its 1.8 billion users' posts (according to many legal analyses, this functional ownership is reinforced legally through such platforms' terms of service).

This leads us to our second development: the rise of a new ethic, which Trebor Scholz refers to as "platform cooperativism."[24] This ethic, which Scholz and others have been working to transform into a movement, seeks to reclaim power for exploited digital labor by building platforms in which the users themselves have a controlling and/or ownership stake. Thus, instead of relying on Facebook for social networking, Uber for connecting drivers with travelers, and Airbnb for connecting hosts with guests, these commercial services can be "cloned" and rebuilt with the needs and interests of diverse stakeholders engineered into their foundations.

If there is a meaningful future for the concept of "collaboration," I believe it has a shared destiny with Scholz's vision of "cooperativism." Theoretically, it may be possible to enjoy the benefits of property and platforms without the crippling monopolization and stratification that has resulted from these economic and technosocial systems in the past. Similarly, it may be possible to rebuild our cultural architecture with pluralism and collectivism at its heart, relying on a path guided by pragmatism and progress rather than a nostalgic yearning for a golden age that never actually transpired. If this is the case, however, we're going to need a better word than "collaborative." Let's begin by rehabilitating some older, simpler words—words like "create," "make," and "art"—and use them in ways that acknowledge their roots in ritual communication and shared practice, as well as their independence from the logic of the marketplace.

Notes

1 Gary Tomlinson, *A Million Years of Music: The Emergence of Human Modernity* (New York: Zone Books, 2015).
2 Walter Benjamin, *The Work of Art in the Age of Mechanical Reproduction* (London: Penguin, 2008).
3 Aram Sinnreich, *Mashed Up: Music, Technology and the Rise of Configurable Culture* (Amherst, MA: University of Massachusetts Press, 2010).
4 Richard Florida, *The Rise of the Creative Class, Revisited* (New York: Basic Books, 2014), 38.
5 James Carey, *Communication as Culture* (London: Routledge, 2009), 18.
6 Mark Rothko, *The Artist's Reality: Philosophies of Art* (New Haven, CT: Yale University Press), 106.
7 Laura Miller, "Thomas Kinkade, the George W. Bush of Art", *Salon.com* (April 9, 2012). Available at www.salon.com/2012/04/09/thomas_kinkade_the_george_w_bush_of_art.
8 Michel Foucault, *Aesthetics, Method, and Epistemology, Vol. 2* (New York: The New Press, 1998).
9 Roland Barthes, *Image, Music, Text* (New York: Hill and Wang, 1977).
10 Martha Woodmansee, "On the Author Effect: Recovering Collectivity," in M. Woodmansee and P. Jaszi (eds.), *The Construction of Authorship: Textual Appropriation in Law and Literature* (Durham, NC: Duke University Press, 1994), 1.
11 Peter Jaszi, "On the Author Effect: Contemporary Copyright and Collective Creativity", in M. Woodmansee and P. Jaszi (Eds.), *The Construction of Authorship: Textual Appropriation in Law and Literature* (Durham, NC: Duke University Press, 1994), 15.
12 The word acquired a secondary political meaning during the World War II era, which no doubt boosted its prevalence in that decade — however, the long, upward arc of its usage continued well after this meaning had receded.
13 Barthes, *Image, Music, Text*.
14 Foucault, *Aesthetics, Method, and Epistemology, Vol. 2*.
15 Axel Bruns, *Blogs, Wikipedia, Second Life and Beyond: From Production to Produsage* (New York: Peter Lang, 2008).
16 George Ritzer and Nathan Jurgenson, "Production, Consumption, Prosumption: The Nature of Capitalism in the Age of the Digital 'Prosumer,'" *Journal of Consumer Culture*, *10*(1), 13–36 (2010).
17 Carey, *Communication as Culture*.
18 Sinnreich, *Mashed Up*.
19 Maurizio Lazzarato, "Immaterial Labor", in P. Virno and M. Hardt (eds.), *Radical Thought in Italy: A Potential Politics* (Minneapolis: University of Minnesota Press, 1996), 132.
20 Michael Hardt and Antonio Negri, *Multitude: War and Democracy in the Age of Empire* (New York: Penguin Books, 2004).
21 Mark Andrejevic, "Social Network Exploitation", in Z. Papacharissi (ed.), *A Networked Self: Identity, Community, and Culture on Social Network Sites* (New York: Routledge, 2011), 82–102.

22 Tiziana Terranova, "Free Labor", in T. Scholz (ed.), *Digital Labor: The Internet as Playground and Factory* (New York: Routledge, 2013), 33–57.
23 Gina Neff, *Venture Labor: Work and the Burden of Risk in Innovative Industries* (Cambridge, MA: MIT Press, 2012).
24 Trebor Scholz, *Uberworked and Underpaid: How Workers Are Disrupting the Digital Economy* (Cambridge: Polity Press, 2016).

6
CONSUMERISM

Pau Figueres

> The excess is with us forever. So let's have a drink of Coke. It's getting warm . . . It's no longer The Real Coke and that's the problem. You know, this passage from sublime to excremental dimension. When it's cold, properly served it has a certain attraction. All of a sudden this can change into shit. It's the elementary dialectics of commodities.
> Slavoj Žižek[1]

The purpose of this chapter is to explain the continuous use of trademark and brand visual material within contemporary art and its relation to remix in the era of hyper-consumerism. The relationship between consumerism, one of the tenets of capitalism, and art is not new. In 1960s pop art, low and high culture came together with everyday things, among which elements from the media, such as brands, appeared as the new main characters in the art scene. The influence of the pop art aesthetic has lasted to the present day, but even if we find similar cyclical problems, mistakes and solutions to those that took place in the second half of the past century, globalization boosts this relationship with refreshing art proposals. Postproduction and the remix of commercial iconography have emerged as different ways of representing consumerism that enable us to reflect on its role in late capitalism and contemporary art practice. In what follows, I discuss how art meets globalization and the extreme increase of commercial material presence—not just by celebrating the liturgy of consuming—but assuming these elements naturally as part of our lives; and the paradox of remix opposite to the idea of appropriation and remix as a result of hyper-consumerism.

The Influence of Pop

Thanks to new business strategies and the deep-rooted connection between consumerism and capitalism, commercial brands have easily coped with barriers caused by the global economic crisis. The fall of the Berlin Wall illustrated the final steps toward a homogeneous society: it is one of the most significant twentieth-century events that contributed to the contemporary notion of *global*. Under this new paradigm, brands transcend national boundaries to unprecedented areas with the arrival and development of new technologies that allow new tools for advertising. High-definition billboards, targeted advertising on Internet browsing or video advertising in streaming are designing the mediascape of consumerism in the global era. Production and consumption excess not only leads to the necessity of residue recycling, more than ever, the demand for an ecology of the audiovisual and art production, justifies the work of recoding, redefining and remixing what already exists. The retrieval of the old idea of selecting an object and using it according to a specific purpose triggers the conditions for postproduction and post-appropriation during the 1990s and remix in the visual arts in the hypermodern[2] era.

The concept of consumption is evident in art history mainly during the 1960s with pop art and later in the 1980s with simulationism[3] in works that redefine existing material from mass media. But a new concern for remixing this material has emerged with the artist of the global era under what we consider the

FIGURE 6.1 Times Square, New York, February 1, 2015. Courtesy of the author.

aesthetics of consumerism. Nicolas Bourriaud states that while the American pop art scene was fascinated by the visual frontality of the marketing spectacle—focusing on packaging, billboards, neon-signs and a whole ensemble of material used by brands to market their products—the European New Realists' approach focused directly on the abstract phenomenon of anonymous consumption by rescuing used objects, becoming pioneers in representing a still-life of the mediascape and the industrial society. However, it is simulationism that brought forth the idea of creation as a way of consumption, exhibiting the object "from the angle of the compulsion to buy, from the angle of desire, midway between the inaccessible and the available."[4]

Undoubtedly influenced by pop art and simulationism, a new concern for remixing this material has emerged with the artist of the global era under what we consider the aesthetics of consumerism. As part of the collective memory, brands are transmitted and spreadable, akin to Dawkins's understanding of the viral nature of memes. Moreover, the dialectics of commodities through different emotional connections have set aside a very important place for brands among our necessities and our desires, encouraging excess and feeding consumerism. As could be expected, with the confluence of low and high culture and later with remix, art complies with this situation and transmits its concern by sharing the idea of spectacle, observing, making commentary, questioning and ultimately by representing the hyperbole of the invisible transcendence of consumerism, through the use of the commercial iconography that surrounds brands. The realms of commercial imagery, from billboards and banners to packaging, logos and typographies, coalesce into an outstanding raw material for artists worldwide, generating the global aesthetics of hyper-consumerism as a definite effect of late capitalism. The new redefining phenomena do not argue about authorship issues, as appropriation artists claim. Stealing is not the purpose, nor the means, of remix. The action of reusing and recycling is an automatic gesture, an attitude that goes further than any ethical question. In this new global picture, the concern, the admiration, as well as the new forms of addressing hyper-consumerism, are brought back by artists in new aesthetic proposals, pointing out the abstract concept and spectacle of excess with no geographic borders of action.

Similar aesthetic approaches to pop art are indeed unavoidable. For better or worse, the resurgence of remix in brands and the elements from the commercial mediascape as part of art production is absolutely reliant on pop art. The aesthetics of pop art obviously share a lot in common with the actual artistic proposals that deal with hyper-consumerism, but we cannot look at them as a simple repetition of style. Behind this exercise there is a different understanding whose awareness leads into a reaction from the art sphere to comment on this phenomenon. While the interest in consumption emerged from the fascination of its novelty, as new raw material and new concerns emerge, consumerism does not represent anything new in contemporary society because it has been radically absorbed by our subconscious. But the trend to continue making use of popular visual materials continues to demonstrate a necessity for psychological integration, it is the concept of hyper-consumerism, the limits of excess that define the new art proposals. The abundant presence of commercial visual stimulus has made brands, once again, part of the palette of material and resources of the artist. Consequently, this situation pushed contemporary artists to vindicate any action of reusing and remixing the image of brands as a must without discussion. While the spectacle of consumption fascinated American pop artists and artists from the New European Realism, hyper-consumption—its aesthetics and its representation—is the concern for part of the community of global artists of the twenty-first century.

Hyper-Consumerism as a Religion

"Capitalism is not good looking" argues Lipovetsky and Serroy in the introduction of their discussion on capitalism in *The Aestheticization of the World*, "in a very polite way."[5] One important difference between today and past societies is the aesthetic value attributed to our landscapes and urbanscapes. Regardless of the fact that human evolution has incorporated new architectonic components to our landscape and industrial revolutions ravaged urban spaces with atmospheric and acoustic pollution, brands have dressed the cities and even natural spots with their own forms. They own the extraordinary faculty to produce a particular attraction for the human eye and brain, and moreover, the invisible essence that feeds a collective imagery whose content is dictated by the brand owners. During more than half a century of visual pollution, we have gained the right to defend the use of the forms of the mediascape; and according to Nicolas Bourriaud, this right can be fulfilled by reactivating, even hacking private property and copyrights and claiming for the necessity that no public image should savor impunity whatsoever.[6] We must assume that a logo belongs to the public space not just because of its presence in the streets, but because it invades our privacy by being prominent in every product we consume.

Looking at hyper-consumerism as the logic and the ultimate way of capitalism towards infinite growth, under Walter Benjamin's idea of capitalism as religion,[7] we can think of brands as something that will lead us into redemption, promising happiness, status, success and a long list of virtues. But brands also appear to guarantee a better life, taking advantage of the insecurities and fears natural to the human condition—the fear of being unable to access the range of new and different products that appear weekly in store windows and make us think of human work as a purifying instrument to reengage with God.

As capitalism stands in for religion, Agamben locates the bank in the place of the celebration of the religious liturgy, where the priests command over credit, manipulate and manage the faith.[8] In this we find a wide range of symbols that help spread the word of money and the religious icon metamorphosed into the image of a brand. If we accept human labor as the liturgy of capitalism, and consumerism as communion, the celebration of the actual liturgy is a non-stop party for believers, who swallow images of brands and thousands of visual stimulus that tease us to consume. But the satisfaction of purchasing disappears once we exit the temples of the cult for consumption, the mall, the store, and the thousands of online shopping sites that offer the Eucharist of shopping without moving from the couch.

We could identify a brand by the design of its logo. We could imagine a brand, as Baudrillard explained, as the heart of advertising differentiating two functions, the designation of a product and the mobilization of emotional connotations.[9] We could locate a brand as a product in a shelf of the supermarket and as the supermarket itself. Or, we could think of a brand as a simple idea. But the complexity of the nature of a brand goes far beyond defining and distinguishing products from others of similar features. Generally, there is a lot more embedded in the objects we consume. In a reference to Marx, Slavoj Žižek clarifies what is hiding under the complexity of a brand, as part of the "excremental" elementary dialectics of commodities. Quoting the Coca-Cola slogan, "Coke is the Real Thing!" we can understand how commodities, are objects full of metaphysical, invisible qualities—the real thing—that cannot be described, but that provoke our desire.[10]

We can hardly refute the idea that, as a result of capitalism and the subsequent advertising industry, brands have taken our society to a point where there is no way back for a natural relationship with consumption according to one's needs. This is what art that reuses and samples brands communicates. Artists, whether engaged or not, use brands and their elements, amazed by both their own metaphysics and visual attributes, bringing forth the powerful functionality of brand design that captures artists' (and anybody's) attention. Are these the visual attributes of brands that remix art reclaims? Or is it somehow the metaphysics of commodities that is being pursued? Could we ever think of a consumption motivating a control system simply by reducing visual commercial pollution? Could we really live in a world without Coca-Cola?[11] Could we actually live in a world without brands and advertising? Is it only death that separates us from the symbolic world?[12]

What has been observed continuously becomes part of global worship. The concept of the brand is the real player in the shaping of what we call the aesthetics of consumerism. Both aesthetic and emotional connotations of a brand are necessary for understanding how the aesthetics of consumerism come about, and why artists use its attributes to represent a complex reality. The consequent relevance that our society has claimed for brands as part of a global collective memory is continuously concerning us according to how it affects art, even to the point of being convinced of vindicating its use, as part of the symbolic imagery that has been settled for all time in the aesthetics of the world. As a matter of fact, this concern pushes many artists to follow different schemes of gathering, reusing, remixing, sampling, re-inhabiting, revising and a complete series of concepts that involve the idea of providing new meanings to commercial iconography.

Reciprocal Manipulations

When we have a look at the instruments that facilitate consumerism, we are not only coping with visual content, but with an invisible psychological warfare that shapes complex graphic strategies based on data collected in focus groups, user studies, and audience surveys. These unseen *agents*, those who promise the functionality, the efficiency, the happiness and the necessity for every product of the market, are the ones that manipulate our habits of consumption. Agents, according to Noam Chomsky,[13] are capable of making women start smoking, thanks to Edward L. Bernays's *Propaganda,* considered the handbook of manipulation for the public relations industry, through which he pretended to organize chaos:

> The conscious and intelligent manipulation of the organized habits and opinions of the masses is an important element in democratic society. Those who manipulate this unseen mechanism of society constitute an invisible government, which is the true ruling power of our country. We are governed, our minds are molded, our tastes formed, our ideas suggested, largely by men we have never heard of. This is a logical result of the way in which our democratic society is organized.[14]

Isn't Coca-Cola being manipulative when it promises "The Real Thing"? What is "The Real Thing"? wonders Žižek.[15] "The Real Thing" is the absence of a physical content in a simple attempt to manipulate our consumer behavior. In front of the most evident manipulation of our codes, the response, in the form of resistance from art, is almost inevitable—a response of manipulating back and claiming the actual manipulation of those signs as something that is addressed to, and belongs to us. Manipulation in terms of remix should be used as a means and inspiration for creation, not as an act of vengeance, but as an act of negotiating, in which manipulation functions as a reciprocal agent. Remix is like a boomerang, the old guarantee of the symbiotic relation between art and advertising.

The commercial strategy that focuses on the use of the emotional force of aesthetics to service desires other than just artistic pleasure is not new, it is the same seduction strategy that capitalism follows to sell its mass production, says Lipovetsky.[16] If we have a look at the old alliance between art and advertising, we cannot ignore the connection between consumerism and remix. Once more, art feeds advertising and advertising feeds art in an infinite loop. Sometimes the borders between both are blurred and even a symbiotic relationship occurs. This symbiotic relationship also works the other way around. Bourriaud reflects on the aesthetics of the flea market:

> An old sewing machine can become a kitchen table, an advertising poster from the seventies can serve to decorate a living room. Here, past

production is re-cycled and switches direction. In an involuntary homage to Marcel Duchamp, an object is given a new idea. An object once used in conformance with the concept for which it was produced now finds new potential uses in the stalls of the flea market.[17]

FIGURE 6.2 Shoe store, Bilbao downtown. Courtesy of the author.

FIGURE 6.3 Pau Figueres. *Sleeping with the Fish*. Courtesy of the author.

After a short walk in the commercial promenade of the European commercial downtown or the American mall, it is not unusual to find a new pair of Nike Air Max I next to thousands of other brand new versions and reproductions of the original ones–new colors and new materials but the same recycled design. The original Nike Air Max I appear as a readymade in a successful attempt of being commercialized under a different concept, which was—with all their metaphysical invisible qualities of the time—used by our parents in the 1980s for the purpose of running, meant for stylish fashion these days. In this case, the object/product loses its original functionality and achieves an abstract one, as a consequence of the effort of the brand to generate a new necessity. The idea of the readymade gives the sneaker a new conception: the same object with a different purpose. What it was meant to be, a cushioning, comfortable, stability revolution, does not offer anything else than status and melancholic pleasure. Many brands have found this strategy an exciting development for creating "new" products, selling the taste for vintage products and feeding the anxiety for consumption in the era of the new flea markets. On the other hand, it is the idea of postproduction that works with the different versions of the same sneaker. Nike recycles and remixes its own product in order to create an infinite range of "new" and exclusive Air Max to satisfy the needs of the consumerist masses. This example could make us reflect once more on how art has an impact not only in advertising, but in production and does not only influence advertising just aesthetically but also conceptually.

This paradigmatic relation between art and advertising in the global era could rather be a love affair between art and capitalism and defined by Gilles Lipovetsky and Jean Serroy as artistic capitalism or the aestheticization of capitalism. One could ask whether it is happening the other way around. And one could, and arguably must, reflect critically on the possibility that art is being overly influenced by the aesthetics of capitalism.

Remixing the Brand

The evolution of the commercial strategies, advertising, marketing and design have transformed brands into the new global saints. The old religious icons have been replaced by a Nike Swoosh, a Coca-Cola Santa, a fast-food clown and a long list of new idols that have homogenized the aesthetics of twenty-first century society, as it is visible in hundreds of examples such as Helmut Smits's successful attempt to turn Coke into water, making its "Real Thing" disappear, Olaf Nicolai's *Big Sneaker* and Guillaume Poulain's *Nike° 1999* inflatables or Superflex's ironic representation of a flooded McDonald's restaurant. To reflect on all the issues discussed above, I developed *The Revolution Will Be Sponsored*,[18] which is an online project that collects the work of 200 different artists that deal with postproduction and the principles of remix related to commercial brands. It hosts a list of 328 brand names, among which Coca-Cola, McDonald's and

FIGURE 6.4 Helmut Smits. *The Real Thing*. Photograph by Ronald Smits. Courtesy of the author.

Nike stands out for their repeated presence, especially in artworks of the past two decades. After looking at these figures, it is not really surprising to find these three corporate brands in the first places of the most chosen consumer and economic valuable brands global rankings.[19] My assessment based on this online art and research project is that, apparently, artists continue to incorporate into their work the forms of the global era, which began to materialize long ago, when consumerism as an ideology of capitalism took its first steps. It is a small wonder that one of the first artworks to represent a Coca-Cola bottle in anticipation of pop art—even before Andy Warhol started art-school—was *Poetry of America* painted by Salvador Dalí in 1943, during his period in America, where we can notice his interests in the relation between art, consumerism and capital.[20]

Aesthetic variables found in works included in *The Revolution Will Be Sponsored* also find a type of vindication through remix strategies of the ubiquitous visual commercial material as the global palette to build new forms. Such is the case of a work like *Logorama*,[21] the hyperbole of life through logos of thousands of brands, transforming each character and each element of the architecture of contemporary life, representing a ridiculous pseudo-reality meeting a grim reality: hyper-consumerism. A logo is a chosen form of recognizing and visually representing the ideas and characteristics of a brand, different invisible attributes that conform to the strategies of a company and its brand. It is through remix that this visual material is used to represent a totally different scenario: on one hand a mere

FIGURE 6.5 Superflex. *Flooded McDonald's*. Courtesy of the artists.

aesthetic work, and on the other, a work of art engaged with a contemporary discourse of hyper-consumerism concern. Using the principles of remix, through sampling parts or even a complete form, a new universe that goes further than the sum of the features of simple logos is born.

Following this line of thought on remix, the omnipresence of brands and logos in our lives has taken other artists further away to use what they already claim as public material in works like Evan and Franco Mattes's (0100101110101101.org) *Nikeground*, a fake Nike advertisement campaign turned into art—an action in which only the famous icon of the brand is sampled, but even a whole set of visual elements to redesign a Nike webpage and diverse promo material is used to claim that:

> Nike like other modern multinational corporations, is not an industry, it is an idea represented by its brand. It is an immaterial identity, an abstract message, an enormous advertising machine that does not produce anything, and limits its efforts to distributing products created far away in another part of the world. Precisely for its immateriality, the perception that people have of Nike is everything there is. Nike's earnings depend on their popularity, and their success depends on the image people have of their products—not in the quality of their products. [. . .] People, in turn, vindicate the right to use these symbols because they belong to anyone who lives through them every day, not those who impose them from above.

Nike's Swoosh is probably the most *seen* logo on the face of the earth, even more than any other religious or political symbol. In effect we have been working for them long enough with our bodies every time we wear brand clothes; it is now the time to reuse all that.[22]

The powerful functionality of brand design manipulation to capture consumers' and of course artists' attention, made brands such as Coca-Cola end up being one of the most remixed brands in the history of art, in an infinite range of art proposals, among which we find works such as Darren Lago's, *Coke 45 BlackPearl*, a gun made out of a Coca-Cola bottle in an example of a humorous and ironic contemporary-assisted readymade. Or the approach to the quintessential emblem of global consumerism, of Gert Robijns's *Fles*, a plastic Coca-Cola bottle and a tin can, both painted black, set face-to-face, proving the victory of the iconic design, in the fight with an anonymous but not less iconic can. More popularly, Ai Weiwei's *Han Dynasty Urn with Coca-Cola Logo* is another example of how the power of this icon seduces in a global scenario that hardly understands physical barriers, giving birth to works that show the confluence of Western and Eastern societies, in another attempt that reveals how the capacity of art to give feedback to hyper-consumerism is as ubiquitous as hyper-consumerism itself.

As we might already suspect, the work behind marketing and brand design, as well as controversial commercial strategies, has probably guaranteed the remix of brands like Nike and Coca-Cola in many artworks. But the need for a continuous growth of consumption offers a vast range of brand designs and brand promises that capture the attention of consumers and artists, becoming the new script of the global consumer society. Works such as *ABC*, an installation produced by Benjamin Verdonck, a collection of handmade logos representing the alphabet, is the perfect analogy of remixing commercial iconography as part of the collective memory, in an effort to recognize how these elements have become the new alphabets of hyper-consumerism.

What can be argued based on the examples presented above is that the action of postproduction and remixing in visual arts is an act of manipulation by itself, as we are using the same codes to approach a viewer who perfectly acknowledges what the huge Nike Swoosh might be. For example, we could define the term as a 3M manipulation,[23] in a process where brands manipulate the targeted audience, and artists manipulate the audience as well as the brand. Looking at this picture from another point of view, it can be argued that artists are conscious of the emerging complicity imposed on the viewer with such well-known everyday objects. To this effect, in my public intervention *The Revolution Will Be Sponsored*, carried out at the entrance of the Palmer Museum of the Pennsylvania State University, which consists of a 17-foot Nike Swoosh composed entirely of pebbles gathered from the museum gardens, we can notice how the aura and the metaphysical strength of the icon exceeds an effort of transformation, when recontextualized with the words of an Instagram user that shared a photo

FIGURE 6.6 Cellular screenshot of the Palmer Museum's Nike Swoosh and an Instagram reaction to it. Courtesy of the author.

of the work with the words "you know you go to the right school when you see this." This is an example of the ambiguity and the complicity that takes place when a very well-known image is remixed. The viewer might be mainly seduced by the power of an existing commercial icon, while on a different level of interpretation, the artwork is making a deeper commentary on other matters.

The commonplace attributes of brands could well explain how the complicity between artist and viewer takes place—complicity that also works as a trap for an audience consumer of all of those brands. The commercial spectacle is responsible for facilitating both an approach to the production of critical knowledge and obscuring the content of the artwork.

Conclusion

Duchamp favored selection more than composition or creation, because the artist was more empowered in the act of selection due to the growing consumer-driven culture that followed the industrial revolution. If we consider his action as the preamble of postproduction and the principles of remix, where the ability is no other than combining two selected items, by creating a new sound from two different sounds, like how we get a new color from mixing two different ones, the editing of a video from existing movie clips and the production of a new commercial universe from reusing a thousand logos in an installation. Both postproduction and remix concepts should escape from the idea of appropriation or re-appropriation and get closer to the idea of using, utilizing and manipulating. The concept of appropriation makes reference to propriety—closer to the capitalist idea of consumption—and it diverges from the contemporary idea of sharing more than owning. Curiously the idea of appropriation with the aim of owning is close to consumerism and actually clashes with the conception of reusing and recycling that has been proposed. However, it is known that when an artwork is commercialized we fall into great contradictions. The artwork transforms itself into a commodity, it has been somehow manipulated. Maybe the price for vindicating the usage of the great icons should respond to the production of non-marketable nature works. Possibly the price has already been paid off by its appearance and re-advertising in the artwork. Perhaps this is the inferred contract that should remain unsigned, nourishing the relationship between art and advertising, between art and brands.

As we are witnessing the evolution of the global mediascape aesthetics, the effort from contemporary art to address the era of hyper-consumerism is taking place, redesigning the new aesthetics of consumerism through different forms of remixing commercial imagery, which differs from its precursors in the fascination and repulsion for the novelty of the effects of global homogenization. Brands and logos, understood as public material for their ubiquity, should make acceptable the use that art freely makes of them. The close relation between hyper-consumerism and remix is seen not just in terms of production and reproduction, but as an aesthetic solution that belongs to a hypermodern era and stands in, symbolically, for worshiping excess.

Notes

1 Transcribed from *The Pervert's Guide to Ideology*, directed by Sophie Fiennes, written and presented by Slavoj Žižek (2012 British Film Institute/Channel Four Television/Bord Scannán na hÉireann/The Irish Film Board), iTunes download 2016.
2 "We live in the era of the aesthetic boom thanks to the capitalism of hyper-consumerism. With the hypermodern era we face a new aesthetic era, a new super-aesthetic society, an empire where the sun of art does never set." Gilles Lipovetsky and Jean Serroy, *La estetización del mundo. Vivir en la época del capitalismo artístico*. In my own translation from the Spanish edition: *The Aestheticization of the World: Living in the Era of the Artistic Capitalism* (Barcelona: Editorial Anagrama, 2015), 31–32.
3 In Chapter 4 of *Unpackaging Art of the 1980s* ("Peter Halley, Jeff Koons, and the Art of Marketing- and Consumption-Analysis") Alison Pearlman defines simulationism: "By the summer of 1986, yet another artistic trend had risen. Simulationism—also known as Neo-Geo, Commodity Art, Neo-Conceptualism, and new Abstraction- was the most prominent trend to captivate the New York art world since Neo-Expressionism, Appropriation, and Graffiti Art [. . .] polemics in response to the trend were defining it along one or more of the following axes: as a continuation of the aims of Appropriation Art (Donal Kuspit's emphasis), as an attempt to represent the simulation principle defined by neo-Marxist theorist Jean Baudrillard (Hal Foster's emphasis)." Alison Pearlman, *Unpackaging Art of the 1980s* (Chicago: University of Chicago Press, 2003), 105–106.

4 Nicolas Bourriaud discusses the differences between the American and European approaches to consumption when talking about the use of objects. *Postproduction: Culture as Screenplay: How Art Reprograms the World* (New York: Lukas & Sternberg, 2005), 26.
5 Lipovetsky and Serroy, *La estetización del mundo [The Aestheticization of the World]* , 7
6 Bourriaud, *Postproduction*, 93.
7 In *Capitalism as a Religion*, Walter Benjamin reflects on how capitalism offers the same answers as a religion does. We can also point out how consumerism can ensure most of those answers too. Walter Benjamin, "Capitalism as Religion [Fragment 74]," *Religion as Critique: The Frankfurt School's Critique of Religion*, edited by E. Mendieta (New York: Routledge, 2005), 259–262.
8 Re-engaging with money, as Giorgio Agamben states: "God didn't die, he became money." Agamben talks about the economic crisis, capitalism as a religion, the role of history in European cultural identity, "bio-politics," the "state of exception" and the fate of contemporary art in an interview with Giuseppe Savà for Ragusanews.com, accessed September 20, 2016
9 Jean Baudrillard, *The System of the Objects* (London: Verso, 2005), 209.
10 In the documentary *The Pervert's Guide to Ideology*, Slavoj Žižek talks about the invisible transcendence of commodities.
11 Quoting Walter White, the main character in the *Breaking Bad* television series, when he wonders: "Do you wanna live in a world without Coca-Cola?" *Breaking Bad*, season 5 episode 7, "Say My Name," directed by Thomas Schnauz and written by Vince Gilligan; created by Thomas Schnauz, Netflix.
12 "There is no outside. Once we enter the symbolic world there is no getting out again unless we lose self-awareness or die. One could somehow get off the grid, severing contact with all media and cultures but, even then, if this rather romantic and delusional decision is made after growing up with the concepts of our current global culture—which in a large part is an extension of Western culture—even then, if you decide to become a hermit, you will negotiate your existence in some context based on those Western principles. From this stance, to think of being outside media—or outside the text, for that matter—is a mute argument with a dead-end." Eduardo Navas talks about how remix functions in art practice in the interview conducted for the exhibition *Pictoplasma: White Noise*, curated by Lars Denicke and Peter Thaler, which took place at La Casa Encendida, Madrid Spain from May 23, to September 8, 2013.
13 Noam Chomsky, *What Makes Mainstream Media Mainstream* (transcribed from a talk at Z Media Institute June, 1997), accessed August 17, 2016, https://zcomm.org/zmagazine/what-makes-mainstream-media-mainstream.
14 Edward L. Benays, *Propaganda* (New York: Horace Liveright, 1928), 9.
15 Žižek, *The Pervert's Guide to Ideology*.
16 Lipovetsky and Serroy, *La estetización del mundo [The Aestheticization of the World]*, 121.
17 Bourriaud, *Postproduction*, 29.
18 https://larevolucionserapatrocinada.wordpress.com.
19 *Brand Footprint Annual Report 2016*, accessed June 12, 2016, www.brandfootprint-ranking.com.
20 Salvador Dalí retreated to the United States to escape from the World War II, and became fascinated by American mass culture. In an attempt to offend him André Breton named him "Avida Dollars" for Dali's obsession for money, he instead took it as a compliment: "En América querer ganar dinero es lo mejor que hay. Voy a triunfar con ese nombre" (In my own translation: "In America being eager for earning money is the best thing there is. I am going to be so successful with that name"). "El Dandi del surrealismo," accessed June 12, 2016, Document1www.elmundo.es/especiales/2013/cultura/dali/extravagancia.html.
21 Logorama, short film animation.

22 Laura Baigorri, La obra de arte como alucinación collectiva. Una conversación con *0100101110101101.org* (In my own translation: The Artwork as a Collective Hallucination: A Conversation with 0100101110101101.org), February 2004, accessed June 20, 2017, www.academia.edu/20061766/La_obra_de_arte_como_alucinaci%C3%B3n_colectiva._Una_conversaci%C3%B3n_con_0100101110101101.org.

23 We decided to use the name of the brand 3M to explain the triple action of manipulation. First, manipulation held by brands towards its target; second, manipulation taken place when the artist targets the audience using a brand's commonplace features; and a third manipulation in terms of remix, taking place when the artist uses the attributes of brands to create his work.

7
COPYRIGHT/FAIR USE

Patricia Aufderheide

Copyright policies are critical to shaping the present and future of what Aram Sinnreich calls "configurable culture," Kembrew McLeod calls "remix culture," and Henry Jenkins calls "spreadable culture." This is a reality across all disciplines and practices, given the protean nature of the remix concept. Remix—reuse of existing material in a new work—can occur in any kind of creative endeavor. For instance, scholars remix existing scholarship when they provide a literature review and quote from previous work. Journalists remix existing journalism when they provide a summary and/or update. Critics remix the work they examine as they weave elements of it into their own comment, critique or analysis. Visual artists who do appropriation art or collage aggressively and consciously remix, but other artists are also and inevitably in dialog with the past as they build upon and refer to previous artwork in their own as well. People who produce vids, memes, mashups and other terms of art from emerging digital practice extend these time-honored creative practices. In all cases, the terms of copyright policy are implicated.

Copyright policy influences the cultural process. In law, copyright determines what of existing cultural production can be taken without permission for new work. In practice it does so by enabling copyright holders to forbid creators to use work, sue them for using it or, in the case of online remix, to command Internet Service Providers to remove work that is suspected of infringement; and by confining the imagination of creators to what they believe that, under copyright, they have the right to do. Thus, copyright considerations occur in the realm of *law* and its legal interpretation; *corporate policies* and practice; and individual *creative practice*.

Copyright Policies

Copyright policy is anchored territorially by national laws. Copyrights are limited monopolies granted to owners (not necessarily creators) of some fixed expression. Copyright policies determine the terms of those limits, which usually include the length of time, the geographic extent, and the scope of monopoly in related forms (derivative products).

Copyright policies also carve out certain uses that override the owners' monopoly right while it is still in play, as discussed in *Reclaiming Fair Use*.[1] Teachers, librarians and people with disabilities typically have some privileges that override those rights. In some places, government or public media have privileges that override monopolies. Also, highly specific carve-outs may exist (for instance, using music in religious services).

Aside from these specific and sometimes quirky overriding clauses, which vary by nation, copyright policies typically also have written into law *user rights* designed to apply to certain kinds of behavior, and thus to anyone using work in a particular way. This kind of user right is structured, generally, in two ways: either by making a list—sometimes a very long list—of different kinds of practices that override monopoly (e.g., using copyrighted material as an illustration in an academic paper), or by creating a general condition (e.g., doing something that is different from the market purpose of the protected work, and that adds value to the culture). The first kind of user right—the most common term for this approach is fair dealing—has the advantage of relative clarity and the disadvantage of rigidity; the second has the advantage of flexibility and the disadvantage of ambiguity.

All of these legal terms have evolved as a result of interests coalescing around demands that the state create favorable conditions to benefit, through monopolies, a class of people or set of practices. Monopolies, by definition, benefit the few at the expense of the many; they are privileges provided by government to those few. The origins of copyright, for instance, are in demands of eighteenth-century incumbent British publishers to the Crown to protect their interests against upstart publishers. The justifications for creating such policies vary in different national territories. In the U.S., the justification for copyright is that it will promote the creation of culture, the "Science" (as in knowledge) in the phrase "Science and the Useful Arts" in the Constitution. Both monopolies and their exceptions and limitations (user rights) are subject to this logic; both in some cases encourage the creation of culture.

Tilting Toward Monopoly

Current copyright law worldwide is extensive, with extremely long and broadly applicable monopolies, with relatively weak user rights. These regimes have evolved along with two overarching trends: the evolution of mass media and large, increasingly global, media companies; and the evolution of freer trade practices implemented and enforced with bilateral and multilateral international treaties. The practical effect has been both to extend and expand the terms of copyright monopolies, and to regularize these terms to some extent across national borders.

This process has been powerfully shaped by U.S. interests, both corporate and geopolitical. Since the 1970s, U.S. media companies, including music, movie, television and software companies, have vigorously, persistently and with both clout and sophistication worked to expand monopoly rights in U.S. copyright law, to extend those terms internationally, and to leverage U.S. diplomacy to advantage U.S.-based protected works. The media corporations found allies among free-trade advocates who were ascendant in the federal government, particularly from the Bill Clinton administration onward. In 1976, a major rewrite of the Copyright Act transformed U.S. copyright law. A process of steady extension of the length of time of monopoly rights was put into place at that time. Also, U.S. copyright was made default; registration and renewal was no longer necessary. International treaty agreements with the U.S. have usually included clauses demanding some conformity to U.S. copyright terms, and often have also included penalties for governments that acquiesce to piracy of intellectual property.

Two kinds of tensions have stressed the functionality of this increasingly international copyright policy. Digital practices by their nature involve the copying of entire files and objects, and such copying also facilitates new kinds of creative practices—for instance, non-consumptive research (searching through entire databases of content for recurring patterns, or mashing up several databases to find patterns across them), remix, mashups and a wealth of practices that use the original work (e.g., vidding) for purposes of criticism or commentary. Second, Internet communication inherently crosses national borders, and thus national copyright regimes, creating new challenges to interpretation of policy. While current practice works on the assumption that the copyright law where work was created, or alternatively where the server housing the work is located, applies; however, as discussed in *Reclaiming Fair Use*, this is practice in the absence of settled international agreement.

The unbalanced nature of copyright in many countries, particularly the largest exporters of intellectual property, has created enormous frustration among creators in the burgeoning DIY remix culture. At the beginning of the twenty-first century, some scholars and activists[2] called for protection of the endangered "commons" of culture, being "enclosed" by monopoly. Others proudly celebrated their role as "pirates" of a copyrighted culture, seizing what they needed, although many in fact were well within the law. For instance, the musical artist calling himself GirlTalk composes work entirely from the work of others, successfully employing fair use to do so, although he is widely looked upon as a copyright-defying pirate. The Swedish Pirate Party has flaunted its support for not only creative but openly illegal consumer practices. Some sought workarounds, such as using Creative

Commons-licensed material in their own work and in turn sharing their work under CC licenses. In DIY digital-culture circles, conversations about the problems with copyright were often phrased in terms of crisis. In the intervening years, the apocalyptic discourse cooled; legal decisions, corporate policies and user habits all contributed. A key feature of the more nuanced copyright environment has been growing awareness and employment of user rights, chronicled in *Reclaiming Fair Use*.

User Rights

In a time of extensive monopoly rights, user rights rise to an unparalleled importance, particularly with digital innovation. The nature of user rights, however, is anchored in the purpose of copyright policy in the national territory. U.S. user rights have been of particular importance internationally. This is partly because of the size of the U.S. market and the heft of U.S. geopolitics. It is partly because, since the explosive success of Google and Facebook, which employ the most expansive U.S. user right of fair use assertively, fair use has recently been strongly linked to digital innovation. Indeed, Google and any form of digital search that copies material could not have been developed in the U.K. or continental Europe, where fair use does not exist. It is partly because of the burgeoning of grassroots, aggregated and remixed content internationally, where traditional user rights usually work awkwardly with emerging cultural patterns.

Fair Use

The most important and most general user right in the U.S. is fair use. It is also the user right attracting the greatest attention in copyright reform internationally. Fair use is also part of the law in Israel, in the same form; in the Philippines, in much the same way; and in variants in South Korea, Singapore, Bangladesh, Sri Lanka, Taiwan and Uganda. It has been actively discussed as part of copyright reform discussions in the U.K. and in Australia. Canada's fair dealing clauses were recently redesigned to work more like fair use in the U.S.[3]

Fair use became part of U.S. law in 1841, with a legal case, *Folsom v. Marsh*, about a biography that copied extensively from a collection of letters. Judge Story articulated four concerns, later known as "factors," to consider when making a decision about fair use: the nature of the original work; the nature of the new work; the amount/value of what was taken; and the effect on the market. These four criteria were included in the 1976 rewrite of the U.S. Copyright Act.

Evolving Definitions of Fair Use

Implementation was initially difficult, with judges puzzled about how to interpret the four general criteria, especially since they were not necessarily equally ranked.

Judges tended to lean heavily on concerns about impinging on the market. In 1990, Judge Pierre Leval wrote a definitive and highly influential law journal article on the subject, establishing standards that have become the norm.[4] He argued that the core concept guiding decision-making should normally be a transformative purpose—whether the new author was using copyright-protected material for a different purpose than the one for which it was originally placed on the market or designed. If the transformative purpose was met, then the next question would be whether the amount/nature of what was used was appropriate to the transformative purpose. If these two considerations were met, then the Constitutional purpose of copyright, to promote culture, had been met. Putting transformativeness (the result of comparing the first two "factors," the nature of the original and the new work) and appropriate amount (the third "factor") in the center meant that the concern about market harm (the fourth "factor") was usually effectively answered. This was because transformative uses would not be in the same sphere as the existing market, and copyright holders cannot lay claim to all potential markets, only ones they actually occupy.

This logic became, over decades, the default reasoning on fair use in the courts. This understanding was consolidated in 2015, in an appeals court ruling written by Judge Leval in the Google Books case.[5] In this lawsuit, major publishers sued Google for copying entire books under copyright and making snippets of them available to searchers in Google Books. The court found definitively that Google had a fair use right to repurpose this material, in the process copying it in its entirety and making only portions available to inform viewers about the book. The purpose was transformative and the amount made available was appropriate.[6] The logic of Google Books was widely applicable.

Making Risk Assessment Easier

Still, many people feared legal and reputational consequences of employing fair use. Statutory damages, or fines, are set very high for copyright infringement, and although they are never actually invoked at the higher end, the dollar figures terrify anyone who gets a cease-and-desist letter. Lack of experience with clearly identified fair use left many with questions about how to calculate risk. While risk is always present when people employ their rights, it is vanishingly low for most common fair use situations. But unfamiliarity and anxiety tended to dampen creators' enthusiasm for fair use, when they knew they were using it. These same people incurred risk, of course, in many other situations—inviting friends over to a party where someone might slip, fall and sue; crossing a street; making a sardonic comment about a public official (treason?) or a competitor (libel?). But knowing the norms made it easy to do risk calculations.

These frustrations led some people, most notoriously the activist legal scholar Lawrence Lessig, to declare that existing user rights, including fair use in the U.S., were too weak to be helpful, providing only a disturbing "grey area" where the little guy, the small-time creator, was at the perpetual mercy of the corporation with its bank of lawyers.

Some people in specific creative communities decided to use the strength of their communities to address insecurity about applying fair use, by establishing field-wide best practices in fair use. Filmmakers, communication and film scholars, academic librarians, creators of open courseware, media literacy teachers, archivists, poets, journalists and visual arts professionals crafted codes of best practices in fair use. Members of these creative communities usually worked closely with Peter Jaszi and myself of American University; we both facilitated their discussions and coordinated legal review from a group of independent experts.[7] Several private funders, including the Rockefeller Foundation, the John D. and Catherine T. MacArthur Foundation, the Ford Foundation, the Andrew W. Mellon Foundation, the McCormick Foundation and the Kress Foundation all contributed to these various efforts. These codes specified the logic to employ to make the concepts of "transformative" and "appropriate" useable in the most common situations for people in that creative community. People created more work that cost less to produce, suffered fewer delays and was sometimes innovative, because they were able to understand when they could employ from others' work without licensing.

The growing importance of remix culture and the centrality of user rights in making it possible generated organizational activity along with political action. The Organization for Transformative Works was created in 2007, representing the interests of remixers, fan-fiction writers, vidders and others who rework popular culture. It offers remixers legal advice and its website and journal also became a resource both for scholars and practitioners. Public Knowledge hosted World's Fair Use Day for several years, starting in 2010. Several creative communities whose codes of best practices had clarified their fair use understanding successfully won their cases for greater access to fair use before the Copyright Tribunal. Filmmakers, professors, students and remixers all won waivers from the penalties in the Digital Millennium Copyright Act of 1998 for breaking encryption on digital media. They successfully made the case that their work in creating new culture was inhibited by not being able to break encryption on others' work so that they could employ fair use.

Corporate Practices Inhibiting Fair Use

Fair users were, by 2016, in a good place before the law. But their rights could be sabotaged by private corporate online behavior, when rights holders claimed they detected infringement. Under the 1998 Digital Millennium Copyright Act (DMCA), Internet Service Providers are free from infringement created by people using their platform, if they respond to any copyright holder's good-faith claim by taking down the offending material.

From 2007 onward, increasingly large providers and large copyright holders alike have used automatic detection of digital matches for copyrighted material.

As well, the major platform for online video, YouTube, instituted an automatic detection system of its own, ContentID. Severe penalties, such as being blocked from the service, are issued by ISPs that find repeated use of copyrighted material, even when it is clearly fair use. The automated identification and takedown process has resulted in exponentially more takedowns, and of course such claims cannot distinguish between legitimate fair use and infringement. A University of California, Berkeley study showed that many of the claims were made in error, often because fair use was being employed.[8] Users can claim fair use in a counter-takedown, and as of 2016 no copyright holder had ever sued a user for infringement. But to do that, users have to feel confident in their rights, since the platforms alert them to their sole responsibility for any infringement claims. Many are too afraid to do anything but complain to each other.

A long-running lawsuit initiated by a user, Stephanie Lenz, against Universal for takedowns of a video showing her toddler dancing to a Prince song in the kitchen (a clear fair use), may trigger some changes. In an interim ruling, the court told copyright holders that automatic detection software was not enough to fulfill the requirement of good faith in believing that a copyright infringement had taken place. That may affect corporate behavior and rein in automated detection as a trigger for takedowns, as the case continues. Also, Google has pledged to defend users who are sued for legitimate fair use. This is a fairly safe promise to make, since no copyright holder has yet sued and no corporate lawyer would

FIGURE 7.1 *Let's Go Crazy* was a YouTube video response project xtine burrough created with students at California State University, Fullerton from 2007 to 2013. For more information, see http://letsgocrazy.info/.

> *Let's Go Crazy* was a YouTube video response project xtine burrough created with students at California State University, Fullerton from 2007 to 2013. For this project, students created parodies of Lenz's original video—often criticizing Prince or the takedown notice issued by Universal Music Group as the primary text in their videos. On Lenz's video response page the sample of Prince's *Let's Go Crazy* song captured in Lenz's video appeared in more than 100 student videos, each protected by fair use while commenting on her original media. See the YouTube playlist, http://tinyurl.com/letsgocrazyvids, or the project page, www.letsgocrazy.info.

counsel proceeding against a clear fair use either. But it demonstrates Google's awareness of the need to support users who employ fair use more than it has done in the past. Some argue that the DMCA's permission for such pre-emptive takedowns should be retired, and others that the law should stipulate more and human work to identify infringement. But others on the copyright holder side of the argument say that the DMCA needs to be strengthened to stiffen enforcement further, and that automatic detection tools are the only way to address the volume of material that needs to be scanned.

Increasingly, creative work lives in an active space between online and offline (Figure 7.1). The Internet and digital tools are fueling ever-more creative possibilities in every cultural and knowledge-generating realm. International governments are cautiously exploring the implications of incorporating the powerful and flexible right of fair use into their own copyright policies. Meanwhile international treaties encourage more and sterner copyright enforcement internationally, without strengthening user rights.

User Knowledge and Action

Knowledge of the user rights available to remixers of all kinds may be a critically important tool to create greater flexibility in copyright for a remix era. If creators understand the rights available to them to reuse copyrighted material without licensing, and assert those rights when challenged with takedowns online, they could see their work restored. Certainly user knowledge builds awareness that can mobilize constituencies for remix-appropriate policy reforms in the future. The 2016 Twitter hashtag #WTFU (what the fair use?!), a *cri de coeur* from frustrated makers vulnerable to arbitrary and inappropriate takedowns, was one demonstration of a growing group of users well aware of their rights and in touch with each other. The efforts of constituencies ranging from vidders and librarians to filmmakers and scholars, demanding and winning DMCA exemptions, is another example of coordinated activity that has had real-world effects. Citizen action played a part in two public processes exploring the advantages of fair use in Australia since 2013, and it was important in Canadian reform expanding fair dealing to be more like fair use. Education about user rights generally is crucial to the evolution of remix culture. Turning creative opportunity into culture depends on finding a balance between monopoly and user rights in copyright, and on makers being confident in their own understanding of their rights.

Notes

1 Patricia Aufderheide and Peter Jaszi, *Reclaiming Fair Use: How to Put Balance Back in Copyright* (Chicago: University of Chicago Press, 2011).
2 These scholars include legal scholars Lawrence Lessig, James Boyle, and Yochai Benkler; they were joined by author David Bollier and cultural studies advocates including Kembrew McLeod.
3 Katz, A. (2013) "Fair Use 2.0: The Rebirth of Fair Dealing in Canada," in *The Copyright Pentalogy: How the Supreme Court of Canada Shook the Foundations of Canadian Copyright Law*, edited by Michael A. Geist, 93–156 (Ottawa, ON: Ottawa University Press).
4 P.N. Leval (1990) "Toward A Fair Use Standard," *Harvard Law Review* 103: 1105–1113.
5 "Judge's Ruling on Google Books Case," *Document Cloud*, www.documentcloud.org/documents/834877-google-books-ruling-on-fair-use.html.
6 U.S. Court of Appeals. 2d Circuit. (2015). 13-4829-cv. Authors Guild v. Google, Inc. Document 230-1, 10/16/2015, 1620658, 48 pp.
7 All the codes reside at cmsimpact.org/fair-use.
8 Jennifer M. Urban, Joe Karaganis and Brianna L. Schofield (2016) *Notice and Takedown in Everyday Practice*, UC Berkeley Public Law Research Paper No. 2755628. Available at SSRN: https://ssrn.com/abstract=2755628.

Bibliography

Aufderheide, Patricia, and Peter Jaszi. 2011. *Reclaiming Fair Use: How to Put Balance Back in Copyright*. Chicago: University of Chicago Press.
Jenkins, Henry, Sam Ford, and Joshua Green. 2013. *Spreadable Media: Creating Value and Meaning in a Networked Culture*. New York and London: New York University Press.
Joyce, Craig, Marshall Leaffer, Peter Jaszi, and Tyler Ochoa. 2006. *Copyright Law*, 7th edn. Newark, NJ: LexisNexis.
"Judge's Ruling on Google Books Case," *Document Cloud*, www.documentcloud.org/documents/834877-google-books-ruling-on-fair-use.html.
Kaplan, Benjamin. 2005. *An Unhurried View of Copyright*, republished (and with contributions from friends). Newark: LexisNexis Matthew Bender.
Katz, Ariel. 2013. "Fair Use 2.0: The Rebirth of Fair Dealing in Canada." In *The Copyright Pentalogy: How the Supreme Court of Canada Shook the Foundations of Canadian Copyright Law*, edited by Michael A. Geist, 93–156. Ottawa, ON: Ottawa University Press.
Leval, P.N. 1990. "Toward A Fair Use Standard." *Harvard Law Review* 103: 1105–1113
Netanel, Neil. 2011. "Making Sense of Fair Use." *Lewis & Clark Law Review* 15(3): 715–772.
Sinnreich, Aram. 2010. *Mashed Up: Music, Technology, and the Rise of Configurable Culture*. Amherst: University of Massachusetts Press.
Urban, Jennifer M., Joe Karaganis and Brianna L. Schofield. 2016. *Notice and Takedown in Everyday Practice*. UC Berkeley Public Law Research Paper No. 2755628. Available at SSRN: https://ssrn.com/abstract=2755628.

8
CREATIVITY

xtine burrough and Frank Dufour

> The true life takes place when we're alone, thinking, feeling, lost in memory, dreaming self aware, the sub microscopic moments.[1]

Writing about creativity is like writing about a memory—it is engulfed in a web of associations, some that are seemingly other-worldly. We are often so engrossed in a creative moment that it is hard to remember how a thing is made once it is finished. This blurry part of the process—the act of production—includes creative acts of sampling and appropriation inherent to remix, which inform our artistic practices. In this chapter, we will begin by establishing the type of creativity that interests us in relation to remix, one that Don DeLillo cites as "true life" in the epigraph; then we locate creativity in a part of the chapter that examines homogeneous and heterogeneous sampling. Finally, we review cases of remix artworks to define creativity in remix by way of these two forms of sampling.

Sisyphus and Other Ghosts

Creativity has come to be one of the most commonly used terms in a context that has very little, if anything to do with artistic creation: accounting software solutions are creative, planning and management of human resources are creative, solutions to just about anything from cleaning your house to following a recipe in a *Real Simple* magazine are described as "creative." Creativity is associated with what is deemed today to be the most valuable intellectual capacity: problem-solving. Within this category of creativity, problems are meant not only to be solved, but to disappear forever, making room for new problems, in a never-ending course of industrial and intellectual progress, perfectly synchronized for neoliberal agendas. We, however, claim a different quality for the problems we wish to deal with: in this chapter we explore the types of problems that remain, embarrassing problems—the ones that do not go away. These magnificent and stupid problems we keep failing to overcome, these simple and familiar, yet terrible obstacles upon which we keep stumbling are what we imagine to be at the root of creativity. The guile of Ulysses brought him back alive to Ithaca through the many problems he encountered. What awaits him there, returning after a 20-year journey, is the death of the faithful Argos. What awaits him here is the embarrassing and eternal problem of primultimacy: each instant of life is altogether a new, first, and unique one; the last one, tinting each moment with the strange color of nostalgia. Our creativity, we believe, relies on this strange sense of something transformed from feeling familiar in an almost dreamlike state, or "a human melancholy made possible by our consciousness, which is the consciousness of something else, the consciousness of an elsewhere, the consciousness of a contrast between past, between present and future."[2] These are the kinds of problems we seek to address on the notion of creativity in remix studies, and we claim that this kind of problem requires a kind of creativity very different from the one that aims to solve problems once and for all.

Transformation

A consciousness that understands contrast between a past, present, and a future can be imagined as a group of senses positioned at the center of a vortex in fluid motion. These senses create understanding, relationship, and dialog with activity. They bring an awareness that fluctuates between keenness and abstraction to the motion surrounding them. Using this metaphor, we position creativity as the gust of transformative motion, ever-changing and ever-aware of its relation to change, at the center of a practice so reliant on change and temporal dialog such as remix.

This notion of creativity can be illustrated as the manifestation of an acute temporal consciousness with one of the first musical remixes created with new recording technologies: concrete music. When Pierre Schaeffer, the inventor of this genre, reflected on 20 years of experimentations in music perception, he suggested that music arises ultimately and only when the listener is not using her perception of the sound objects to learn about the world from these objects, but to learn about herself. Music arises as the poignant description of human consciousness expressed in the language of objects.[3]

The search for what Schaeffer calls a balanced sound object is the initial phase of composition in concrete music. There are two possible origins for the sound object: the intentional creation of such sound by means of recording and processing, and the extraction of this object from a pre-existing recorded stream of sounds. In both cases, the composer is guided through this process by the search of a form, something that would display over time a particular manifestation of one or several auditory qualities such as pitch, color, mass, grain, harmonic timbre, and so on. The attention in this process is not guided by searching for the unheard, the novelty, or the originality of this form, but rather by the exploration of an entity that would be preserved through the extraction of this form from the context in which it first appeared: a recording session with musical and non-musical instruments, or a pre-existing composition of forms such as a song, the soundtrack of a film, or any other organized collection of sounds.

The first consequence of this extraction is the severance of the sound from its cause: neither the musical instrument nor the syntactic succession of forms is present to assign from the past the temporal position of the sound. Liberated from the causal chronology, the freed object stands by itself in a context only determined by the flow of its own existence and the composer's intention. In this relative temporal autonomy, the sound object identity is no longer solely determined by its past, as an effect of a pre-existing causal chain, but by its possible future as one of the objects within a new arrangement determined by the relationships created between its inner qualities and the qualities of the other objects. This disposition is the main characteristic of what Schaeffer termed the "concrete" compositional practice. Its initial phase is deeply anchored within the real and concrete experience of the sound object and the emergence of its aural qualities through the act of reduced listening. Unlike the traditional or abstract compositional practice whose initial phase is the invention of an ideal or virtual form, i.e., the musical idea, progressively actualizing itself through notation, orchestration, and finally interpretation; the concrete practice operates on a scale between the actuality of the sound and the virtual potential of the form. We will use this notion of a spectrum between the actuality of the object and the virtual, poetic potential for a relational object to define the creativity embedded in two types of practices.

Homogeneous and Heterogeneous Samples

Creativity is manifested in these practices in two different ways: in the first, what we will call the abstract practice, creativity resides essentially within the composer's mind from where it coordinates and organizes the formal creational process. This manifestation is also temporally anchored in the past, suggesting or imposing to the listener a clear alignment of temporalities orienting the present activity of listening to the musical piece toward the future of its final resolution. Relevant examples of such compositional practice can be drawn from works by composers from the Baroque period, such as J.S. Bach—the contrapuntal form of any of his fugues, while progressively revealing itself throughout the present activity of listening, is only fully achieved and perceived with the final entry and tonal resolution. This abstract compositional practice becomes radicalized over time, leading to the mathematical principles of dodecaphonic composition invented by Arnold Schoenberg perfecting the abstraction of the musical material, by reducing it to numbers and imposing the pre-existing development of their mathematical series to the actualization of the piece. Within the context of this practice, creativity is mostly engaged in the identification and manipulation of abstract entities, or minimal syntactic units that are read as freely as possible of any meaning—they are entirely detached from any previous existence. The musical note from a traditional abstract piece of music is always radically new, pure, and unaffected by previous uses. The sense of liberty, and further the creativity awarded to the composer, is entirely constructed on the premise of the compositional units' purity and severance from any previous formation of meaning. Further, it is possible to identify within this practice, not only one type of creativity, but also one major type of sample or unit: homogeneous samples, which are identical in kind and acquire meaning only in the processes of substitution or combination. Operating with such homogeneous samples, or remixing them, is primarily an organizational practice relying on rules of repetition, contrast, duration, order, and frequency.

Heterogeneous samples (different in kind, sizes, and qualities) rely on their attachments to intrinsic individual meanings. Operating with such samples calls for different practices than when constructing a work with homogeneous samples. The founding principle for creative use of heterogeneous samples is the acknowledgment of the sample's linguistic meaning and meaningfulness as a cultural and political operator. The initiating act of artistic creativity for the remixer of heterogeneous samples is the act of making oneself available to the language of the sample: seeing, hearing, and feeling the expression of the sample and accepting the humble role of the translator of this voice within the remix. The main operation or creative act is then relational and consists in creating the context for the samples to play in dialog with each other, for exchange, alteration, and a transfer of meanings by way of metaphors, analogies, and poetic attachments of form with meaning. Using the heterogeneous sample as the creative thread that unites many remix practices, we will consider it in examples that rely on various strategies for making meaning, and that, instead of solving problems, aim to transform the viewer's state of consciousness from the static here and now to a fluid realm of possibilities.

In Practice

Cory Arcangel's *Drei Klavierstücke op.11* (Figure 8.1) proposes an oxymoronic synthesis of these two creative practices by assigning each note of a Schoenberg score to video samples of cats playing the actual tone on a piano before recombining all of these samples in accordance with the original score. This project synthesizes our ideas by taking Schoenberg's formal strategy as a starting point for creative operation, rather than a landing that becomes definitive of the creative object. Remixing cat videos—representative of a comical, if banal, form of online communication—to Schoenberg's formal, "high-brow" modern art composition creates a communicative message that inverts the meme-status of each component in the remix. At once the cats become elevated to the status of

FIGURE 8.1 Cory Arcangel, *Drei Klavierstücke op. 11*, 2009. Three YouTube videos, www.coryarcangel.com/things-i-made/2009-003-dreiklavierstucke-op-11.

high culture and the Schoenberg composition is reduced to the low-life cachet of the online cat. This inversion, a relational activity rooted in the poetics of juxtaposition, relies on the viewer's understanding of the past—the signification of the cats and the Schoenberg score—and willingness to re-understand these signifiers as a future potential expressed in Arcangel's creative work.

Assuming *Drei Klavierstücke op.11* can be used to represent both abstract and formal compositional strategies and remix practices, we will now examine remix practices that take a relational approach to the homogeneous and heterogeneous sample in works that use extraction, just like Schaeffer's sound object removed from pre-existing recorded streams of sounds, to express creativity in relation to context, political messages, and formatting tropes. To demonstrate these relationships, we will analyze three remixes, one for each of Navas's primary types of remix: extended (Douglas Gordon's *24-Hour Psycho*), selective (Jonathan McIntosh's "Donald Duck Meets Glenn Beck in Right Wing Radio Duck"), and reflexive (Megan MacKay's "Ray Rice Inspired Makeup Tutorial").[4]

Douglas Gordon's 24-Hour Psycho

The extended remix lengthens the media object, as in an "extended version" of a song created for play in a dance club. While this transformation is common in audio practices, it can also be used as a way of understanding Douglas Gordon's 1993 art film, *24-Hour Psycho* (Figure 8.2), as a remix. Gordon's iteration of *Psycho* lengthens the frames of Hitchcock's thriller, transforming the film from its

FIGURE 8.2 Norman Bates in front of the Bates Mansion as seen during the *Psycho* section of the Universal Studios Studio Tour in Hollywood. Source: Alfred A. Si on Wikipedia.

original 109 minutes to a 24-hour film marathon, displaying *Psycho* at a rate of approximately two frames per second. While Gordon's transformation is often considered a work of appropriation art among fine art or museum audiences, his methodology creates an extended play of the film similar to extended disco songs of the 1970s. Doubling as a work of appropriation and an extended remix (the two in fact go hand-in-hand), Gordon's work lengthens the sample size—it is a copy of the entire movie, with the seemingly invisible addition of time. The paradox of this invisible addition resulting in a heightened visual experience of the work contributes to a transformation in dialog with remix as a heterogeneous treatment to a homogeneous sampling. Like Arcangel, Gordon creates a communication that turns inward on itself, but this time the pair of signifiers is not two separate pieces of recombined media, instead it is a homogeneous set of film stills that are remixed in time—a compositional or formal dimension of the media in which the film stills are the "pure" compositional units. Gordon's extended play was remixed both on the grounds of its cinematic composition and viewing experience. Like Schaeffer's freed object, this creative transformation of Hitchcock's *Psycho* gains its own possible future in an audience who will undoubtedly experience a fluctuation between keenness and abstraction while viewing Janet Leigh in slow motion.

Jonathan McIntosh's "Donald Duck Meets Glenn Beck in Right Wing Radio Duck"

In "Donald Duck Meets Glenn Beck in Right Wing Radio Duck," Jonathan McIntosh's version of the popular Disney duck character is unemployed, and has fallen behind on mortgage payments when he hears the voice of redemption in a radio infomercial (Figure 8.3). Donald Duck says, "I'm so discouraged. I've tried so hard."[5] Then he hears the radio countdown to Glenn Beck's show. Beck's voice booms through the radio, "I think a lot of people feel like they're alone and they just want to give up."[6] Donald Duck talks back in agreement with Beck's radio persona. Beck emotes with nationalistic rhetoric before declaring, "The ideas that built America are being lost and perverted."[7] Beck blames Marxists, Communists, and anti-capitalists. Donald Duck begins to take cover from the oncoming reign of liberal terror—presumably Pluto the Marxist, Goofy the Communist, and Mickey Mouse the anti-capitalist—acting out the fear Beck successfully implanted by preying upon Donald Duck's despair. Beck declares, "There is a perfect storm formulating and it is here."[8] As Donald Duck switches between various radio stations the news worsens. The list of threats to America include "Obama himself, Al Qaeda, Iran, Islamic Jihadists, terrorists, Venezuela, immigration,"[9] and more. Donald Duck locks himself in his house just before Beck's voice alerts him that the enemy is: inside the house! In a psychotic, dreamlike series of clips Donald Duck is terrorized before he hears Beck land on "We invite you to join up for $9.95 a month . . . It is gonna explain everything that is going on."[10] When Donald Duck receives Beck's extremist machine it immediately invalidates him, "Donald Duck, isn't that the name of some stupid Disney cartoon?"[11] The machine tells Donald he can ask any question. When Donald, in full duck-rage, shows his notice of foreclosure, the machine replies, "Oh! Sucks to be you, du'n it?"[12] The extremist slips away from Beck's original, sympathetic position and espouses new rhetoric that condemns Donald Duck for his laziness: "it happens, you lost, move on . . . Get a job!"[13] The video ends with Donald declaring, "This is the end of you"[14] before shooting the machine, and as a result, creating a hole in the wall of his house.

A selective remix undergoes a transformation by way of addition or subtraction.[15] This type of remix is especially popular in political remix video because of the persuasive power of juxtaposition. To create this parody, McIntosh remixed 50 classic Disney cartoons to demonstrate how right-wing media paradoxically appears sympathetic while fear-mongering, and espouses nationalist views that prioritize security at the expense of racist, heteronormative, and violent behavior. In an interview with Henry Jenkins, McIntosh said political remix video

> can be a blunt tool that uses ridicule as a way to expose hypocrisy, illuminate tropes, and talk back to power—but it is a little harder to use the form in more subtle ways (especially if you still want to get the lolz).[16]

FIGURE 8.3 Jonathan McIntosh, "Donald Duck Meets Glenn Beck in Right Wing Radio Duck," 2010. Political remix on YouTube, http://popculturedetective.agency/2010/right-wing-radio-duck-donald-discovers-glenn-beck.

The "more subtle ways" that McIntosh refers to must relate to creativity. It is harder to achieve because creativity does not lend itself to easy solutions.

Expanding upon Bakhtin's understanding of the "dialogic nature of certain texts," Mark Nunes argues in the "Parody" chapter of this book that "What we witness in remix, then, is the dialogic made even more concrete through a literal act of cutting up source material and arranging digital 'scraps'—forcing them to speak to one another in unintended ways."[17] While the Disney clips and the Beck audio speak to each other by their arrangement, they also gel to create a synecdoche of right-wing politics.

Like many overtly political works in remix culture, this video speaks back to authority by using voices of power in juxtaposition with elevated voices of those underserved. Here, a heterogeneous sampling is necessary for the language-based fluidity of signifiers embedded in each video clip.

Megan MacKay's "Ray Rice Inspired Makeup Tutorial"

The reflexive remix acts as an interpretation of the original work of art with which it is in dialog—it could be extended, or it could be transformed by the addition or subtraction of materials—but the primary motivation for this methodology is to extend the dialog of an original work of art by alluding to it in a remix while challenging "the 'spectacular aura' of the original."[18] Megan MacKay creates videos with feminist messages using a variety of tropes common to the online video format. In "Ray Rice Inspired Makeup Tutorial" she subverts the YouTube make-up video tutorial formula to express a feminist critique of Ray Rice (Figure 8.4). A former American running back, Rice played in the National Football League for the Baltimore Ravens until the day the second video of his assault on his then fiancée (now wife) was released.[19] Two videos were made public by TMZ Sports.

FIGURE 8.4 Megan MacKay, "Ray Rice Inspired Makeup Tutorial," 2014. YouTube makeup tutorial, https://youtube/zyNa9kqq8mk.

In the first (released February 19, 2014) Rice drags Janay Rice's body out of an elevator. In March, Rice was indicted on aggravated assault charges. In July, the NFL suspended Rice from two games. The second video (released September 8, 2014) shows Rice punching Janay in the face during the same elevator incident. On the same day he was suspended indefinitely by the NFL. The description MacKay assigns to her tutorial, published in September 2014, is "A new makeup look inspired by America's new favourite spousal abuser."[20]

A description of MacKay's video follows:

MacKay appears facing the camera—presumably her computer's camera, sitting on the edge of her bed. She is seen in a medium close-up shot. While the camera focuses on her face the viewer can also see the closed doors to her bedroom, where a poster hangs reading "Do your thing & don't care, we like it."[21] MacKay moves through the usual steps in a makeup tutorial, inserting commentary throughout.

She begins, "So the first step, as always, is foundation. And I'm using a new shade I just bought called the NFL," she goes on to say, "I really like this color, because it'll cover up anything just to save face."[22] In the next step she applies eye primer while explaining,

> I'm using one other color called, um, Intersectional Feminism. And a lot of people complain, like, "Why do I have to use Intersectional Feminism, you know, like, why does my feminism have to include people of all genders and races and orientations? Like, why, you know?" And to those people, generally the best thing to do is, um, read a f>ing history book.[23]

She looks in the mirror, applies makeup, looks in the camera, but never breaks her tutorial persona while weaving a narrative of Rice's case, The NFL, and intersectional feminism into the work. She applies eye shadow:

Your crease color is #27 which is Ray Rice's jersey number for the Baltimore Ravens—or former jersey number, I guess. It's so hard to get used to people getting fired for doing bad things, you know? And the other color you're going to be using is #25, which in the state of Maryland is the number of years you serve in prison for felony assault.[24]

MacKay moves on to eyeliner, called "Women are Objects," she says, "And you're just gonna want to ring your eyes like all the way around, um, like a wedding ring."[25] She adds mascara, "Mismanaged Rage," and bronzer, "Orange You Sad That the American News Source Most Dedicated to Truthful Journalism Turned Out to be TMZ."[26] As she continues brushing her face with bronzer she says, "Rub it in the NFL's face, you know what I mean? Like, just rub it in."[27] Finally, she adds lipstick called, "We Can Do Better." Before applying the lipstick she says, "Millions of North American women are violently or verbally assaulted by their domestic partner, and we find reasons not to help them. And that's why I choose to put on We Can Do Better today."[28] She ends the video with a statement that links to resources are available beneath the video on the YouTube page, at last breaking from her character to acknowledge, without parody, the seriousness of the issue her remix video critiques.

Here we make the case for an "aura" connected to the formula of a tutorial video rather than clips seen in the original footage. In fact, if one watches the MacKay video without sound (and without reading the captions), it appears no different from thousands of other makeup tutorials published on YouTube. In this reflexive remix, Megan MacKay extends the trope of the makeup tutorial to include feminist commentary—that is, she presents the virtual potential of the makeup tutorial as feminist platform—while remaining to act (or to be made up, as it is) as a makeup tutorial.

Coda

Creative remix projects are transformative, fluid platforms on which knowledge or assumptions from the past are revealed in a new consciousness. The units of meaning are always part of a code, such as a set of formal or linguistic rules, or tropes that govern political or media formats. Creativity bridges these codes in remix practices just as Christian Metz suggests codes are bridged in cinema, where

> no sovereign code exists which imposes its minimal units, which are always the same, on all parts of all films. These films, at the contrary, have a textual surface—which is temporal and spatial—a fabric in which multiple codes come to segment each for itself, their minimal units, which throughout the entire length of the filmic discourse, are superimposed, overlap, and intersect, without their boundaries necessarily coinciding.[29]

Schaeffer's "language of objects" is located within this temporal and spatial fabric, creatively remixed with a heterogeneous set of samples. While we could have selected from hundreds of well-known remixes to demonstrate the use of homogeneous and heterogeneous sampling, we focused on four works that illustrate creative remix practices based on the ways in which the work's compositional units are rearranged or manipulated. Arcangel's use of Schoenberg's composition strategy and Gordon's extended cinematic play present remixes that juxtapose homogeneous samples to transform the message encoded in the original works (online cat videos and Hitchcock's *Psycho*, respectively). McIntosh and MacKay's remixes utilize heterogeneous samples to transform the linguistic connection to the original works. For McIntosh, the Disney cartoons featuring Donald Duck are in dialog with conservative political agendas broadcast on talk radio. MacKay pirates a common YouTube trope, the makeup tutorial, to present a feminist message. While the visuals in MacKay's video appear as a homogeneous series of video clips, we posit the rhetorical samples MacKay is basing this work on also includes every makeup tutorial that precedes this one. In sum, these case studies demonstrate creatively liberated media objects, extensions that transform messages, inverted tropes, and, we believe, moments of "true life."

Notes

1 Don DeLillo, *Point Omega* (New York: Scribner, 2010), 17.
2 Vladimir Jankélévitch, *L'Irréversible et la Nostalgie* (Paris: Flammarion, 1974), 368.
3 Pierre Schaeffer, *Le Traité des Objets Musicaux* (Parisr: Le Seuil, 1966), 659–62.
4 Eduardo Navas, "Regressive and Reflexive Mashups in Sampling Culture," in *Mashup Cultures*, ed. Stefan Sonvilla-Weiss (New York: Springer Wien, 2010), 157–77. Also available at http://remixtheory.net/?p=444
5 Jonathan McIntosh, "Donald Duck Meets Glenn Beck in Right Wing Radio Duck," YouTube (October 2, 2010), https://youtu.be/HfuwNU0jsk0.
6 Ibid.
7 Ibid.
8 Ibid.
9 Ibid.
10 Ibid.
11 Ibid.
12 Ibid.
13 Ibid.
14 Ibid.
15 Navas, "Regressive and Reflexive Mashups in Sampling Culture."
16 Jonathan McIntosh, "Interviewed by Henry Jenkins about DIY Remix Video" (December 20, 2010), http://popculturedetective.agency/2010/henry-jenkins-interview.
17 Mark Nunes, "Parody and Pastiche" in *Keywords in Remix Studies*, eds. Eduardo Navas, Owen Gallagher, and xtine burrough (New York: Routledge, 2018, pp. 217–29).
18 Ibid.
19 See a timeline of the Ray Rice case online, for instance in Rebecca Elliot, "Everything You Need To Know About the Ray Rice Case," *Time* (11 September 2014), http://time.com/3329351/ray-rice-timeline/ or Louis Bien, "A complete timeline of the Ray Rice assault case," *SBNation* (28 November 2014), www.sbnation.com/nfl/2014/5/23/5744964/ray-rice-arrest-assault-statement-apology-ravens.

20 Megan MacKay, "Ray Rice Inspired Makeup Tutorial," YouTube (12 September 2014), https://youtu.be/zyNa9kqq8mk.
21 Ibid.
22 Ibid.
23 Ibid.
24 Ibid.
25 Ibid.
26 Ibid.
27 Ibid.
28 Ibid.
29 Christian Metz, *Language and Cinema* (Berlin: Walter de Gruyter, 1974), 194.

Bibliography

DeLillo, Don. *Point Omega*. New York: Scribner, 2010.
Jankélévitch, Vladimir. *L'Irréversible et la Nostalgie*. Paris: Flammarion, 1974.
MacKay, Megan. "Ray Rice Inspired Makeup Tutorial." September 12, 2014. https://youtube/zyNa9kqq8mk.
McIntosh, Jonathan. "Donald Duck Meets Glenn Beck in Right Wing Radio Duck." October 2, 2010. https://youtube/HfuwNU0jsk0.
Metz, Christian. *Language and Cinema*. Berlin: Walter de Gruyter, 1974.
Navas, Eduardo. "Regressive and Reflexive Mashups in Sampling Culture." In *Mashup Cultures*, edited by Stefan Sonvilla-Weiss, 157–77. Vienna: Springer, 2010.
Nunes, Mark. "Parody and Pastiche." In *Keywords in Remix Studies*, edited by Eduardo Navas, Owen Gallagher, xtine burrough. New York: Routledge, 2017.
Schaeffer, Pierre. *Le Traité des Objets Musicaux*. Paris: Le Seuil, 1966.

9
CUT-UP

Janneke Adema

> **To Make a Dadaist Poem**
> Take a newspaper.
> Take some scissors.
> Choose from this paper an article the length you want to make your poem.
> Cut out the article.
> Next carefully cut out each of the words that make up this article and put them all in a bag.
> Shake gently.
> Next take out each cutting one after the other.
> Copy conscientiously in the order in which they left the bag.
> The poem will resemble you.
> And there you are—an infinitely original author of charming sensibility, even though unappreciated by the vulgar herd.
> Tristan Tzara (1920)[1]

The cutting up and subsequent rearranging of media forms as part of a creative or critical practice has a long material history. Only recently has this culminated in the well-known digital technique by which we transfer text, images, or data from one place to another via cut, copy and paste keyboard commands. The expression "cut and paste" originates from manuscript and film editing, originally involving actual scissors and glue, but collage and assemblage techniques date back to the invention of paper (see for example the decorative pasting of papers in chine-collé). Extended forms of cutting (and pasting) can be seen among others in modern art collages such as those introduced by Braque and Picasso; in the literary cut-up techniques of Brion Gysin, William Burroughs, and Kathy Acker; in photomontage, including works by Dada artists such as Raoul Hausmann and Hannah Höch; the later work of feminist artists such as Martha Rosler and Barbara Kruger; and in remixed music and video, eventually culminating in today's digital and online mixed media remixes.

The actual cut-up "method" or technique, however, became most famous when adopted in the 1950s and 1960s by one of its main proponents: beat writer William Burroughs. Burroughs used the cut-up method as an experimental form of writing to produce a set of three novels in the Nova Trilogy—*The Soft Machine* (1961), *The Ticket That Exploded* (1962) and *Nova Express* (1964)—and to create tape-works (several tapes spliced into each other)[2] and films.[3] His literary experiments had a great and long-lasting influence on the development of avant-garde art and literature and on the subsequent adoption and adaptation of the cut-up method.[4] Burroughs has, however, always been clear in crediting artist Brion Gysin for coming up with the actual method, while also stating influences from surreal and modern artists such as Tristan Tzara, James Joyce, John Dos Passos and others. Gysin famously "discovered" the cut-up technique "while cutting a mount for a drawing," where he "sliced through a pile of newspapers with [his] Stanley blade ... [He] picked up the raw words and began to piece together texts that later appeared as 'First Cut-Ups' in *Minutes to Go*."[5] Both Gysin and Burroughs emphasized that the cut-up was a textual adaptation of methods originating in the visual arts, where Gysin famously stated that "writing is fifty years behind painting"[6] and Burroughs concurred that "the cut-up method brings to writers the collage."[7]

Next to practicing cut-up as a method, both Burroughs and Gysin have extensively theorized it in various co-authored publications, for example in the collection *The Third Mind* (1978), which included both cut-up fiction and literary essays. Burroughs, for whom all literature is cut-ups, describes the cut-up as a textual practice that could be seen as a democratic *method* or an *instruction* even— an innovative literary approach at that time: "Cut-ups are for everyone. Anybody can make cut-ups. It is experimental in the sense of being *something to do*. Right here write now."[8] Gysin and Burroughs argued that these methods of writing, where narratives are created out of the cutting and splicing, the rearranging and juxtaposing of various texts in a random way (from cut-ups to fold-ins) would free the words of their underlying meaning and from their societal and linguistic constraints. As such, the cut-up method would expose the texts' true, deeper meanings. This attempt to escape preconditioning based on a specific mode of experimentation with non-linear narratives and discontinuity was seen as undermining authority, as breaking down the control system. Forms of aleatory and non-linear writing would undo the constraints of word order, emphasizing the mutability of words. In this sense, as Chris Land has argued, "[the cut-up] opens a space for undecidability, a momentary stutter, where interpretation of meaning is unclear and new logics of sense can emerge from the text."[9] Yet at the same time in its practice of re-combining various source-texts, the cut-up served as a valuable metaphor for what postmodern theorists of the time (i.e., Bakhtin, Kristeva, Derrida, Barthes) theorized as "intertextuality" in literature. For these theorists, Robin Lydenberg explains, "any literary text is an intersecting network of many texts spliced, crossed and merged."[10] Both Barthes and

Burroughs perceive intertextuality as extending into our discursive and experiential life in the world—which, according to Burroughs, we experience as a constant cut-up.[11]

Commonplace Books

Where the cut-up and fold-in methods as applied by Grusin and Burroughs in their various publications were subsequently popularised, their direct origin was already prevalent in surrealist and modernist avant-garde experiments of the 1920s. Tristan Tzara famously composed a method of how to compose a Dadaist poem, a *poésie découpé* based on aleatory techniques, where André Breton and the surrealists experimented among others with the creation of *cadavre exquis* or exquisite corpses, collaboratively created fold-in drawings and poems. Yet next to avant-garde, modernist, postmodernist and digital sensibilities, the cut-up can be seen to have early modern roots. We can observe it in literature (i.e., Shakespeare and his contemporaries),[12] but more commonly, practices of physically cutting and pasting texts to create new manuscripts as a form of "remixing" can be traced back to the practice of compiling scrapbooks or so-called commonplace books. Commonplacing, as a method or approach to reading and writing, involved the gathering and repurposing of meaningful quotes, passages or other clippings from published books by copying and/or pasting them into a blank book. Often this meant the copying of quotations by hand but it could also involve the actual cutting and pasting of materials—especially with the proliferation of printed matter in the eighteenth century—and the inclusion of all kinds of annotations from drawings to graphs and visuals. Commonplace books were both utilized and theorized as information management devices, used by well-known practitioners such as John Locke, Carl Linnaeus and Thomas Jefferson. Yet commonplacing also functioned as a pedagogical tool, as something that could aid one's intellectual development. As a highly personal compendium, they also served as a memory aid and an aspirational device. From a feminist perspective, scrapbooks and commonplace books were an important aspect of identity formation, situating women, as Amy Mecklenburg-Faenger has argued, "within a larger narrative of citizenship and national progress."[13] For example, as English scholar Whitney Trettien—who studied the cut-and-paste biblical harmonies made by the women of Little Gidding during the 1630s—emphasizes, commonplacing was an active creative practice, where "remix practitioners of the early modern period often chopped apart printed texts and images not only to slice up but splice together new (and newly coherent) narratives."[14]

The cut-up method as practiced by Burroughs and Tzara is usually seen as fundamentally different from commonplacing, where the former is inherently random, based on chance, and the latter is heavily curated. Yet, as Adam Smyth argues, this difference tends to be overstated, where "the author snipping up text according to Tzara's rules necessarily makes a series of conscious choices: most obviously, which source text to select."[15] Chris Land similarly emphasizes that Burroughs on the one hand theorized cut-up as a chance operation, but that he also put forward the notion that cut-up was actually a quite deliberate operation, attentive to the materiality of its source-texts.[16] Similarly, cutting up text shouldn't necessarily be seen as a destructive gesture (where it is often associated with censorship or criticism) as for early modern readers cutting up text was a way to engage with them, as something that happened alongside reading and writing, a different mode of textual consumption and production.[17] Cutting texts was not a taboo but a very common and widespread practice, where at that time, as Smyth argues, the book was still materially negotiable and the willingness to remake the book "reflects the fact that the coherent, bound, unannotated, 'complete' printed book was not yet the dominant medium for conveying text."[18] Texts were not yet neatly confined to codex books where many slippages still occurred.

Commonplacing as a cut-up format and practice can therefore be envisioned as a form of writing. Cutting and writing were not fundamentally different acts of textual production, where both are based on a process of selection, curation, and re-combination.[19] For example Whitney Trettien defines the "deep history of reading and writing as material, combinatory practices", where cutting up texts should be seen as both a readerly and writerly act.[20] Here it becomes clear how commonplace books, again both as a format and a practice, challenged simple dichotomies between readers and writers, where readers become writers through the act of commonplacing.[21] But there are further narratives beyond the reader/writer binary that this method complicates, including the still often upheld linear or teleological discourse in book history, which sees the codex and print book as a stable and fixed format. The cut and paste practices exemplified in commonplace books both complicate this vision and showcase the overlapping worlds of manuscripts/the written word and print.[22] Similarly engagement with the notion of cutting and pasting as a writerly interactive method also disturbs neat divisions between print and digital, between the codex book as a material form and the digital as an epistemology[23] while also challenging the rhetoric that situates remix in an inherently digital practice.[24]

The Digital Cut-Up

The kinds of media, technology, and materials people use and have access to have played an important role in the development of cut-up and cut, copy, and paste practices. It influences how people can engage with their source materials, based on the degree of openness of various media and technology in regards to manipulation. In this respect, Eduardo Navas distinguishes three stages of mechanical reproduction "which set the ground for sampling to rise as a meta-activity in the second half of the twentieth century," namely the rise of early photography in the 1830s, the collage and photomontage experiments from the 1920s and the introduction of Photoshop in the late 1980s.²⁵ Technological developments in the realm of copying and media reproduction (i.e., the mimeograph, Xerox) especially meant a move away from cutting apart and splicing together original media, towards a practice that left the original work intact, which was important for the further popularization of the method. It was Lawrence Tesler who invented the cut, copy, and paste commands we now use for our text editors (where word processing is in many ways structured around these three respective features) while working for Xerox Palo Alto Research Center between 1973 and 1976. Apple then further popularized the cut/copy-and-paste commands through the Lisa (1983) and Macintosh (1984) operating systems.²⁶

These technological developments led to a boost in the development of remix cultures and practices, opening up the reworking of words, sounds and visuals to a wider population. The ability to automatically randomize texts with the aid of computer software or algorithms stimulated technological experiments in combinatorial poetry, where the first poetry composed using computer operations dates back to Theo Lutz's 1959 "stochastic" or random variation poems.²⁷ Permutation poems, already created by people such as Gusin, could now be generated automatically from databases by digital algorithms, enabling the digital alteration and permutation of words though programmatic procedures and techniques. Text-generating initiatives such as these are examples of "cyborg-poetry" or machine writing, which, with its emphasis on machinic and computer agency, has contributed to a further disruption of the hegemony of human intentionality in literature.²⁸ The ability of the computer or of algorithms to randomly select word sequences and to collect and recombine online materials has been incremental for the development of and experimentation with conceptual literature and automatic poetry, culminating in today's digital cut-up engines and scripts (online generators that automatically pass texts through algorithmic formulae), movements such as Flarf (poetry created out of the combination of phrases from random web searches), and Kenneth Goldsmith's uncreative writing, which involves a repurposing and appropriation of existing texts and works, which then become materials or building blocks for further works.²⁹

Cutting-Up Remix Theory

Entangled with these technological developments are societal and discursive structures that have simultaneously influenced the use and development of cut-up practices. Here the controversy sparked by cutting up and reusing already existing materials has mainly to do with how this practice complicates and poses a challenge to notions such as originality, single authorship, and the ownership of works (established through copyright). It is through its engagement with these issues in particular that remix theory has contributed significantly towards the theorization and contextualization of "cutting" and the cut-up. "Cut, copy, and paste" functions as a powerful metaphor for the concept of remix as a whole. For example, Eduardo Navas argues that remix is supported by the practice of cut, copy, and paste.[30] Yet at the same time the variety of overlapping, yet not necessarily always compatible terms used to describe remix (e.g., mashups, sample, collage), tends to lead, as David Gunkel has established, to terminological mix-ups.[31] One could argue, however, that this "variable, multiple and diverse" nature of remix terminology, exemplifies the fluid nature of remix and remix theory. These various terms, as Gunkel argues, each add their own perspective to the concept and practice of remix, where the diversity of sources and viewpoints towards remix as a whole, provides us with "the opportunity for revealing the various dimensions or facets of [remix]."[32] Taking this terminological confusion into consideration, and being aware that the practice of cut-up has been described using a variety of metaphors within remix theory, as a field, remix theory has engaged both practically and discursively with the above-mentioned issues of authorship, originality, and ownership in relation to "cutting" and the cut-up, in important ways.

One of these divergent terms is patch-writing (also known as collage-writing), in which disconnected bits of writing are pasted together in a work or collage, which, as a form of writing or as a cut-up method is relatively common to remix and appropriation art and theory. What is interesting in this respect is how collage as an artistic method has been more accepted than patch-writing in literature or science. It is more controversial in these latter contexts due to a discursive structure that tends to emphasize originality and single authorship and, as such, accusations of unoriginality and plagiarism abound in these realms. Within remix theory, however, there has been a tendency for theory-writing itself to be performative and to apply the patch-writing or cut-up method to its written reflections on remix. Most famously this has been explored in Jonathan Lethem's essay "The Ecstasy of Influence," and in David Shield's *Reality Hunger*.[33] We see this practice, too, in Mark Amerika's *Remixthebook* (as well as in some of his other works) and in Paul D. Miller aka DJ Spooky's *Rhythm Science*.[34]

Paul D. Miller—aka DJ Spooky, That Subliminal Kid, named after a character in Burroughs's novels—writes about flows and cuts in his artist's book *Rhythm Science*, which is accompanied by a "WebTake" built around a database of keywords extracted from the book. Readers are encouraged to create their own re-combinations of these keywords, in the process creating their own remix of the text. For Miller, the flow of language has direct consequences for his conceptualization of identity; he argues that our identity (which is plural) comes about through our engagement and immersion with the material, through the cuts that we make, where the collage or the cut-up becomes our identity.[35] Mark Amerika cuts-up "source material," where he applies a form of patch-writing in the 12 essays that comprise his multimodal and versioned publication *Remixthebook*. As part of this writing method, Amerika develops a new form of new media writing, one that constitutes a crossover between the scholarly and the artistic, and between theory and poetry. Similar to Miller, Amerika also explores multiple flux personae in his work, through which he critiques the unity of the self.[36]

Beyond this critique of the linearity of writing, and of the concept of the individual author, remix theorists and practitioners have also been active in using cut-up methods to reconfigure the original works they cut or borrow from, complicating the fixed and stable nature of works. We see this most clearly in the work of vidding artists, for example, who re-edit television and film clips into new videos called vids or fanvids. Vidding is practiced by artists such as Vicki Bennett (*People Like Us*), Luminosity, and Elisa Kreisinger. Similar to commonplace books, the cutting up of videos serves as a critical engagement with the works themselves, where the re-cutting and recomposing of source material is part of a critical textual engagement.[37] Beyond an engagement with the work itself, however, these practices are also involved in adopting an affirmative position towards the production of a more diverse world, following the ethical imperative to cut well.[38]

The Post-human Cut

One further aspect where the concepts and practices of the cut and the cut-up method have been of essential importance is in how, through our entanglement as human beings with language and the technology of writing, any experimentation with writing and the discourse around it actively reconfigures our human subjectivity. In their book *Life after New Media*, media theorists Sarah Kember and Joanna Zylinska focus specifically on the cut in photography, while analyzing the notion of the cut in the work of Barad, Derrida, Bergson, and Deleuze and Guattari, among others. Kember and Zylinska argue that "cutting is fundamental to our emergence in the world, as well as our differentiation from it."[39] Through the act of cutting (i.e., in photography or in writing) we become individuated, as we shape our temporally stabilized selves while actively forming the world we are part of and the matter surrounding us. Through cutting we enact both separation and relationality where an "incision" becomes an ethical imperative, a "decision." Therefore, they argue, if we have to inevitably cut in the process of becoming (to shape it and give it meaning) how is it that we can cut well?

Chris Land theorizes the cut-up method in a similarly post-human manner, as an inherently performative act (instead of a representational one), that necessarily implies a radical reconfiguration of human subjectivity. This claim is made by way of an analysis of the work of Burroughs, where Land demonstrates that for Burroughs *the* human consists of a symbiotic relationship of body and word-virus (where famously for Burroughs "language is a virus").[40] In this sense Burroughs's linguistic experimentation with the theory and practice of the cut-up, has—through its specific focus on the relationship between language, technology and embodiment—been an affirmative practice, enabling new modes of becoming mainly suppressed in the literary narrative traditions structured around humanism and subjectivity.[41] Burroughs's aim was to annihilate this humanist self to escape the control of language through the cut-up. For him, therefore, cut-up is both a theory of language and a theory of subjectivity.

Land makes the fundamental argument that in the work of Burroughs cut-up is not a representational technique, in the sense of an attempt to represent our subjective experience ("the cut-up nature of lived experience") more accurately. Instead it is an active, affirmative, and performative technique, whereas Land states:

> for Burroughs language is neither a neutral means of representing an objective, external reality, nor a tool for expressing an authentic, subjective interior. Language and writing are material elements within the reproduction of the social. They actively produce social subjects through their connection with, and inscription of, bodies and other material objects. For this reason language is never neutral or innocent.[42]

In this sense we can argue that cut-up as a form of writing breaks with this (modernist) logic of representation and is a performative and critical intervention both in the production of language, in our own reproduction of ourselves *through* language and with that of our "becoming-with and becoming-different from the world."[43] To cut well then means not to close or fix things down, but to enable—for example, through techniques such as the cut-up—both the duration of writing and, entangled with that, the vitality of our becoming.

Notes

1. Tristan Tzara, "To Make a Dadaist Poem," in *Seven Dada Manifestos and Lampisteries*, trans. Barbara Wright (John Calder, 1977), 39.
2. Robin Lydenberg, "'Sound Identity Fading Out': William Burroughs' Tape Experiments," in *Wireless Imagination: Sound, Radio and the Avant-garde*, ed. Doug Kahn (MIT Press, 1992).
3. Rob Bridgett, "An Appraisal of the Films of William Burroughs, Brion Gysin, and Anthony Balch in Terms of Recent Avant Garde Theory," *Bright Lights Film Journal*, February 1, 2003, http://brightlightsfilm.com/appraisal-films-william-burroughs-brion-gysin-anthony-balch-terms-recent-avant-garde-theory/.
4. Edward S. Robinson, *Shift Linguals: Cut-Up Narratives from William S. Burroughs to the Present* (Rodopi, 2011).
5. Brion Gysin, "Cut-Ups: A Project for Disastrous Success," in *A William Burroughs Reader*, ed. John Calder (Picador, 1982), 272.
6. Brion Gysin, "Cut-Ups Self-Explained," in William S. Burroughs and Brion Gysin, *The Third Mind* (Viking Press, 1978).
7. William S. Burroughs, "The Cut-up Method of Brion Gysin," in William S. Burroughs and Brion Gysin, *The Third Mind* (Viking Press, 1978).
8. Ibid., emphasis in original.
9. Chris Land, "Apomorphine Silence: Cutting -up Burroughs' Theory of Language and Control," *Ephemera: Theory in Politics & Organization* 5, no. 3 (2005): 462.

10 Robin Lydenberg, *Word Cultures: Radical Theory and Practice in William S. Burroughs' Fiction* (University of Illinois Press, 1987), 46.
11 Lydenberg, Word Cultures.
12 Bruce R. Smith, *Shakespeare | Cut* (Oxford University Press, 2016), https://global.oup.com/academic/product/shakespeare—cut-9780198735526.
13 Amy L. Mecklenburg-Faenger, *Scissors, Paste and Social Change: The Rhetoric of Scrapbooks of Women's Organizations, 1875–1930* (Ohio State University, 2007).
14 Whitney Trettien, "Remixing History," *Remixthebook*, September 1, 2012, www.remixthebook.com/by-whitney-trettien.
15 Adam Smyth, "Cutting and Authorship in Early Modern England," *Authorship* 2, no. 2 (September 20, 2013): 2, www.authorship.ugent.be/article/view/790.
16 Ibid., 460.
17 Ibid., 3.
18 Ibid., 9.
19 Ibid.
20 Whitney Anne Trettien, *Computers, Cut-Ups and Combinatory Volvelles: An Archaeology of Text-Generating Mechanisms* (Thesis, Massachusetts Institute of Technology, 2009), http://dspace.mit.edu/handle/1721.1/54505.
21 Jennifer Lei Jenkins, "Cut and Paste: Repurposing Texts from Commonplace Books to Facebook," *The Journal of Popular Culture* 48, no. 6 (December 1, 2015): 1374–90.
22 Smyth, "Cutting and Authorship in Early Modern England," 6.
23 Trettien, "Computers, Cut-Ups and Combinatory Volvelles."
24 Margie Borschke, "The Extended Remix. Rhetoric and History," in *The Routledge Companion to Remix Studies*, ed. Eduardo Navas, Owen Gallagher, and xtine burrough (Routledge, 2015).
25 Eduardo Navas, *Remix Theory: The Aesthetics of Sampling* (Springer, 2012), 11.
26 Larry Tesler, "A Personal History of Modeless Text Editing and Cut/Copypaste," *Interactions* 19, no. 4 (July 2012): 70–5.
27 Christopher Funkhouser, "First-Generation Poetry Generators. Establishing Foundations in Form," in *Mainframe Experimentalism: Early Computing and the Foundations of the Digital Arts*, ed. Hannah Higgins and Douglas Kahn (University of California Press, 2012), 245.
28 Lori Emerson, "Materiality, Intentionality, and the Computer-Generated Poem: Reading Walter Benn Michaels with Erin Mouré's Pillage Land," *ESC: English Studies in Canada* 34, no. 4 (December 1, 2008): 45–69.
29 Kenneth Goldsmith, *Uncreative Writing: Managing Language in the Digital Age* (Columbia University Press, 2011).
30 Navas, *Remix Theory*, 65.
31 David J. Gunkel, *Of Remixology: Ethics and Aesthetics After Remix* (MIT Press, 2015), 3.
32 Ibid., 30–1.
33 Jonathan Lethem, "The Ecstasy of Influence: A Plagiarism," *Harpers*, no. 1881 (2007): 59–72; David Shields, *Reality Hunger: A Manifesto* (New York: Vintage, 2011).
34 Mark Amerika, *Remixthebook* (University of Minnesota Press, 2011); Paul D. Miller, *Rhythm Science* (MIT Press, 2004).
35 Miller, *Rhythm Science*, 24.
36 Amerika, *Remixthebook*, 28.
37 Francesca Coppa, "An Editing Room of One's Own: Vidding as Women's Work," *Camera Obscura* 26, no. 2 (January 1, 2011): 123.
38 Sarah Kember and Joanna Zylinska, *Life After New Media: Mediation as a Vital Process* (MIT Press, 2012); Janneke Adema, "Cutting Scholarship Together/Apart. Rethinking the Political Economy of Scholarly Book Publishing," in *The Routledge Companion to Remix Studies*, ed. Eduardo Navas, Owen Gallagher, and xtine burrough (Routledge, 2014).

39 Kember and Zylinska, *Life After New Media*, 21.
40 Land, "Apomorphine Silence," 450.
41 Ibid., 451.
42 Ibid., 461.
43 Kember and Zylinska, *Life After New Media*, 75; Karen Barad, *Meeting the Universe Halfway: Quantum Physics and the Entanglement of Matter and Meaning* (Duke University Press, 2007).

Bibliography

Adema, Janneke. "Cutting Scholarship Together/Apart. Rethinking the Political Economy of Scholarly Book Publishing." In *The Routledge Companion to Remix Studies*, edited by Eduardo Navas, Owen Gallagher, and xtine burrough. Routledge, 2015.
Amerika, Mark. *Remixthebook*. University of Minnesota Press, 2011.
Barad, Karen. *Meeting the Universe Halfway: Quantum Physics and the Entanglement of Matter and Meaning*. Duke University Press, 2007.
Borschke, Margie. "The Extended Remix. Rhetoric and History." In *The Routledge Companion to Remix Studies*, edited by Eduardo Navas, Owen Gallagher, and xtine burrough. Routledge, 2015.
Bridgett, Rob. "An Appraisal of the Films of William Burroughs, Brion Gysin, and Anthony Balch in Terms of Recent Avant Garde Theory." *Bright Lights Film Journal*, February 1, 2003. http://brightlightsfilm.com/appraisal-films-william-burroughs-brion-gysin-anthony-balch-terms-recent-avant-garde-theory/.
Burroughs, William S., and Brion Gysin. *The Third Mind*. Viking Press, 1978.
Coppa, Francesca. "An Editing Room of One's Own: Vidding as Women's Work." *Camera Obscura* 26, no. 2 77 (January 1, 2011): 123–30.
Emerson, Lori. "Materiality, Intentionality, and the Computer-Generated Poem: Reading Walter Benn Michaels with Erin Mouré's Pillage Land." *ESC: English Studies in Canada* 34, no. 4 (December 1, 2008): 45–69.
Funkhouser, Christopher. "First-Generation Poetry Generators. Establishing Foundations in Form." In *Mainframe Experimentalism: Early Computing and the Foundations of the Digital Arts*, edited by Hannah Higgins and Douglas Kahn. University of California Press, 2012.
Goldsmith, Kenneth. *Uncreative Writing: Managing Language in the Digital Age*. Columbia University Press, 2011.
Gunkel, David J. *Of Remixology: Ethics and Aesthetics After Remix*. MIT Press, 2015.
Gysin, Brion. "Cut-Ups: A Project for Disastrous Success." In *A William Burroughs Reader*, edited by John Calder. Picador, 1982.
Jenkins, Jennifer Lei. "Cut and Paste: Repurposing Texts from Commonplace Books to Facebook." *The Journal of Popular Culture* 48, no. 6 (December 1, 2015): 1374–90.
Kember, Sarah, and Joanna Zylinska. *Life After New Media: Mediation as a Vital Process*. MIT Press, 2012.
Land, Chris. "Apomorphine Silence: Cutting -up Burroughs' Theory of Language and Control." *Ephemera: Theory in Politics & Organization* 5, no. 3 (2005): 450–71.
Lethem, Jonathan. "The Ecstasy of Influence: A Plagiarism." *Harpers*, no. 1881 (2007): 59–72.
Lydenberg, Robin. *Word Cultures: Radical Theory and Practice in William S. Burroughs' Fiction*. University of Illinois Press, 1987.
Lydenberg, Robin. "'Sound Identity Fading Out': William Burroughs' Tape Experiments." in *Wireless Imagination: Sound, Radio and the Avant-garde*, edited by Doug Kahn. MIT Press, 1992.

Mecklenburg-Faenger, Amy L. *Scissors, Paste and Social Change: The Rhetoric of Scrapbooks of Women's Organizations, 1875–1930*. Ohio State University, 2007.

Miller, Paul D. *Rhythm Science*. MIT Press, 2004.

Navas, Eduardo. *Remix Theory: The Aesthetics of Sampling*. Springer, 2012.

Navas, Eduardo, Owen Gallagher, and xtine burrough. *The Routledge Companion to Remix Studies*. Routledge, 2015.

Robinson, Edward S. *Shift Linguals: Cut-Up Narratives from William S. Burroughs to the Present*. Rodopi, 2011.

Shields, David. *Reality Hunger: A Manifesto*. Vintage, 2011.

Smith, Bruce R. *Shakespeare | Cut*. Oxford University Press, 2016.

Smyth, Adam. "Cutting and Authorship in Early Modern England." *Authorship* 2, no. 2 (September 20, 2013). http://www.authorship.ugent.be/article/view/790.

Tesler, Larry. "A Personal History of Modeless Text Editing and Cut/Copypaste." *Interactions* 19, no. 4 (July 2012): 70–5.

Trettien, Whitney. "Remixing History." *Remixthebook*, September 1, 2012. http://www.remixthebook.com/by-whitney-trettien.

Trettien, Whitney. *Computers, Cut-Ups and Combinatory Volvelles: An Archaeology of Text-Generating Mechanisms*. Thesis, Massachusetts Institute of Technology, 2009. http://dspace.mit.edu/handle/1721.1/54505.

Tzara, Tristan. "To Make a Dadaist Poem." In *Seven Dada Manifestos and Lampisteries*. Trans. Barbara Wright. John Calder, 1977.

10
DECONSTRUCTION

David J. Gunkel

The term "deconstruction," which has often been utilized to characterize both the practice and theoretical importance of remix, is itself the product of remix, specifically Jacques Derrida's appropriation and reconfiguring of material drawn from other sources. The word, as Derrida has explained and acknowledged, was originally appropriated from and devised as a means of translating Martin Heidegger's *Destruktion* and the task of critically analyzing the history of Western ontology, which was supposed to have been the subject of the second volume of his career-defining 1927 *magnum opus*, *Being and Time*. In fact, the way Derrida explained all of this in the "Letter to a Japanese Friend" sounds a lot like the practice of remix:

> When I chose this word [deconstruction], or when it imposed itself on me—I think it was in *Of Grammatology*—I little thought it would be credited with such a central role in the discourse that interested me at the time. Among other things I wished to translate and adapt to my own ends the Heideggerian word *Destruktion*.[1]

So what exactly is deconstruction? And how does it relate to the theory and practice of remix?

Default Setting

Descriptions, definitions, and depictions of both the process and product of remix—whether provided in popular media or academic efforts at what is now called "remix studies"—have subsequently appropriated the term in order to define or characterize what remix is, how it comes to be produced, or how it reworks and repurposes existing content. Consider the following examples derived from the current literature (emphasis added):

> For the mash-up to proliferate, two key technological developments were necessary: an abundance of available source material, which, by the late 1990s, had amassed on the Internet, and cheaper music software that facilitated the *deconstruction* and reconstruction of songs.[2]
>
> Tom Moulton was another remix innovator who helped change the complexion of pop music . . . He *deconstructed* songs by boosting the hooks, lengthening instrumental passages, building layers of rhythm that beefed up the percussion breaks, and other tricks.[3]
>
> So there is this DJ who goes by the name Danger Mouse. He decided one day to try a little art project. So the Jay-Z album is called *The Black Album*. Well, there's this little group out of Liverpool that came up with an album called *The White Album* years and years ago. Danger Mouse decided to *deconstruct* the *White Album* into snippets, which could be played as an accompaniment for Jay-Z's vocals. The result was called *The Grey Album*.[4]
>
> "Remixing Information Without Programming," introduces mashups without demanding programming skills from you and teaches skills for *deconstructing* applications for their remix potential.[5]

Add to this list *Wired* magazine's "Mashup DJ Girl Talk Deconstructs Samples from *Feed the Animals*," which features a cleverly designed infographic—a multicolor timeline (bent into the shape of a circle) complete with graphical icons of source material and precise time index numbers—to dissect, identify, and exhibit the 35 individual samples that comprise the remixed composition "What's it All About."[6]

As is evident from these representative samples, the word "deconstruction," or its verbal variant "to deconstruct," has been typically understood and operationalized as a synonym for decomposition, reverse engineering, or a kind of destructive analysis or dismantling.[7] In this way, de-construction (written with the hyphen to emphasize the negative prefix "de") is positioned as the opposite, undoing, or reversal of construction. Whereas "construction" denotes the process of assembly or the putting together of different elements in order to create a unified whole, i.e., a drumbeat is combined with a guitar melody and vocal line, "deconstruction" is assumed to be the decomposition of something into its constitutive parts. Hence remixing has been characterized as "deconstruction" insofar as the DJ, remix artist, or web mashup programmer takes some already existing application or content, a popular song for instance, and disassembles it by extracting each individual constitutive element, such as isolating the drum beat from its accompanying vocal and guitar lines. For this reason, deconstruction is commonly situated as the reversal or undoing of construction and the necessary antecedent to efforts at reconstruction.

This particular employment of the word is not unique to remix; it is consistent with similar usage in other areas of contemporary culture. Physicist Brian Greene, for instance, takes apart and examines the original components of the physical universe under the title "Deconstructing the Big Bang," while Steve Ettlinger exposes and examines the constitutive elements of processed food in *Twinkie, Deconstructed*. In the field of building construction, the word "deconstruction" is routinely used to identify an alternative strategy to demolition: "Bulldozing a house and burying the shattered structure in a hole in the ground sounds perverse . . . an alternative is *deconstruction*, which simply means systematically dismantling a building and salvaging its parts for reuse."[8] And in the culinary arts, celebrity chefs like Graham Elliot (dis)assemble "deconstructed salads"[9] by arranging separate piles of greens, vegetables, and dressing on a plate. Although this employment of the word has its utility, it is not entirely accurate and as such misses the full potential and opportunity that "deconstruction" releases and makes available.

Deconstructing Deconstruction

According to Derrida, the word "deconstruction," to begin with a negative characterization, does not mean to take apart, to un-construct, or to disassemble. Despite this now rather widespread and popular misconception, deconstruction is not a form of destructive analysis, a kind of demolition, or the process of reverse engineering. As Derrida himself has said quite explicitly (and on more than one occasion), "the de- of deconstruction signifies not the demolition of what is constructing itself, but rather what remains to be thought beyond the constructionist or destructionist schema."[10] Deconstruction, therefore, names something entirely other than what is understood and delimited by the conceptual opposition situated between the terms "construction" and "destruction." So what exactly is deconstruction? Here is how Derrida described the practice in an interview from 1971:

> What interested me then, which I am attempting to pursue along other lines now, was . . . a kind of *general strategy of deconstruction*. The latter is to avoid both simply *neutralizing* the binary oppositions of metaphysics and simply residing within the closed field of these oppositions, thereby confirming it. Therefore we must proceed using a double gesture, according to a unity that is both systematic and in and of itself divided, according to a double writing, that is, a writing that is in and of itself multiple, what I called, in "The Double Session" a *double science*. On the one hand, we must traverse a phase of *overturning*. To do justice to this necessity is to recognize that in a classical philosophical opposition we are not dealing with the peaceful coexistence of a *vis-à-vis*, but rather with a violent hierarchy. One of the two terms governs the other, or has the upper hand. To deconstruct

the opposition, first of all, is to overturn the hierarchy at a given moment . . . That being said—and on the other hand—to remain in this phase is still to operate on the terrain of and from the deconstructed system. By means of this double, and precisely stratified, dislodged and dislodging, writing, we must also mark the interval between inversion, which brings low what was high, and the irruptive emergence of a new "concept," a concept that can no longer be, and never could be, included in the previous regime.[11]

If we take this apart—if we "deconstruct" it, to redeploy what would, by comparison, need to be characterized as the "wrong" (or at least "insufficient") sense of the word—we can extract and identify a number of important features.

First, deconstruction names a way—what Derrida calls a "general strategy"—to intervene in "the binary oppositions of metaphysics." According to the insights provided by the twentieth-century innovations of structuralism and poststructuralism, what we know and are able to say about the world can be characterized and arranged in terms of conceptual opposites. Mark Dery expands on this idea:

> Western systems of meaning [what Derrida, following Heidegger, calls "metaphysics"] are underwritten by binary oppositions: body/soul, other/self, matter/spirit, emotion/reason, natural/artificial, and so forth. Meaning is generated through exclusion: The first term of each hierarchical dualism is subordinated to the second, privileged one.[12]

In other words, human beings organize and make sense of the world through terminological differences or conceptual dualities, such as mind/body, male/female, good/bad, being/nothing, and so on.

Furthermore for any of these conceptual oppositions, the two terms are never situated on a level playing field; one of the pair is predetermined to hold more power than the other. Or as Derrida characterizes, "we are not dealing with the peaceful coexistence of a *vis-à-vis*, but rather with a violent hierarchy." In the conceptual opposition (or "metaphysical duality") that identifies sexual difference, for example, the terms "male" and "female" have not been situated as equal partners. The former has already been granted a kind of privilege over the latter (seen, perhaps, most directly in the Judeo-Christian tradition, where God first creates Adam—the prototype of man—from whom Eve is then derived) and this bias has historically produced and been used to justify misogynistic prejudice, exclusion, and oppression. Deconstruction constitutes a mode of critical intervention that takes aim at these problematic conceptual oppositions in such a way that does not simply neutralize them or remain within the hegemony of the existing order. It therefore comprises a general strategy for challenging existing ways of organizing reality and formulating alternative possibilities for thinking.

Second, in order to do this, deconstruction consists of a complicated double gesture or what Derrida also calls "a double science." This two-step procedure necessarily begins with a phase of inversion, where a particular duality or conceptual opposition is deliberately overturned by siding with the traditionally deprecated term. This is, quite literally, a *revolutionary* gesture insofar as the existing order is inverted or turned around; and it is precisely what occurs in the "default" understanding of deconstruction described above. In the standard conceptual opposition situated between the terms "construction" and "destruction," the first term is generally considered to be the positive element. The other term is defined as its flipside—the negative and opposite of this positive component. Deconstruction begins by flipping the script and privileging destruction over construction. In terms of remix, the cutting apart of existing media content deliberately threatens the integrity of the original composition and the authority of its author. It is, therefore, a violent operation that puts emphasis on destruction or at least disassembly. But this is only half the story. This conceptual inversion, like many revolutionary gestures—whether social, political, or artistic—actually does little or nothing to challenge the dominant system. In merely exchanging the relative positions occupied by the two opposed terms, inversion still maintains, albeit in an inverted form, the conceptual opposition in which it operates. Simply flipping the script, as Derrida concludes, still "resides within the closed field of these oppositions, thereby confirming it."[13]

For this reason, deconstruction also entails a second phase or operation. "We must," as Derrida describes it, "also mark the interval between inversion, which brings low what was high, and the irruptive emergence of a new 'concept,' a concept that can no longer be, and never could be, included in the previous regime."[14] This new "concept" is, strictly speaking, no concept whatsoever, which does not mean that it is simply the opposite of the conceptual order, for it always and already exceeds the system of dualities that define the conceptual order, as well as the non-conceptual order with which the conceptual order has been articulated.[15] For this reason, this "undecidable"[16] new concept occupies a position that is in-between or in/at the margins of a traditional, binary pair. It is simultaneously neither/nor and either/or. It does not resolve into one or the other of the two terms that comprise the conceptual order nor does it constitute a third term that would mediate their difference in some kind of a synthetic unity. It is positioned in such a way that it both inhabits and operates in excess of the conceptual oppositions by which and through which systems of meaning have been organized and articulated. And it is for this reason, that the new concept cannot be described or marked in language except (as is exemplified here) by engaging in what Derrida calls a "bifurcated writing," which compels the traditional philosophemes to articulate, however incompletely and insufficiently, what necessarily resists and displaces all possible modes of articulation.[17]

Perhaps the best illustration of deconstruction's two-step operation is available in the term "deconstruction" itself. In a first move, deconstruction flips the script by putting emphasis on the negative term "destruction" as opposed to construction. In fact, the apparent similitude between the two words "deconstruction" and "destruction" is a deliberate and calculated aspect of this effort. But this is only step one. In the second move of this "double science," deconstruction introduces a brand new concept, the concept of "deconstruction." The novelty of this concept is marked, quite literally, in the material of the word itself. "Deconstruction," which is fabricated by combining the "de" of "destruction" and attaching it to the opposite term "construction," is a neologism that does not quite fit in the existing order of things. It is an exorbitant and intentionally undecidable term that names a new conceptual possibility. This new term, despite first appearances, is not the mere polar opposite of construction but exceeds the conceptual order instituted and regulated by the terminological opposition situated between construction and destruction.

Deconstruction and Remix

Deconstruction, therefore, names a mode of critical intervention that is simultaneously both more and less than a mere revolutionary operation. It comprises both the inversion of a classic metaphysical opposition and the irruptive emergence of a new concept that exceeds the grasp of the existing system and puts all elements of the established order in question. This formulation supplies a more radical set of critical possibilities for understanding the role and function of remix. As deconstruction, remix is more than the process of simply taking things apart in order to reassemble new and interesting re-combinations. This first phase of revolutionary destructive analysis is undoubtedly necessary. In addition, deconstruction also releases new opportunities that challenge the existing conceptual order and its authority.

Although this might sound rather abstract, we can, following the suggestion of Paul D. Miller (aka DJ Spooky), already find an example in a rather unlikely place: Ralph Waldo Emerson's essay "Originality and Quotation." Although Emerson's text predates both the emergence of remix and the theory and practice of deconstruction, his essay elucidates remix as deconstruction *avant la lettre*:

> Our debt to tradition through reading and conversation is so massive, our protest so rare and insignificant—and this commonly on the ground of other reading or hearing—that in large sense, one would say there is no pure originality. All minds quote. Old and new make the warp and woof of every moment. There is no thread that is not a twist of these two strands.[18]

In this short passage, Emerson identifies the existing opposition situated between the concepts "original" and "copy." From very early on, copies have been positioned as derived and deficient representations or images of some pure and pristine original. This conceptual order has been in place since at least Plato, where it finds expression in both the *Phaedrus* and the *Republic*, continues through the modern period with texts like Walter Benjamin's *The Work of Art in the Age of Mechanical Reproduction*, and informs contemporary efforts with digital technology and intellectual property law and copyright. Emerson does not just reverse this longstanding value system; he deconstructs it. He inverts the existing hierarchy by privileging the deprecated term (the copy or the act of copying) and fabricates a new concept, what he calls "quotation," that is not quite just another form of copying but something that challenges this entire tradition, demonstrating that the idea and ideal of a "pure original" is originally a derived fiction.

Remix as deconstruction taps into this Emersonian effort, releasing, in both theory and practice, a disturbing but revitalizing reconfiguration of Western axiology—the theory of value in both moral and aesthetic terms. Conceptualized in this way, remix is more than a temporary fad that shakes things up just for the fun of it (although it can do that, of course, but its critical application takes priority.) Instead remix comprises a crucial and critical intervention in the way we perceive, conceptualize, and make sense of our world, in art, creativity, technology, aesthetics, ethics, law, and so on. Remix, therefore, is more than just a juxtapo-sition of unlikely things. It is a carefully calculated and deliberate intervention in the material of contemporary culture that fabricates what Miller calls "new zones of representation," [19] questioning all the elements of the established order.

A particularly good illustration of this can be heard in DJ Danger Mouse's seminal mashup of the Beatles and Jay-Z on *The Grey Album*. According to Danger Mouse (aka Brian Burton), *The Grey Album* is not just a clever recombination of prefabricated audio components. "A lot of people just assume I took some Beatles and, you know, threw some Jay-Z on top of it or mixed it up or looped it around, but it's really a deconstruction. It's not an easy thing to do."[20] In recombining the music of the Beatles with the vocal delivery of Jay-Z, Burton did more than just throw different things together; he synthesized a critical and calculated intervention in the material of popular culture, creating both disturbing and revealing short circuits that challenge existing standards and practices in the culture industry.

Responses to this kind of effort typically begin with direct (and even violent) opposition but often end with attempts at recuperation and domestication. Although EMI initially issued an infamous cease and desist letter to try to shut down and control the "damage" wrought by *The Grey Album*, the corporation then tried to repurpose Burton's efforts by creating its own mashup of Jay-Z and Linkin Park. This is not hypocrisy or even a ruthless business strategy; it is, as Derrida has pointed out, the necessary and predictable response to all efforts of deconstruction. Because the conceptual oppositions or existing systems of power, in which deconstruction works, comprise the very logic and possibility of being able to say anything at all, "the hierarchy of dual oppositions always seeks to reestablish itself."[21] Consequently, the result of deconstruction always runs the risk of becoming re-appropriated into the conceptual order by which it comes to be articulated, explained, understood, and commodified.[22]

This facet is clearly evident in the history of deconstruction itself. Despite Derrida's explicit statements to the contrary—namely, that "the de- of deconstruction does not name the opposite of construction"—deconstruction has been continually (mis)understood and explained through association with forms of destructive analysis that come to be defined through opposition to the (positive) work of construction. And these efforts at re-appropriation are (for better or worse) firmly established in the literature of remix studies, where "deconstruction" has been typically utilized as a synonym for decomposition, dissection, and reverse engineering. In other words, the way that deconstruction has been routinely (mis)understood and utilized in the literature of remix and remix studies is itself a necessary and unavoidable aspect of deconstruction. For this reason, deconstruction must remain, as Derrida finally insists, something of "an interminable analysis."[23] It is "interminable" mainly because the critical work of deconstruction is never able to achieve finality. It must continually struggle against both the efforts of its opponents, who seek to marginalize, demonize, or even criminalize it, and its advocates, who unfortunately work to re-inscribe its transgressions within the existing conceptual field that it targets in the first place.

Notes

1 Jacques Derrida, "Letter to a Japanese Friend," trans. David Wood and Andrew Benjamin in Peggy Kamuf (ed.), *A Derrida Reader: Between the Blinds* (New York: Columbia University Press, 1991), 271.
2 Michael Serazio, "The Apolitical Irony of Generation Mash-Up: A Cultural Case Study in Popular Music," *Popular Music and Society* 31(1) (2008): 81.
3 Kembrew McLeod and Peter DiCola, *Creative License: The Law and Culture of Digital Sampling* (Durham, NC: Duke University Press, 2011), 59.
4 David Earl, *LMMS: A Complete Guide to Dance Music Production* (Birmingham: Packt Publishing, 2012), 167.
5 Raymond Yee, *Pro Web 2.0 Mashups: Remixing Data and Web Services* (New York: Apress, 2008), xxx.
6 Angela Watercutter, "Mashup DJ Girl Talk Deconstructs Samples from *Feed the Animals*," *Wired* 16.9 (2008): 92. www.archive.wired.com/special_multimedia/2008/pl_music_1609.
7 Understood in this way, "deconstruction" would share certain affinities with other critical efforts in contemporary culture that go by other names, such as "hacking." For more on this affiliation between poststructuralist theory and the DIY practices of the "computer underground," see David J. Gunkel, *Hacking Cyberspace* (Boulder, CO: Westview Press, 2001).
8 Jennifer Roberts, *Redux: Designs that Reuse, Recycle, and Reveal* (Salt Lake City, UT: Gibbs Smith, 2005), 126, emphasis in original.
9 Lucy Lean, *Made in America: Our Best Chefs Reinvent Comfort Food* (New York: Welcome Books, 2011), 118.
10 Jacques Derrida, *Limited Inc.*, trans. Samuel Weber and Jeffrey Mehlman (Evanston: Northwestern University Press, 1993), 147.

11 Jacques Derrida, *Positions*, trans. Alan Bass (Chicago: University of Chicago Press, 1981), 41–42, emphasis in the original.
12 Mark Dery, *Escape Velocity: Cyberculture at the End of the Century* (New York: Grove Press, 1996), 244.
13 Derrida, *Positions*, 41.
14 Ibid., 42.
15 Jacques Derrida, *Margins of Philosophy*, trans. Alan Bass (Chicago: University of Chicago Press, 1982), 329.
16 Derrida, *Positions*, 43.
17 Ibid., 42.
18 Ralph Waldo Emerson, "Quotation and Originality," in *The Collected Works of Ralph Waldo Emerson, Vol. III: Letters and Social Aims* (Cambridge, MA: Harvard University Press, 2010), 94.
19 Paul D. Miller, *Rhythm Science* (Cambridge, MA: MIT Press, 2004), 33.
20 Matthew Rimmer, *Digital Copyright and the Consumer Revolution: Hands off My iPod* (Northampton, MA: Edward Elgar Publishing, 2007), 132.
21 Derrida, *Positions*, 42.
22 Brian Burton represents a good example of this kind of re-appropriation into the established order, from his initial position as an antagonistic outsider. As a direct result of the online popularity of *The Grey Album*, Burton was head-hunted to produce a commercially successful Gorillaz album, subsequently formed the group Gnarls Barkley, achieved a global number one hit with the single, "Crazy," and went on to win numerous Grammy Awards.
23 Derrida, *Positions*, 42.

Bibliography

Benjamin, Walter. 1969. *Illuminations*. Trans. H. Zohn. New York: Schocken Books.
Derrida, Jacques. 1981. *Positions*. Trans. Alan Bass. Chicago: University of Chicago Press.
Derrida, Jacques. 1982. *Margins of Philosophy*. Trans. Alan Bass. Chicago: University of Chicago Press.
Derrida, Jacques. 1991. "Letter to a Japanese Friend." Trans. David Wood and Andrew Benjamin. In Peggy Kamuf (Ed.), *A Derrida Reader: Between the Blinds*, 270–276. New York: Columbia University Press.
Derrida, Jacques. 1993. *Limited Inc*. Trans. Samuel Weber and Jeffrey Mehlman. Evanston: Northwestern University Press.
Dery, Mark. 1996. *Escape Velocity: Cyberculture at the End of the Century*. New York: Grove Press.
Earl, David. 2012. *LMMS: A Complete Guide to Dance Music Production*. Birmingham: Packt Publishing.
Emerson, Ralph Waldo. 2010. "Quotation and Originality." In *The Collected Works of Ralph Waldo Emerson, Vol. III: Letters and Social Aims*, 93–107. Cambridge, MA: Harvard University Press.
Ettlinger, Steve. 2008. *Twinkie, Deconstructed: My Journey to Discover How the Ingredients Found in Processed Foods Are Grown, Mined (Yes, Mined), and Manipulated into What America Eats*. New York: Hudson Street Press.
Greene, Brian. *The Fabric of the Cosmos: Space, Time, and the Texture of Reality*. New York: Vintage Books, 2005.
Gunkel, David J. *Hacking Cyberspace*. Boulder, CO: Westview Press, 2001.

Heidegger, Martin. 1962. *Being and Time*. Trans. John Macquarrie and Edward Robinson. New York: Harper & Row.

Lean, Lucy. 2011. *Made in America: Our Best Chefs Reinvent Comfort Food*. New York: Welcome Books.

McLeod, Kembrew and Peter DiCola. 2011. *Creative License: The Law and Culture of Digital Sampling*. Durham, NC: Duke University Press.

Miller, Paul D. 2004. *Rhythm Science*. Cambridge, MA: MIT Press.

Plato. 1982. *Phaedrus*. Trans. H. N. Fowler. Cambridge, MA: Harvard University Press.

Plato. 1987. *Republic*. Trans. Paul Shorey. Cambridge, MA: Harvard University Press.

Rimmer, Matthew. 2007. *Digital Copyright and the Consumer Revolution: Hands off My iPod*. Northampton, MA: Edward Elgar Publishing.

Roberts, Jennifer. 2005. *Redux: Designs that Reuse, Recycle, and Reveal*. Salt Lake City, UT: Gibbs Smith.

Serazio, Michael. 2008. "The Apolitical Irony of Generation Mash-Up: A Cultural Case Study in Popular Music." *Popular Music and Society* 31(1): 79–94.

Watercutter, Angela. 2008. "Mashup DJ Girl Talk Deconstructs Samples from *Feed the Animals*." *Wired* 16(9): 92. www.archive.wired.com/special_multimedia/2008/pl_music_1609.

Yee, Raymond. 2008. *Pro Web 2.0 Mashups: Remixing Data and Web Services*. New York: Apress.

11
DIY CULTURE

Akane Kanai

DIY culture emerges at a particular social and historical conjuncture in which the saturation of mass media in everyday culture in the West figures prominently. There are many debates about the position of DIY as an ideological movement, its value and meaning for people who engage in it, and its potential for resistance against corporate control over production. But first, it is important to understand that this culture does not necessarily comport a simple definition, and is connected to multiple overlapping concepts in its status and significance as *amateur* production. In what follows, I discuss DIY's synergies and tensions with Remix discourse[1] through tracking discussions of DIY in debates on mainstream and subcultural production, convergence culture, and individualization. Like Remix, DIY must be understood in the context of advanced capitalism in which there is substantial pressure to position the self, like other cultural products, as innovative rather than "derivative."[2] Given the highly individualistic framework underpinning this position, this account maintains a focus on gender as a central dynamic, as a means of engaging with assumptions of power and individuality in DIY discourses.

Amateur Production and its Significance

If DIY as an acronym may simply be boiled down to "do it yourself," its parameters are less clear. DIY is often referred to in conjunction with the understanding that DIY production is not professional.[3] Jean Burgess has more recently coined the influential term "vernacular creativity" to broadly encompass everyday DIY forms of creation in a context where, in some fields like digital media, amateur production is not simply a minority but a majority activity and dominant forms of media are constantly remediated.[4] Vernacular, like the term "amateur," is associated with mundane activity that has traditionally been understood as informal, illegitimate; indeed, less than hegemonic,[5] part of the reason for which scholars have been interested in its potential to disrupt dominant culture.

Vernacular culture and Remix discourses coincide in their emphasis on appropriation of mass culture. Appropriation in these discourses may be seen as politically significant if we have reference to critiques of the traditional divide between producers and consumers of culture. Frankfurt School theorists Theodor Adorno and Max Horkheimer argued that commercial mass culture results in the production of culture that suits the interests of the powerful, and produces inauthentic, predictable, cookie-cutter goods to sate the needs of comfort and security of the masses, as part of their alienation.[6] Amateur production, then, has always been of interest in relation to challenging existing structures of power and their repetition. The sense that some production can be considered amateur and thus possibly done by "ordinary people" is loaded with political significance. Rather than being produced by a technical elite as part of a system of mass production, amateur production speaks to the possibility of social connection, creativity, and authenticity, for people who have historically constituted part of the masses, the end of the cycle of cultural consumption, rather than the originators of culture.

This analysis finds some similarities in the arguments made by legal scholar Lawrence Lessig about the stifling effects on society when culture and art are narrowly construed as property.[7] Arguing for the power of remix culture, from Lessig's perspective, art and culture ought to be understood as social artifacts through which people feel connection and find meaning in a world that is "saturated" with commercial culture. Why should commerce uniquely control the ways in which people consume culture, when all culture, Lessig argues, is based on some form of mimicry and recombination?[8] Using the example of Candice Breitz, an artist who films ordinary people re-enacting and singing songs by their favorite artists ranging from John Lennon to Michael Jackson, Lessig argues that such "rewriting" of media through their redoing must be understood as part of the social enjoyment of culture, which tends to be unduly restricted in its current commercialized form (Figure 11.1).[9]

Amateur production, then, may be understood as a way for the masses to speak back in a form of democratic cultural participation, and, while not true of all remix practices, many may fall under this DIY amateur umbrella. Amateur production that involves remix opens up opportunities to express social value beyond pure commercial interests. Lessig suggests that the media relationship set up in traditional patterns of consumption may be likened to a CD-ROM that is designated "read-only"; in remix culture, DIY may be expressed as "read-write."[10] Exceeding the narrow commodification of culture, and the continuing control over it through broadcast structures that maintain the right of producers to control it, amateur remix may become a means of protest. If controlling the means of production, as critiqued by Adorno and Horkheimer, results in control

FIGURE 11.1 Screenshot of Candice Breitz's work on Vimeo.

over culture and audiences, the notion of production carried out by "ordinary people" suggests the possibility of greater freedom and empowerment. Yet, there is a need for specificity in how such terms are used and how amateur culture is evaluated, as well as a need to be mindful of certain tensions between DIY and remix discourses.

Mass Culture versus Subculture and Other Value Judgments

A strong current of DIY culture borrows its aesthetics from the 1970s British punk movement, and its content from resistant, anti-capitalist, anti-bourgeois sentiment,[11] and as such, DIY has often been associated with "counterculture" as opposed to mainstream, or mass commercial production. The feminist creativity of Riot Grrrl groups in the 1990s is one high-profile example. Predominantly based in the U.S. cities Olympia and Seattle, Riot Grrrl bands such as Bratmobile and Bikini Kill were well-known for inaugurating a new age of feminist politics embracing agency and empowerment through a DIY ethos. DIY acts ranged from producing zines to writing on one's body: a simple move that proclaimed that "anyone" could produce their own culture in resistance to dominant mass-manufactured trends.[12]

Punk DIY production has often been of interest to cultural studies scholars as it demonstrates resistance in artistic expression; but if the question is of *democratic* involvement, how inclusive can it be? In relation to debates over "Riot Grrrls versus Spice Girls" in 1990s feminist scholarship, Catherine Driscoll argues that too much emphasis was placed on the political ruptures made

> See also Chapter 13, "Feminism."

possible by Riot Grrrl music, without taking into account their possible audiences.[13] While the Spice Girls were critiqued for commodifying Riot Grrrl feminism into a commercial, limited pop "girl power," Driscoll notes that such distinctions in feminist value did not properly take into account the way in which Riot Grrrl productions were not culturally accessible for a mass of girl consumers.[14]

The Spice Girls may be seen as a paradigmatic example testing some of the tensions between "commercial" Remix and "authentic" DIY discourses. Arguably, the Spice Girls' ostensibly anti-DIY, commercially produced nature enabled feminist discourses to be "sampled" and redistributed for popular audiences. The Spice Girls, Driscoll argues, in being portrayed as "every girl," wearing clothes accessible from high street stores, appearing in music videos, produced a vernacular that was similar to the content of girls' magazines, circulated in the limited spaces available for many girls,[15] and created a form of culture that was available for girls to appropriate, recycle and remix. Such mass culture circulation constituted a stark contrast with the subcultural Riot Grrrl circulation through zines and music venues.[16] Although the Spice Girls were seen as overly manufactured, indeed, the opposite of DIY, they were able to reach girls and raise questions of empowerment in ways that often Riot Grrrl bands and the communities they established did not.

Scholars, indeed, have often overlooked the connection of DIY with mainstream culture. As Driscoll and Gregg suggest, cultural studies scholars have tended to devote attention to what is "hip, cool and emergent under the radar of mainstream political and popular culture"[17] at the expense of culture that is *prima facie* less exciting. Girls' amateur production is often automatically considered to be less DIY: their remix culture, more derivative. In the U.S., Mary Kearney notes the neglect of girls' fan writing, scrapbooks, collages and scripts written in celebration of their favorite stars in the early twentieth century.[18] This non-digital remix activity was promoted by commercial movie magazines that encouraged girls to send in works that poached from traditional movie texts in creative ways.[19] Kearney's labor of retrieving and valuing this work suggests that such youthful, feminine fan labor may still not often be considered "subcultural" and, as such, not part of the DIY "canon."

Beyond these distinctions in mass and subculture, the sophistication of amateur production in itself may indicate unequal distributions in who may be able to participate. As such, DIY or vernacular culture must be understood as not simply "open to everyone", but carry its own distinctions in terms of cultural capital, competency and know-how in what is sampled. Burgess argues, for example, that in the Lomography movement of the 1990s, its amateur production was positioned as avant-garde, mixing the everyday with a playful aesthetic that is deliberately positioned against standard photography.[20] As such, enthusiasts of DIY culture must be careful not to posit a simple dichotomy between industry power and consumer disempowerment, but note hierarchies of power within consumer communities.

Convergence Culture Debates

As this discussion has shown, DIY culture is historically diverse. Recently, it has attracted renewed interest in the wake of its connection to remix cultures in the expansion of digital cultures that allow consumers to show how they sample the world. In advanced industrial economies, the Internet has been largely mainstreamed,[21] and the growth of Web 2.0 platforms in particular in the late 2000s shows how the Internet has been incorporated into everyday social life.[22] In contrast to the primarily elite male spaces of MUDs (multi-user domains) of the 1990s, social network sites are widely used among young people and teenagers with regular access to the Internet, and it appears that women and girls are an active demographic of users.[23] This access to digital media has led to debates over consumer empowerment, participation and voice in cultural production. However, claims about the everyday amateur production facilitated by digital media need to be located within a long series of cultural and technological interventions.[24]

Henry Jenkins, one of the best-known proponents of fans' engagement with media through creative forms of remix, argues for the opportunities fostered by media "convergence" made possible through affordances of digital media production. In this culture, Jenkins sees an extension of the possibilities of audiences to participate and have a voice.[25] In "convergence culture," the active participation of audiences alters the relationship between technologies, industries and markets and the mechanisms through which culture may be created.[26] Rather than the traditional dictating of content to audiences, in convergence culture, audiences' collective intelligence, seen in sophisticated fan engagement in remix culture, is mobilized in commercial production.[27] Most visible in media genres such as reality and lifestyle TV and film, traditional media producers now rely on audience know-how; for example, drawing on audience expertise in the 2000s in the making of the *Lord of the Rings* trilogy by director Peter Jackson.[28] Now that audiences have a share, media is more "their own," even though, as Jenkins acknowledges, the audience must of necessity be somewhat commoditized in this process.

Yet, Jenkins's articulation of convergence culture has attracted much contestation from sociologists and cultural studies scholars, in terms of separating the emergence of digital participation from everyday life, and evaluating such "opening up" to audiences as value-neutral or positive. This model of the knowing, sophisticated, participatory audience of DIY culture has been critiqued for ignoring the way audience knowledge and creativity is co-opted and used against their interests. Scholars such as Mark Andrejevic, for example, view the premise of interactive media as a means of obscuring the still enduring inequalities between consumers and producers.[29] Rather than collapsing those distinctions, Andrejevic argues, DIY audience know-how is used and *sold back to them*; voting participation in reality shows such as *American Idol* does not allow audience empowerment, but the customization of the audience into further niche markets that are more easily targeted.[30]

In another critique of the convergence culture thesis, scholars have argued that the creative remixing audience based on whom Jenkins and similar proponents tend to make their case for convergence culture, are not representative of the general public. Bird asks: "are we all produsers now?"[31] Skeptical of the widespread applicability of portmanteau terms in which consumption and production are conflated, Bird notes that those who "count" as produsers—usually highly engaged, erudite fans—are an elite minority.[32] Couldry similarly suggests that a continuing focus on stratification and differentiation is needed in these times of rapid change.[33] While celebratory accounts of amateur production figure prominently in the understanding of convergence culture, Couldry argues that such examples are not representative of digital participation.[34] For example, in relation to fans, often those that are responsible for the most developed forms of remix, are precisely those that are not typical as they demonstrate an above-average level of immersion in the fictional worlds of media from which they draw inspiration.[35] The high-intensity consumption that is needed for those who produce the engaged remix that Jenkins, for example, promotes as new forms of collective intelligence and participation, is not representative. Further, scholars suggest that there is often a subversion of the promise of DIY, resulting in the continuing exploitation of consumers, with their production co-opted and made the property of platforms and traditional media producers.[36]

The DIY Self: Individualization and Identity in a Neoliberal Context

From another perspective, digital DIY culture has been of interest in terms of understanding, not necessarily how people may change culture, but how they understand and negotiate it through remix. For scholars who have traditionally held a strong interest in the active audience, DIY culture may show how people engage in and interpret social questions and issues. Digital remix, then, in which people articulate readings of their favorite forms of popular culture demonstrates the ways in which people actively understand the culture they consume, rather than passively absorbing its messages.[37] This is not simply restricted to fans, but applies to audiences more generally in their interpretation of celebrity personality or the signification of media narratives more generally. For example, in my own research, I have examined how young women on Tumblr build their own digital identities through remixing the star text of actress Jennifer Lawrence in the selective use of GIFs from the star's interviews and filmic moments. In the Tumblr blogs, it is notable that Lawrence is sampled in ways that correspond with changing norms and ideals of contemporary femininity.[38]

Feminist scholars have long been interested in the political possibilities of women screening themselves, the question being: with the new affordances of digital media, could DIY self-production provide an authenticity and power that mass representation could not?[39] Such interest can be seen in scholarship on Cam

Girls, early adopters who actively involved the self in amateur content in the late 1990s and early 2000s, continuing to debates over the possibilities of self-production in social media more broadly today.[40] To this day, however, no definite answers have been found for this question. In the wake of the popularization of amateur videos on platforms like YouTube, scholars such as Sarah Banet-Weiser have suggested that instead of disrupting corporate values, individuals have instead largely taken on commercial understandings of themselves in their DIY self-production.[41] If the DIY self can be thought of as a remixed self, the distribution of select samples of the self in digital spaces similarly takes place along capitalist logics. In scholarship tracking young women's DIY self-production in particular, scholars have noted that self-branding is seen as a common-sense, responsible, self-actualizing practice.[42] Thus, in a "post-girl power and postfeminist context," producing the self according to logics of consumer feedback, self-regulation, self-monitoring and investment on platforms such as YouTube appears to be a dominant framework for producing amateur content, to the disappointment of scholars who had hoped for a rupture in this commercial paradigm.[43]

DIY, then, can be understood, not simply as the amateur production of culture, but as a way of articulating selfhood in ways that reflect contemporary preoccupations with renovation, revamping and adaptation in relation to capitalism's bottom line, that are also found in Remix discourses more broadly.[44] Social theorists such as Anthony Giddens[45] and Zygmunt Bauman[46] have argued that the emphasis on DIY may be seen as a result of late modernity in which people are increasingly disembedded from the relations that used to predict their life paths. In this context, we see increasing obligations on individuals to construct their own life, to appropriate and rework the right cultural resources, and to forge their own trajectories without the support of traditional kinship and employment structures; self-branding thus becomes a logical expression of DIY selfhood.[47] This individualization thesis has notably been critiqued for the overemphasis on individuality as a neutral construct with disregard to race, gender, ethnicity, sexuality, ability and geography.[48] Yet, I suggest individualization provides a useful means of understanding how the *self* has become much more incorporated in DIY culture across digital and other forms of media. DIY selfhood, in a contemporary Western context, appears promising but is necessarily premised on already-existing access to resources that may be appropriated to improve, create and remix the self.

Conclusion

This chapter has shown how socio-political and economic contexts frame our understanding and investments in DIY as part of Remix, as well as the tensions between these discourses. There remain burning questions about the politics, purpose and potential of DIY. Scholars have historically been attentive to its political potential through examining resistance in subcultures, but sometimes reproduce misplaced value judgments about consumers of mass culture. Recent work has emphasized the political nature of classifying the "creative/active/original" versus the "repetitive/passive/reproductive," the latter being attached to girls, fans and the masses in general. Across these debates, particularly in relation to the potential of convergence culture and the way in which the self has become a DIY remix project, there are still continuing questions of how DIY culture may resist or subvert dominant formations of production and power.

Notes

1 Eduardo Navas, *Remix Theory: The Aesthetics of Sampling* (Vienna: Springer-Verlag, 2012). I follow Navas in adopting the capitalized term Remix to refer to it as a discourse.
2 Ibid.
3 Jean Burgess, *Vernacular Creativity and New Media* (Queensland University of Technology, 2007); Jean Burgess and Joshua Green, *YouTube: Online Video and Participatory Culture* (Cambridge: Polity Press, 2009).
4 Ibid.
5 Ibid.
6 Theodor Adorno and Max Horkheimer, *Dialectic of Enlightenment* (New York: Seabury Press, 1972).
7 Lawrence Lessig, *Remix: Making Art and Commerce Thrive in the Hybrid Economy* (New York: The Penguin Press, 2008).
8 Ibid.
9 Ibid.
10 Ibid.
11 Teal Triggs, "Scissors and Glue: Punk Fanzines and the Creation of a DIY Aesthetic," *Journal of Design History* 19, no. 1 (2006).
12 R. Şahin et al., "Riot Grrrls, Bitchsm, and Pussy Power: Interview with Reyhan Şahin/Lady Bitch Ray," *Feminist Media Studies* 16, no. 1 (2016).
13 Catherine Driscoll, "Girl Culture, Revenge and Global Capitalism: Cybergirls, Riot Grrls, Spice Girls," *Australian Feminist Studies* 14, no. 29 (1999).
14 Ibid.
15 Ibid.
16 Ibid.
17 Catherine Driscoll and Melissa Gregg, "Convergence Culture and the Legacy of Feminist Cultural Studies," *Cultural Studies* 25, no. 4–5 (2011): 568.
18 Mary Celeste Kearney, *Girls Make Media* (New York: Routledge, 2006).
19 Ibid.
20 Burgess, *Vernacular Creativity and New Media*.
21 Amanda Lenhart, "The Democratization of Online Social Networks," Pew Internet and American Life Project, www.pewinternet.org/2009/10/08/the-democratization-of-online-social-networks.
22 Ibid.
23 Ibid.
24 Ibid.
25 Henry Jenkins, *Convergence Culture: Where Old and New Media Collide* (New York: New York University Press, 2006); "Rethinking 'Rethinking Convergence/Culture'," *Cultural Studies* (2013).
26 Jenkins, *Convergence Culture: Where Old and New Media Collide*.
27 Ibid.
28 Ibid.

29 Mark Andrejevic, *Reality TV: The Work of Being Watched* (Lanham: Rowman & Littlefield Publishers, 2004).
30 Ibid.
31 S. Elizabeth Bird, "Are We All Produsers Now?," *Cultural Studies* 25, no. 4–5 (2011).
32 Ibid.
33 Nick Couldry, "More Sociology, More Culture, More Politics," *Cultural Studies* 25, no. 4–5 (2011).
34 Ibid.
35 Ibid.
36 Tiziana Terranova, "Free Labor: Producing Culture for the Digital Economy," *Social Text* 18, no. 2 (2000).
37 Sonia Livingstone, "The Challenge of Changing Audiences: Or, What Is the Audience Researcher to Do in the Age of the Internet?," *European Journal of Communication* 19, no. 1 (2004).
38 Akane Kanai, "Jennifer Lawrence, Remixed: Approaching Celebrity through DIY Digital Culture," *Celebrity Studies* 6, no. 3 (2015).
39 Amy Shields Dobson, *Postfeminist Digital Cultures: Femininity, Social Media, and Self-Representation* (London: Palgrave Macmillan, 2015).
40 Feona Attwood, "Through the Looking Glass? Sexual Agency and Subjectification Online," in *New Femininities: Postfeminism, Neoliberalism and Subjectivity*, ed. Rosalind Gill and Christina Scharff (Basingstoke: Palgrave Macmillan, 2011); Theresa M Senft, *Camgirls: Celebrity and Community in the Age of Social Networks* (New York: Peter Lang, 2008).
41 Sarah Banet-Weiser, *Authentic TM: The Politics of Ambivalence in a Brand Culture* (New York: New York University Press, 2012).
42 Ibid.
43 Amy Shields Dobson and Anita Harris, "Post-Girlpower: Globalized Mediated Femininities," *Continuum: Journal of Media & Cultural Studies* 29, no. 2 (2015).
44 Navas, *Remix Theory: The Aesthetics of Sampling*.
45 Anthony Giddens, *Modernity and Self-Identity: Self and Society in the Late Modern Age* (Cambridge: Polity Press, 1991).
46 Zygmunt Bauman, *The Indivdiualized Society* (Malden, MA: Polity Press, 2001).
47 Dobson, *Postfeminist Digital Cultures: Femininity, Social Media, and Self-Representation*.
48 Beverley Skeggs, *Class, Self, Culture* (London: Routledge, 2004).

Bibliography

Adorno, Theodor, and Max Horkheimer. *Dialectic of Enlightenment*. New York: Seabury Press, 1972.
Andrejevic, Mark. *Reality TV: The Work of Being Watched*. Lanham: Rowman & Littlefield Publishers, 2004.
Attwood, Feona. "Through the Looking Glass? Sexual Agency and Subjectification Online." In *New Femininities: Postfeminism, Neoliberalism and Subjectivity*, edited by Rosalind Gill and Christina Scharff, 203–14. Basingstoke: Palgrave Macmillan, 2011.
Banet-Weiser, Sarah. *Authentic TM: The Politics of Ambivalence in a Brand Culture*. New York: New York University Press, 2012.
Bauman, Zygmunt. *The Individualized Society*. Malden, MA: Polity Press, 2001.
Bird, S. Elizabeth. "Are We All Produsers Now?" *Cultural Studies* 25, no. 4–5 (2011): 502–16.
Burgess, Jean. "User-Created Content and Everyday Cultural Practice: Lessons from YouTube." In *Television as Digital Media*, edited by James Bennett and Niki Strange, 311–31. Durham: Duke University Press, 2011.

———. *Vernacular Creativity and New Media*. Queensland University of Technology, 2007.
Burgess, Jean, and Joshua Green. *YouTube: Online Video and Participatory Culture*. Cambridge: Polity Press, 2009.
Couldry, Nick. "More Sociology, More Culture, More Politics." *Cultural Studies* 25, no. 4–5 (2011): 487–501.
Dobson, Amy Shields. *Postfeminist Digital Cultures: Femininity, Social Media, and Self-Representation*. London: Palgrave MacMillan, 2015.
Dobson, Amy Shields, and Anita Harris. "Post-Girlpower: Globalized Mediated Femininities." *Continuum: Journal of Media & Cultural Studies* 29, no. 2 (2015): 143–4.
Driscoll, Catherine. "Girl Culture, Revenge and Global Capitalism: Cybergirls, Riot Grrls, Spice Girls." *Australian Feminist Studies* 14, no. 29 (1999): 173–93.
Driscoll, Catherine, and Melissa Gregg. "Convergence Culture and the Legacy of Feminist Cultural Studies." *Cultural Studies* 25, no. 4–5 (2011): 566–84.
Giddens, Anthony. *Modernity and Self-Identity: Self and Society in the Late Modern Age*. Cambridge: Polity Press, 1991.
Jenkins, Henry. *Convergence Culture: Where Old and New Media Collide*. New York: New York University Press, 2006.
———. "Rethinking 'Rethinking Convergence/Culture.'" *Cultural Studies* (2013): 1–31.
Kanai, Akane. "Jennifer Lawrence, Remixed: Approaching Celebrity through DIY Digital Culture." *Celebrity Studies* 6, no. 3 (2015): 322–40.
Kearney, Mary Celeste. *Girls Make Media*. New York: Routledge, 2006.
Lenhart, Amanda. "The Democratization of Online Social Networks." Pew Internet and American Life Project, www.pewinternet.org/2009/10/08/the-democratization-of-online-social-networks.
Lessig, Lawrence. *Remix: Making Art and Commerce Thrive in the Hybrid Economy*. New York: The Penguin Press, 2008.
Livingstone, Sonia. "The Challenge of Changing Audiences: Or, What Is the Audience Researcher to Do in the Age of the Internet?" *European Journal of Communication* 19, no. 1 (2004): 75–86.
Milner, Ryan. *The World Made Meme: Discourse and Identity in Participatory Media*. University of Kansas, 2012.
Navas, Eduardo. *Remix Theory: The Aesthetics of Sampling*. Vienna: Springer-Verlag, 2012.
Şahin, R., C. Scharff, C. Smith-Prei, and M. Stehle. "Riot Grrrls, Bitchsm, and Pussy Power: Interview with Reyhan Şahin/Lady Bitch Ray." *Feminist Media Studies* 16, no. 1 (2016): 117–27.
Senft, Theresa M. *Camgirls: Celebrity and Community in the Age of Social Networks*. New York: Peter Lang, 2008.
Skeggs, Beverley. *Class, Self, Culture*. London: Routledge, 2004.
Terranova, Tiziana. "Free Labor: Producing Culture for the Digital Economy." *Social Text* 18, no. 2 (2000): 33–58.
Triggs, Teal. "Scissors and Glue: Punk Fanzines and the Creation of a DIY Aesthetic." *Journal of Design History* 19, no. 1 (2006): 69–83.

12
FAN CULTURE

Joshua Wille

On July 19, 2016, some four months after the meteoric debut and decline of *Batman v Superman: Dawn of Justice* at the box office,[1] Warner Bros. released an extended "Ultimate Edition." The new R-rated cut provided audiences with approximately 30 additional minutes to appreciate director Zack Snyder's cinematic vision, and yet within the next month one could find at least ten other feature-length versions of *Batman v Superman* on the Internet, many released within just days of each other. Unlike corporate sanctioned alternative cuts destined to find their way onto the third disc of a Blu-ray boxed set, these different versions of *Batman v Superman* are fan edits made on the personal computers of

FIGURE 12.1 Screenshot of "*Man of Tomorrow*—Trailer 2" by YouTube user JobWillins.

people with pseudonyms such as slendernyan, PlzDieNow, JobWillins, and MajorPineapple (Figure 12.1).[2] Rather than merely speculating about what else could have been made from the dearth of digital material provided in the extended cut of *Batman v Superman*, these fan editors used the content of the film itself as their medium for creative and critical expression. Through these fan edits, which variously excised and reorganized scenes from the film, modified the color grading of the visuals, and even recombined elements from *Batman v Superman* and *Man of Steel* (2013), members of the audience essentially stood from their proverbial seats in the cinema and resolved to tell their own versions of the story. Following this example, in this chapter, a conscientious look into fan editing will reveal appreciable intersections between fan culture and the broader field of remix: fan edits are generally created by amateurs and are intentionally noncommercial; fan edits are sourced from popular media and have continually increased in technical sophistication; and the public reception of fan edits is regularly impeded by logistical problems and evidence of social inequities.

Appropriation, Transformation, and Participation

The case of *Batman v Superman* is not the first time that a film had inspired so many fan edits—in fact, each of the films that comprise *The Lord of the Rings*, *The Hobbit*, and *Star Wars* series have inspired numerous feature-length fan edits in recent years—but it represents an unprecedented surge of fan edit production based on a single film. Media fans are people who devote great amounts of time, effort, and resources to celebrate, criticize, and recreate media texts in diverse ways, and this particular response to *Batman v Superman* exemplifies the astonishing creative agency of fans. The galaxy of fan culture, which encompasses a dynamic range of idiosyncratic traditions and practices, is broadly shaped by principles of appropriation, transformation, and participation. Whether they write fiction or produce their own films based on existing characters and narrative worlds, construct garments and props based on beloved characters, or recombine digital content ripped from films and television shows to make custom music videos, speculative promotional trailers, or feature-length remixes, fans continually find remarkable ways to appropriate, transform, and participate with media.

In the past few decades, many diverse extensions of fan culture have thrived in the wake of consumer digital technologies, and fans have helped recreate the fabric of contemporary popular culture. Henry Jenkins argues that because of an increased visibility of grassroots participation in the early twenty-first century, media companies have cultivated a new economy

> where fan tastes are ruling at the box office (witness all of the superhero and fantasy blockbusters of recent years); where fan tastes are dominating television [. . .], where fan practices are shaping the games industry (where today's modders quickly get recruited by the big companies).[3]

To Jenkins, these developments illustrate that fandom increasingly plays a major role in the lives of consumers.[4] Drawing from computer terminology regarding the capability to modify data stored on disk, Lawrence Lessig provides a useful model for broadly describing this historical change with his models of "Read/Only" (RO) culture and "Read/Write" (RW) culture. Lessig explains that in the RW culture of the nineteenth century, before the phonograph fixed music performances in tangible recordings, amateurs freely reinterpreted popular songs using the same instruments as professionals. However, the popularization of records, tapes, and other commercial formats during the RO culture of the twentieth century cemented authoritarian concepts of recorded media and conditioned common people to strictly consume, to merely "read" the culture around them instead of augmenting it. In the twenty-first century, continuous innovations in digital technologies and the emergence of the Internet have replaced contemporary tools of cultural production and distribution into the hands of everyday people, reviving participation and awareness in amateur creativity and signaling a return to RW culture.[5]

However, coinciding with the popularization of traditionally marginalized interests such as comic books and fantasy literature, wider exposure to fan culture precipitates confrontations among fans, media companies, and the law. Cinematic fan edits exemplify creative phenomena that have evolved significantly in the midst of dramatic changes in consumer technology and policy governing digital media and networked audiences.

Conflicts between Creativity and Copyright

Most scholarly appraisals of contemporary fan editing are unfortunately brief, but they typically reference *The Phantom Edit*, a seminal recut of *Star Wars Episode I: The Phantom Menace* (1999) that was created by Mike J. Nichols and traded among fans beginning around the year 2000 before spreading widely on the Internet the following year (Figure 12.2). Nichols, who initially obscured his identity with the pseudonym The Phantom Editor, is a professional film and television editor who recut *Episode I* in his spare time in an attempt to improve the narrative pacing and depiction of characters in the film. Nichols considered *The Phantom Edit* to be an editing experiment as well as a means to enter a creative dialog with Star Wars creator George Lucas,[6] but Star Wars fans and members of the press variously embraced it as a breakthrough for contemporary fan culture or condemned it as unethical.[7] Lucas and company initially expressed goodwill toward remixes like *The Phantom Edit* but recanted when reports surfaced that bootleg copies of the fan edit were being sold to the public.[8] Nichols was not involved in any sales of his project, but he publicly apologized for the fallout of *The Phantom Edit*, explaining that it was a "well-intentioned editing demonstration."[9]

The practice of remixing cinema has been part of fan culture for decades, but several factors elevated *The Phantom Edit* in 2001 to the status of a fan-editing

138 Joshua Wille

FIGURE 12.2 Screenshot of *The Phantom Edit*, a recut of *Star Wars Episode I: The Phantom Menace* by Mike J. Nichols on YouTube.

touchstone, including the development of large-capacity hard disk drives and the popularization of peer-to-peer file sharing technology. The fact that *Episode I* is regarded as a vexing film among many Star Wars fans made it a subject primed for reinterpretation, and Nichols brought a professional editor's sensibility for reshaping story and characters to *The Phantom Edit*. Moreover, its viewers were part of an audience that had been gradually conditioned to accept textual variation in Hollywood cinema. For them, wide commercial releases of the *Star Wars* Trilogy "Special Editions" (1997), *Apocalypse Now: Redux* (2001), and the extended editions of *The Lord of the Rings* (2002–2004) essentially offered more footage for fans to rework. Reflecting on the emergence of *The Phantom Edit* at that particular time, Peter Rojas observed, "We are headed towards a new conceptualization of a film as a permanent work-in-progress, which exists in multiple permutations, and can always be tinkered with in the future, whether by the director or by anybody else."[10] During that formative period, *The Phantom Edit* acted as a catalyst for the emergence of contemporary fan editing. It became a gateway text for newcomers to the burgeoning fan edit subculture that had already begun to take shape online, demonstrating to increasing numbers of fans that powerful tools for remaking cinema according to their own designs were within their grasp.

Thousands of new fan edits have been made since *The Phantom Edit*, but its notoriety has overshadowed much scholarly discourse about fan editing and contributed to a dysfunctional legacy in which *The Phantom Edit*, the most referenced fan edit, is increasingly not representative of fan editing practice.[11] *Episode I* and the Star Wars prequel films are perennial favorites for revision, but the field of fan editing has broadened to reinterpret more film and television genres. Contemporary fan editors rebuild narratives, perform extensive aesthetic modifications, and merge texts into surprising hybrids of film, television, and video game media. A casual online search will yield dozens of remarkable projects such as Alex Daily's *The Marvel Age* (2015), a comprehensive recombination of the Marvel cinematic universe into a serialized television show format, or Neglify's *Scream—The Giallo Cut* (2012), a bold version of the horror film *Scream* (1996) remixed in the style of an Italian exploitation film. Fan editors and restorationists have honed their skills in dedicated discussion forums at FanEdit.org and OriginalTrilogy.com and established their own conventions regarding the tools they utilize, their standards of quality, and the legitimacy of their craft.

Many conversations about fan edits will inevitably lead to a question about whether such works are legal. Fan editors generally claim that their works are protected by the fair use provisions of the U.S. Copyright Act of 1976, which safeguard certain noncommercial uses of copyrighted material without permission. Furthermore, a prevailing principle in communities like FanEdit.org is that all participants should "own the original," to support the work of the original filmmakers by owning a legitimate copy of all the film or television sources used in a given fan edit.

> See Chapter 7, "Copyright/Fair Use."

The Phantom Edit was initially assembled from a digitized videocassette copy of *Episode I*, although Nichols eventually reconstructed the project based on the subsequent DVD release. Contemporary fan editors have since expanded the range of their resources to Blu-ray and other commercial digital releases. Fan editors, like many fan vidders and video essayists, employ specialized software to decrypt the Digital Rights Management (DRM) implementations in these formats and harvest useful material. They typically use nonlinear video editing and visual effects software to create their projects, which are often developed over a series of draft versions shared with fellow fans who critique the work in community forums such as FanEdit.org and OriginalTrilogy.com.

FanEdit.org has fostered a dynamic community in part due to its development of the Internet Fanedit Database (IFDb), a reference website akin to the Internet Movie Database. A typical listing in the IFDb provides essential information about a fan edit such as its title, source texts, and runtime, as well as a list of changes made to the film. That section of the listing is comparable to the conventional changelog that typically accompanies versioned software releases, which similarly vary from broadly written summaries to exhaustive descriptions of every minute alteration. The release of every fan edit assumes that potential viewers have a degree of familiarity with its sources in addition to the presumption that viewers own the originals. In turn, the community has developed expectations of audiovisual quality and editing competence for every listing in the IFDb. New fan editors must submit their work for peer evaluation by members of FanEdit.org, who either approve the work or provide constructive criticism to improve the project. Once fan editors have proven their skills by earning a listing in the IFDb, they are free to create listings for their subsequent projects. FanEdit.org encourages criticism of every fan edit, and each listing in the IFDb includes a ratings and reviews section for participants to register their praise or complaints. "Favorite Edit of Month" competitions, which are regular community polls to determine the most popular works, have contributed to the development of a critical community at FanEdit.org.

Fan edits also emerge from online discussion forums or in enclaves of Reddit centered on specific fandoms, such as *The Lord of the Rings* and *Godzilla*. Indeed, most of the first wave of *Batman v Superman* fan edits were announced in Reddit forums designated for fans of *Man of Steel*, *Batman v Superman*, and DC Comics. Unlike FanEdit.org and OriginalTrilogy.com, which are online communities dedicated to fan edits and independent film restorations, not all sites of fannish discourse necessarily welcome such unauthorized and non-canonical artifacts. For example, the moderators of the popular Reddit forum /r/StarWars routinely suppress references to fan edits such as Harmy's *Star Wars Despecialized Edition*.[12]

Further, fan edits spontaneously appear on popular video streaming services such as YouTube and Vimeo, which permit rudimentary discussion in the comments section associated with every video. Although the ease of accessing these services provides rich opportunities to connect with many viewers, fan edits released on YouTube and Vimeo are more frequently targeted for removal following a Digital Millennium Copyright Act (DMCA) takedown request from the copyright holder of the original film or television program. The Content ID system on YouTube automatically checks every uploaded video against a database of copyrighted reference files, and fan edits are often blocked by that system because they inherit so much audiovisual content from their source media, albeit in new configurations. Some fan editors on YouTube have circumvented Content ID detection by arbitrarily altering the color palette and playback speed of their projects, perhaps unwittingly enacting further aesthetic transformation.[13]

In addition to robotic content blocking systems, popular video streaming services like YouTube and Vimeo are untenable sites for fan edit distribution because of the human factor. The destructive pattern typically goes like this: an online journalist or film blogger discovers a fan edit and publishes a complimentary article about it; other journalists and bloggers recycle it into their own articles about the fan edit, driving greater amounts of web traffic to the video. This provokes the original copyright holder and results in the sudden removal of the fan edit. Witness the brief celebrity of nuxwarboy's *Mad Max: Black & Chrome*, a fan edit uploaded to Vimeo that approximated director George Miller's highly anticipated alternate version of *Mad Max: Fury Road* (2015). Miller, inspired by "slash dupe" prints of films that are traditionally used for timing music scores, requested that Warner Bros. include in the Blu-ray release a version of *Fury Road* in black and white with an isolated musical score.[14] After news circulated that this second version would not be packaged with the initial retail editions of the film, journalists discovered nuxwarboy's fan edit on September 22, 2015, and set a viral machine into motion by embedding the Vimeo video directly in their articles.[15] Consequently the fan edit was purged from Vimeo the next day, which journalists like Timothy Geigner claimed he had predicted, "immediately after I shared the fan project . . ."[16] As a recourse, nuxwarboy posted links to the dozens of articles that were generated about the fan edit and expressed hope that the fervor would encourage Warner Bros. to eventually release Miller's black and white version of the film.[17]

Rather than wagering their uploads on the alluring yet precarious platforms of YouTube and Vimeo, many fan editors turn to less regulated means of distribution such as file locker websites and torrents, which provide somewhat more reliable file storage solutions because of their relative obscurity, but consequently limit the size of their audience. Instead of reaching potentially millions of viewers on YouTube, the choice to release fan edits through these comparatively underground channels narrows their scope to people who are willing to access those generally less convenient and controversial systems.[18]

Although many fan edits manage to avoid removal due to their obscurity, there are other cases in which fan edits persist online quite possibly because of prestige. Filmmaker Steven Soderbergh was notably one of the plaintiffs in a fateful 2006 lawsuit against CleanFlicks, a company that the court found to have trafficked in unauthorized censored versions of Hollywood films. In their fight with CleanFlicks, professional filmmakers argued against what they perceived as violations of their artistic authority, but Soderbergh himself was criticized elsewhere for publishing his own homegrown film revisions.[19] Since 2014, Soderbergh has freely shared his fan edits of films such as *Psycho* (1960 and 1998 adaptations), *Heaven's Gate* (1980), and *Raiders of the Lost Ark* (1981) to visitors on his website using an implementation of the Vimeo platform. Critics such as David Post challenged these works, asking whether Soderbergh "thinks that he has some kind of 'artistic license' to do what he denies to others, that his creativity is somehow more valuable than the creativity of others?"[20]

Although it has been widely reported that actor Topher Grace created fan edits based on films like the Star Wars prequel trilogy and *Close Encounters of the Third Kind*, none of Grace's projects have been substantiated by a public release. Reportage generally maintains that Grace screened his fan edits for a private audience of entertainment industry friends and journalists but withheld the works from the public due to concerns about legal reprisals from film companies such as Lucasfilm. But perhaps Grace's fears were unfounded; despite DMCA enforcements that effectively sever public access to fan edits made by other people, the enigma that Soderbergh's fan edits have been widely publicized and yet remain online suggests that Hollywood could be partial to its own.[21]

The tribulations of *Mad Max: Black & Chrome* notwithstanding, the case of Peet Gelderblom's groundbreaking *Raising Cain: Re-cut* (2012) illustrates how fan edits not made by celebrities might prosper, if at least their work reaffirms the creative vision of the original filmmakers. *Raising Cain: Re-cut* was initially an unauthorized fan edit that approximated director Brian De Palma's original narrative structure for *Raising Cain* (1992), based on an early screenplay draft that had been leaked online. Gelderblom published the work and an accompanying video essay under the auspices of *IndieWire*, and the project surprisingly avoided removal despite widespread attention. In praise of the fan edit, De Palma sought to include it in the Blu-ray release of the film. Thus, Gelderblom supervised a high-definition reconstruction of his project for the home video distributor Shout Factory, thereby elevating his fan edit to the status of De Palma's "Director's Cut" in 2016.[22] *Raising Cain: Re-cut* is an example of fan labor that was subsumed into a commercial product and overcame the recurrent dilemmas of how a contemporary fan edit can reach an audience as well as how to preserve the work for the sake of posterity. With the designation of "Director's Cut," *Raising Cain: Re-cut* will rest comfortably on the shelves of auteur-devoted cineastes who might otherwise reject the transformative implications and authorial transgressions of a fan edit.

A Permanent Work-in-Progress

A key concept in all extensions of fan culture is its propensity for change, to evolve in response to new social movements, economic conditions, and technological innovations. Some fan editors have already begun to explore new approaches to sharing their creative work without the entanglements of cumbersome file sizes that necessitate large data storage and associations with controversial distribution channels, as well as accusations of copyright infringement. Approaching cinema from a software perspective, one nascent method is to abandon the practice of uploading digital copies of fan edits and instead share their respective video editing project files, as illustrated in Scott Monaghan's 2016 "open source" fan edit, *Star Wars: Fall of the Jedi*.[23]

As a repository for his fan editing project files, Monaghan used GitHub, which supports documentation of versioning and fosters collaboration with other software developers. Open-source software distributed on GitHub ranges from fully formed installation packages to raw code that must be compiled in order for programs to take shape. Likewise, the tradition of distributing fan edits as fully rendered digital videos can be compared to complete software packages, while an "open source" project such as *Fall of the Jedi* represents an uncompiled version. Although the "open source" approach in a fan edit like *Fall of the Jedi* potentially clears the fan editor of any risk in sharing copyrighted media, it introduces extra steps for viewers. In addition to downloading the *Fall of the Jedi* project files, viewers must obtain their own ostensibly legal digital copies of the three Star Wars prequel films and scrub them of DRM if necessary, then apply the project files to the source videos in order to render the complete fan edit. In nonlinear video editing software, project files record all of the changes an editor makes; they are variations on the basic principle of an Edit Decision List (EDL), which is essentially a recipe for a computerized editing system to automatically conform video sources into a desired configuration. Although the use of a proprietary project file means that *Fall of the Jedi* is not open source in the true sense of software development, it suggests a new methodology for sharing fan edits in which the creative work is laid bare for inspection and further revisions. In that sense, it encourages the principles of appropriation, transformation, and participation that characterize fan culture.

Theory and practice of cinema as software is in the vanguard of Lessig's revitalized RO culture, and fans continue to push us toward that horizon. Hastened by the proliferation of alternative film versions from Hollywood as well as the unrelenting spread of fan edits, audiences have arguably grown more accustomed to a pluralistic understanding of cinema in the digital age. For some of them, like fan editors and those who know how to find their transformative works, the theatrical release of a film like *Batman v Superman* might as well have been a hyperextended trailer for the new standard of cinema: a permanent work-in-progress.

Notes

1. Pamela McClintock, "Box Office: Inside *Batman v. Superman*'s Historic Drop-off," *The Hollywood Reporter*, April 4, 2016, www.hollywoodreporter.com/news/box-office-inside-batman-v-880143.
2. Among the first fan edits of *Batman v Superman: Dawn of the Justice*, released between June and August 2016, were: *Batman v Superman-Dawn of Justice Remastered* by slendernyan (https://redd.it/4qi3ct), *Son of Krypton v Bat of Gotham* by PlzDieNow (https://vimeo.com/174358987), *Man of Tomorrow* by JobWillins (http://jobwillins.tumblr.com/post/148151789297/about-man-of-tomorrow), *Batman vs. Superman: The Osom Fanedit* by theosomfanedit (https://theosomfanedit.wordpress.com/2016/08/10/the-osom-fanedit-batman-vs-superman-english/), *Batman V Superman: Cut of Justice* by cutofjusticeeditor (https://cutofjustice.wordpress.com), *Batman v Superman Fanedit* by mostlikelymu (https://redd.it/4xgfx6), *Batman: Dawn of Justice* by Linus Otis (http://fanboyedit.wixsite.com/batman), *Batman vs Superman: No Justice* by Reese Evans (https://redd.it/4xodaz), *Batman v Superman: Ultimate Edit* by Mr_Liney97 (https://batmanvsupermanedit.wordpress.com), and *Batman V Superman: Dawn of Justice—The Vigilante Cut* by MajorPineapple (https://redd.it/4xrwen).
3. Henry Jenkins, "Afterword: The Future of Fandom," in *Fandom: Identities and Communities in a Mediated World*, ed. Jonathan Gray, Cornel Sandvoss, and C. Lee Harrington (New York: NYU Press, 2007), 360.
4. Ibid, 361.
5. Lawrence Lessig, *Remix: Making Art and Commerce Thrive in the Hybrid Economy* (New York: The Penguin Press, 2008), 28–31.
6. Mike J. Nichols, *Star Wars Episode I.II: The Phantom Edit*. DVD commentary, 2001.
7. Joshua Wille, "Fan Edits and the Legacy of *The Phantom Edit*," *Transformative Works and Cultures*, no. 17 (2014): 3.10–3.12.
8. Andrew Rodgers, "Lucas Unhappy about *Phantom Edit* Distribution," *Zap2it*, June 14, 2001, http://web.archive.org/web/20070804061419/http://movies.zap2it.com/movies/news/story/0,1259,—-7033,00.html.
9. Andrew Rodgers, "Phantom Editor Apologizes," *Zap2it*, June 28, 2001, http://web.archive.org/web/20051030080759/http://www.zap2it.com/movies/news/story/0,1259,---7311,00.html.

10 Peter Rojas, "Hollywood: The People's Cut," *The Guardian,* July 24, 2002, www.theguardian.com/film/2002/jul/25/internet.technology.
11 Wille, "Fan Edits and the Legacy of *The Phantom Edit,*" 1.7.
12 The /r/StarWars forum guidelines state that discussions about projects like *Star Wars: Despecialized Edition* are welcomed, provided they do not direct readers to any copyright infringing material: www.reddit.com/r/StarWars/wiki/rules#wiki_subreddit_rules. However, the moderators of /r/StarWars purge most of these submissions regardless of their actual content.
13 Both of these methods were already in practice by unscrupulous pirate accounts on YouTube whose operators regularly upload unmodified copies of films and television content.
14 Russ Fischer, "*Mad Max: Fury Road*—Eight Awesome Facts About the Making of the Film," *SlashFilm*, May 22, 2015, www.slashfilm.com/fury-road-trivia/3/.
15 Examples of the dozens of online articles that fatefully publicized nuxwarboy's *Mad Mad: Black & Chrome* include: Kyle Hill, "Finally Witness a Black and White Cut *of Mad Max: Fury Road,*" *Nerdist*, September 22, 2015, http://nerdist.com/finally-witness-a-black-and-white-cut-of-mad-max-fury-road/; Mike Sampson, "Watch *Mad Max: Fury Road* in Black & White," *Screencrush*, September 23, 2015, http://screencrush.com/mad-max-fury-road-black-white/; Rob Beschizza, "Watch *Mad Max: Fury Road* in Glorious Shiny Monochrome," *BoingBoing*, September 23, 2015, http://boingboing.net/2015/09/23/watch-mad-maxfury-road-in-glo.html; Kevin Jagernauth, "Watch: *Mad Max: Fury Road* Presented in Black and White," *IndieWire*, September 23, 2015, www.indiewire.com/2015/09/watch-mad-max-fury-road-presented-in-black-and-white-259414/; Charlie Jane Anders, "*Mad Max: Black & Chrome* is *Fury Road* the Way George Miller Intended It," *io9*, September 23, 2015, http://io9.gizmodo.com/mad-max-black-chrome-is-fury-road-the-way-george-mil-1732519536.
16 Timothy Geigner, "*Mad Max Fury Road* Re-Edit Taken Down Because Of Course It Was," *Techdirt*, September 25, 2015, www.techdirt.com/articles/20150923/12251132348/mad-max-fury-road-re-edit-taken-down-because-course-it-was.shtml.
17 In late 2016, Warner Bros. finally began to release an authorized black and white version of *Mad Max: Fury Road* on worldwide home media as well as in a limited theatrical run in the United States. Although director George Miller previously described his black and white version as having an isolated music score, comparable to a silent film, the commercially available alternative version retained the full audio mix. Warner Bros. branded it the "Black and Chrome Edition." However, Miller evidently did not refer to it by that title in interviews or during an introductory video that precedes it on Blu-ray. Given the brief but significant publicity of nuxwarboy's September 2015 fan edit, *Mad Max: Black & Chrome*, it is reasonable to question whether Warner Bros. appropriated the title "black and chrome" from the fan edit.
18 Joshua Wille, "Dead Links, Vaporcuts, and Creativity in Fan Edit Replication," *Transformative Works and Cultures*, no. 20 (2015): 1.3.
19 Mike Masnick, "Steven Soderbergh Fought to Make Re-Editing Films Illegal, Now He's Re-Editing Famous Films," *Techdirt*, January 15, 2015, www.techdirt.com/articles/20150114/17225129702/steven-soderbergh-got-judge-to-say-that-re-editing-films-is-not-fair-use-now-hes-re-editing-films-posting-them-online.shtml.
20 David Post, "Steven Soderbergh, Copyright Infringer?" *Washington Post,* January 16, 2015, www.washingtonpost.com/news/volokh-conspiracy/wp/2015/01/16/stephen-soderbergh-copyright-infringer/.
21 Soderbergh's alternate cut of *2001: A Space Odyssey* (1968) is a notable exception, which he apparently removed at the request of Warner Bros. and the estate of Stanley Kubrick: http://extension765.com/soderblogh/23-the-return-of-w-de-rijk. In another case, limited access to *Heaven's Gate: The Butcher's Cut*, Soderbergh's 2014 revision of *Heaven's*

Gate, inspired fan editor Take Me To Your Cinema to recreate the project and, consequently, introduce new changes to the film. For more on these creative side effects, as well as a critical perspective on promulgation of Topher Grace's fan edits, see Wille, "Dead Links, Vaporcuts, and Creativity in Fan Edit Replication," 4.1–4.11.

22 Peet Gelderblom, "Changing Cain: How My Fan-Edit Became a Brian De Palma Director's Cut," Directorama.net, July 26, 2016, www.directorama.net/2016/07/26/changing-cain-fan-edit-brian-de-palma-directors-cut/.

23 Although *Star Wars: Fall of the Jedi* is not the first fan edit to be shared as metadata instead of a complete video, it is remarkable because of Monaghan's utilization of GitHub, an established site for collaborative software development, and his preparation of a remix kit for aspiring viewers to assemble.

Bibliography

Anders, Charlie Jane. "*Mad Max: Black & Chrome* is *Fury Road* the Way George Miller Intended It." *io9*, September 23, 2015. http://io9.gizmodo.com/mad-max-black-chrome-is-fury-road-the-way-george-mil-1732519536.

Beschizza, Rob. "Watch *Mad Max: Fury Road* in Glorious Shiny Monochrome." *BoingBoing*, September 23, 2015. https://boingboing.net/2015/09/23/watch-mad-maxfury-road-in-glo.html.

Doctorow, Cory. "Topher Grace Turns All Three *Star Wars* Prequels into One Short, Punch 85-min Hypermovie." *BoingBoing*, March 12, 2012. http://boingboing.net/2012/03/12/topher-grace-turns-all-three-s.html.

Fischer, Russ. "*Mad Max: Fury Road*—Eight Awesome Facts About the Making of the Film." *SlashFilm*, May 22, 2015. www.slashfilm.com/fury-road-trivia/3/.

Fuster, Jeremy. "*Mad Max: Fury Road* 'Black & Chrome' Cut Gets German Release." *The Wrap*, July 5, 2016. www.thewrap.com/mad-max-fury-road-black-chrome-cut-gets-german-release.

Geigner, Timothy. "*Mad Max Fury Road* Re-Edit Taken Down Because Of Course It Was." *Techdirt*, September 25, 2015. www.techdirt.com/articles/20150923/12251132348/mad-max-fury-road-re-edit-taken-down-because-course-it-was.shtml.

Gelderblom, Peet. "Feature Film with Video Essay: Brian De Palma's *Raising Cain* Is Re-cut." *IndieWire*, January 31, 2012. www.indiewire.com/2012/01/feature-film-with-video-essay-brian-de-palmas-raising-cain-is-re-cut-132482/.

———. "Changing Cain: How a Fan-Edit Became a Brian De Palma Director's Cut." *Directorama.net*, July 26, 2016. www.directorama.net/2016/07/changing-cain-fan-edit-brian-de-palma-directors-cut/.

Hill, Kyle. "Finally Witness a Black and White Cut of *Mad Max: Fury Road*." *Nerdist*, September 22, 2015. http://nerdist.com/finally-witness-a-black-and-white-cut-of-mad-max-fury-road/.

Jagernauth, Kevin. "Watch: *Mad Max: Fury Road* Presented in Black and White." *IndieWire*, September 23, 2015. www.indiewire.com/2015/09/watch-mad-max-fury-road-presented-in-black-and-white-259414/.

Jenkins, Henry. "Afterword: The Future of Fandom." In *Fandom: Identities and Communities in a Mediated World*, edited by Jonathan Gray, Cornel Sandvoss, and C. Lee Harrington. New York: NYU Press, 2007.

Lessig, Lawrence. *Remix: Making Art and Commerce Thrive in the Hybrid Economy*. New York: The Penguin Press, 2008.

Masnick, Mike. "Steven Soderbergh Fought to Make Re-Editing Films Illegal, Now He's Re-Editing Famous Films." *Techdirt*, January 15, 2015. www.techdirt.com/articles/20150114/17225129702/steven-soderbergh-got-judge-to-say-that-re-editing-films-is-not-fair-use-now-hes-re-editing-films-posting-them-online.shtml.

McClintock, Pamela. "Box Office: Inside *Batman v. Superman*'s Historic Drop-off." *The Hollywood Reporter*, April 4. www.hollywoodreporter.com/news/box-office-inside-batman-v-880143.

Nichols, Mike J. *Star Wars Episode I.II: The Phantom Edit*. DVD commentary.

Post, David. "Steven Soderbergh, Copyright Infringer?" *Washington Post*, January 16, 2015. www.washingtonpost.com/news/volokh-conspiracy/wp/2015/01/16/stephen-soderbergh-copyright-infringer/.

Rodgers, Andrew. "Lucas Unhappy about *Phantom Edit* Distribution." *Zap2it*, June 14, 2001. http://web.archive.org/web/20070804061419/http://movies.zap2it.com/movies/news/story/0,1259,---7033,00.html.

———. "Phantom Editor Apologizes." *Zap2it*, June 28, 2001. http://web.archive.org/web/20051030080759/http://www.zap2it.com/movies/news/story/0,1259,---7311,00.html.

Ryan, Mike. "Topher Grace's *Star Wars* Edits Explained: Actor Discusses Editing Three Prequels into One Film." *Huffington Post*, April 26, 2012. http://www.huffingtonpost.com/2012/04/26/topher-grace-star-wars_n_1454526.html.

Sampson, Mike. "Watch *Mad Mad: Fury Road* in Black & White." *Screencrush*, September 23, 2015. http://screencrush.com/mad-max-fury-road-black-white/.

Sciretta, Peter. "Topher Grace Edited the *Star Wars* Prequels Into One 85-Minute Movie and We Saw It." *Slashfilm*, March 7, 2012. www.slashfilm.com/topher-grace-edited-star-wars-prequels-85minute-movie.

———. "Trailer and Report From Topher Grace's Edit of *Close Encounters of a Third Kind*." *Slashfilm*, February 21, 2014. www.slashfilm.com/trailer-and-report-from-topher-graces-remix-of-close-encounters-of-a-third-kind/.

Wille, Joshua. "Fan Edits and the Legacy of *The Phantom Edit*." *Transformative Works and Cultures* 17 (2014) http://dx.doi.org/10.3983/twc.2014.0575.

———. "Dead Links, Vaporcuts, and Creativity in Fan Edit Replication," *Transformative Works and Cultures* 20 (2015). http://dx.doi.org/10.3983/twc.2015.0663.

Wright, Larry. *Refocused Media*, June 29, 2016. www.refocusedmedia.com/post/146671510935/fury-road-black-and-chrome-edition-included-on.

13
FEMINISM

Karen Keifer-Boyd and Christine Liao

What do grrrls really (really) want? In the *Project Everyone*[1] feminist remix, girls from around the world dance to the popular Spice Girls' *Wannabe* song but the music video takes on new meaning. Revealing what they really really want today, primarily to end violence against girls and to have access to quality education, these grrrls are even spicier than the Spice Girls. Using the twentieth birthday of the Spice Girls' song as an opportunity for a feminist remix, *Project Everyone* calls attention to issues that need to be addressed to achieve equity for women. The witty viral music video makes viewers smile, dance, and sing along, but the feminist remix is also a powerful way to form coalitions to work toward equity and justice around issues such as education, wages, violence, ownership, freedom, access, participatory governance, and human rights.

A *feminist remix* is a creative resistance and cultural production that talks back to patriarchy by reworking patriarchal hierarchical systems privileging men. Patriarchy is based on a view that there is a natural/normal order in which men are superior. Patriarchy, rooted in essentialist views of gender differences, requires coercion and violence to maintain dominance of men and subordination of women. Some feminists seek to reform social hierarchies within the patriarchal system, and others work to radically overturn the system. Some combine both reform and radical transformation. A primary goal of feminist remix is to disrupt patriarchy as it intersects with other forms of oppression (e.g., racism, classism, ableism) by envisioning non-hierarchal systems of integrative power for co-creation of the present and future.

Remix is an important strategy that feminists have used to challenge patriarchy and other systems of oppression and to pursue social justice. Thus, feminist remix is political in nature. As feminist remix artist Elisa Kreisinger declares:

> Remix and feminism go hand in hand. For young women and girls, it's a way to take back our identities from corporate commodification and the use of appropriation in the remix process allows for images of woman and femininity to be rearticulated and redefined by the author. As a result, women become authors, resignifying the practices, discourses, and institutions on which oppression is based in real time.[2]

Although feminist remix strategies predate the use of computers, it is the convenience of digital technologies and the Internet that engages a wider audience to create and distribute remix works. As technology and social media have become increasingly important in our daily lives, feminist remix has become a powerful way to advance feminist goals.

Feminist media theories have influenced feminist remix works, especially regarding stereotypes, gender portrayals, and what is privileged, absent, belittled, threatened, attacked, and erased in the media. New materialism feminist theory embraces the post-identity potential of new media platforms yet is situated in embodied experiences of women. The feminist remix, *Distaff [Ain't I Redux]* (2008)[3] by artist Sian Amoy grapples with all of these issues simultaneously in "mute" juxtapositions on a split screen, each side with a different film montage. On the right side, sports media film footage—a tennis match with close-ups of tennis stars Venus and Serena Williams, is interspersed with the eye of a young Black woman, perhaps the artist's eye, staring at the viewer. Presented on the left side of the screen are cartoon images of derogatory Mammy caricatures ridiculing young Black women, and of Black women as devalued domestic workers. The juxtaposition calls attention to the continuation of stereotypes in the media portrayal of Black women, yet, in this remix, the male gaze is turned on itself.

The above example shows that issues such as stereotypes of and discrimination against women are great concerns and critical subjects of feminist remix. The following intertwines the histories of feminist remix to provide a broad understanding of its strategies, and to discuss feminist remix in relation to feminist media theories of cyborg, cyberfeminism, intersectionality, and the male gaze. In our discussion, we include examples of different methodologies that feminists have used to practice remix. These examples reflect a variety of issues concerning feminists but they also have a common goal— disrupt and dismantle patriarchal systems. It is important to note that although these examples are selected to illustrate feminist remix, not all the artists self-identified as feminist activists. We recognize a feminist remix work not by self-identification, but through the message conveyed in the work interpreted by viewers. The art/remix might start with a personal goal, but "it automatically becomes political when seen by the public."[4] Given that feminism and feminists are frequently misunderstood as misandrous by a misogynistic society, these remix works stem from historical discourse of carnal art, biotechnological assemblage, posthumanism, and embodied avatar, which convey feminist remix as creating new narratives toward gender justice.

Remix: From Photomontage to Femmage to Cyborg Bodies of Assemblage

The wave metaphor for feminist histories of activism introduced in the 1970s was a useful strategy in the United States to rewrite new understandings of the Suffrage movement as women's activism that did not come to a halt in 1920 when women in the U.S. were granted the right to vote. Today, as the *Project Everyone* remix indicates, women's calls for safety in both public and private spheres, enfranchisement, education and career opportunities, reproduction rights, among other issues, have not peaked and receded as the wave metaphor suggests but are rather part of an ongoing global struggle. Feminist remix plays a role in breaking the wave metaphor from notions that obscure the differences among women and what they need and want.

Remix, as an artistic subversion of content and context in the male/female dichotomy, arguably began in the early twentieth century, typically in the art form of photomontage. A feminist remix subverts the limitations of gender social expectations in which women are marginalized and controlled by patriarchal norms. Berlin Dada artist Hannah Höch used photomontage to deconstruct the concept of women in the early twentieth century by deconstructing female representation. In her photomontage works, various images—often including bodies or body parts, machinery, and typography—reconstruct the female body, calling attention to stereotypes of women. Her work *The Gymnastics Teacher* (*Die Gymnastiklehrerin*, 1925) juxtaposes a silhouette of a supposedly ideal thin woman's body with a full frontal image of a hefty woman wearing an apron, suggesting domestic service. In her 1924–30 photomontage series *From an Ethnographic Museum* (*Aus einem ethnographischen Museum*), she remixed "beautiful" European women's bodies with museum artifacts, such as African masks, male bodies, and bodies of color to question the representation of a woman's body as simultaneously primitive and infantile while being put on a pedestal as a precious specimen or trophy to display and own. Höch's Dadaism blends genders, ethnicities, and ages, suggesting that identities are not absolute but fluid. Her photographic collages are arguably precursors to feminist remix videos. Collage as photomontage remains an important methodology for feminist remix.

To recognize the powerful opportunities of using collage, extended as assemblage of objects, as strategies for conveying feminist messages, Miriam Schapiro and Melissa Meyer coined the term *Femmage*.[5] Throughout the history of feminist remix, re-constituting the female body as empowered and with agency is a continuous theme as well as calling attention to stereotypes, misogyny, sexism, and violence to women. Feminist surrealist paintings, such as Leonor Fini's *Dithyrambe* (1972), also predate Donna Haraway's "Cyborg Manifesto,"[6] which theorized and proclaimed women's agency in assemblages that challenged narrow views of women. Martha Rosler's photomontage series *Body Beautiful, or Beauty Knows no Pain* (1966–72), which combines female body parts with a stove, lighter, and cargo, is an assemblage of bodies and machines. Barbara Kruger's *You Are Not*

Yourself (1982), *We Are Not What We Seem* (1988), and *Your Body is a Battleground* (1989) challenge social expectations that women desire to be consumed by pleasing others. Kruger's combination of text and image, mimicking advertisement strategies of bold statements with social motives to sell desire for products, continues to be generative in producing feminist remix strategies of mimicking mass media forms to dismantle master narratives with edgy humor and irony.

The female body continues to be objectified and commodified. Recognizing that women's social and economic conditions have not greatly improved, Haraway's "Cyborg Manifesto"[7] sought to create a metaphor and new identity for women in the era of technology. Since then, the cyborg has become an important concept for feminist remix. Artists exploring cyborgian feminist theory include Lynn Hershman Leeson, Lee Bul, Mariko Mori, Cao Fei, and Natasha Vita-More. "Standing at the threshold separating the human and the posthuman, the cyborg looks to the past as well as the future."[8] Cyborg remixes, in effect, have extended from photomontage in the early twentieth century to sculpture, new media installations, online virtual worlds and avatars, design and even human body alterations such as the work of ORLAN.

Referred to as anti-aesthetics, ORLAN uses cosmetic surgery as a remix medium. ORLAN's "Manifesto of Carnal Art" "is not against aesthetic surgery, but against the standards that pervade it, particularly, in relation to the female body, but also to the male body. Carnal Art must be feminist."[9] Beginning in 1994, ORLAN's "Self-Hybridizations" digital photographic series ushered in pro-technological ethics and aesthetics, situated between cyborg and posthumanism, questioning human embodiments and gender identities. In "The Reincarnation of Saint-ORLAN," a series of performance-surgeries, ORLAN morphed herself with respect to ideal features of the feminine as depicted by male artists in the history of art.

Modifying toy bodies as culture jamming, a practice that provides critical intervention by tactically using the affordances of media, is intended to unveil and critique media representations of women and gender stereotypes. For example, the Barbie Liberation Organization (BLO) project, created by RTMark[10] in 1993, involved physically switching the voice box of Barbies and GI Joes, and placing these toys on store shelves, which were then purchased by unaware buyers. A phone number on the packaging, to call if the product is defective, brought the voice box remix to the attention of the news media. The shoppers, news media respondents, BLO's surgery on the plastic bodies, and manufacturers of femininity and masculinity all contributed to the remixing of bodies through biotechnological assemblage.

Cyberfeminism Posthumanist Remix

In the early 1990s, net art emerged. VNS Matrix's *A Cyberfeminist Manifesto for the 21st Century* (1991) "was a project in multiple media that gave vivid expression to the emerging political position of cyberfeminism, which saw new technology as an opportunity to disrupt society's patriarchal norms, and to have fun doing it."[11] Cyberfeminism emphasized "multiplicity, nomadicity and connectivity,"[12] thus, cyberfeminism is anti-thesis.[13] In order to intervene in political and social conditions, the challenge of feminism in the era of technology, cyberfeminists found themselves in the space of "the post-human, the cyborg, or the hyper-cyborg . . . the monstrous, and unrepresentable."[14] The works from cyberfeminists are often remixed works. This can be seen in VNS Matrix's iconic poster for their manifesto—a human body combined with animal parts, technology, molecular geometry, and text—creating new species and aesthetics, which empowered a new generation of feminists.

Cyberfeminists' works are concerned with gender, power, body, desire, identity, subjectivity, agency, and other related issues surrounding high and low tech, digital and bio-technology, as well as the environment and health. Cyberfeminism is an important antecedent of posthumanism. Since the publication of Katherine Hayles's book *How We Became Posthuman*,[15] feminist scholars theorizing a cyborgian state of being[16] "challenge individualist and disembodied notions of what it means to be human in a virtual age."[17] Posthumanism is a way to inclusively rethink human subjectivity and consider the processes that constitute the subject and embodiment.[18] Posthumanists recognize entanglements of human subjectivity and non-human agency. Thus, a posthuman aesthetic is a hybridity of human and non-human, envisioning a collective past, present, and future.

The online character "GashGirl/Doll Yoko" created by artist Francesca da Rimini is an example of remix from a strategic, essentialist standpoint[19] to emphasize the centrality of women in the development of posthuman aesthetics. Doll Yoko resides in *Dollspace* (da Rimini, Dominguez, and Grimm, 1997–2001), which is a hypertext fiction, a complex web environment with links, music, and remix images. She represents unwanted female children as posthuman, "evolving from the dark abysses of patriarchal capitalism . . . and at the same time dead and alive . . . deeply paradoxical figure[s], situated in an in-between space."[20]

Feminist Remix Counter-Narratives of Intersectionality

Intersectionality theory[21] as an analytical tool in feminist remix works considers the multiple intersecting oppressions experienced by women of color, and other marginalized groups, such as those experiencing disability, poverty, or those who identify as gender creative, transgender, lesbian, gay, or bisexual. For example, Evelin Stermitz's remix, *Women at War* (2010), mixes pornographic images of women collected on the Internet masked with high contrast filters of blood red and black color and journalistic reports of the horrors of violence against women and girls.

Creating counter-narrative is a way to bring awareness of the intersectionality of oppression against women. Feminist remix is a way to create counter-narratives.

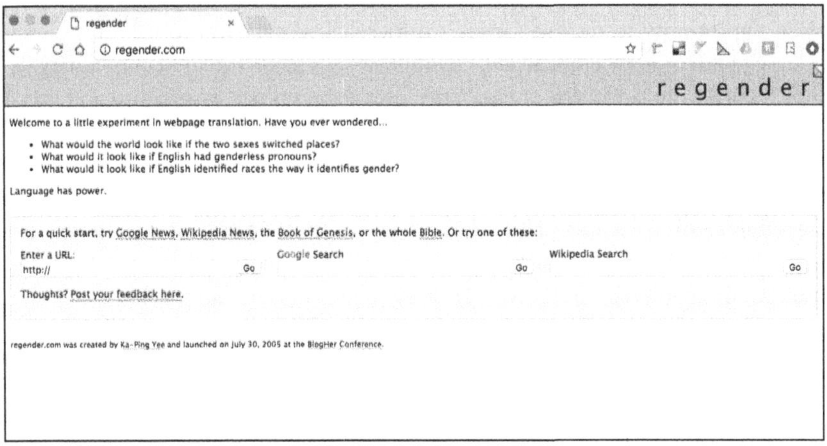

FIGURE 13.1 Screenshot of Regender.com.

One form of feminist remix is vidding, re-editing film or TV into music videos, a practice that dates back to 1975.[22] There are many other forms of feminist remix, such as net art, interactive applications, and social media hashtag movements. Strategies used to create remixed music or music videos include changing lyrics, vidding and remaking music videos. *Hotline Bling Remix*[23] changes the lyrics of the song *Hotline Bling*,[24] which feminists had criticized for putting forth the view that women should stay at home. The remixed song provides a feminist perspective of agency by flipping the original lyrics about how women should behave. Remixing the song *All About that Bass, Bitch in Business*[25] strategically changes the lyrics and re-makes the music video. Students at the Columbia Business School created the remix, which uses humor to imagine a women-centered business world instead of the men-centered business reality. Both remixes provide a counter-narrative to patriarchal ideology and practice.

A feminist remix can also take the form of interactive applications. As this art form often involves computer coding, it enables the use of data visualization to represent the reality of (in)equality. Regender.com is an example of net art as a feminist remix in which users can enter a URL and the website's text reverses male/female gender pronouns and gender specific terms and names, such as King/Queen and Joe/Jane, on the page searched (Figure 13.1).

Creating interactive applications as a tool to raise awareness of issues related to gender inequality is another type of feminist remix with code. *Are Men Talking Too Much?* is an online tool that can be used to record the talking time of men and women during a meeting or conversation. Another kind of tool reveals the hidden inequality in job advertisements. *Gender Decoder* allows people to check the gender codes embedded in job ads. These applications were developed to interrupt existing media systems and empower the user to think critically and take action. Each of these tools and strategies can be one-dimensional if not understood from the intersection of other marginalized positions in relation to gender. As new narratives and tools are created, understanding the intersectionality of oppression is critical to the success of counter-narratives. Calling attention to the multiplicity of positionality of the subject of the remix as well as the viewer should be made apparent in the remix.

Fe/Male Gaze Remix: Avatars and Embodiment

The *male gaze*, a term coined by Laura Mulvey[26] to frame a prominent feminist media theory in the twentieth century, draws attention to the dominance of media productions that assume heterosexual White males as viewers and privilege their desires. In her essay "Visual Pleasure and Narrative Cinema," she conceives that viewing is embedded in a patriarchal system, and that male pleasure is at the root of gender power imbalances in cinema. Feminist artists have created works to subvert the male gaze using strategies of masquerade and self-portrait.[27] Artists such as Karin Mack, Ewa Partum, Cindy Sherman, Lynn Hershman Leeson, Nona Faustine, and Violet Overn remix their own bodies with other objects or identities to challenge the male gaze. For example, Karin Mack's surreal photography *Demolition of an Illusion (Zerstörung einer Illusion,* 1977) fused an image of a woman who looks back to the viewer with nails and wires confronting the pleasure of the male gaze. Ewa Partum's *Change* (1974) applied makeup to appear old on one side of her face. The juxtaposition of a young and aging face destabilizes the male gaze desire of young and beautiful women. The masquerade and self-portrait strategies used by artists such as Cindy Sherman, Lynn Hershman Lesson, Nona Faustine, and Violet Overn all aim the camera on themselves to actively construct narratives and embody multiple identities.

Embodiment in the virtual space, for instance, through avatars, becomes a way to overturn the male gaze and simultaneously embody fantasy and fluid identities that empower the person behind the avatar. Avatar, as assemblage, blurs boundaries between the real and the virtual. In Cao Fei's work *i.Mirror* (2007) the artist embodies herself through her avatar China Tracy, a remix of real and virtual interrogating the male gaze fantasy in a posthuman virtual space.

Video games are another realm in which the male gaze is privileged. An early example of the feminist intervention and criticism of video games and gender, VNS Matrix's computer art game *All New Gen* (1993) offers an alternative point of view to male gaze video games.[28] In the game, "female 'cybersluts' and 'anarcho cyber-terrorists' hack into the databanks of Big Daddy Mainframe, an Oedipal embodiment of the techno-industrial complex, to sow the seeds of a New World Disorder and end the rule of phallic power."[29] Images, animations, and videos in the game combine plastic, constructed female bodies with imaginative creature bodies creating representations of bodies as parody.

In the early days of the Internet, men were the primary creators of cyberspace. As a parody, the remix music video *Too Many Dicks in Video Games* created by Anita Sarkeesian, creator of the *Feminist Frequency* website,[30] is a video collaged from different video gameplay scenes, with mostly male characters and violent actions, to highlight malestream video games' representation. The video was inspired by another remix video, *Star Trek Dance Floor* created by Sloane, which criticizes the mostly-men Star Trek series.

In the age of social media, there are new issues facing women. While the Internet is a powerful tool for spreading information, validity is not screened. The malicious intention of spreading derogatory misinformation and misogynist information about women continues online. An example of this is "GamerGate," a scandal that involved a feminist videogame developer who was initially targeted by her ex-boyfriend and later became a target of misogynists.[31] Similarly, Anita Sarkeesian received harassment and death threats after she started a Kickstarter campaign to create a video series analyzing and critiquing the video game industry's representation and treatment of women in video games. Both instances highlight areas in which women are treated with hostility. The malicious attacks and degradation of women in video games are creatively resisted by many feminist remix works that use the games as source material to subvert the normalizing of violence toward women.

Feminist Remix Nodes

Feminist remix works exist in different media formats and practices. Remediation, the representation or extension of media works from one format to another, is a transformative media practice that "borrows, modifies, samples, and remixes existing content, forms and expressions to create new works, relationships, interactions and meanings."[32] The overall goal of feminist remix is to disturb, expose, and/or challenge existing established patriarchal ideologies and systems that have undermined women's rights and equality in society. Feminists use a variety of media and methodologies to achieve these objectives. For example, as previously discussed, the remix of the Spice Girls' *Wannabe* song recreates the music video and inserts feminist messages of the desires of girls and young women for equity in education, careers, and wages. A different methodology can be seen in Elisa Kreisinger's feminist video remix *Mad Men: Set Me Free*. Remixing women's words from movie clips to create a music video for the 1966 song "You Keep Me Hangin' On," she created a work that shows women's frustrations. These two examples use different methods—the former remade the music video and the latter reused existing movie clips.

Places that promote, publish, and archive individual feminist remix works are nodes that enable the works to spread and be seen. Some nodes also act as a regenerative machine, which allows remixes to be remixed, or the site itself is a remix. ArtFem.TV[33] is an example of a feminist remix node. ArtFem.TV is an online site that acts as an online television program, which shows feminist video art. New media artist Evelin Stermitz created the site in 2008 and since then it has continued to grow. Many of the videos curated in the site are examples of remix video art works.[34] The site is itself a feminist remix, which aims at promoting feminist video, as well as digital and performance art.

Feminist remix works, as discussed in this chapter, put feminist goals and theories into practice. Whether it is the representation of women's bodies in the media, equality and social justice for women, envisioning a new world for women, or whether it is high- or low-tech—feminist remix is activism. Works on the web and social media can potentially go viral and become more influential with the power to create change, making remix an effective venue for feminist activism. The boundaries of feminist remix are ever-expanding with changing technologies. However, at its core it is a creative art form that challenges patriarchal systems. As feminist remix artist Kreisinger advocates: "don't blame the media, become the media."[35] Using existing media to create feminist remix is actively participating in creating a *gender just* media landscape and society.

Notes

1 Project Everyone, *#WhatIReallyReallyWant* . . . www.youtube.com/watch?v=sZQ2RUFd54o.
2 Kreisinger, "What Is a Remix, Exactly?," para. 5.
3 The video is archived on ArtFem.TV at http://artfem.tv/TEST/id;20/action;showpage/page_type;video/page_id;Distaff_by_Sian_Amoy_flv/.
4 Sameshima, *Seeing Red—A Pedagogy of Parallax: An Epistolary Bildungsroman on Artful Scholarly Inquiry*, 268.
5 Schapiro and Meyer, "Waste Not Want Not: An Inquiry into What Women Saved and Assembled—FEMMAGE."
6 Haraway, "A Cyborg Manifesto: Science, Technology, and Socialist-Feminism in the Late Twentieth Century."
7 Ibid.
8 Hayles, "The Life Cycles of Cyborgs: Writing the Posthuman," 322.
9 ORLAN, "Manifesto of Carnal Art," para. 8.
10 It is worth noting that RTMark is a group of anonymous men and women. Their work demonstrated that everyone, not just women, can participate in feminist remix.
11 "Net Art Anthology: A Cyberfeminist Manifesto for the 21st Century," para. 1.
12 Ferrando, "A Feminist Genealogy of Posthuman Aesthetics in the Visual Arts," 7.
13 Evans, "'We Are the Future Cunt': CyberFeminism in the 90s."
14 Old Boys Network, "Call for Contributions," 14.
15 Hayles, *How We Became Posthuman: Virtual Bodies in Cybernetics, Literature, and Informatics*.
16 Volkart, "The Cyberfeminist Fantasy of the Pleasure of the Cyborg."
17 Du Preez, *Gendered Bodies and New Technologies*, 74.
18 Ferrando, "The Body."
19 Spivak, *In Other Worlds: Essays in Cultural Politics*.
20 Volkart, "The Cyberfeminist Fantasy of the Pleasure of the Cyborg," 110–11.
21 Crenshaw, "Demarginalizing the Intersection of Race and Sex: A Black Feminist Critique of Antidiscrimination Doctrine, Feminist Theory and Antiracist Politics."
22 Coppa, "An Editing Room of One's Own."
23 *Hotline Bling Remix* video: www.youtube.com/watch?v=dAwGBlI5b8Q.

24 Original *Hotline Bling* video: www.youtube.com/watch?v=uxpDa-c-4Mc.
25 *Bitch in Business* video: www.youtube.com/watch?v=oPD0L0M7rtA.
26 Mulvey, "Visual Pleasure and Narrative Cinema."
27 CuratingtheContemporary, "Subverting the Male Gaze."
28 Breeze, "Attack of the CyberFeminists."
29 Evans, "'We Are the Future Cunt': CyberFeminism in the 90s," para. 7.
30 *Feminist Frequency* is a popular site that examines media and gender. The site, although not exclusively, contains remix videos, which are created as a way to critique media gender inequality. It also offers resources of feminist remix videos produced by Sarkeesian as well as remix tools.
31 Quinn, "5 Things I Learned as the Internet's Most Hated Person."
32 Lievrouw, *Alternative and Activist New Media*, 219.
33 Stermitz, "Artfem TV."
34 Stermitz, "Women's Images Re-Edited: The Critical Remix within Feminist Context."
35 Slajda, "'Don't Blame the Media, Become the Media,'" para. 10.

Bibliography

Breeze, Mary-Anne. "Attack of the CyberFeminists." *Switch: Electronic Gender: Art at the Interstice* 4, no. 1 (1998). http://switch.sjsu.edu/web/v4n1/art_mez.html.

Coppa, Francesca. "An Editing Room of One's Own: Vidding as Women's Work." *Camera Obscura: Feminism, Culture, and Media Studies* 26, no. 2 (January 1, 2011): 123–30.

Crenshaw, Kimberlé Williams. "Demarginalizing the Intersection of Race and Sex: A Black Feminist Critique of Antidiscrimination Doctrine, Feminist Theory and Antiracist Politics." *University of Chicago Legal Forum* 1989, no. 1 (1989): 139–67.

CuratingtheContemporary. "Subverting the Male Gaze." *CuratingtheContemporary (CtC)*, November 7, 2014. https://curatingthecontemporary.org/2014/11/07/subverting-the-male-gaze-femininity-as-masquerade-in-untitled-film-stills-1977-1980-by-cindy-sherman/.

Du Preez, Amanda. *Gendered Bodies and New Technologies: Rethinking Embodiment in a Cyber-Era*. Newcastle upon Tyne: Cambridge Scholars, 2009.

Evans, Claire L. "'We Are the Future Cunt': CyberFeminism in the 90s." *Motherboard*, November 20, 2014. https://motherboard.vice.com/read/we-are-the-future-cunt-cyberfeminism-in-the-90s.

Ferrando, Francesca. "A Feminist Genealogy of Posthuman Aesthetics in the Visual Arts." *Palgrave Communications* 2 (May 10, 2016): 16011.

———. "The Body." In *Post- and Transhumanism: An Introduction*, edited by Robert Ranisch and Stefan Lorenz Sorgner, 213–26. New York: Peter Lang, 2014.

Haraway, Donna. "A Cyborg Manifesto: Science, Technology, and Socialist-Feminism in the Late Twentieth Century." In *Simians, Cyborgs, and Women: The Reinvention of Nature*, 149–81. New York: Routledge, 1991.

Hayles, N. Katherine. *How We Became Posthuman: Virtual Bodies in Cybernetics, Literature, and Informatics*. Chicago, IL: University of Chicago Press, 1999.

———. "The Life Cycles of Cyborgs: Writing the Posthuman." In *The Cyborg Handbook*, edited by Chris Hables-Gray, Heidi J. Figueroa-Sarriera, and Steven Mentor, 321–35. New York: Routedge, 1995.

Kreisinger, Elisa. "What Is a Remix, Exactly?," September 23, 2011. https://elisakreisinger.wordpress.com/2011/09/23/what-is-a-remix-exactly/.

Lievrouw, Leah A. *Alternative and Activist New Media*. Cambridge: Polity, 2011.

Mulvey, Laura. "Visual Pleasure and Narrative Cinema." *Screen* 16, no. 3 (1975): 6–18.
"Net Art Anthology: A Cyberfeminist Manifesto for the 21st Century." *Rhizome Net Art Anthology*, October 27, 2016. http://anthology.rhizome.org/a-cyber-feminist-manifesto-for-the-21st-century.
Old Boys Network. "Call for Contributions." In *Cyberfeminism. Next Protocols*, edited by Claudia Reiche and Verena Kuni, 13–17. New York: Autonomedia, 2004.
ORLAN. "Manifesto of Carnal Art," n.d. www.orlan.eu/bibliography/carnal-art/.
Project Everyone. *#WhatIReallyReallyWant* . . . , 2016. www.youtube.com/watch?v=sZQ2RUFd54o.
Quinn, Zoe. "5 Things I Learned as the Internet's Most Hated Person." *Cracked*, September 16, 2014. www.cracked.com/blog/5-things-i-learned-as-internets-most-hated-person/.
Sameshima, Pauline. *Seeing Red—A Pedagogy of Parallax: An Epistolary Bildungsroman on Artful Scholarly Inquiry*. Youngstown, NY: Cambria Press, 2007.
Schapiro, Miriam, and Melissa Meyer. "Waste Not Want Not: An Inquiry into What Women Saved and Assembled—FEMMAGE." *Heresies I*, 78 (1977).
Slajda, Renee. "'Don't Blame the Media, Become the Media': Feminist Remix as Utopian Practice." *Barnard Center for Research on Women*, May 30, 2013. http://bcrw.barnard.edu/blog/dont-blame-the-media-become-the-media-feminist-remix-as-utopian-practice/.
Spivak, Gayatri Chakravorty. *In Other Worlds: Essays in Cultural Politics*. London: Methuen, 1987.
Stermitz, Evelin. "Artfem TV." *Artfem TV*, 2008. http://www.artfem.tv/.
———. "Women's Images Re-Edited: The Critical Remix within Feminist Context." *Visual Culture and Gender* 8 (2013): 21–30.
Volkart, Yvonne. "The Cyberfeminist Fantasy of the Pleasure of the Cyborg." In *Cyberfeminism. Next Protocols*, edited by Claudia Reiche and Verena Kuni, 97–130. New York: Autonomedia, 2004.

14
INTELLECTUAL PROPERTY

Nate Harrison

One of the challenges in any discussion about intellectual property is that it necessarily remains abstract. This abstraction arises from the fact that intellectual property is everywhere and yet nowhere at the same time. It shapes modern life in dramatic ways, while its ubiquity and naturalization leaves it nearly invisible. Much like the Chinese proverb in which fish cannot recognize the water that surrounds them, we have difficulty seeing and therefore describing adequately that which is all around us. And it is all around us: anyone who has sampled recordings in the creation of a new remix, or downloaded electronic books from Amazon, or clicked "I Agree" after scrolling through a lengthy software licensing agreement, or, for that matter, purchased a car with an onboard computer control system, or taken prescription medication, or even sipped a can of Coke, has interacted with intellectual property. In the following paragraphs, I'll lay out the history of intellectual property as a principle, and as a term. I'll then show how approaches to intellectual property have shifted over recent decades, through examples drawn from cultural practices as well as court rulings. These examples foreground critical issues surrounding authorship, intellectual labor, (now global) economies, and the creative freedom to remix.

Origins of Intellectual Property

To begin, it should be immediately pointed out that sampled-based music, or prescription pills, or any of the items listed above are not intellectual property in and of themselves. This is to say: intellectual property is none of those *things*. Rather, copyrights, trademarks, patents, and trade secrets are a set of legally regulated social relations. More practically, intellectual property can be conceived of as a set of legal mechanisms that grant particular rights for creations of the mind. U.S. Court of Appeals Judge Richard Posner and economist William Landes further define intellectual property as

> ideas, inventions, discoveries, symbols, images, expressive works (verbal, visual, musical, theatrical), or in short any potentially valuable human product (broadly, "information") that has an existence separable from a unique physical embodiment, whether or not the product has actually been "propertized," that is, brought under a legal regime of property rights.[1]

Although Landes and Posner do not link intellectual property with corresponding legal rights per se, for our purposes, it is worth unpacking just how "property" functions here. In order to do that, we must visit the origins of the concept of intellectual property, as it is documented in the United States Constitution.

Clause 8 of Article I, Section 8 of the U.S. Constitution grants Congress the power "To promote the Progress of Science and useful Arts, by securing for limited Times to Authors and Inventors the exclusive Right to their respective Writings and Discoveries."[2] While it does not mention them explicitly, this clause is generally understood as the origin of copyright and patent law in the United States. The purpose of the clause the Framers had in mind was twofold. On the one hand, it would provide the citizenry with an incentive to create and innovate. With the legally backed assurance that they could exclusively exploit (for financial gain) what they made, creators would be motivated to write books, or develop technologies. We might think of this incentive as the clause's "short-term" goal. On the other hand, the "limited times" granted to those creators meant that their monopolies would eventually expire and, in the long term, the ideas and expressions they produced would become accessible for all to use, in turn helping to cultivate the intellectual enrichment of a newly born nation. The accretion of the public domain lies at the heart of Clause 8. Despite the fact that in our contemporary moment the concept of intellectual property may seem to sit comfortably within the logic of absolute property rights, it is instead a mechanism designed to balance the needs of individuals and the national public good.

The term "intellectual property" appears at least as early as the 1860s in England, when inventors and other specialists employed it to argue that legal protections should be given to new discoveries and technological advancements in the same way that creative expressions are granted protection through copyrights.[3] Its usage becomes more pronounced in the second half of the twentieth century with the emergence, especially in the West, of post-industrial or "information" economies. Such economies have been characterized by the dominance of value production derived through intangible goods or services—in short, the cubicle worker replaced the factory worker, producing fewer automobiles than computer software.[4] Apple's iTunes is but one example of intellectual property in action: consumers purchase media content through the company's service, but are not securing physical copies of music albums, movies, or books so much as buying access to digital versions that may be transmitted to a variety of devices. Even as their media libraries expand, consumers own no actual property, but rather a collection of licenses that Apple, and the content industries, ultimately control. It is this control over information and its commodification that forms the crux of the debate over the boundaries of intellectual property.

Authorship, Labor, and Culture as Rental

For many critics, intellectual property rights have expanded substantially in recent years, leaning too far in favor of individual (and, importantly, corporate) interests at the expense of the notion of sharing ideas and creativity as a common good. The force of this criticism becomes apparent when we look at the changes made to copyright in the United States over the past several decades. In that time, the law seems to have become only more author-centric. For example, the Copyright Act of 1976 shifted in favor of the author in three key respects. First, it lowered the threshold for what constitutes protected expression to such a degree that virtually anything short of a math equation or list of alphabetized names (i.e., "facts") qualifies. Second, the Act lifted the requirement that works be registered with the federal Copyright Office; the moment expressions became "fixed in a tangible medium" they would be granted protection. These changes mean, in effect, that any napkin doodle is copyrighted the moment it is scrawled. Third, and perhaps most crucially, the Copyright Act of 1976 increased the term length of protection, from a possible maximum of 56 years to life of the author plus 70 years. For works made for hire, the term increased to a fixed 75 years.[5]

In 1998, two amendments to copyright were enacted that further augmented the rights of the author. The Copyright Term Extension Act increased the length of copyright to life of the author plus 70 years, and 95 years for works made for hire.[6] In the same year, the Digital Millennium Copyright Act (DMCA) proposed criminal penalties for those who would develop technologies that circumvented encryption systems on copyrighted materials—for instance, designing code that could break into read-only electronic books, or descramble commercial DVDs so that they might be copied, even if the copying was valid.[7] As recently as 2015, the DMCA prohibited auto owners from attempting to repair their own vehicles by reconfiguring the computer systems within them. Only after continued public pressure did the Library of Congress (which oversees copyright regulation) acquiesce that owners modifying their own cars and trucks was not *de facto* copyright infringement.[8]

Of course, from the point of view of enterprising authors and their labor, none of these changes to copyright law appears entirely unreasonable. Especially for those who depend directly on the protection of their intellectual property for a living—say, for instance, an independent software developer, or a commercial photographer who licenses her or his images—the intellectual work performed in the creation of new expressions might justify robust laws. Yet the reality is that within the creative industries today, a great deal of the intellectual property produced is not owned by those who author it. Works made for hire, freelance, and contract work, in the form of photography, graphic design, audio engineering, 3D modeling, and the like, often become properties that large corporations exploit. Hollywood and the music industry are obvious examples, entities whose profitability depends on legions of innovative, creative laborers. Viewed through the lens of the division of labor, then, intellectual property is conceived of as an ideological instrument. Propping up the "inspired genius" of individuation as a foil for furthering their economic interests, corporations use intellectual property to help ensure that the line—however now blurry—between producers and consumers of content remains definite, and calculable. Producers own properties; consumers merely "rent" them, and are further pressured not to tamper with their rentals, through laws that punish copying, collaging, remixing, redistributing, and appropriation generally. The economic status quo, the authority of the propertied class, remains intact.

The most egregious examples of the distilled instrumentalization of intellectual property are to be found in so-called copyright and patent "trolls," companies that manufacture no product, perform no service, but rather exist to secure creative assets and, moreover, police the creative industries for potential infringements. Within "golden age" hip hop, Bridgeport Music, Inc. is the most notorious of copyright trolls.[9] Bridgeport owns the rights to much of the back catalog of soul and funk music, including the work of George Clinton. The company has taken scores of hip hop artists to court seeking compensation for alleged infringements, and along the way changed the genre, one founded on the inventive collaging of snippets of old music into new compositions, for the worse. *Bridgeport Music, Inc. v. Dimension Films* (2005) pitted the sample-trolling company against NWA, who lifted a two-second guitar riff from a George Clinton recording in the creation of the track "100 Miles and Runnin'."[10] Ultimately a federal court essentially declared that any sampling, regardless of length or how recognizable it is, constitutes copyright infringement. "Get a license or do not sample," the opinion starkly decreed.[11] Given the outcomes of this and other cases in the late 1980s and 1990s, it would simply be too cost-prohibitive today for a major record label to produce such seminal and sample-laden albums as Public Enemy's *It Takes a Nation of Millions to Hold Us Back* (1988), De La Soul's *3 Feet High and Rising* (1989), or the Beastie Boys' *Paul's Boutique* (1989).[12]

New Approaches to Intellectual Property

The litigious environment surrounding much of hip hop, as just one indicator of the corporate efforts to secure culture as private property for rent, takes on a further ominous tone when we zoom out and consider intellectual property on a global scale. The World Intellectual Property Organization (WIPO), an agency under the United Nations founded in 1967 to "lead the development of a balanced and effective international intellectual property (IP) system that enables innovation and creativity for the benefit of all," is criticized for privileging the business interests of Western nations at the expense of the needs of poorer peoples and developing countries.[13] The patenting of medical technologies and pharmaceuticals rake in billions of dollars for U.S. corporations, while innovation stagnates because new IP becomes too costly to develop. One need only look to the health crises in parts of Africa, or the exorbitant prices for prescription medication in the United States, as examples of corporate intellectual property regimes that have gone awry. Now, with treaties between nations such as the Agreement on Trade-Related Aspects of Intellectual Property Rights (TRIPS) and the Trans-Pacific Partnership (TPP), a new, global intellectual property order, modeled after United States laws and corporate lobbyist trade prerogatives, is arising. Advocates believe these agreements will help international trade to everyone's advantage, while critics decry them as neo-authoritarian measures that ultimately seek to quash not just innovation and creativity but also fairness, and justice, on a global scale.[14]

Yet the picture painted above need not be so bleak. If we survey, at the very least, the current condition of what we might generally call "remix culture," it is not. On the contrary; by many measures, people are copying, reconfiguring, and sharing information and culture as never before. From amateur documentary videos to "bedroom" electronic music producers, from the spreading of memes appropriated from mass entertainment to Ivy League schools offering free courses online, it might even be said that we are living in the most creative period in human history.[15] Of course, remix practices have become of interest to academia—the book you are reading now is proof of that interest. Appreciably, the desire to change attitudes about and relationships with IP are increasingly evident.

To be sure, companies such as Disney and Mattel will continue to vigorously defend their IP in Mickey Mouse and Barbie. Hip hop artists will continue to run the risk of legal action through unlicensed sampling. And proud mothers such as Stephanie Lenz will continue to receive DMCA take-down notices for the videos they upload that contain copyrighted music in the background.[16] Yet in this last example, after YouTube removed a video Lenz had recorded of her children dancing to Prince's "Let's Go Crazy," she filed a counter-claim against Universal Music Group, the copyright holder of the song. Lenz argued that her use was authorized under copyright's fair use doctrine, which holds that in some circumstances, the copying of protected materials is not infringement.[17] Notably, the federal appeals court ruled that content producers like Universal are obligated to consider whether such videos satisfy fair use requirements before deciding to request that they be removed. *Lenz v. Universal Music Corp.* (2015) is considered not only a win for Lenz, but also a decision that defines fair use not merely as an affirmative defense against possible infringing action, but an actual right that may be asserted in the everyday copying and sharing of content.

Other recent legal disputes, including *Cariou v. Prince* (2013) and *Authors Guild v. Google* (2015), further illustrate just how sympathetic U.S. courts have become to copying and transforming intellectual property. In the former case, artist Richard Prince produced a series of paintings by appropriating a suite of photographs taken by Patrick Cariou. The photographer sued Prince for copyright infringement. After the District Court initially ruled in favor of Cariou, the Circuit Court reversed the decision, finding that the majority of Prince's works were sufficiently transformative and thus fair use; the rest in question were remanded back to the lower court. Specifically, the Circuit Court clarified that appropriations such as Prince's need not criticize or even refer back to their sources in order to be considered fair use, in a way that parody, for instance, necessarily does (Prince claimed his paintings were not meant as commentary on Cariou's images but new "remixes" in their own right).[18] This left the question as to what qualifies as fair use in artistic expression far from answered. Then, the decision in *Author's Guild* seemingly went a step further. The circumstances in that case involved information giant Google digitally scanning millions of physical books in order to index them into a searchable database for public research. While the books' contents would not be wholly available to users for download, Google copied the volumes in their entirety, giving the for-profit company control over vast amounts of information, and leverage over much of the future of accessible knowledge. Yet the court ruled that even non-expressive and blatant reuses such as Google's are transformative, performing a service vital to the public.[19]

In tandem with these lawsuits there have also been grassroots efforts to educate creative communities about the fair use doctrine. Patricia Aufderheide, one of the contributors to this book, has played a central role in developing fair use "best practices" for artists, filmmakers, academics, and others who work with protected materials and might otherwise be reluctant to exercise their right to copy in light of draconian intellectual property laws.[20] One of the core principles in this fair use advocacy is the notion that the doctrine should not be considered as a special exception to copyright, but rather one of its defining features, without which the law would not properly function (the reader will recall that copyright is originally designed as a balance between individual rights and public good). This is to say that if you agree with fair use, you must also agree with the concept of copyright itself (and by extension, intellectual property).

This last point is an important one to reflect upon. In the ethical and legal battles over the contours of intellectual property, the various positions taken have become increasingly polarized. In response to the apparent overreach of corporate copyright through stricter laws, opponents have, in some cases, sought to jettison them altogether. In more extreme examples, we encounter groups such as the Pirate Bay, a peer-to-peer file sharing service whose supporters believe any and all knowledge should be shared freely and widely through the Internet. The Pirate Bay's antagonism is primarily against the "property" part of intellectual property. Less subversive but no less significant are "copyleft" efforts such as the free software movement and Creative Commons, which have championed knowledge sharing by instituting practices and policies that help people regulate the distribution of their work as they see fit. In all of these cases, the solutions proposed (even the illegal file-sharing of protected materials) seek to compensate for the perceived failings of intellectual property law to adequately address the realities—and potential—of twenty-first-century knowledge production and distribution.[21]

For those who believe intellectual property is yesteryear's idea, left over from a pre-industrial era and positioned now mostly to serve the interests of a few, working towards its obsolescence seems the proper option. For those who believe in the ideals of intellectual property, and accept legislative shortcomings as projects to improve upon, working towards new licensing schemes such as Creative Commons, or towards strengthening the fair use doctrine are more apt courses of action. Yet so much of the thinking around these decisions depends on how we position ourselves within the chains of cultural production. While we may have little sympathy for entertainment executives whose bonuses shrink because of movie or music pirating, we might not be so cavalier about dismissing the concerns of those who pay the bills by directly selling the works they create. In an ongoing lawsuit, Richard Prince is again being sued for copyright infringement for appropriating Instagram users' photos.[22] Other than existing as enlarged canvases (and not small, digital images on screens), Prince's "portraits" are identical copies of the pictures he appropriates, and they sell for $90,000 each. Should a court rule that these self-serving artworks qualify as instances of fair use, it will call into question the very limits of copying protected materials and potentially open the flood gates for similar takings. Or more simply, a positive fair use decision will raise the question: what, in the name of artistic expression, can't be copied? Photographers everywhere should be watching this case closely.

Intellectual Property: From the Legal to the Ethical

In conclusion, I return to the abstract, but in the form of simple questions. Where do you, the reader, the potential remixer, stand? How do you value your creative labor? Can a price—economic or otherwise—be placed upon it? Is the euphoric feeling of sharing freely, of connecting with others, compatible with a belief in being fairly compensated for your work? How to define fair compensation? How would you feel if someone copied your Instagram photos outright, and sold them as works of art for large sums of money? But also: what do you think about life all around us being caught up in property rights regimes? How do you feel about the fact that Instagram controls (and can exploit) whatever content is using its service? Our understanding of the concept of intellectual property depends on your answers. Perhaps we should be concerned less with laws—and lawsuits—than with our ethical, or even moral, positions, always with an eye towards being fair to both ourselves and others (which makes it no less difficult a task). A friend of mine recently gave me a painting as a gift. It is a multicolor, geometric composition, with a single sentence that might provide guidance for future generations of remixers: *Copy the Art of Others as You Would Want Them to Copy Your Work.*

Notes

1 William M. Landes and Richard A. Posner, *The Economic Structure of Intellectual Property Law* (Cambridge, MA: Harvard University Press, 2003), 1.
2 Article I, Section 8, *Constitution of the United States*, www.senate.gov/civics/constitution_item/constitution.htm#a1_sec8 (accessed January 5, 2017).
3 See Adrian Johns, *Piracy: The Intellectual Property Wars from Gutenberg to Gates* (Chicago, IL: University of Chicago Press, 2011).
4 The larger narrative of an information economy is fraught with complications. The entire concept of intellectual labor, required of such economies, implies a workforce that has acquired needed technical skills through access to both higher education and new technologies. The lower and working classes, often ending up not in college classrooms but on factory floors, have been mostly excluded from this process. With the decline of traditional, industrial production in the U.S. (offshored to countries with cheaper labor forces), economic opportunities for the factory class have likewise fallen off. Trump's "Make America Great Again" slogan is precisely an expression of the anxiety brought about by this post-industrial condition.
5 See "Copyright Laws of the United States, and Related Law Contained in Title 17 of the United States Code," www.copyright.gov/title17/circ92.pdf (accessed January 11, 2017).
6 See "Sonny Bono Copyright Term Extension Act," www.copyright.gov/legislation/s505.pdf (accessed January 11, 2017).
7 See "H.R.2281—Digital Millennium Copyright Act," www.congress.gov/bill/105th-congress/house-bill/2281 (accessed January 11, 2017).
8 See David Kravets, "U.S. Regulators Grant DMCA Exemption Legalizing Vehicle Software Tinkering," *Ars Technica*, http://arstechnica.com/tech-policy/2015/10/us-regulators-grant-dmca-exemption-legalizing-vehicle-software-tinkering/ (accessed January 11, 2017).
9 See http://bridgeportmusicinc.com/index.html (accessed January 15, 2017).
10 The formal comparison between George Clinton's "Get Off Your Ass and Jam" and NWA's "100 Miles and Runnin'" is shown in the 2007 documentary *Good Copy Bad Copy*, www.youtube.com/watch?v=WEKl5I_Q044 (accessed February 2, 2017).
11 *Bridgeport Music, Inc. v. Dimension Films*, 410 F.3d 792 (6th Cir. 2005), http://fsnews.findlaw.com/cases/6th/04a0297p.html (accessed January 16, 2017).
12 For further reading about copyright, samples, and hip hop music, see Kembrew McLeod and Peter DiCola, eds., *Creative License: The Law and Culture of Digital Sampling* (Durham, NC: Duke University Press, 2011).
13 See www.wipo.int/about-wipo/en/ (accessed January 15, 2017).
14 See the Electronic Frontier Foundation's web video outlining the implications that the TPP will have on users' rights in digital spaces: www.youtube.com/watch?v=p3KlrfjcjV4 (accessed January 16, 2017).
15 See, for example, Harvard University's free online courses, www.edx.org/school/harvardx (accessed January 17, 2017).
16 See Ben Sisario, "YouTube 'Dancing Baby' Copyright Ruling Sets Fair Use Guideline," *New York Times*, www.nytimes.com/2015/09/15/business/media/youtube-dancing-baby-copyright-ruling-sets-fair-use-guideline.html?_r=0 (accessed January 17, 2017).

17 On fair use, see Section 107, Title 17 of the United States Code, www.copyright.gov/title17/circ92.pdf (accessed January 17, 2017).
18 *Cariou v. Prince*, 714 F. 3d 694 (2nd Cir. 2013), https://scholar.google.com/scholar_case?case=5845890683658306826&hl=en&as_sdt=6&as_vis=1&oi=scholarr (accessed January 23, 2017).
19 *Authors Guild v. Google, Inc.*, 804 F. 3d 202 (2nd Cir. 2015), https://scholar.google.com/scholar_case?case=2220742578695593916&hl=en&as_sdt=6&as_vis=1&oi=scholarr (accessed January 23, 2017). For more information on the case, see Chapter 7, "Copyright/Fair Use" in this volume.
20 To download codes of best practices, see http://cmsimpact.org/program/fair-use/ (accessed January 24, 2017).
21 On the free software movement, see www.gnu.org/philosophy/free-software-intro.html (accessed January 25, 2017); on Creative Commons, see https://creativecommons.org (accessed January 27, 2017).
22 See Eileen Kinsella, "Outraged Photographer Sues Gagosian Gallery and Richard Prince for Copyright Infringement," *Artnet News*, https://news.artnet.com/exhibitions/laurie-anderson-heart-of-a-dog-times-square-400736 (accessed January 26, 2017).

Bibliography

"Bridgeport Music, Inc." Accessed January 15, 2017. http://bridgeportmusicinc.com/index.html.
"Constitution of the United States." Accessed January 5, 2017. www.senate.gov/civics/constitution_item/constitution.htm#a1_sec8.
"Copyright Laws of the United States, and Related Law Contained in Title 17 of the United States Code."
Copyright.gov. Accessed January 11, 2017. www.copyright.gov/title17/circ92.pdf.
Christensen, Ralf, Andreas Johnsen, and Henrik Moltke. *Good Copy Bad Copy*. 2007. Accessed February 2, 2017. www.youtube.com/watch?v=WEKl5I_Q044.
Electronic Frontier Foundation. "TPP: The Biggest Threat to the Internet You've Probably Never Heard Of." Accessed January 16, 2017. www.youtube.com/watch?v=p3KlrfjcjV4.
"Fair Use, Free Speech & Intellectual Property." Accessed January 24, 2017. http://cmsimpact.org/program/fair-use/.
"H.R.2281—Digital Millennium Copyright Act." Accessed January 11, 2017. www.congress.gov/bill/105th-congress/house-bill/228.
Harvard University. "HarvardX." Accessed January 17, 2017. www.edx.org/school/harvardx.
"Inside WIPO." Accessed January 15, 2017. www.wipo.int/about-wipo/en/.
Johns, Adrian. *Piracy: The Intellectual Property Wars from Gutenberg to Gates*. Chicago, IL: University of Chicago Press, 2011.
Kinsella, Eileen. "Outraged Photographer Sues Gagosian Gallery and Richard Prince for Copyright Infringement." *Artnet News*. Accessed January 26, 2017. https://news.artnet.com/exhibitions/laurie-anderson-heart-of-a-dog-times-square-400736.
Kravets, David. "U.S. Regulators Grant DMCA Exemption Legalizing Vehicle Software Tinkering." *Ars Technica*. Last modified October 27, 2015. Accessed January 26, 2017. http://arstechnica.com/tech-policy/2015/10/us-regulators-grant-dmca-exemption-legalizing-vehicle-software-tinkering/.

Landes, William M., and Richard A. Posner. *The Economic Structure of Intellectual Property Law*. Cambridge, MA: Harvard University Press, 2003.

McLeod, Kembrew and Peter DiCola. *Creative License: The Law and Culture of Digital Sampling*. Durham, NC: Duke University Press, 2011.

Sisario Ben. "YouTube 'Dancing Baby' Copyright Ruling Sets Fair Use Guideline." *New York Times*. Accessed January 17, 2017. www.nytimes.com/2015/09/15/business/media/youtube-dancing-baby-copyright-ruling-sets-fair-use-guideline.html?_r=0.

"Sonny Bono Copyright Term Extension Act." Accessed January 11, 2017. www.copyright.gov/legislation/s505.pdf.

United States Court of Appeals for the Second Circuit. "Cariou v. Prince." Accessed January 23, 2017. https://scholar.google.com/scholar_case?case=5845890683658306826&hl=en&as_sdt=6&as_vis=1&oi=scholarr.

———. "Authors Guild v. Google, Inc." Accessed January 23, 2017. https://scholar.google.com/scholar_case?case=2220742578695593916&hl=en&as_sdt=6&as_vis=1&oi=scholarr.

United States Court of Appeals for the Sixth Circuit. "Bridgeport Music, Inc. v. Dimension Films." Accessed January 16, 2017. http://fsnews.findlaw.com/cases/6th/04a0297p.html.

15
JAZZ

T Storm Heter

At the intersection of remix and jazz, I propose that strategies of musical repetition have been a central part of jazz culture since its inception in 1920s America. Jazz musicians helped pioneer the technique of intensive listening from records in order to copy sound. Approaching turntables as tools for active listening, jazz musicians manually looped small sections of their favorite records to copy licks and riffs, which they then integrated into their performances. While jazz musicians were not alone in developing active listening techniques in the early period of the turntable, players as diverse as Bix Beiderbecke[1] and Lester Young[2] have described the turntable as central to their sound.

Remix theorists have shown the importance of the turntable in DJ culture; in turn, I examine the turntable in jazz, arguing that jazz musicians make them active tools for musical creation.[3] I suggest that jazz culture is an important precursor to remix culture. With recent technology, we see convergences of jazz and remix cultures.

Four Approaches to the Turntable in Jazz

In the American South in the 1920s when Race Records boomed, musicians began lifting the needles of their turntables to create loops. Lester Young, for instance "liked to get with the record and play along."[4] Musicians like Young could focus on one short phrase at a time and by way of repeated listening, they would eventually be able to copy the music of others. The musician could also slow down the turntable (e.g., by softly placing a thumb on the table) and listen to a tricky phrase at a reasonable tempo, allowing for easier imitation. According to one 1920s jazz musician, in " those days you'd buy the record [and] play it, play it, play it, and write it note for note . . . I learned on the clarinet first from the record."[5] This same method of looping and tempo alteration has been used by jazz musicians for generations.

In the late 1960s, jazz "Play-A-Long" records were introduced, and since that time they have become a standard method for learning improvisation. The records are specially designed for interactive playback. Play-A-Long records gave their user control over the playback experience. Unlike traditional records, the Play-A-Long records placed discrete musical information on the left and right channels so that unwanted instruments could be muted. Play-A-Long records are mixed so that users can eliminate whichever instrument they wish to play themselves. Users wishing to mute, say, the bass line of a recording, could pan right and hear only the drums and piano. Instead of practicing by playing one's instrument on top of the canonical solos, the user would hear only the backing rhythm section.

More recently, two pieces of software have been developed. The "Amazing Slow Downer" (ASD, released in 2001) allows users to create loops with precision and without manually resetting a record each time. The major innovation of ASD is that it provides users the ability to slow the tempo of a recording without pitch alteration. We might think of the ASD as a rather sophisticated turntable—one that allows precise loops of any duration from any point in a recording at any speed and at any pitch.

The Stretch Music app, released in 2015, accompanied the album *Stretch Music* by trumpeter Christian Scott. The app is a virtual mixing board that incorporates and surpasses the technologies above: looping (with greater control, and less labor), tempo alteration (with greater functionality, since the speed can be slowed without pitch alteration), and the ability to selectively adjust the levels of instruments during looped playback. With Scott's *Stretch Music* project, we have a release that is simultaneously a Play-A-Long record and a traditional commercial record. The release marks a new moment in jazz culture because *Stretch Music* was released as a *remixable* album.

Turntable as Tool: Learning from Records

To understand repetition in jazz culture, one must look at the turntable as a tool. The practice of learning from records began with the record boom of the 1920s. Musicians copied riffs and licks by looped listening. Jazz players like Lester Young learned from records because it is difficult to learn to play jazz from only listening to in-person live performances where too much information is presented, too quickly for learning but on pace for enjoyment (both for the master players and listeners). Without the possibility of repeated, slowed listening, only highly accomplished players would hear, let alone be able to copy, difficult music. From this standpoint, jazz culture is connected to the birth of the commercial record and the technology of the turntable. Jazz would not emerge as a national phenomenon in the U.S. until records and turntables were available for cheap at-home use. Jazz spread primarily because of records. In its earliest days, roughly 1914 to 1917, jazz spread slowly through the sale of ragtime sheet music, touring Vaudeville acts, riverboat bands, and regional brass bands.

In the late 1910s, when jazz culture was just beginning, the idea of making a record was unusual, and jazz artists were ambivalent about recording. Famously, the New Orleans cornet player Freddie Keppard (1889–1933) was offered a record deal and declined on the grounds that he did not want to make it easier for lesser players to copy him. Keppard feared that recorded repetition would destroy his live performance career. Louis Armstrong (1901–1971), just one generation younger than Keppard, became the most famous jazz musician in history because he recorded.

Having a permanent record of an improvised performance that could be played back repeatedly at will was a game changer. Records became reliable sources for efficient copying. Because most jazz music is improvisational, records are an important form of communication. Early, non-improvised forms of jazz such as ragtime spread through the sale of sheet music.[6] Improvised jazz, however, needed to be recorded to be copied.

JazzAdvice.com

Learning from records is a key part of jazz education. An entry at the webpage JazzAdvice.com entitled "Inspiration for Improvisers," lays out how the aspiring jazz player should learn her craft.[7] The entry begins: "All you truly need is one great record. Try this exercise. For the next couple of months (or two), pick one record from your collection and focus on it exclusively." The student should pay special attention to hearing and transcribing solos. The entry stresses the importance of repetition and intense study: "By studying this one record intently, you'll learn much more than glossing over fifty records." Repeated listening will make it possible for the musician to "transcribe a chorus of a solo or even an entire solo to ingrain the changes and pick up some language along the way."[8] The quoted passage speaks to a cultural continuity between jazz musicians in the 1920s and today—they learn to improvise from record listening, usually aided by loops and tempo alterations.

Repetition and Remix

Musical repetition is an important part of jazz culture, both for musicians learning jazz and those performing it. But the main techniques of repetition in jazz were too early to be considered part of remix culture. Jazz musicians were primarily copying from the world when employing licks and riffs. Jazz musicians who actively used turntables might be considered early precursors of DJs. An important part of DJ culture is also learning from records the way generations of jazz players have done.[9]

Are jazz musicians "sampling" when they learn to copy sound from records? No, although the practices are related. According to Remix Theory, sampling requires copying from a pre-existing source, rather than from the world. The jazz version of "cut/copy, paste" is manual, not mechanical. The jazz musician is like a painter who has taken a photo of a tree and now paints a picture of the tree from the photo. These jazz techniques might be considered the musical foundations out of which genuine sampling would emerge.

In a recent interview, the contemporary jazz saxophonist Joshua Redman distinguished three types of repetition in jazz performance: "riffing" in order to get a crowd excited, repetition for the sake of explicating a motif, and machine-like cutting and pasting of "licks" into a song form.[10] Redman praises the tenor player Sonny Rollins for his non-mechanical playing: "You don't ever get the sense that he's sitting back, outside of himself, thinking about the architecture . . . You don't ever get the sense that he's playing licks . . . It never sounds like, 'two-five, lick, insert.'"[11]

Redman is skeptical of jazz musicians who follow the formula "two-five, lick, insert." "Two-five" refers to a common chord progression in jazz. A "lick" refers to a short musical phrase that can be copied or borrowed and used in a novel musical context. In short, the "two-five, lick, insert" is a primitive, non-mechanical equivalent of "cut/copy, paste." Redman goes so far as to mildly criticize the virtuoso tenor Illinois Jacquet for using "riff-based repetition to get the band and the crowd going. That's very powerful and exciting, but it's a kind of specific device."[12]

Building on Redman's brief comments we might say that there is a spectrum of repetition that occurs when jazz musicians copy music. Redman suggests a ranking. First there is playing a "lick" in a performance context, which Redman sees as the least interesting type of sampling, because the player is using a rote pattern without flexibility, without innovation and without the creation of a new relationship among the sampled musical element and the performance. Slightly better is the type of non-mechanical sampling employed by saxophonist Illinois Jacquet, which might be called riff-based sampling. A riff can be distinguished from a lick, in so far as the riff is a short musical element—usually rhythmic—that is repeated dramatically in order to generate excitement and energy. Riffing is the pre-modern equivalent of a break beat loop: the artist finds an especially powerful short rhythmic sequence and repeats it. Lastly, Redman describes the kind of non-mechanical sampling used by his hero Sonny Rollins. Redman analyzes a performance of Rollins's theme song, *St. Thomas*. He comments, "As symmetrical as it is, it still has the element of surprise. It's not bland; it's not derivative." Redman hears a special quality in Rollins's use of repetition: it is always fresh, new and interesting, "even when he plays something that you know he's played before."[13]

The notions of the lick, the riff and what jazz musicians call "quoting" are all related to, but different from, sampling in remix culture. Quoting is the practice of playing a recognizable, short phrase from an unrelated song during a performance. It is not uncommon for jazz musicians to quote popular music, canonical solos, or even themselves, while soloing. Similar to sampling, in quoting a musician incorporates rhythmic, harmonic or melodic information from another source; but unlike sampling the copying is not mechanical.[14]

A significant difference between sampling in remix culture, and the jazz techniques above is that while jazz musicians do "cut/copy, paste," *in a sense*, they employ ear training and traditional instrumental technique (embouchure, bowing, fingering, sticking, breath support, etc.) for producing copies. Jazz musicians spend years building up enough technique to be able to copy what they hear.

Further, as the Redman interview shows, to say that a jazz musician plays "mechanically" is not usually a compliment; mechanical playing is considered a mark of musical immaturity or lack of ability. A master of non-mechanical playing, Rollins is able to solo on his theme song, *St. Thomas*, which he has played live perhaps more than a hundred times, without turning his performance into a regressive listening experience for the audience, or for himself.

Jazz and Stages of Mechanical Reproduction

The emergence of jazz culture can be considered part of the second stage of mechanical reproduction. The model stayed mostly the same from the 1920s until the late 1960s when *academic* jazz culture emerged.[15]

The technological change that accompanied the birth of academic jazz culture was the "Play-A-Long" record. Jazz educator Jamey Aebersold released the first of his Play-A-Long records in 1967. The Aebersold Play-A-Long series is still running strong, with more than 130 records available now, and no end in sight.[16]

As Eitan Wilf shows in *School for Cool*, Play-A-Long technology is a central element of today's academic jazz culture.[17] As markets for jazz educators emerged, more efficient methods of teaching jazz were sought. Instead of students learning to play jazz "on the street" by having gigs and live performances, students turned to Play-A-Long records and university settings such as classes, clinics, camps, and ensembles. Ironically, as Wilf shows, the boom in academic jazz did not accompany a rise in the popular consumption of jazz; the opposite happened. Jazz musicians were not only learning their craft in universities; universities also became the main performance context for jazz musicians.

The secret to the success of the Play-A-Long record is not only in providing musicians with their own convenient rhythm section, but also in allowing the user to change the listening experience by panning stereo left or right to eliminate instruments. Each replay would become a different experience, defined by the needs of the user. Like the old method of copying from canonical records, the key to success would be hours and months of repeated playing of the same record, usually the same song.

The phenomenology of practicing with the Play-A-Long record is different than practicing against a commercial recording. Instead of listening to whether the user is matching the soloist, the user listens to how her solo sounds against the rhythm section. As the musician grows in sophistication, she is expected to hear more of what's happening in the rhythm section and to react accordingly. While a beginner might hear only a difference between a major and a minor chord, a more sophisticated user will hear the difference in how the chord is voiced, and react accordingly. Play-A-Long records are often marketed according to the prominence of the backing musicians; the better the rhythm section, the more there is for the budding soloist to hear and react to.

To summarize, the Play-A-Long record changed how jazz musicians learned from records. Having copied solos from canonical records, the musician could now have a user-activated experience where she could hear herself play solos in a context akin to live performance. Through successive listening, the user would unlock more and more information from the archived rhythm section.

So, what forms of musical repetition are involved in the Play-A-Long? I argue that the Play-A-Long technology has the possibility to produce *reflexive* performances that in turn are predecessors of remixes. Such performances are "allegorical" and retain the "aura" of the original, while also challenging audiences by substantially modifying original copied material.[18] Take the Aebersold Play-A-Long record Volume 6 "Charlie Parker—All 'Bird.'" The rhythm section on this record is impressive: Kenny Barron (piano), Ron Carter (bass) and Ben Riley (drums), yet none of these musicians is Charlie Parker. The Play-A-Long tracks on their own would constitute "versions" of the original Parker recordings. Those who buy Volume 6 are interested in reaching back to the aura of Charlie Parker's canonical 1940s records. The student places himself in the shoes of Parker, invoking the idea of "what Parker would have played over this chord change." The record is not just a *version*, however, because each time the user replays the record she can adjust the playback experience, based on which musical information in the archive she chooses to foreground.

Ironically, the same interactive technology that can produce reflexive performances can also give rise to *regressive* practices. It is a common joke among jazz musicians today to talk about the "Berklee sound," referring to musicians trained at Berklee College of Music, the leading jazz conservatory in the world. At Berklee, jazz musicians learn to "cite with exactitude"[19] by mastering the routine of the Play-A-Long record, and by transcribing and copying extremely complex solos by canonical artists. By any measure, Berklee musicians are some of the best trained in the world, so why has the "Berklee sound" attained a certain stigma?

Nate Chinen argues that because jazz conservatories are both big business and "the primary means of exposure and training for aspiring jazz students," the result is a "jazz-educational industrial complex."[20] Wilf hypothesizes that the Berklee sound is a result of canonizing a relatively small number of musicians and styles (Parker, Coltrane, Miles, Shorter), and a curriculum that is focused on transcribing and copying *exactly* the solos of canonical recordings.[21] If Chinen and Wilf are correct about conservatory culture, then we may worry that user-activated jazz technologies are being subverted by the logic of efficiency.[22] At this point I turn to two recent jazz remix technologies.

The Amazing Slow Downer

The release of the ASD software in 2001 changed how jazz musicians used the "turntable." According to the software company Roni Music, the ASD "provides the means to slow down the music, so you can learn the music in real-time by playing it from a CD, MP3, WAV, AIFF, MP4, or WMA."[23] The ASD allows "increasing the music speed up to twice the normal rate—making pitch adjustments in semi-tones at full or lower speed—setting loop points—using keyboard shortcuts."[24]

ASD software fixed a common problem with traditional turntables: as the user slowed down the tempo of a recording, the pitch changed. Copying music at a slower tempo required the user to switch keys. The ASD gave users playback control: a riff could be played at any tempo, at any pitch. The user could also create loops of any length, from any part of the recording.

What types of emulative strategies are available to ASD users? Let's begin by asking whether learning to play by using ASD is *allegorical*. It would seem that practicing with ASD consists of retaining the "text" or "code" of the original recording. Assume the user is learning Coltrane's *A Love Supreme*, although very slowly and in a different key from the recording. Such a practice clearly retains the aura of the original.[25]

ASD remixes embrace another important element of remix culture: recycling. JazzAdvice.com tells us not to buy new records, since one good solo "has enough language in it to transform your playing."[26] JazzAdvice.com ties remixing to the authority of an "original" recording, but also admits that there is musical, cultural information contained in the original that can only be found through critical, engaged repetitious listening.[27]

To summarize, the ASD is specifically designed as a tool for reflexive performance and embraces cultural recycling. ASD emulative strategies tend to be extended, selective or allegorical. However, while the ASD is a significant tool that allows the listener to repurpose the musical composition, it does not fully engage the possibilities of new media and remix culture.

Christian Scott, *Stretch Music* and the Stretch Music App

Christian Scott's project represents a significant crossover between jazz and remix cultures. *Stretch Music* is not a traditional record and not a Play-A-Long record; it is what we might call a *remixable album*. The Stretch Music app allows the user to manipulate a canonical jazz recording. Scott's album is both for listening and for practicing. The album/app release challenges the sharp separation between public performance and practicing. Users who purchase both the album and app have access to a novel remix technology. The app is a downloadable mixing board that turns the listener/user into a studio engineer.[28] By the standards of remix theory, the app constitutes a form of new media.[29]

In a recent promotional YouTube video, Scott demonstrates the software in front of a live audience.[30] Scott can be heard remixing his own record, while playing improvised figures over the top. The video is an archived performance of a jazz remix session—but is Scott performing, practicing, or both? Scott's approach to jazz is clearly influenced by remix. Scott, born in 1983, grew up listening to hip hop, which shows in his music. Scott's familiarity with remix culture inspired his inventive concept of what constitutes an album. His *remixable album* challenges the idea that a record is a stable archive that can be copied precisely. With Scott's release, jazz culture moves more fully in line with remix culture. Specifically, Scott's app/album is a technology of *regenerative* remixing.

By giving the user a remixable file of his record, Scott prioritizes functionality[31] and moves away from traditional ideas of textual authorship and artistic control. In the past, jazz artists have closely guarded master recordings and final mixes. For example, for the film *Miles Ahead* (2015) jazz musician Robert Glasper was given access to Davis's masters, which had not seen the light of day for more than 50 years. From this material, Glasper produced remixes for the Robert Glasper/Miles Davis album, *Everything is Beautiful*. The album contains potent examples of reflexive remixes, but does move into the stage of the regenerative remix. Glasper's music (like Scott's) is heavily influenced by remix culture and hip hop in particular. But Glasper's release, unlike Scott's, was not released as remixable.

In sum, Scott's Stretch Music project marks an important stage in the confluence of remix culture and jazz culture.

Conclusion

I have examined repetition in jazz, specifically the use of the turntable, arguing that jazz musicians helped pioneer active listening practices that would be foundational to how remix functions in our current times. Jazz musicians have used looping and mechanical copying techniques to create their sound. Repetition plays a special role in jazz culture. The turntable, the Play-A-Long record, and now the ASD and the Stretch Music app, provide musicians with the means to culturally recycle riffs, licks, melodies and solos. With the most recent jazz remix technology, Stretch Music, jazz musicians have a tool for *regenerative* remixing. Stretch Music is a user-activated album/tool. Scott's creation of a *remixable* jazz record blurs the difference between practicing and performing, giving the user greater control to determine the album's function. A reflection of both jazz culture and remix culture, Scott's project points the way forward for jazz players who have grown up listening to both Coltrane and NWA.

Notes

1 James Lincoln Collier, *Jazz: The American Theme Song* (New York: Oxford University Press, 1993), 152.
2 Burton W. Peretti, *The Creation of Jazz* (Champaign: University of Illinois Press 1992), 105.
3 The third and fourth technologies I examine are digital media applications, not literal turntables.
4 Peretti, *The Creation of Jazz*, 105.
5 Ibid.
6 Performances of Scott Joplin's "Maple Leaf Rag" (1899), for instance, did not tend to vary from person to person or region to region. The syncopated, improvised music of New Orleans musicians such as Keppard and Armstrong, on the other hand, had to be heard live to be understood.
7 www.jazzadvice.com/too-much-information-not-enough-knowledge.
8 Ibid.
9 Thank you to Eduardo Navas for this observation.
10 Ben Ratliff, *The Jazz Ear: Conversations Over Music* (London: Macmillan, 2008).
11 Ibid. 130.
12 Ibid. 132.
13 Ibid. 130.
14 Like the literary practice of allusion quoting is a form of intertextuality, often used to wink at fellow jazz musicians. Some jazzers frown on quoting, while other thrive on it. Once when I was listening to a live jazz performance with a fellow musician, he looked up at the stage and signed, "Oh him . . . he's one of those people who has to quote 'pink panther' every solo he takes." Bill Goodwin, the drummer for Phil Woods quartet, told me a story about one of the band's tours when the quoting had become so frequent that the band mates created a rule for evening performances—who ever caved first and put a quote in their solo would have to buy the first round of drinks for the night.
15 The beginnings of academic jazz culture can be traced to 1947, when University of North Texas became the first university to offer a degree in jazz studies. By the late 1950s, Stan Kenton pioneered the jazz summer camp, and by 1968, jazz educators created National Association of Jazz Educators (NJAE) to unify pedagogical efforts.
16 The Aebersold record series spawned dozens of imitators, such as the Hal Leonard "Jazz Play-Along" series. The Leonard line is also thriving, with hundreds of recordings and more than 30 differed subcategories within its Jazz Play-Along line.
17 Eitan Y. Wilf, *School for Cool: The Academic Jazz Program and the Paradox of Institutionalized Creativity* (Chicago: University of Chicago Press, 2014).
18 This is relevant to how Navas discusses different forms of remixes. Eduardo Navas, *Remix Theory: The Aesthetics of Sampling* (Vienna: Springer-Verlag, 2012), 67.
19 Ibid., 114.
20 www.npr.org/sections/ablogsupreme/2012/10/26/163741653/a-brief-history-of-jazz-education-pt-1 .
21 Wilf, *School for Cool*, 124, 139.
22 This worry is consistent with Navas's discussion of repetition as regression in the work of Jacques Attali and Tracy McMullen. See Navas, *Remix Theory*, 114–115.
23 www.ronimusic.com.
24 Ibid.
25 Take a second scenario, where the user also selectively remixes through the looping feature of ASD. Now we have a looped phrase, not in the original key and not at the original tempo. We still are operating at the level of allegory, since the purpose of the

loop is not to create an autonomous piece of culture, but to bring the player closer to Coltrane's exact pitches, rhythms and inflections.
26 www.jazzadvice.com/too-much-information-not-enough-knowledge.
27 Ibid.
28 The Stretch Music app is a mixing tool with a difference. Unlike Garageband or ProTools, it is not a general mixing tool for use in home or professional studio mixing. The tool works with just one commercially released album. The album can remix at will; the user controls whether the remix is pedagogical (used mostly as a practice tool) or otherwise.
29 "What is particular to new media is that the user plays a crucial role in activating the material, as the DJ does when s/he plays with vinyl records." Navas, *Remix Theory*, 75.
30 www.youtube.com/watch?v=v5eBHyh0o54.
31 Navas, *Remix Theory*, 73.

16
LOCATION

Dahlia Borsche, translated by Jill Denton

In the digital age, artifacts of cultural production can no longer be attributed mono-dimensionally to a single location. Similarly, locations, which at one point were current and went unchallenged in classic ethnological research, can now hardly be described in mono-cultural terms. The essentialist notion of a hegemonic cultural space has meanwhile ceded to complex cultural and transcultural references of self-referential protagonists. Eduardo Navas speaks in this context of a regenerative culture comprised of individual modules that can be recombined in endless variations.[1]

Yet this "remix culture" to which Navas refers is neither placeless nor located solely in virtual space. Remix culture (and indeed any cultural practice) *takes place* in a very literal sense, and its links with a location are a crucial indicator of style, genre, and so on, while remaining a primary classifier. Research into the location of culture (in particular in postcolonial studies), developed more or less apace with rapid digitization and the increasingly global reach of remix culture, and culminated in discourse that prompted what has come to be known as the transdisciplinary spatial turn. In this chapter, I intend to examine the interplay of the remix culture phenomenon and those theories of location and articulation that have been explicated to date in, and in relation to, postcolonial studies as well as in spatial theories prompted by the Actor Network Theory (ANT). My intention is not only to inquire where remix culture takes place, but also to demonstrate, first, how very much the practices of remix culture shape and give voice to the global order; and, second, how shifts within this order in turn spark and sustain remix practices.

Locating Remix (Culture)

The principle of recycling or of building on existing tangible and intangible cultural components is implicit in every cultural legacy known to mankind and by no means dates only from the first collage experiments of the early twentieth century avant-garde, as well as the *musique concrète* cut-and-paste techniques of the French composer Pierre Schaeffer and his circle. However, the advent of digital archives in which cultural artefacts can be stored and their availability maintained, perhaps indefinitely, has lent the recycling or building-on phenomenon a new dimension, one that is wholly distinct from previous cultural practices, and not only in terms of its pace. Not least thanks to the rise of remix as a creative act, this discrete phenomenon is now subsumed under the term "remix culture." The term encompasses all manner of cultural expression, from literature to the visual arts to music and so forth, although it originated in the pop music scene, more specifically in relation to DJ culture, in the latter half of the twentieth century. The remix concept first took hold in dub, a variation on Jamaican reggae, then in dance-floor variations on 1970s disco and then, more firmly, in the 1980s hip hop scene, before ultimately gaining fully fledged status as an independent art form in the electronic dance music context, at the latest by the 1990s. But music has a special role within remix culture not only because the latter term was coined in sound-based contexts. Also from the specific perspective of remix cultures and location, the observation of music-related phenomena is highly diagnostic. Sound, by its very nature, and even if in digital form, can hardly be pinned down to a specific place. I sought to express this thus, in an earlier paper:

> Sound has no place. Sound is immaterial and dynamic, conceivable solely as motion, for sound is nothing other than air that is made to vibrate. True, such vibrations permeate a certain space, but they also fade away, remain intangible. This is why even the sound-based art form, music, can never be pinned down to a specific place. Indeed it is difficult to say exactly where music is manifest: in a score, perhaps, of which generally several versions exist? In cultural memory, which is equally elusive? In the knowledge of those who perpetuate or make music, in concerts and performances? In the brains of the listeners, who process sound waves? Or in a recording, a CD or a file? There are no simple and, as a rule, only unsatisfactory answers to the question: "Where is music?"[2]

And one might likewise ask: "Where are remix cultures?" The cultural practices subsumed under this term are composed of countless set-pieces incessantly recombined in endless variations—and they make nonsense of notions such as "origins" and "original."[3] They are bereft of meaning also (or particularly) when references to location are brought into play.

"Schizophonia" is the term that sound-ecologist R. Murray Schafer coined back in the 1970s to highlight this phenomenon:[4] the confusion of the senses prompted by an inability to instantly locate the source of a sound, i.e., an inability to *place* a sound. It was only with recording techniques (starting with Edison's phonograph of 1877) that it became possible to separate sounds from the local specificities of their production. Previously, all sounds could only ever be heard at their point of origin and for as long as they lasted. Sound recordings and sound storage put an end to this, however. Thanks to the digital revolution, sounds today are more placeless than ever, deterritorialized; and they constantly reveal their capacity to break free and take root again, time after time, and to thereby continually generate new associations and meanings. And these dynamics have not only accelerated dramatically over the past few decades, but apply in equal measure to all other remix culture phenomena. Artifacts now switch location, are deconstructed, taken apart, mixed, recycled, alienated or appropriated quite literally at the speed of a single mouse click. Take, for example, an art-house film that references various global dance cultures and in which the actors' costumes and choreography draw on aspects of American hip hop as well as Japanese manga and South African rites while the genre code itself evokes classic film noir; and the director is British-born perhaps, but the production company is New York-based and most of the action unfolds on Berlin's backyards. The list could continue, so which location does the film represent? This fictitious case demonstrates how closely a sense of place is tied up with practices that instill a sense of identity, respectively how the traditional practice of attributing identity to a person or thing in terms of location is challenged by remix practices.

On Location and Hybridity

Similarly, various postcolonial theorists have challenged the notion of place-bound cultural identities, although Homi Bhabha's *The Location of Culture* (1994) is the landmark publication.[5] In this pioneering study, Bhabha turned the spotlight on the political dimension of locating culture by describing processes of cultural hybridization and the political implications of cultural identification strategies; and he thus made a far-reaching contribution to the then still relatively young discipline of postcolonial studies. Bhabha investigates processes of identity construction in the light of colonization, decolonization and re-colonization. His concept of hybridity seeks to undermine the binary oppositions that have hitherto structured perceptions of established cultures. Such simple dichotomies, posits Bhabha, are inadequate to grasp the complexities of the socio-political relations that shape identities. His concept of cultural hybridity implies that all cultures have always been hybrid and that all cultural formations are in a constant process of hybridization.[6] Simultaneously, he demonstrates that the agency of the colonized subject is no less than that of the colonizer, and that hybridization and the exertion of influence must be considered from a broad range of perspectives and the most diverse orientations.

Interestingly, one of his core concepts with regard to cultural hybridity is a location-based concept, although the location admittedly is fictitious, a mere metaphor. This "Third Space" is the place of transition, the point at which various identities meet, and at which friction and also ruptures occur. Bhabha does not mean by this only the simple accumulation of various influences, the adaptation or integration of cultural practices, but points out that encounters in this metaphorical space give rise to something new.

> The intervention of the Third Space of enunciation, which makes the structure of meaning and reference an ambivalent process, destroys this mirror of representation in which cultural knowledge is customarily revealed as an integrated, open, expanded code. Such an intervention quite properly challenges our sense of historical identity, of culture as a homogenizing, unifying force, authenticated by an originary Past, kept alive in the national tradition of the People. In other words, the disruptive temporality of enunciation displaces the narrative of the Western nation, which Benedict Anderson so perceptively describes as being written in homogeneous, serial time.[7]

Bhabha—like many of his peers both in postcolonial studies[8] and related late twentieth-century fields (such as post-structuralism or social constructivism)—explicitly refutes an essentialist notion of culture. The theory of essentialism, in brief, posits that cultures are homogeneous and self-contained entities with specific and necessary characteristics. This understanding of culture in turn fosters a notion of art that revolves around the work of art as the central figure. Essentialist notions of culture maintain the erroneous but persistent idea that an artwork somehow exists in and of itself, as an object with no connection at all to its contexts of production and reception—an idea fostered by the misleading expression "a piece of art." Scholars have long since mistakenly assumed that art can be treated as an object, and that works of art and cultural traditions can be studied and read as complete, unchanging entities. Yet to do so is not only to neglect the dynamic character of cultural formations but also to misread performance or communication (if they are considered at all) as mere by-products of the latter.

Such essentialist notions of culture are rooted in a concept of space known at least since the time of Albert Einstein under the name "container" but which advocates of the spatial turn have meanwhile completely debunked. The container concept suggests not only that space is a fixed, limited entity but also (since a container contains) that it has content. The concept was established *inter alia* by Isaac Newton, who took it as the premise of classical mechanics.[9] Building on the absolutist spatial concept of antiquity, he regarded space as being infinite, homogeneous and above all independent of the bodies in motion within it. In the twentieth century this deterministic concept of space underpinned the expansionist aspirations of fascist ideologies.[10] The container concept of space has moreover led to a practice that, above all when used for the purposes of identity politics, is highly problematic: namely, it considers a location (primarily a country) and a culture as synonyms, as if simply the act of drawing geographical borders were enough to distinguish cultural practices from one another as well as to fix their limits and impact. National identities are rooted not only in a common legislation but also to a great extent on cultural attributions. Especially in colonized, conquered or newly founded states, as in times of upheaval or post-war reconstruction, the myth of a locality's "own" culture is revived or simply invented in order to better cement the sense of collective identity among the more or less arbitrarily thrown together members of a labile community. Whether it is a case of right-wing movements recalling nationalist hymns or minorities invoking their cultural traditions as a means to counter cultural hegemony, the intent is always to foster or strengthen a sense of common identity. Culture serves in such cases to stake out certain territory, either ideological or (as with national borders) geopolitical. The practice of cultural mapping can therefore reveal a great deal about social orders, about power and empowerment, about political interests and resistance.[11]

On Remix and Mediation

Theories and practices of remix culture and the theoretical deliberations formulated in parallel in regards to the spatial turn hence pose a serious challenge to our established understanding of culture. Although the spatial turn has been driving new concepts in the sciences for decades, the idea that culture is generally site-specific is seemingly so self-evident as to remain a rarely challenged *topos*.[12] That the idea has taken root linguistically is obvious when we speak of culture "taking place."[13] The idea that culture and place are mutual determinants is so widespread and so deeply anchored in our conception of culture that it cannot be easily dismissed. On the contrary, location is still indisputably the classifier of choice, especially in the dynamic and flexible cultural products of remix culture.

To name a place is to offer easy orientation. Like personal names, the name of a place or a genre gives us an instant frame of reference, not least in music-related forms of culture.[14] A place name evokes associations and not infrequently allows a measure of aesthetic categorization or at least some insight into the personal background of whoever can call it home. Classifications of this sort are quickly snapped up in various fields, in the tourism sector, for example. The associations triggered by art thus become a trademark, an image, and hence a cliché; yet they generally remain potent nonetheless. Such clichés in turn help cement those frames of reference established by linking together various locations; and such links, once cemented, simplify the matter of attribution. Thus explicit reference to an artist's nationality is still commonplace in event programs and advertisements. An artist's background is not only named but also emphatically used as a marketing tool—and it often plays a role also in the staging of an event.[15] Likewise in artists' biographies and music journalism, to define a person or genre by naming numerous attributes is almost standard practice. Another reason to define the biographies of musicians, artists and producers in these terms is their respective credibility rating. Just as an artist's degree of credibility (cred) determines her or his ranking within a global hierarchy, so, too, her location assures a measure of orientation. To rank venues, cities or regions serves to put people "on the map" in terms of their geography or style, and hence, with nothing more than a few words or intimations, guarantees any reader capable of reading a map some insight into reassuring mines of information. Since the 1970s, cartographic tools have become an increasingly popular means to visualize complex cultural processes in various disciplines.

The major reason why locations still play an essential role not only in talk about remix culture but also in conceptions and configurations of it is the significance of the respective contexts in which it emerges and takes place. Digital art may be sourced, produced, encrypted, decrypted, dispatched and read in virtual spaces, but these virtual spaces and likewise digital data are always and everywhere bound up in a complex and polymorphous network of relationships. The contexts in which art takes place are constitutive of it to a significant degree: specific local factors—be it the role of, and value attributed to, art in a society; the resources there; the opportunities for education and performance; the legal framework and societal norms; the types of cultural venue and their attendant habitus—all have an enormous influence on the production and perception of culture. And such influence of whatever sort is inscribed in the configuration of meaning. Art is always embedded in local cultural practices, value systems, social structures or rituals and hence constitutes a cryptic system of signs that can be read (decrypted) only by those familiar with the aforementioned factors. Accordingly, art outside of its original context is subject to a transformation that automatically embeds it in a new system of signs.

My intent here, however, is not to simply reiterate a text-context dualism (that would, by the way, serve merely to perpetuate the old space-as-container trope) but, rather, to argue that cultural productions and all their parameters—including location—must be thought about in relational terms. Cultural phenomena gain their meaning through the interplay of various parameters. This alone explains why the same elements, once differently recombined (for example, at a different location) engender quite other associations and levels of meaning. The crucial point is that contexts themselves, unlike the traditional space-as-container trope, are permanently in flux. Locations are not fixed reference systems but serve, rather, as building blocks in the remix system. A location, be it a studio, a neighborhood, a concert hall or other public venue, not only influences the art that is performed live, heard, practiced, recorded or played back there but does so differently on each occasion. These variations also have an impact on locations, which absorb influences and then impart them further. A location is never the same from one moment to the next. In other words, locations are actants of cultural practice.

To regard culture as practice is no longer a groundbreaking idea. The performative turn has long since ensured that performance and practice rank among the leading topics in art-related research. Moreover, a group of scholars has been seeking for some time to accomplish a further turn by once and for all dispelling the last remnants of the classical notion that art is a representation or an object. Prompted by Actor Network Theory (ANT),[16] new paths to describing, localizing and analyzing social issues have been trodden in recent years in many disciplines— tellingly, also in the fields of geography and musicology. In geography it was first and foremost Sarah Whatmore, who succeeded in turning the discipline topsy-turvy with her controversial book *Hybrid Geographies* (2002), in which she posited that "geographies are not pure or discrete but hybrid and constituted through relations."[17] In musicology it is authors such as Antoine Hennion or Georgina Born who have drawn inspiration from ANT. A central premise for Born is that music must be imagined not as a representation but as a myriad of mediations. Neither music nor society exists "per se," i.e., in and of itself, in a vacuum, since each is the outcome of instances of mediation, which is to say, of agency. Music takes place on many different levels simultaneously. It is a diffuse and heterogeneous assemblage, "an aggregation of sonic, social, corporeal, discursive, visual, technical and temporal mediations."[18] It is not only a social practice but also generates social factors (for example, in the form of imagined communities). In this reading, to locate music is of relevance only when it serves to explain a certain practice, i.e., when it brings to light associations and agency; and, moreover, it only ever takes place on imaginary, transient maps.

If one extrapolates this argument in relation to remix culture, which is to say, if one regards remix culture as an aggregation of multiple mediations, then an explanatory model for various phenomena unfolds, one that can be observed in the location processes of these practices. As I briefly suggested above, a shift in meaning from the original to the transitional has taken place within remix practices. Artistic ambitions are no longer focused primarily on creating something new, on bringing forth "an original." At the zenith of remix culture are genres such as mashup, advocates of which seek explicitly to cobble together new creations from found material, which they either leave "as found" or reconfigure. References here are often consciously left visible yet the various strands attesting to origin or background may well be cut and pasted in such a way as to (intentionally) render their geographical classification impossible. This, of course, does not lessen the importance of originality. But remix culture no longer sets much store either by the concept of 'the original' or, in consequence, the origin of a thing. This is evident also from certain countertrends, which merely represent the other side of the coin, however, without refuting the fundamental concept. For example, artists such as Matthew Herbert endeavor to prove and legitimate the originality of their tracks and artistic oeuvre by assuring transparency with regard to the origins or sources of the sounds they use. In his manifesto, Herbert expressly forbids the use of pre-recorded material and calls upon all artists to use only sounds that they personally have discovered and recorded.[19] The appeal of his albums lies precisely in his treatment of source material: for example, he devotes one album completely to body noises and another to a pig that from its birth to its slaughter was his constant companion.[20]

But this approach, even in the work of Herbert, is simply a response to the development of digitization, just one way among many of playing the game; for without sleeve notes it would be impossible to decrypt the traces of his sounds. Therefore, even with this work ethic he cannot escape the fundamental shifts in meaning. For the shifts and metamorphoses in the practices of remix culture are so fast and so radical that such decryptions occur not so much wherever one tries to impart and to understand their origin but, rather, in the transitions, in the remixes or, to use Homi Bhabha's term, in the Third Space. Not that Bhabha, in his reading of hybridity, is concerned with tracing back to source, or deducing from, origins that must fundamentally be regarded as discrete—in the sense of this term as it has traditionally been used in biology. Bhabha, with his Third Space concept, opens up a space in which ruptures and paradoxes can occur and frictions arise, a space that reverberates with the actors who pass through it. He is concerned not with the origins of each actor, not with the possibility of tracing these exhaustively but, rather, with the potential that is unleashed at each point of rupture. Remix culture has no need of this origin to which Matthew Herbert still wants to cling but instead manifests itself time after time in practice; and despite this restless motion, it remains a stable means of forging identity. Mediation theory as defined by Georgina Born is a helpful means to grasp the great diversity and contrariety of transcultural processes, to address the dynamics between global remix streams and local variations, and to understand the permeability, fluidity and motion of remix cultures.

Perspectives (on Locating Remix)

To refute the importance of location, or of the original, in remix culture phenomena is, of course, not to imply that differences should be ignored. I am not at all in favor of diluting or denying local differences, or of the homogenization so long anticipated by critics of globalization. On the contrary, I believe that remix culture is the best medium through which to experience global diversity. But at the same time it irrefutably opens our eyes to the fact that cultural processes are fluid, permanently in flux, and that creativity and innovation are often particularly strong at points where cultural production is ambivalent, hybrid and transgressive. Or, to put it another way, there are of course significant differences between the various multifaceted remix culture phenomena, which, as I said above, can be explained at least in part by the contexts in which they originate. Admittedly, the outcomes no longer necessarily allow conclusions to be drawn about the latter's exact location. As Schafer's term schizophonia so aptly describes, remix culture practices typically no longer deliver that which was hitherto considered to be a reliable orientation aid.

Location processes have not become any less important in light of this development. It is more imperative than ever to question the strategies and interests that underpin localization. Mapping is not innocent. Thomas Swiss, John Sloop and Andrew Herman have written in this regard of the need for "a cartography of sound as a territory of power."[21] Remix culture can be read as a harbinger of an ever-more rapidly networking hybrid world in which borders shift and dissolve. Transcultural processes can serve then to foster understanding of migratory movements, new forms of social community and ways to overcome national states; and also to foster appreciation of the enormous potential and opportunities inherent to accelerated hybridization processes. In addition, taking remix culture seriously as a research topic opens up scope for new concepts and approaches articulated by self-referential actors in reflective and complex spaces of negotiation and action; and this not only refutes deterministic concepts of space but also sets up a genuine alternative to them.

Notes

1 Eduardo Navas, '"Regenerative Culture," 2016, accessed November 3, 2016, http://norient.com/academic/regenerative-knowledge-culture-part-15/.
2 Dahlia Borsche, "Locating Music," 2016, accessed November 3, 2016, http://norient.com/academic/locating-music/.
3 Walter Benjamin early posited that technical reproduction would put an end to the spheres of authenticity and originality in art (the aura of a work of art); Walter Benjamin, "The Work of Art in the Age of Mechanical Reproduction," in *Zeitschrift für Sozialforschung*. Paris: Librairie Felix Alcan, 1936.
4 R. Murray Schafer, *The Tuning of the World* (New York: Knopf, 1977).
5 Homi Bhabha, *The Location of Culture* (New York: Routledge, 1994).
6 Ibid., p. 129.
7 Ibid., p. 37.
8 For example, Edward Said, *Orientalism* (New York: Vintage Books, 1978).
9 Susanne Rau, *Räume. Konzepte, Wahrnehmungen, Nutzungen* (Frankfurt and New York: Campus Verlag, 2013), pp. 32ff.
10 Ibid., p. 61.
11 See Thomas Swiss, John Sloop and Andrew Herman, "Mapping the Beat: Spaces of Noise and Places of Music," in *Mapping the Beat: Popular Music and Contemporary Theory*, edited by Thomas Swiss, John Sloop and Andrew Herman (Malden, MA: Blackwell, 1998).
12 John Connell and Chris Gibson, *Sound Tracks. Popular Music, Identity and Place* (London: Routledge, 2003), pp. 90f.
13 Wim van der Meer, "The Location of Music: Towards a Hybrid Musicology," 2005, accessed November 3, 2016, www.academia.edu/340910/The_Location_of_Music_Towards_a_Hybrid_Musicology

14 Rau, *Räume*, p. 59.
15 A growing trend among artists in recent years has been to refuse such categorization. See, for example, Tara Transitory aka One Man Nation, a performance artist who does not wish to be identified in terms of gender or nationality and therefore withholds the relevant information as best they can.
16 For further information, see, for example, Bruno Latour, *Reassembling the Social: An Introduction to Actor-Network-Theory* (Oxford: Oxford University Press, 2005).
17 Sarah Whatmore, *Hybrid Geographies: Natures Cultures Spaces* (London: Sage, 2002).
18 Georgina Born, "Mediation Theory," in *The Routledge Reader of the Sociology of Music*, edited by John Shepherd and Kyle Devine (London: Routledge, 2015) 359.
19 Herbert, "Manifesto," accessed November 22, 2016, http://matthewherbert.com/about-contact/manifesto/.
20 Herbert, "Bodily Functions" (K7 Records/soundlike 2001); "One Pig" (Accidental 2011).
21 Swiss et al., "Mapping the Beat," p. 17.

Bibliography

Benjamin, Walter. "The Work of Art in the Age of Mechanical Reproduction." In *Zeitschrift für Sozialforschung*. Paris: Libraire Felix Alcan, 1936.
Bhabha, Homi. *The Location of Culture*. New York: Routledge, 1994.
Born, Georgina. "Mediation Theory." In *The Routledge Reader of the Sociology of Music*, edited by John Shepherd and Kyle Devine. London: Routledge, 2015.
Borsche, Dahlia. "Locating music." *Norient.com*, 2016. Accessed November 3, 2016. http://norient.com/academic/locating-music/.
Connell, John, and Gibson, Chris. *Sound Tracks. Popular Music, Identity and Place*. London: Routledge, 2003.
Herbert. "Manifesto." Accessed November 22, 2016. http://matthewherbert.com/about-contact/manifesto/
———. "Bodily Functions." K7 Records/soundlike 2001.
———. "One Pig." Accidental 2011.
Latour, Bruno. *Reassembling the Social: An Introduction to Actor-Network-Theory*. Oxford: Oxford University Press, 2005.
van der Meer, Wim. "The Location of Music: Towards a Hybrid Musicology," 2005. Accessed November 3, 2016, www.academia.edu/340910/The_Location_of_Music_Towards_a_Hybrid_Musicology.
Navas, Eduardo. "Regenerative Culture." 2016. Accessed November 3, 2016, http://norient.com/academic/regenerative-knowledge-culture-part-15/.
Rau, Susanne. *Räume. Konzepte, Wahrnehmungen, Nutzungen*. Frankfurt and New York: Campus Verlag, 2013.
Said, Edward. *Orientalism*. New York: Vintage Books, 1978.
Schafer, Murray. *The Tuning of the World*. New York: Knopf, 1977.
Swiss, Thomas, Sloop, John, and Herman, Andrew, eds. *Mapping the Beat: Popular Music and Contemporary Theory*. Malden, MA: Blackwell, 1998.
Whatmore, Sarah. *Hybrid Geographies: Natures Cultures Spaces*. London: Sage, 2002.

17
MASHUP

Nate Harrison and Eduardo Navas

The origin of the word "mashup" remains vague. In terms of common usage it dates back to at least the 1960s, though Charles Dickens used the term as early as the 1850s to describe two characters (Mr. and Mrs. Mashup) in one of his stories.[1] In the early 2000s, the term mashup commonly described a particular practice of combining two music recordings.

As the word became more popular, mashup began to be applied to the process of combining other materials. In media this included memes, videos, and still images. Music mashups became even more popular as producers incorporated corresponding video edits as part of an overall multimedia expression. Subgenres eventually developed, such as critical and political remix videos, as well as mashup memes. The concept of the mashup was eventually extended to software development, and became an all-encompassing descriptive term for the general amalgam of two sources that, be it music, image, or code, retained a clear recognition between its various elements. Mashup is often used in direct relation to the act of remixing. While the two terms, mashup and remix, are often used interchangeably, there are some notable differences. This becomes clear once we outline the history of mashup. In what follows, we consider the basic meaning of the term mashup, and then describe its evolution from music to software and culture at large. We end with a reflection on how mashups open the possibility of a third meaning that points to different ways of engagement with remixed source material.

Definition of Mashups

The terms "mashup" and "mash up" in English appear in print in the 1850s (Figures 17.1).[2] The way the words have been used appears to allude simply to bringing two or more things together, as in mashing potatoes with other ingredients such as lentils and meat.[3] From the 1960s to 1980s, the term appeared in Caribbean literature.[4] "All he foot get mashup" denoted that a person's foot or leg was physically injured.[5] Attributing a definitive source of origin for the term is likely impossible. Yet one can infer from reviewing the literature that mashup usually implies the combination of at least two things, or to smash or destroy something. These connotations are worth keeping in mind because they both play an aesthetic role in many creative productions that are considered mashups.

Used as a verb in the context of music, "mash" can be traced back at least to Jamaican patois from the early 1970s. In the island's reggae and dancehall music, MCs would occasionally proclaim "mash it up!" as a way to build energy during performance. To "mash," then, was a general call to succeed, to do well, to push the music's "vibe" forward, not unlike hip hop MCs shouting "put your hands in the air!" In one example, the UK roots band Steel Pulse's pro-marijuana 1977

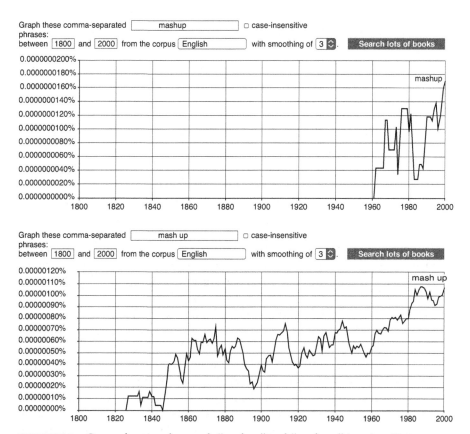

FIGURE 17.1 nGrams showing the words "mashup" and "mash up" in print. Note that some of the material found online in the 1960s are actually scans of publications from previous years.

FIGURE 17.2 "Mash Down" by the Roots, 1977.

anthem "Makka Splaff (The Colly Man)," we hear "Mash it Grizzly!"—a directive to percussionist Steve "Grizzly" Nisbett, who responds with a bombastic drum fill.[6]

To mash also gives music a political dimension. Just as the term was used as a call to build up, so too it could be a signal to tear down, or wipe away. Both the up and down variations retain a positive and cathartic element—both express a process of purification. More specifically, following the Jamaican Rastafari movement and its criticism of imposed Western values (crass materialism, colonialism, racial injustice), to mash *down* is to destroy, to purge, to resist. In the 1977 track "Mash Down," the Roots tell listeners: "We're going to mash down principalities and wickedness," in reference to doing away with the corrupt Babylon culture foisted onto otherwise peaceful and natural people (Figure 17.2).[7]

Just how these Jamaican uses of "mash" carry forward into contemporary music mashup culture can be perceived to some degree when we look at the way the word was used in Caribbean literature, as Jamaican diaspora took place during the 1960s.[8] Thus, while one could argue that there seems to be no direct link from earlier manifestations to the common usage found in music and culture at large, it certainly is not unreasonable to surmise some sort of relation, if only because so many aspects of remix culture today can be traced back to Jamaican reggae, dub, and dancehall music. Following these earlier moments, the term appears to denote a particular subset of remix music practices, crossing over to the United States and other parts of the world in the early 2000s that are characterized by the concept of combining two songs together. Soon after, the definition expanded even further, with mashup being used to describe a certain strain of software development. The term at the time of this writing designates generally all types of combinations, from music to video editing to software.

Music Mashups

In typical formulations, music mashups consist of the vocal track of one song overlaid on the instrumental track of another. The contrast between the two recordings as they are heard together reveals the artistic intent, and is not without historical precedent. Before music mashups developed into a fully fledged genre of remix, audio collage artists had experimented with splicing together bits of analog audio tape and vinyl records to produce a *third recording*. Examples include Christian Marclay's avant-garde turntablism, John Oswald's "plunderphonics," and Negativland's culture-jamming audio collages. The most notorious early, proto-mashup is Negativland's "U2," which layered music from the Irish pop group U2's "I Still Haven't Found What I'm Looking For" with an expletive-laden rant from Casey Kasem, one of the most familiar and family-oriented top-40 pop radio voices in the United States (Figure 17.3). The resulting sonic train

FIGURE 17.3 Negativland, "U2," EP released in 1991.

wreck landed Negativland in legal trouble: U2's record labels sued the band for copyright and trademark infringement.[9]

Moving from parody and media critique to homage, one of the first recordings to define mashup as a music genre was "A Stroke of Genie-us" by Roy Kerr, also known as Freelance Hellraiser, released in 2001. Kerr combined the pulsing rock of NYC-based alternative band the Strokes's "Hard To Explain" with pop diva Christina Aguilera's vocals in "Genie in a Bottle."[10] Soon thereafter, mashup productions abounded. Other notable artists include Mark Vidler, working under the alias Go Home Productions, whose "Ray of Gob" from 2003 combined the Sex Pistols "God Save the Queen" with Madonna's "Ray of Light."[11] In 2004, Brian Burton, operating as Danger Mouse, released *The Grey Album* (Figure 17.4), which sampled the *a cappella* rap from Jay-Z's *The Black Album* with instrumentation from the Beatles' *White Album*.[12] Danger Mouse's new creation quickly became one of the most

> For more on *The Grey Album*, see Chapter 10, "Deconstruction."

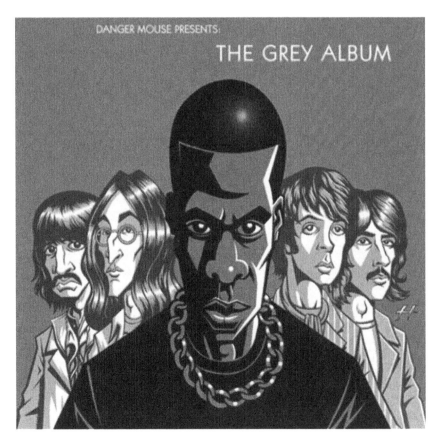

FIGURE 17.4 Danger Mouse, *The Grey Album*, released in 2004.

well-known and controversial mashups of its time when the original copyright holders demanded that the album cease distribution. Terry Urban, Girl Talk, 2ManyDJs, DJ Earworm, and Tom Caruana are just a few of the mashups artist to gain critical and commercial success for their innovative mashup productions in the first decade of the twenty-first century. At this point, mashup as an established genre of music is ubiquitous, with music festival stalwarts such as those mentioned above appearing in playlists alongside unknown bedroom studio musicians. On a formal level, mashups have become increasingly sophisticated, with artists collaging and reconfiguring dozens of songs in the space of mere minutes.

The rise of music mashup culture would not have been possible without parallel developments in digital audio technologies. In the early 2000s, new computer software solutions made it possible to manipulate audio data in ways that were not previously available to average users. Software offerings such as Ableton Live introduced the ability to easily decouple audio *frequency* from audio *speed*, in real time. Anyone who has played vinyl records on a conventional turntable will recall that slowing down (or speeding up) the rate of the record's rotation also shifts the pitch of the music. Playing records faster than they are intended produces the "chipmunk" effect to vocal tracks. Newer software algorithms removed this limitation, allowing users to adjust the tempo of a recording while maintaining its pitch, or, conversely, to alter the pitch while keeping the tempo. This made it possible to "lock" two songs of originally different styles to a master tempo, ensuring that they were precisely in sync. Additionally, since pitch became a variable unto itself, songs originally produced in differing keys could be adjusted and blended harmoniously. Users found they could combine songs from almost any genre together into new and unusual, yet still musically coherent, expressions.

Music mashups fly in the face of many conventions. Like remix in general, they call into question long-established notions of authorship, artistic labor, and originality. Mashups also subvert standard methods of distribution. Emerging at the outset of Web 2.0 and social media, mashups are forms of expression made for and by the Internet. It is online—source materials often reside there in the first place—where mashups ultimately live as new expressions ready for download. Traded around the Internet for little or no money, they embody the "free culture" aesthetics of recycling and sharing.[13] They also provoke the ire of copyright holders, which is why, in the early 2000s, mashups were also sometimes referred to as "bootleg remixes," unauthorized reinterpretations of one-hit wonders and obscure tracks alike. Mashups continue to test the boundaries of copyright law as well as the ethics of creativity.

Mashups, like other remix practices, sprout from DIY initiatives. Given that the Internet, in conjunction with new software technologies, helped empower everyday computer users operating outside the specialized field of professional audio production, music mashups can be placed on the continuum of remix as amateur cultural phenomenon. Mashups are a type of digital folk music. Just as young people in the Bronx "misused" turntables when they repurposed them as music instruments and in turn invented hip hop, so too have technically savvy younger generations realized the potential of manipulating computer data towards a new aesthetics. And it is not merely music that is mashed up; any type of data, from video footage to Microsoft Word documents can be used, even abused, in order to create something new that paradoxically thrives on the recognition of the combined elements.

Mashups and Memes

Like software developments in the audio domain, still and moving image editing options, aided by speedy Internet circulation, also opened up creative avenues for everyday users. Long the staple for retouching and color correcting images, Adobe's Photoshop application would become an essential tool in the service of combining images and text together in order to produce new meanings for old pictures. At this point, mashing up images and text in the hope that they "go viral" as memes has become so commonplace that smart phone applications, such as Make a Meme+, Meme Producer, and Meme Generator, now exist to make the process easier. In short, anyone can make a mashup meme. Thus, no definitive example can be offered. There is, however, a common format: one or two images, positioned one on top of the other or side by side, with a pithy phrase or two written (often in the typeface Impact). The sources in meme creation often come from still shots from Hollywood films or television shows, but just about any image can be used. The accompanying text messages can range from the nonsensical to the hyper-partisan.

Multiple contributors to this volume collaborated on Chapter 18 for a discussion on the keyword "Memes."

Meme mashups have also gained popularity as videos uploaded to the Internet and as visuals screened in live performances. New video hardware and software tools such as Roland's DVJ-1000 and the Vegas editing platform have come into wider use, with the effect that the boundary between mashing up music and moving image collage is practically seamless. Moreover, the syncing of music mashups with corresponding archival video of musicians' performances have yielded an entirely new, hybrid remix artist: the "VJ." The UK audio/video mashup group Eclectic Method combine footage of the Jackson 5 or James Brown with contemporary electronic music to deliver a schizophrenic dance club visual experience (Figure 17.5).[14]

The musical collective The Gregory Brothers have produced some of the more notable Internet video mashup memes over the past several years. Their *Songify the News* (previously *Autotune the News*) is a series of videos featuring clips taken from local TV news reporting and "talking head" news shows mixed with green-screened live musical performances of members of the group.[15] Many of their videos provide entertaining vignettes into current events, although like some past

FIGURE 17.5 Eclectic Method, screen shot from "Eclectic Method—A Brief History of Sampling."

artists who appropriate from mass media content, there can be an ambiguity to the messaging. They are at once an indictment and trivialization of media sensationalism.

The Internet meme achieves its highest status, and perhaps loses its vitality, when it reaches a state of self-awareness. There is no better example than the "Hitler/Downfall" video mashups. In contrast to the complex editing found in the examples above, these memes, all taken from the 2004 German film *Downfall*, recycle the same scene—Hitler in his final moments within a Berlin bunker—swapping out only the English subtitles in order to deliver their message. In one video, the doomed leader lashes out at his inner circle after discovering the iPhone 7 has no headphone jack; in another, he decries Britain leaving the European Union. Yet its ultimate expression is found in a version in which Hitler's attack is directed at the meme itself: he assails his military advisers for allowing the "Radiohead Lotus Flower" meme mashup to surpass it in popularity.[16] It could be said that the longest-lasting mashup memes are those that include within them a statement about their own role in contemporary media consumption.

Mashup memes tend to take on many forms, including copying from all possible sources of media. The "Downfall" and "Lotus Flower" examples are a case in point.[17] In the former, it is text—in the form of subtitles—that is mashed against image and sound. In the latter, it is sound against not just image, but styles of editing (fast, slow, and selective omission of frames, among other strategies) that provides the creative drive for the respective memes.

Software Mashups

In technical terms, code is the common link between music mashups, meme mashups, and what has come to be known as "software mashups." Computing made sampling and all other types of music manipulation configurable, which then enabled the treatment of sound as data. The term mashup was used in relation to software around the year 2006, in parallel to the rise of music mashups.[18] Software mashups are networked applications; they cannot function unless they are able to access data from two or more sources. The term is now part of the technical vernacular of software development. Both Techopedia and Wikipedia define software mashups as web applications—as webpages that bring two or more sources together in a new presentation.[19] Techopedia more explicitly states that this combination creates "a new service." While these definitions may not be academic, they are what most people will encounter when searching for the definitions of software mashups, insofar as they describe the vernacular, and are what most individuals engaged in developing software will read. The definitions are also evidently driven by commercial, or at least utilitarian, interests.

Software mashups became common in the initial stages of Web 2.0. Early examples include news feeds, as well as maps with specific local information. The basic principle of all mashups is the extraction of information from two or more sources. Mashups repurpose sources for a different function, thereby potentially creating a new use from their pre-existing purposes. An early example that is no longer active is Pipes by Yahoo![20] This particular type of mashup would provide access to dynamic information directly from the database. What Pipes by Yahoo! explored early on was the possibility, which is now taken for granted, that users could customize, to a sophisticated level, the type of information that they accessed from day to day. Pipes, in its own way, provided users with the same possibilities made available by early Google news feeds, when users customized their personal portal news page. In software mashups, the actual code of the copied applications is not accessed; such mashups are usually combined with a type of "binding" technology. One can think of pre-existing applications (or "apps") as building blocks designed for modular implementation. A basic and early software mashup technique is described as "scraping"; it consists of lifting material from the front pages of various websites to aggregate it. This practice is now commonly exercised online whenever web developers embed prepared scripts that are made available across online platforms, such as YouTube, Instagram, or Flickr. Other types of mashups actually embed or incorporate material directly from databases, according to permissions allocated by the online entity with an Application Programming Interface (API).[21] Using an API, developers aggregate specific information for their platform, which provides a unique experience for the user. Pinterest is a clear example of this type of approach, which in effect creates a platform for sharing unique content, based on borrowed data as well as the relation of selections to and by each user. What can be noted in the above examples is that a software mashup is only stable as long as the sources offering the information maintain open APIs.

The conceptual and cultural role of mashups changed dramatically when they evolved from the music realm to a more open media space such as the web. While the software mashup operates mostly for lucrative purposes closely justified with practical use and convenience for users, it has been shown repeatedly that social media platforms, which allow narrow and specific API access to their content, are being repurposed in the service of social change as a response to major current events.[22] For example, the mashing of information to be shared continuously played a significant role in the Arab Spring, which relied on social media in order to communicate and organize activist actions in countries such as Egypt and Tunisia.[23] Mashups also played a role in the Charlie Hebdo events, as people in France organized acts of peaceful resistance against terrorist attacks.[24] In these cases, all types of information were shared, from locations on maps to images from specific areas, which were then accessed across social media platforms such as Facebook and Twitter.

There are thousands of software mashups available at the time of this writing. Some examples include Trendsmap,[25] which continues to implement the text over map approach explored early on by Google and Yahoo![26] Another notable mashup that functions more as a work of art is "Spell with Flickr,"[27] which uses Flickr's API in order to mashup images of letters in a "ransom-note" style, spelling out phrases entered by the user.

The concept of mashing pre-existing data has led to an exponential increase in online content development. In turn, the idea of repurposing information allows network culture to increase its activity to a degree that would be impossible if the sharing of content were not understood as a vital strategy for communication, as well as the growth of global markets. In a sense, then, the term mashup has been co-opted for the sake of the growth of an emerging "productivist" culture, which itself is a hybrid of property interests and an open sharing of information.

Mashups as Third Meaning

Mashups are ubiquitous. They are the contemporary embodiment of remix culture. And while the remix can be understood as a type of general collage practice whose sources may not be readily identifiable, the same cannot be said of mashups in particular. A defining characteristic of the mashup, whether it is music, image, or software, is that its elements operate together but remain discrete. Indeed, part of the success of the mashup has to do with the thrill of being able to identify these elements as they take on new meanings in the process of their combination. An evolved form of the *third meaning*, to invoke Roland Barthes, is produced.[28] This is especially the case in creatively expressed mashups, which oblige us to reexamine our own relationships to both their content and form.

The third meaning, for Barthes, is particularly pronounced in carefully selected still images from films. He tends to privilege images that offer a state of ambiguity, which, in turn, put in question the context of the image. Barthes focuses on images that expose the slippage of meaning within the overall narrative of a story. His basic theory of the third meaning, which is an early post-structural reflection that in effect questions early structural theories, exposes the instability of conventional understanding within a carefully structured narrative. The third meaning—that slippage in understanding is today generally considered to be part of all forms of communication, and is essential to creative productions that strive to provide an ambiguous or open-ended reading, while also pointing to how they are themselves structured.

Mashups certainly take the aesthetics of the third meaning in their own way. Music in particular, due to the art form's close relation to the abstract and open-ended experience, is ripe to explore the third meaning when combining elements that show the instability of the sign, demanding a reaction from the listener. The mashup is an "obtuse" form of signification that exposes the instability of its elements (content and form) as they are brought together. The obtuse meaning is the product of a fourth, semiological element called *signifiance* (following the research of Julia Kristeva). In its own way, the mashup brings together two elements that already possess several signifiers and signifieds (pre-existing concepts and forms). Such elements can be mashed up in ways that may come off as inconceivable, or perhaps even violent or destructive. The undecidability in meaning is produced when one hears two or more elements at play that seem autonomous, yet are bound as one new expression that both fights and embraces itself while exuding something completely different. This can help explain why some of the most acclaimed mashups, particularly in music, bring together compositions that would not immediately seem to complement each other. Music genres that would seem incongruous—country and hip hop, bubblegum pop and black metal—blend naturally, though the results certainly vary.

One of the affective results is that of the feeling of nostalgia, as evoked by Vidler's "Ray of Gob," or DJ Earworm's megamixes, known as United States of Pop, which mash all of the top 40 hits at the end of each year.[29] Another example is found in the recent album *Mouth Moods*, in which producer Neil Cicierega takes the listener on an aural journey through 1990s pop music.[30] Anyone who experienced the decade firsthand will immediately identify with Cicierega's mix. It has the capacity to induce memories that are nonetheless made strange, as layered snippets of tracks contrast with one another. Old meets new, fragments of history reshape future listening traditions, experienced in the present.

Yet mashups are more than new formalizations of past content. Decidedly more critical in his intent, mashup video artist Jonathan McIntosh remixes pop culture in order to expose its ideological aspects. McIntosh's 2009 video mashup "Buffy vs. Edward: *Twilight* Remixed" intercuts clips from the TV series *Buffy the Vampire Slayer* with scenes from the film *Twilight* to jab at the gender stereotypes, and male sexual aggression, that permeates mass entertainment.[31] In 2010, McIntosh parodied right wing political talking points in the mashup "Donald Duck Meets Glenn Beck in Right Wing Radio Duck," in which the viewer encounters a working-class

This mashup is discussed at length in Chapter 8, "Creativity."

Donald Duck eventually resisting the sway of radio talk show host Glenn Beck. Beck reacted to the video by calling it "some of the best propaganda" he'd ever seen.[32] More recently McIntosh has repurposed his mashup approach to produce short documentaries that fall under critical remix videos, thus joining the ranks of Elisa Kreisinger, Diran Lyons, Desiree D'Alessandro, Anita Sarkeesian, and Owen Gallagher, among many others. Mashups, arguably, are the most transparent form of cultural recombination currently being produced, in any form, from music to text to video to software. The mashup proudly displays the way we bring ideas and forms together. For all of its controversy, it is an unabashed form of remix that openly presents itself as such.

Notes

1. Charles Dickens, "Literal Claims," *Household Words* (Leipzig: Bernhard Tauchnitz, 1856), 252
2. See the ngrams for "mashup" and "mash up" at https://books.google.com/ngrams/graph?content=mashup&year_start=1800&year_end=2000&corpus=15&smoothing=3&share=&direct_url=t1%3B%2Cmashup%3B%2Cc0#t1%3B%2Cmashup%3B%2Cc0; https://books.google.com/ngrams/graph?content=mash+up&year_start=1800&year_end=2000&corpus=15&smoothing=3&share=&direct_url=t1%3B%2Cmash%20up%3B%2Cc0, accessed March 15, 2017
3. Henry Doubleday Research Association. Newsletter, Issues 52–58, 1973, 48 https://books.google.com/books?id=HOcnAQAAIAAJ&q=%22mashup%22&dq=%22mashup%22&hl=en&sa=X&ved=0ahUKEwiYgKaCoKnSAhVFWCYKHQ9pDRUQ6AEIIDAB, accessed March 15, 2017,
4. Earl Lovelace *A Brief Conversion and Other Stories* (Austin: Pearlson Education,1988); see also N. Ramadevi, *The Novels of V.S. Naipaul: Quest for Order and Identity* (Ann Arbor: Prestique Books, 1996), 49.
5. Dennis Solomon, *The Speech of Trinidad: A Reference Grammar* (Kingston: University of West Indies, 1993), 54.
6. Steel Pulse, "Makka Splaff," www.youtube.com/watch?v=uqr1tuCfMMw, accessed March 15, 2017
7. The Roots, "Mash Down 12," www.youtube.com/watch?v=aoCZNIrz2o4, accessed March 14, 2017. Thank you to Peter Becker for helping trace the earlier Jamaican references.
8. A good account of this can be found in Dick Hebdige, *Cut 'N' Mix* (New York: Routledge, 1987).
9. See Negativland, *Fair Use: The Story of the Letter U and the Numeral 2* (Concord, CA: Seeland, 1995).
10. Freelance Hellraiser, "A Stroke of Genie-us," www.youtube.com/watch?v=ShPPbT3svAw , accessed March 14, 2017.
11. Go Home Productions, "Ray of Gob," www.youtube.com/watch?v=wrjSlTeTpNc , accessed March 14, 2017.
12. Danger Mouse, *The Grey Album*, www.mixcloud.com/SoulCoolRecords/danger-mouse-the-grey-album/, accessed March 14, 2017.
13. See Lawrence Lessig, *Free Culture: How Big Media Uses Technology and the Law to Lock Down Culture and Control Creativity* (New York: Penguin, 2004).
14. See www.eclecticmethod.net/video/, accessed March 14, 2017.
15. See www.thegregorybrothers.com, accessed March 14, 2017.

16 "Hitler Learns of Radiohead's Lotus Flower Video Parodies," www.youtube.com/watch?v=Fvo45_kXogs (accessed March 14, 2017).
17 For an extensive analysis of these memes see Eduardo Navas, "Modular Complexity and Remix: The Collapse of Time and Space into Search," *Anthrovision* 1.1, 2013, https://anthrovision.revues.org/324, accessed March 8, 2017.
18 Christian Bizer, Richard Cyganiak, and Tobias Gauss "The RDF Book Mashup: From Web APIs to a Web of Data," Document1www.online-journals.org/index.php/proceedings/article/viewFile/229/161, accessed March 15, 2017.
19 https://en.wikipedia.org/wiki/Mashup_(web application hybrid) and www.techopedia.com/definition/5373/mashup, accessed March 15, 2017.
20 This site is no longer online. Wikipedia provides a decent summary of how it functioned: https://en.wikipedia.org/wiki/Yahoo!_Pipes.
21 There are many resources online that provide this general information. For a concise reference see "Content Development Guidelines," Akana, http://docs.akana.com/cm/learnmore/api_admin_content_guidelines.htm, accessed March 15, 2017.
22 See Eduardo Navas, "Remix[ing] Theory," in *Remix Theory: The Aesthetics of Sampling* (Wien, New York: Springer, 2012), 100–108.
23 Phillip N. Howard et al., "Opening Close Regimes: What was the Role of Social Media during the Arab Spring," http://collectiondevelopment.library.cornell.edu/mideast/Role%20of%20Social%20Media%20During%20the%20Arab%20Spring.pdf, accessed March 15, 2017.
24 Mark Deuze, "A Call for Comparison in Social Media," *Social Media + Society*, http://journals.sagepub.com/doi/pdf/10.1177/2056305115580333, accessed March 15, 2017. The article actually refers to a rather popular post on *The Guardian*: Jane Martinson, "Charlie Hebdo: A Week of Horror When Social Media Came into its Own," Document1www.theguardian.com/media/2015/jan/11/charlie-hebdo-social-media-news-readers, accessed March 15, 2017.
25 Trendsmaps, http://trendsmap.com/, accessed March 14, 2017.
26 Tweetping, https://tweetping.net/, accessed March 14, 2017.
27 "Spell with Flickr," http://metaatem.net/words/, March 14, 2017.
28 Roland Barthes, "The Third Meaning," in *Image, Music, Text* (New York: Hill & Wang, 1977), 52–68.
29 "United States of POP Series," http://djearworm.com/UnitedStateOfPop.php, accessed March 14, 2017.
30 See Neil Cicierega, "Mouth Moods," https://soundcloud.com/neilcic/mouth-moods, accessed March 14, 2017.
31 See "Donald Duck Meets Glenn Beck in Right Wing Radio Duck," www.youtube.com/watch?v=HfuwNU0jsk0, accessed March 14, 2017.
32 See "Insider Video of Glenn Beck Responding to Donald Duck Remix (2010)," www.youtube.com/watch?annotation_id=annotation_406592&feature=iv&src_vid=HfuwNU0jsk0&v=1ytW9l7TBI8, accessed March 14, 2017.

Bibliography

DiCola, Peter and Kembrew McLeod. *Creative License: The Law and Culture of Digital Sampling*. Durham, NC: Duke University Press, 2011.
Gunkel, David. J. *Of Remixology: Ethics and Aesthetics After Remix*. Cambridge, MA: MIT Press, 2015.
Hebdige, Dick. *Cut 'N' Mix: Culture, Identity and Caribbean Music*. New York: Routledge, 1987.
Hegarty, Paul. *Noise/Music: A History*. New York and London: Continuum, 2008.

Kuenzli, Rudolf and Kembrew McLeod. *Cutting Across Media: Appropriation Art, Interventionist Collage, and Copyright Law.* Durham, NC: Duke University Press, 2011.

Reynolds, Simon. *Retromania: Pop Culture's Addiction to Its Own Past.* New York: Faber & Faber, 2011.

Shifman, Limor. *Memes in Digital Culture.* Cambridge, MA: MIT Press, 2013.

Sinnreich, Aram. *Mashed Up: Music, Technology and the Rise of Configurable Culture.* Amherst and Boston: University of Massachusetts Press, 2010.

Sonvilla-Weiss, Stefan. Editor. *Mashup Cultures.* Wien and New York: Springer, 2010.

Sullivan, Paul. *Remixology: Tracing the Dub Diaspora.* London: Reaktion Books, 2014.

Veal, Michael E. *Dub: Soundscapes & Shattered Songs in Jamaican Reggae.* Middletown, CT: Wesleyan University Press, 2007.

18
MEMES

Authored in Collaboration with Contributors

Authors included in *Keywords in Remix Studies* contributed a meme of their choice for this chapter. Authors were asked to share their thoughts as openly as possible, which resulted in some entries being longer than others. Each author is attributed at the end of their respective entries. This collaborative approach aims to provide an intertextual relation among the selected memes and the chapter contributions. In this way, this chapter functions as a megamix of the many interests at play throughout the essays in the compilation.

> an 'internet meme' is a hijacking of [an] original idea [but] instead of mutating by random change and spreading by a form of Darwinian selection, they are altered deliberately by human creativity. Unlike with genes (and Dawkins' original meaning of "meme"), there is no attempt at accuracy of copying; internet memes are deliberately altered.[1]

Political Memes

My suggestion for a meme would be the use of the image of Princess Leia as an icon of the Women's Marches protesting Donald Trump's inauguration to president (Figure 18.1). There are many versions of this image but this one is a good example.

The selection of this particular image is most likely a byproduct of two factors—the return of *Star Wars* as a core text in contemporary popular culture (and especially the image of Princess Leia from *A New Hope* as seen most recently in *Rogue One*) and the public awareness surrounding the death of actress Carrie Fisher just a few weeks before the marches. Recalling Fisher had led to greater public awareness of her off-screen personality, including her outspoken feminism and her criticisms of Donald Trump through the years. These two popular memories

FIGURE 18.1 Princess Leia as an icon of the Women's Marches, 2017.

come together to insure the widespread embrace of this particular meme in the first wave of protest following Trump's transition to power.

Henry Jenkins et al.[2]

The pussyhat is a symbol of protest against rape culture in which sexual assault is perpetuated by behaviors such as those exhibited by men at the highest leadership positions in the United States (Figure 18.2).

From a new materialism perspective, I have selected an object—the pussyhat—as a meme. It is not only the object or its pattern circulated on the Internet but the making of the object and the wearing of it by millions of women throughout the world with variations but distinctly a pussyhat; and then posting the photos of wearing a pussyhat as part of a protest march. The pussyhat functions as a meme on the terms of its continued use, reuse, and circulation.

Karen Keifer-Boyd

The Koi Dance (Love Dance) from a Japanese TV drama became a video meme in late 2016 in Japan and beyond. The dance was originally the ending music video of a TV drama that raised discussions about compensation for women's work as housewives. Many people, including the U.S. Embassy in Tokyo (Figure 18.3) recreated the dance video and it became a social phenomenon in Japan.

FIGURE 18.2 Karen Keifer-Boyd wearing the pussyhat at the Women's March in 2017.

FIGURE 18.3 The Koi Dance (Love Dance) as an online video meme.

Although, similar to many other memes, for most people, the intention to participate and recreate the dance video was fun, entertaining, and trending, the popularity of the dance video meme brought attention to the TV drama and, subsequently, the issues of often invisible economic impact of housewives and the equality of men and women in marriage. I consider this an example of meme that had a social impact.

Christine Liao[3]

Although this meme is stereotypical in its presentation (white Impact font, appropriated image from the 1980s), it nonetheless performs what memes ought to: critical reflection of the status quo. In their better iterations, they destabilize the present by defamiliarizing the commonplace, putting politics front and center (Figure 18.4).

Nate Harrison

FIGURE 18.4 "Smoking in the boys' room" becomes "Vaping in the gender neutral bathroom" in this meme critical of the status quo.

FIGURE 18.5 La Paz Dancing Zebra Meme, available on green screen for global remix opportunities.

A March 2017 transnational meme that exemplifies sharable culture is the La Paz, Bolivia zebra, introduced on John Oliver's show *Last Week Tonight* (Figure 18.5). The dancers in zebra costumes are a Bolivian strategy for reducing traffic jams and increasing traffic safety. To "Make the news more bearable," Oliver shared 24 minutes of footage of dancing zebras recorded on a green screen on his website. He suggested that dancing zebras, when added to other painful moments, bring about a new way to think of the moment. That is, Oliver suggests remix as a strategy for reimagining the world's problems.

xtine burrough[4]

Memes to Rewrite Culture

I submit the *Civil War* meme (Figure 18.6), in which fans create various hilarious arguments between Steve and Tony as the impetus for *Captain America: Civil War*, such as Figure 18.6 and the brilliant "It's pronounced jif" (which, by the way, it is). Other examples below show fans rewriting and re-performing popular culture.

Francesca Coppa[5]

My choice for a meme is "old school"—a kind of a proto-meme or a meme *avant la lettre*. It is the postcard made famous by Jacques Derrida in *La Carta Postale* (Figure 18.7). It is a weird anomaly and the perfect image of remix. The image shows Plato dictating to Socrates behind his back. The image not only inverts

Memes **207**

FIGURE 18.6 The *Civil War* meme provides fans a platform for generating new arguments between characters.

the usual understanding of the relationship between Socrates ("he who does not write") and Plato ("the writer who recorded the words of Socrates") but shows how remix can make an author say something other than what he originally meant to say.

David Gunkel

My favorite meme is an oldie-but-goodie: it's an image of Mandy Patinkin as Inigo Montoya in the film *The Princess Bride*. Unlike many photo memes, which keep one static element (the image) while offering thematic variations on the overlying text (e.g., Scumbag Steve, Philosoraptor, and so on), the text surrounding Mandy's image is almost always the same. It's a snippet of his dialogue from the film:

> You keep using that word.
> I do not think it means what you think it means.

FIGURE 18.7 Postcard from the cover of Jacques Derrida's *La Carta Postale*.

This line refers to a very specific context in the film *The Princess Bride*—the villain, played by Wallace Shawn, repeatedly exclaims that it would be "inconceivable" for his elaborate plans to be foiled by a masked man following his party.[6] Repeatedly, the inconceivable turns out to be the inevitable. Montoya, a mercenary swordsman, offers this pithy analysis to his criminal employer after several such letdowns (Figure 18.8).

I guess what I love most about this meme (other than the priceless expression on Patinkin's face) is that, in its immutability, it points to a universal truth of the human condition. Over and over again, the circumstances, which we believe to be "inconceivable"—either because of our hubris, or the narrowness of our purview, or both—manifest themselves as reality. And over and over again, the language we use to tame the wilderness of our sensoria, to build a predictive model for the unpredictable world, comes up short. We slip into routines, using words as stand-ins for genuine reflection, and this sets us up to get it wrong, again and again.

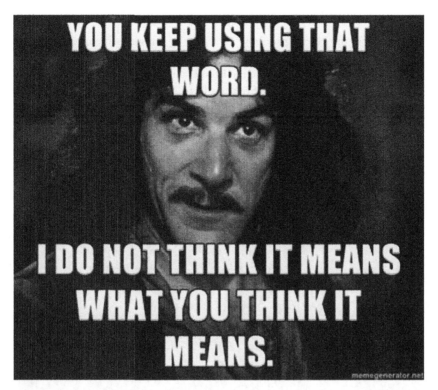

FIGURE 18.8 Mandy Patinkin as Inigo Montoya from *The Princess Bride* reimagined as a meme for his often cited quote, "You keep using that word. I do not think it means what you think it means."

Once upon a time, in the analog days of the twentieth century, we had no social mechanism to observe or remedy this kind of cognitive tic. Today, thanks to the wonders of social media, our hubris can be checked with a cut-and-pasted smirk and a snippet of movie dialogue. Just like a well-timed swat from a Zen master's switch, the image awakens us from our solipsistic ruminations, and offers us the opportunity for enlightenment by forcing us to confront head-on the limitations of our linguistic minds. And, as with some of Zen's most enduring wisdom, we can best understand the dictum in the form of a haiku:

> YOU KEEP USING THAT
> WORD. I DO NOT THINK IT MEANS
> WHAT YOU THINK IT MEANS

Aram Sinnreich[7]

Memes as Parody

This clip from the Norwegian show *Øystein og jeg* transposes the modern idea of the "IT-helpdesk" to early medieval times (Figure 18.9). In this video a monk explains to a colleague how to use the latest technology, a "book." It depicts the shift in information technology from scrolls to codex bound books (reminding us that, yes, the book is also a technology), yet at the same time it functions as a satire on media change today and our ongoing adaptation to new technology, from mobile phones to iPads and Kindles. This video has gone viral and been translated into several languages while also inspiring various remakes.

Janneke Adema[8]

FIGURE 18.9 Original film still from *Øystein og jeg* on Norwegian Broadcasting (NRK) in 2001, with Øystein Backe (helper) and Rune Gokstad (desperate monk). Written by Knut Nærum.

My meme contribution is the *Downfall* parody memes known as "Hitler finds out ..." or "Hitler Reacts to ..." (Figure 18.10). I learned about these viral videos while doing research on music video mashups. These parodies consist of various excerpts from a film released in 2004 titled *Downfall*, which focuses on Hitler's last days, before he committed suicide. In the scene, Hitler is told by key members of his inner circle that Berlin is surrounded and will soon fall. Hitler becomes very upset because he was not told the truth sooner, and rants at length until he eventually accepts the inevitability of defeat.

The parodies add subtitles to the original footage in a few languages, including English, that have nothing to do with what Hitler is actually saying in German. Some of the early memes show him ranting about the lack of features of the iPad, his realization that Pokémon do not exist, and his disbelief that Kanye West

Memes **211**

FIGURE 18.10 A parody meme created with footage from *Downfall*.

was rude to Taylor Swift when West interrupted Swift's acceptance speech at an MTV video awards to tell her that Beyoncé was a much better music artist. Many of these memes were removed because takedown notices were issued aggressively at this time, but the meme lives on and includes rants on Trump becoming nominated for the United States presidency. This meme is interesting because it is able make fun of one of the most disturbing moments in the history of the world as a means to reflect on the insanity of a man who took modern civilization on a very dark path for several years.

Eduardo Navas[9]

This *Dumb and Dumber* meme ironically talks about the poor capacity of the Spanish Prime Minister to talk in his mother tongue and his poor knowledge of English. The text on the meme is a word-for-word translation of one of his most hilarious statements (Figure 18.11).

Pau Figueres

FIGURE 18.11 *Dumb and Dumber*.

Memes that Re-Popularize Culture

You on Kazoo is the stuff of remix dreams (Figure 18.12). It is hard to imagine this content ever existed as an earnest attempt at children's programming. The opening safety advisory ("Remember: don't run, jump, or dance while playing the kazoo") greets its audience with the following advice: "We hope you play along and have fun with this video." And that is exactly what many Internet users have chosen to do. Kazoo Kid remixes operate within a meme logic that depends upon repetition (recognizable citation) and difference (alteration of content.) And as with any good meme, its circulation *as a meme* is far more recognizable and well-known to Internet audiences than the originating video. Kazoo Kid remixes operate within an open-ended ecology of parodied works that cite and remix each other in an ongoing circulation. But unlike straight-up parodies, which attempt to undermine the authority of an originating text, Kazoo Kid memes are made up of equal parts tribute and mockery, placing them more within the realm of pastiche than parody.

Mark Nunes [10]

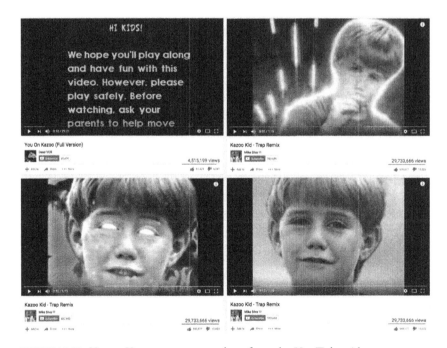

FIGURE 18.12 *You on Kazoo* meme screenshots from the YouTube video.

Rickrolling is an established online practice of bait-and-switch whereby an unsuspecting victim is provided with a web URL that is seemingly relevant to the topic at hand, but when they click the link it redirects to Rick Astley's

FIGURE 18.13 "Never Gonna Give You Up" YouTube video for Rick Astley's 1987 pop-single.

uber-cheesy 1987 hit single "Never Gonna Give You Up" (Figure 18.13). The URL is frequently disguised as a shortlink (e.g., goo.gl or bitly.com) to lure in and trick even experienced web users. Whenever somebody inadvertently encounters Rick Astley's song by clicking on a link they thought was something else, they are said to have been rickrolled.

Although this meme reached peak popularity in 2008, it is still going strong in 2017, with countless derivatives and remixed variations now in online circulation. The original 2007 RickRoll'D YouTube video has over 76 million views, while Rick Astley's official "Never Gonna Give You Up" has amassed over 300 million views since 2009, largely as a result of the meme's popularity.

Owen Gallagher [11]

Insider Memes

FIGURE 18.14 René Magritte's *The Treachery of Images* is appropriated into a meme.

This reworking of Magritte (Figure 18.14) relies on knowledge of art history and modern meme culture (the phrase is taken from a quote falsely attributed to a rapper supposedly being asked if he was guilty of a crime). Like a mustache on the Mona Lisa, it forces us to reconsider our relationship to notions of value, art, and reality. And, it's also funny.

Rebecca Tushnet [12]

This does not meet Shifman's definition of "meme"[13]—but it speaks to my own work of how young women remix Jennifer Lawrence in their own identity work (Figure 18.15).

Akane Kanai [14]

FIGURE 18.15 Jennifer Lawrence meme as representation of identity.

FIGURE 18.16 Imminent Ned meme used as an announcement for an upcoming fan edit.

Appropriating a foreboding catchphrase from the television series *Game of Thrones*, this "Imminent Ned" image macro states: "Brace yourselves/*Batman vs Superman* fan edits are coming . . ." (Figure 18.16). It was shared with me by a fan editor named "JobWillins" on June 27, 2016, just a few weeks before the home video release of *Batman v Superman: Dawn of Justice* (2016). The sarcastic image accurately predicted the astonishing surge of fan edits based on the film. It also reflects an emerging trend on social media in which audiences increasingly anticipate, and even demand, new fan edits to confront what some consider to be Hollywood's recent misfires, like *The Hobbit* trilogy and DC Comics superhero films.

Joshua Wille[15]

Notes

1. Olivia Solon, "Richard Dawkins on the Internet's Hijacking of the Word 'Meme'," *Wired* (June 20, 2013) www.wired.co.uk/article/richard-dawkins-memes.
2. www.yahoo.com/style/princess-leia-and-wonder-woman-emerge-as-icons-in-womens-anti-trump-marches-221231196.html.
3. www.youtube.com/watch?v=7xuXlpvWw1I.
4. Dancing Zebra Meme from John Oliver's Last Week Tonight: www.hollywoodreporter.com/news/john-oliver-just-add-zebras-footage-trump-budget-987285 and www.youtube.com/watch?v=-Z668Qc0P4Q).
5. Meme image source: http://i1.kym-cdn.com/photos/images/original/000/896/362/b54.jpg. See http://knowyourmeme.com/memes/captain-america-civil-war-4-pane-captain-america-vs-iron-man and www.smosh.com/smosh-pit/memes/captain-america-civil-war-memes. Relatedly, check out this—not quite a meme but the Civil War of the Roses: cosplay as meme, cosplay as fan performance. http://datura-riot.tumblr.com/post/151057360021/civil-war-of-the-roses-thank-you-to and www.buzzfeed.com/juliareinstein/this-is-the-future-liberals-want?utm_term=.si4Le0e6g#.fc5RYnYXk.

6 William Goldman, *The Princess Bride*, 1987.
7 http://knowyourmeme.com/memes/you-keep-using-that-word-i-do-not-think-it-means-what-you-think-it-means.
8 Medieval Helpdesk: https://youtu.be/pQHX-SjgQvQ For a gif commenting on the book see "Turning Pages," by Annett Höland (2010): www.paperscissors stone.ch/Translation/Turning-Pages. Annett Höland's description of this animated gif: "The idea for this animation of found gif animations of books came up when thinking about the relationship between the printed book and its digital brother while writing a contribution to the Writing Marathon 2010 coordinated by Andrea Lioy: "(. . .) When surfing the Web, one cannot help but notice that the Internet itself resembles the form of the book in many ways or even tries to emulate the experience of reading a book. How come that electronic book readers, such as the Amazon Kindle or the iPad, imitate the very sensual act of turning the pages of a printed book?"
9 http://knowyourmeme.com/memes/downfall-hitler-reacts and www.youtube.com/watch?v=WEKUIOURVRw.
10 http://knowyourmeme.com/memes/you-on-kazoo
11 http://knowyourmeme.com/memes/rickroll; www.youtube.com/watch?v=dQw4w9WgXcQ; www.youtube.com/watch?v=oHg5SJYRHA0
12 www.pinterest.com/pin/455778424761446253.
13 Limor Shifman, *Memes in Digital Culture* (Cambridge, MA: MIT Press, 2014), 2.
14 http://knowyourmeme.com/memes/people/jennifer-lawrence. [Editors' note: This is a meme but not one that follows a specific form. Rather it is the concept of Lawrence being carefree about things and likeable, which is revisited in diverging forms.]
15 https://twitter.com/JobWillins/status/747586113368252416.

19
PARODY

Mark Nunes

If parody always reveals itself in double, calling attention to both itself and its target, then remix literalizes this doubling as a play of both substance and form. While many modes of parody mimic genres and distort content, remix parody samples directly from its source material, recontextualizing that material in ways that destabilize meaning and intent. Parody always depends upon legible citations of an originating work in order to operate as such; remix parody, however, quite literally appropriates what it cites, placing words, sounds, and images into a dialogic relationship with one another that undermines the authority of any singular text. This chapter explores the dialogic nature of remix and its connection to parody, with particular attention to the role of parody remix in the realm of political discourse. The chapter concludes with a discussion of how remix operates within a larger media ecology of samplings and citations, creating a more ambivalent form of appropriation that functions as pastiche.

The Dialogic of Remix

Bakhtin's discussion of the "interanimation" of hybrid texts provides a particularly useful lens for exploring how parody operates within a remix aesthetic, and how remix activates the destabilizing power of parody.[1] Bakhtin calls attention to the dialogic nature of certain texts—texts in which styles and modes of discourse not only conflict with one another, but "relate to each other as do rejoinders in a dialogue; there is an argument between languages, an argument between styles of language . . . [a] dialogue between points of view, each with its own concrete language that cannot be translated into the other."[2] Parody, Bakhtin argues, is "an intentionally dialogized hybrid" in which the conflicting and incongruent "languages and styles actively and mutually illuminate one another."[3] In his discussion of ancient Greek parodies of important epic and tragic heroes, for example, Bakhtin argues that parody ruptures the authority of the authoritative text, and in doing so, "forces us to experience those sides of the object that are not otherwise included in a given genre or a given style."[4] The dialogic quality of parody, then, does more than offer a mockery of one language or style through the filter of an incongruent reiteration; it marks a zone of "intense struggle and interanimation" between conflicting discourses, revealing new discursive possibilities inherent within any given text.[5]

To connect Bakhtin's dialogism more directly to a discussion of remix, we might turn to his description of Cyprian Feast parodies for a fitting precursor:

> But how was it constituted? The entire Bible, the entire Gospel, was as it were cut up into little scraps, and these scraps were then arranged in such a way that a picture emerged of a grand feast at which all the personages of sacred history from Adam and Eve to Christ and his Apostles eat, drink and make merry. In this work a correspondence of all details to Sacred Writ is strictly and precisely observed, but at the same time the entire Sacred Writ is transformed into carnival, or more correctly into Saturnalia.[6]

The "cut-up" here provides a metaphor for the dialogic act of parody, or more precisely the creative freedom to place even the most sacred of received material within a "zone of crude contact" in which new relations between parts results in new discursive possibilities.[7] What we witness in remix, then, is the dialogic made even more concrete through a literal act of cutting up source material and arranging digital "scraps"—forcing them to speak to one another in unintended ways.

As Martin Irvine notes, the "dialogic engine" inherent in remix is as much generative as it is citational, creating new points of semiotic contact between texts.[8] When remix operates as parody, it does so because this generative interanimation creates a Bakhtinian zone of crude contact between digital scraps and fragments that might otherwise never admit they had anything to say to one another. Yet speak they do, and often in surprising ways. Consider, for example, movie trailer parodies, which, as Peter Kragh Jensen notes, reveal both the way in which film as a medium formally constructs meaning through a montage of clips, as well as the stylistic markers of a recognizable genre that make the trailer legible as such.[9] Drawing on Bakhtin, Jensen argues that while all parodies operate as "intentional hybrids," remix parodies call attention to the "semantic contingency of moving images" in a more direct fashion, showing the seams of this contingent meaning-making in its generative moment.[10] In a parodic version of the Kuleshov effect, clips are placed in dialogic relation to one another through the act of montage, and in doing so, give rise to a genre inconsistent with the intended framing of the originating film. Jensen points to Robert Ryang's "Shining" trailer (Figure 19.1) as a widely circulated and highly successful instance of parody remix, in

FIGURE 19.1 Robert Ryang's remix of clips from *The Shining* transforms the horror/thriller film into a father/son buddy pic: "I'm your new foster father . . . I'd do *anything* for you."

which Stanley Kubrick's classic horror/thriller film *The Shining* is transformed into a feel-good father/son movie through a rearrangement of clips (and the addition of a new voiceover and soundtrack).[11] As with the Cyprian Feast, this cut-up operates as a parody by undermining the authority of the originating text, and does so in a way that reveals the contingency of meaning in any given text. We witness through the operation of this remix parody the generative potential of the text itself—that meaning emerges through dialogic interaction, and that no single discourse can fully contain the potential of the text.

The Politics of Crude Contact

This dialogic interanimation of fragments allows sampled clips to speak for—and against—themselves in ways that give rise to commentary that is immanent to the remix text itself. This aspect of remix parody, coupled with its ability to level even the most elevated rhetoric, has made it a particularly powerful intervention within the political mediascape. Consider, for example, the remix parody "Candidate Obama Debates President Obama on Government Surveillance."[12] This appropriation and rearrangement of clips from televised press conferences into a new, dialogic relation points out the inconsistencies in Obama's position on National Security Agency (NSA) surveillance in a way that is not overlaid onto the remix video as a critique or commentary, but that emerges from the dialogic relation of Obama's "double-voicing" on this issue. Note as well that this remix does not distort its source material ("correspondence . . . is strictly and precisely observed" as Bakhtin might say) but instead it challenges the authority of what are normatively framed as authoritative statements by altering the genre of their presentation from press conference to point-counterpoint debate. It is worth noting as well that while this remix lacks humor, it nevertheless operates as parody through its intent to reframe the originating texts within a new and incongruous dialogic relation.

Remixes of political campaign advertisements create a similar opportunity for individuals to place political rhetoric within a zone of crude contact where, much like with movie trailer parodies, the dialogic interaction of undistorted, directly sampled material creates a new, incongruous genre that undermines the authority of the originating text. As Tryon notes in his analysis of Phil de Vellis's "Vote Different" remix, which combined Hillary Clinton's YouTube channel content with Apple Computer's "1984" advertisement, the intertextual dialog between Hillary Clinton's 2008 campaign rhetoric and the "Big Brother" imagery of the Apple ad called into question the authenticity of the candidate's invitation to openness, conversation, and grassroots participation during the Democratic primaries.[13] While the "Vote Different" campaign ad ends with an explicit call to support Barack Obama (and to "see why 2008 won't be like '1984'"), this remix reframes Clinton's cheery, welcoming rhetoric within a darker genre that does its critical work of parodic commentary long before the viewer sees the final redirect to the Obama campaign website in the final frame (Figure 19.2). In effect, Clinton's own words from her official YouTube channel are utilized to provide a critique of Hillary Clinton as "Big Brother" through recontextualized, interanimating citations. The remix parody operates without mockery or mimicry of either the Apple "1984" ad or Hillary Clinton's YouTube content. Rather, remix creates this zone of crude contact in which two incongruous semiotic frames—Apple's icons of the iconoclastic and Hillary Clinton's indices of earnestness—work for and against each other to level the political rhetoric of a presidential candidate.

As Debord and Wolman note in their discussion of *détournement*, a similar cut-up strategy used to destabilize the dominant messages of a highly mediated society:

> when two objects are brought together, no matter how far apart their original contexts may be, a relationship is always formed . . . The mutual interference of two worlds of feeling, or the bringing together of two independent expressions, supersedes the original elements and produces a synthetic organization of greater efficacy.[14]

It is for this reason that with remix, no critical overlay is needed, since commentary emerges through this moment of dialogic interaction—and political agency

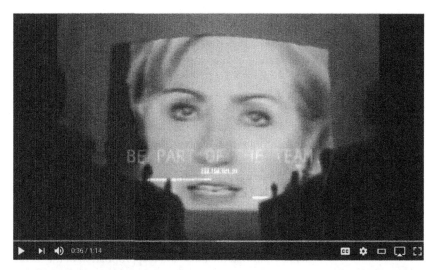

FIGURE 19.2 Phil de Vellis's "Vote Different" replaces Big Brother with Hillary Clinton, creating political parody through dialogic recontextualization.

expresses itself in the very act of arranging these cut-ups. As Russell notes in her discussion of "fake news" and other détourned texts, such as Jonathan McIntosh's remix of Glenn Beck's conspiracy theory ruminations over Donald Duck cartoons, such acts mark "the emergence of a space for dissent being carved out in the middle of the spectacle," expressed through the act of recontextualizing and recirculating mass media political discourse.[15] Remix creates an opportunity for the audience of this political

> This remix is covered at length in Chapter 8, "Creativity."

rhetoric not only to comment on and reply to this discourse, as one might expect in a traditional model of the public sphere, but to manipulate it more directly, placing the most elevated of texts into the hands of citizens and creating a zone of crude contact no less unsettling of authority than the Cyprian Feast travesties of the Holy Writ.

While scholarly and popular press alike have long commented on the leveling effects of digital networks, and the potential for the Internet to provide a platform for a more direct, participatory democracy, what many first-generation theorists of the digital public sphere did not envision was the extent to which increased participation in democracy would take the form of increased production, manipulation, and circulation of political media content. Henry Jenkins calls attention to this shift in what he has called "Photoshop for Democracy," arguing that with the increased ability for individuals to manipulate images, citizens now have the means of creating political commentary through the reuse and reappropriation of the media content that makes up the majority of our contemporary political discourse.[16]

> Henry Jenkins co-authored Chapter 20, "Participatory Politics," for this book.

Remix, here presented as a form of digital collage, allows "amateurs ... to insert their images and thoughts into the political process" by placing visual content into new, dialogic relations.[17] This form of photographic remix, from "Lt. Kerry's Foreign Leader Fan Club Band" (which Jenkins references), to more recent iterations (such as "The Deplorables") enacts parody's dialogic power through a digital cut-up of images that creates a moment of political commentary.[18] The political impact of these appropriating parodies, and their interaction with the mainstream media from which they sample, first came to the fore in the 2004 U.S. Presidential Primaries, most notably, perhaps, with Howard Dean—the first politician to "live by the Internet, die by the Internet."[19] Howard Dean's late-night, post-Iowa Caucus gaffe certainly did not play well on national television, but had this content aired in a pre-participatory culture mass media moment, his "I Have a Scream" speech (as it was soon dubbed) would have faded after a few news cycles. But with this sound bite available online, scores of users could remix this content into mashup songs and videos that would live on much longer, and circulate through a much wider range of cultural networks. The power of remix is marked by its ability to destabilize ownership claims on political rhetoric: who gets to speak, what circulates, and in what context. And much as Russell notes on the role of fake news within the media ecology of "serious" news, Jenkins describes these sorts of "noisy" irruptions within the political process as "not a momentary disruption of the corporate signal, but the new way the system operates" and as a new form of political agency within an altered mediascape.[20]

> See Chapter 9, "Cut-up."

It is worth noting that the political "work" of these "I Have a Scream" remixes is quite different from the parodic commentary of détourned texts and remixed campaign ads such as "Vote Different." Here, the dialogic interanimation of texts is fundamentally an act of leveling lofty rhetoric and placing it into an arena of free play, revealing the tenuous hold that this rhetoric held on the high ground in the first place. There is no "argument" present here; rather, the recontextualization of political speech is its own message, revealing the all-too-frequent emptiness of political content and form. Unlike the "Candidate Obama Debates President Obama on Government Surveillance" parody—or any other example from this genre of remixed politicians debating themselves—which would seem to critique political flip-flopping on various issues, this leveling genre of parody remix appears more intent on revealing the vacuity of the entire political process. Jonny Wilson's "Obama vs. Romney Debate Remix," for example, creates a commentary on the two candidates as either not speaking to anything of substance, or in effect not disagreeing on any points of substance.[21] Likewise, "Obama on Acid" parodies both the form of the White House address as well as the authority of the office itself, rather than the content of the speech or its rhetorical devices.[22] In a similar move, Hugh Atkin's "Will the Real Mitt Romney Please Stand Up"—which presents a remix of the presidential candidate's words as a rap to the tune of Eminem's "The Real Slim Shady"—reveals a parodic construction of Mitt Romney that is no more or less a construct (the remix would seem to suggest) than the persona presented through the political process.[23] Other genres of political parody remix reveal the rhetorical tics of a public figure—such as "Donald Trump Says 'China.'"[24] In this example, several stump speeches and press interviews are edited to remove almost all content except the presidential candidate saying "China," reducing his entire political rhetoric to a single word. Here, the commentary that emerges is pretty clear—Trump has nothing to say, other than the word "China." But as the word repeats itself, and interacts dialogically with itself in an odd echo chamber, we see the baseness of the rhetoric itself exposed not through critical commentary, but through crude repetition.

EDM, Vaporwave and Crude Pastiche

It is important to remember that a parody remix cannot exist in a vacuum; not only does the form depend upon a larger media ecology in which samples of source material circulate and speak to one another, but they also reference other versions of other remixes, so that each iteration of a parody offers a legible citation both to its source texts and to other remix parodies. Not only do we find, for example, an entire genre of remix parodies in which politicians debate themselves; we also have multiple versions of Obama v. Obama that reference and remix each other. Remix parodies operate as part of a larger media ecology of remix in which one work samples and remixes another. Consider, for example, the Bombs Away remix "China All the Time," a video that not only presents a parody remix, but also shows the production of that remix, starting with a sample from "Donald Trump Says 'China'" ("I love China") and documenting the editing of this fragment with another sampled comment ("Somebody's doing the raping") to produce the phrase "I love doing the raping" (Figure 19.3).[25] Further editing from the "Donald Trump Says 'China'" remix creates a keyboard sample, which is then combined with original scorings to give us a full-out Electronic Dance Music (EDM) track, available for download and purchase. As such, "China All the Time" offers a parody remix in which parodic commentary appears muted—if not entirely absent. To the extent that this remix operates as parody, it does so through citation of other political parody remixes rather than through explicit

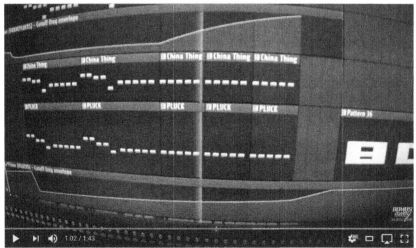

FIGURE 19.3 "I love doing the raping." Bombs Away documents its ambiguously political remix of a pre-existing parody remix, transforming parodic commentary into a lyrical refrain.

critique (although certainly having Donald Trump declare "I love doing the raping" offers a rather blunt character critique).

In this regard, it may be more accurate to classify "China All the Time" as pastiche, rather than parody. Jameson famously defines pastiche as "blank parody," a postmodern mode of engagement "without any of parody's ulterior motives, amputated of the satiric impulse, devoid of laughter and of any conviction that along the abnormal tongue you have momentarily borrowed, some healthy linguistic normality still exists."[26] While we need not fully embrace Jameson's assessment of pastiche as "devoid of laughter," we do see in this definition a logic of remix sampling in which abnormalization becomes normalized—or to put it in other terms, the recognition that sampling and citation are symptomatic of a contemporary mode of creative production, not a parasitic afterthought. As Richard Dyer notes, "parody implies a sure position outside of that to which it refers, one of secure judgment and knowledge," whereas pastiche "is more inside the problem of judgment and knowledge, more ready to acknowledge that it doesn't have all the answers, doesn't know exactly what to think."[27] In this context, then, we might see the Bombs Away remix operating as pastiche rather than parody, to the extent that it references a musical form in a way that counts on its audience recognizing the form without necessarily concerning itself with judging the content from which it samples. We find a similarly ambivalent engagement with citation and dialogism in a wide range of videos that produce music dependent upon the audience identifying how these citations operate within a broader media ecology of circulating content. Mike Diva's "Kazoo Kid-Trap Remix," for example, draws upon two sets of remix sub-genres—"Kazoo Kid" parodies and Trap remixes.[28] The result is a work that is dialogic, in that both forms interanimate each other, but ambivalent in its parodic critique, in effect asserting itself as a "legitimate" EDM remix (or perhaps no more or less legitimate than any other remix).

As Dyer notes, one needs to see the citation and recognize its imitation in order for pastiche to operate.[29] While pastiche "imitates other art in such a way as to make consciousness of this fact central to its meaning and affect," such dialogic relation can only occur within a community of exchange that recognizes and acknowledges it.[30] It is fitting to discuss the electronic music sub-genre of vaporwave in this context, to the extent that, as with pastiche, its aesthetic has been framed as postmodern.[31] But what is relevant to our discussion here is not the ambiguous relation of vaporwave to the "cultural logic of late capitalism" (to borrow from Jameson) but rather how ambivalent citation operates within a community of exchange. In 2016, a number of mainstream websites started to take note of an emerging "micro-genre" of remix that combined vaporwave tracks with sequences from the television series *The Simpsons*, filtering those clips with the kinds of stylistic features that are typical of vaporwave, namely a glitched, "VHS-aesthetic."[32] As with many remix micro-genres, an initial remix of "Bart on the Road" led to additional variants on a theme, until a recognizable set of

FIGURE 19.4 Simpsonwave and other pastiche remixes maintain an ambivalent relation to sampled sources, making it difficult to distinguish parodic and authentic citations.

citations began to circulate under the label of Simpsonwave (Figure 19.4).³³ This micro-genre operates as pastiche to the extent that it depends upon citational references to a musical form (vaporwave), and does so within a dialogic context (remixed with clips from *The Simpsons*) that creates an ambivalent frame for judging the authenticity or legitimacy of the final product in any other context than its ability to circulate within a recognizable, citational framework. It is not surprising, then, that one of the first commentaries on the micro-genre, and a number of commentaries afterward, would ask "Is S I M P S O N W A V E a joke?" indicating the difficulty one has in pastiche teasing out the sincere from the parodic citation.³⁴ The result is a video remix that is imitative of a musical micro-genre, but one that also comments on the micro-genre itself, and does so without maintaining the critical distance implied in parody.

Parody, Pastiche, and the Ecology of Remix

As with parody, pastiche remix operates by creating these dialogic moments that generate new meaning through reference to pre-existing citation. Rather than thinking of pastiche as "blank parody," what differentiates the two in the context of remix has more to do with how these referential frames operate. In pastiche, citation is not only predicated upon an originating text, but also the fact that these texts operate and circulate within a wider media ecology. To some extent then, pastiche performs a corrective to parody similar to parody's corrective to the authority of the originating text. As with the ongoing circulation of memes that repeat and alter a recognizable citational frame, pastiche remix assumes from the start that other remixes came before it, and others will come after.

While discussions of parody and pastiche often frame parody as a more "authentic" engagement with commentary and critique, pastiche provides its commentary by revealing the inherent and ongoing iterability that occurs within all circulating media environments. Parody and pastiche alike point to a similar generative element that operates within remix—that is, a dependence upon recognizable citation, and the transposition of these sampled materials into a new relation that reveals broader potential for meaning-making than the source texts can contain. This logic depends upon a larger media ecology of circulating fragments, such that any one remix can serve as a referent for ongoing rearrangements of dialogic relations. In effect, while not every remix can claim the critical commentary of parody's dialogic challenge to authority, no remix can escape from pastiche's basic structure of citation, iteration, and recirculation.

Notes

1 M.M. Bakhtin, *The Dialogic Imagination* (Austin: University of Texas Press, 1981), 76–82.
2 Ibid.,76.
3 Ibid.
4 Ibid., 55.
5 Ibid., 77.
6 Ibid., 70.
7 Ibid., 26.
8 Martin Irvine, "Remix and the Dialogic Engine of Culture: A Model for Generative Combinatoriality." in *The Routledge Companion to Remix Studies*, ed. Eduardo Navas, Owen Gallagher, and xtine burrough (New York: Routledge, 2015), 27.
9 Peter Kragh Jensen, "Clever Mashups: Online Parodies and the Contingency of Meaning," *Continuum: Journal of Media & Cultural Studies* 27, no. 2 (2013): 284.
10 Ibid., 291.
11 Ibid., 283; Robert Ryang, "Shining," February 27, 2006, www.youtube.com/watch?v=sfout_rgPSA.
12 "Candidate Obama Debates President Obama on Government Surveillance," June 10, 2013, www.youtube.com/watch?v=7BmdovYztH8.
13 Chuck Tryon, "Pop Politics: Online Parody Videos, Intertextuality, and Political Participation," *Popular Communication* 6 (2008): 210–211; Phil de Villis, "Vote Different," March 5, 2007, www.youtube.com/watch?v=6h3G-lMZxjo.
14 Guy Debord and Gil Wolman, "Methods of Détournement," in *Situationist International Anthology*, ed. and trans. Ken Knabb (Berkeley, CA: Bureau of Public Secrets, 1981), 9.
15 Adrienne Russell, *Networked: A Contemporary History of News in Transition* (Malden, MA: Polity, 2011), 126; Jonathan McIntosh, "Donald Duck Meets Glenn Beck in Right Wing Radio Duck," October 2, 2010, www.youtube.com/watch?v=HfuwNU0jsk0.
16 Henry Jenkins, *Convergence Culture: Where Old and New Media Collide* (New York: NYU Press, 2006), 208.
17 Ibid., 222.
18 Ibid., 221; "Hillary Clinton's 'Basket of Deplorables' Gaffe," *Know Your Meme*, September 2016, http://knowyourmeme.com/memes/events/hillary-clinton-s-basket-of-deplorables-gaffe.
19 Keith Olbermann, "The Howard Dean Re-mix," January 22, 2004, www.nbcnews.com/id/4029843/ns/msnbc-countdown_with_keith_olbermann/t/howard-dean-re-mix/#.V-QPEhhQA1I.

20 Russell, *Networked*, 126; Jenkins, *Convergence Culture*, 215.
21 Jonny Wilson, "Obama vs. Romney Debate Remix," October 4, 2012, www.youtube.com/watch?v=vc0EUodAEN0.
22 "Obama on ACID!" December 27, 2010, www.youtube.com/watch?v=Ymsket VqJEg.
23 Hugh Atkin, March 19, 2012, "Will the Real Mitt Romney Please Stand Up (feat. Eminem)," www.youtube.com/watch?v=bxch-yi14BE.
24 "Donald Trump Says 'China,'" August 28, 2015, www.youtube.com/watch?v=RDrfE9I8_hs.
25 Bombs Away, "Donald Trump Remix Video-Future House [Bombs Away—China All the Time.,] October 12, 2015, www.youtube.com/watch?v=J7TWHj-7ycQ.
26 Fredric Jameson, *Postmodernism: Or, the Cultural Logic of Late Capitalism* (Durham, Duke University Press, 1991), 17.
27 Richard Dyer, *Pastiche* (New York: Routledge, 2007), 46.
28 Mike Diva, "Kazoo Kid-Trap Remix," February 2, 2016, www.youtube.com/watch?v=g-sgw9bPV4A.
29 Dyer, Pastiche, 3.
30 Ibid., 4.
31 See for example: Grafton Tanner, *Babbling Corpse: Vaporwave and the Commodification of Ghosts* (Hants: Zero Books, 2016).
32 See, for example: Sandra Song, "What is Simpsonwave? A Brief Introduction Via the Microgenre's Lucien Hughes," *Paper* June 6, 2016 www.papermag.com/what-is-simpsonwave-a-brief-introduction-via-scene-staple-lucien-hughe-1843964229.html.
33 "Bart on the Road," December 3, 2015, www.youtube.com/watch?v=W_rC-495Z_A; "Simpsonwave," *Know Your Meme*, July, 2016, http://knowyourmeme.com/memes/simpsonwave.
34 "Is S I M P S O N W A V E a Joke?" May 26, 2016, www.youtube.com/watch?v=olXUTyk7FP4.

Bibliography

Atkin, Hugh. "Will the Real Mitt Romney Please Stand Up (feat. Eminem)." March 19, 2012. www.youtube.com/watch?v=bxch-yi14BE.
Bakhtin, M.M. *The Dialogic Imagination*. Austin: University of Texas Press, 1981.
"Bart on the Road." December 3, 2015. www.youtube.com/watch?v=W_rC-495Z_A.
Bombs Away. "Donald Trump Remix Video-Future House [Bombs Away—China All the Time.]" October 12, 2015. www.youtube.com/watch?v=J7TWHj-7ycQ.
"Candidate Obama Debates President Obama on Government Surveillance." June 10, 2013. www.youtube.com/watch?v=7BmdovYztH8.
Debord, Guy and Gil Wolman. "Methods of Détournement." In *Situationist International Anthology*. Ed. and trans. Ken Knabb. Berkeley, CA: Bureau of Public Secrets, 1981, 8–14.
Diva, Mike. "Kazoo Kid-Trap Remix." February 2, 2016. www.youtube.com/watch?v=g-sgw9bPV4A.
"Donald Trump Says 'China.'" August 28, 2015. www.youtube.com/watch?v=RDrfE9I8_hs.
Dyer, Richard. *Pastiche*. New York: Routledge, 2007.
"Hillary Clinton's 'Basket of Deplorables' Gaffe." *Know Your Meme*. September 2016. http://knowyourmeme.com/memes/events/hillary-clinton-s-basket-of-deplorables-gaffe.

Irvine, Martin. "Remix and the Dialogic Engine of Culture: A Model for Generative Combinatoriality." In *The Routledge Companion to Remix Studies*, ed. Eduardo Navas, Owen Gallagher, and xtine burrough. New York: Routledge, 2015, 15–42.

"Is S I M P S O N W A V E a Joke?" May 26, 2016. www.youtube.com/watch?v=olXUTyk7FP4.

Jameson, Fredric. *Postmodernism: Or, the Cultural Logic of Late Capitalism*. Durham: Duke University Press, 1991.

Jenkins, Henry. *Convergence Culture: Where Old and New Media Collide*. New York: NYU Press, 2006.

Jensen, Peter Kragh. "Clever Mashups: Online Parodies and the Contingency of Meaning." *Continuum: Journal of Media & Cultural Studies* 27 no. 2 (2013): 283–293.

McIntosh, Jonathan. "Donald Duck Meets Glenn Beck in Right Wing Radio Duck." October 2, 2010. www.youtube.com/watch?v=HfuwNU0jsk0.

"Obama on ACID!" December 27, 2010. www.youtube.com/watch?v=YmsketVqJEg.

Olbermann, Keith. "The Howard Dean Re-mix." January 22, 2004. www.nbcnews.com/id/4029843/ns/msnbc-countdown_with_keith_olbermann/t/howard-dean-re-mix/#.V-QPEhhQA1I.

Russell, Adrienne. *Networked: A Contemporary History of News in Transition*. Malden, MA: Polity, 2011.

Ryang, Robert. "Shining." February 27, 2006. www.youtube.com/watch?v=sfout_rgPSA.

"Simpsonwave." *Know Your Meme*. July 2016. http://knowyourmeme.com/memes/simpsonwave.

Song, Sandra. "What is Simpsonwave? A Brief Introduction Via the Microgenre's Lucien Hughes." *Paper*. June 6, 2016. www.papermag.com/what-is-simpsonwave-a-brief-introduction-via-scene-staple-lucien-hughe-1843964229.html.

Tanner, Grafton. *Babbling Corpse: Vaporwave and the Commodification of Ghosts*. Hants: Zero Books, 2016.

Tryon, Chuck. "Pop Politics: Online Parody Videos, Intertextuality, and Political Participation." *Popular Communication* (2008) 6: 209–213.

de Villis, Phil. "Vote Different." March 5, 2007. www.youtube.com/watch?v=6h3G-lMZxjo.

Wilson, Jonny, "Obama vs. Romney Debate Remix," October 4, 2012, www.youtube.com/watch?v=vc0EUodAEN0.

20
PARTICIPATORY POLITICS

*Henry Jenkins and Thomas J Billard,
with Samantha Close, Yomna Elsayed,
Michelle C. Forelle, Rogelio Lopez, and Emilia Yang*

Imagine how Donald Trump would fit into the bloodthirsty world of Westeros as depicted on HBO's cult fantasy series *Game of Thrones*.[1] In an anonymously circulated video posted in February 2016, Trump rejects Daenerys and her army of refugees in the name of drawing the line against "radical Islam," solicits the Night Watch in his efforts to build a massive wall to keep out "illegal aliens," and discusses his plans to waterboard and torture terrorist suspects with "Littlefinger," Tyrion Lannister, and Lord Varys.[2] "Game of Trump" not only remixes footage, but also digitally inserts Trump into iconic sequences to comic effect (Figure 20.1). But the video is good for more than just a few laughs, offering a concise summary of Trump's "medieval" positions at a time when he was the front-runner for the Republican nomination. Seen through this lens, electing Trump seems about as desirable as getting an invitation to the "Red Wedding."[3]

This chapter considers remix as a form of participation at a time when the infrastructures and skills associated with participatory culture are inspiring new kinds of civic engagement and political participation. We might define a participatory culture as one with relatively low barriers to artistic expression and civic engagement, strong support for creating and sharing one's creations, and some type of informal mentorship whereby what is known by the most experienced is passed along to novices.[4] In an ideal participatory culture, members believe their contributions matter and feel some degree of social connection with one another. A participatory culture provides a context in which people can find their voice, acquire skills at media production and circulation, forge community ties, develop shared reference points and meanings, and build a repertoire of common practices, all of which may be, and increasingly are being, deployed towards political ends. *Convergence Culture: Where Old and New Media Collide* predicted such a shift:

FIGURE 20.1 Screenshot from "Winter is Trumping."

> These forces [towards digital democracy] are apt to emerge first in cultural forms—a changed sense of community, a greater sense of participation, less dependence on official expertise, and a greater trust in collaborative problem-solving ... Yet these forms of popular culture [among them political remix videos] also have political effects, representing hybrid spaces where we can lower the political stakes (and change the language of politics) enough so that we can master skills we need to be participants in the democratic process.[5]

Over the past decade, participatory practices, such as appropriation and remix, have moved from the periphery to become increasingly central to the ways that American politics operate. What once seemed strange becomes progressively less so, and with this shift, more and more people, especially young people, are finding ways to contribute to movements for social change. We could illustrate these processes through any number of examples, from the DREAMer movement to Occupy Wall Street to #BlackLivesMatter to the Arab Spring, but we are going to focus this discussion around the role of remix practices in U.S. presidential campaigns. Here, we can see the intersection between participatory politics and more institutionalized forms of civic engagement.

Convergence Culture cited a 2004 video, released by the political action group True Majority, which remixed news footage with shots from the reality television series *The Apprentice* to depict Donald Trump taking George W. Bush into the boardroom to fire him for being a "failed" president. This example was striking for the use of political remix by an organization with more than 300,000 members. Four years later, parody videos were introduced into the YouTube-CNN debate between the Democratic candidates. The leading Republican nominee, Mitt Romney, was so flustered by this cartoonish spectacle that he refused to participate in a debate utilizing the same format.[6] During this period, scholars[7] sought to better understand the terms of our participation—in culture and in politics—and more recently,[8] to understand what kinds of mechanisms of translation might bridge between the two.

From Participatory Culture to Participatory Politics

All cultures are participatory, but different cultures invite or facilitate different degrees of participation. For example, in a traditional folk culture, many are invited to participate (e.g., through crafts or folk dance), skills are passed along informally, and individual authorship is favored less than cooperative engagement. By contrast, in mass culture, the means of production are highly concentrated and most people are consumers but not producers. A networked society offers more opportunities to produce and share culture than within mass culture. Early writing on participatory culture highlighted fandom as a space where significant numbers of people deployed popular fiction resources for their own storytelling and media-making practices.[9] Fandom might be described as a mode of participatory culture in which people apply folk culture logics to mass culture contents. However, over the past two decades, more people have expanded their communication capacities, acquired skills within a range of online and offline communities, used new media platforms and practices to find their voice, and gained greater access to the means of media production and circulation. These skills and opportunities are not evenly distributed so we need to speak of a *more participatory* culture or of participatory *sub*cultures, but they are impacting the ways significant numbers of youth are introduced into the political process.

Building on this framework, the MacArthur Foundation launched the Youth and Participatory Politics (YPP) research network, a multidisciplinary group of researchers who have been working together for the better part of a decade mapping the political lives of American youth. YPP tells us that participatory politics practices,

> are focused on expression and are peer based, interactive, and non-hierarchical, and they are not guided by deference to elite institutions ... The participatory skills, norms, and networks that develop when social media is used to socialize with friends or to engage with those who share one's interests can and are being transferred to the political realm.[10]

YPP researchers found that a high percentage of American youth (41 percent according to their 2012 survey) have engaged in some form of participatory politics, and that this percentage has continued to grow over time. Practices such as making memes, commenting on blog posts, or circulating remix videos are becoming a widespread element in the political repertoire of this generation. Moreover, the research suggests that 43 percent of white, 41 percent of black, 38 percent of Latino, and 36 percent of Asian-American youth have engaged in participatory politics practices, showing much greater parity across race than more institutional forms of politics, such as voting.

Not surprisingly, young people are choosing to engage with politics through platforms such as Twitter, Facebook, Tumblr, or Instagram, where they spend much of their social time, and are seeking to conduct politics through different mechanisms than their parents' generation. These findings are consistent with other data on social media usage, such as that from the Pew Center for the Internet & American Life,[11] showing that 61 percent of millennial youth get political news from Facebook in any given week, a much larger percentage than turn to any other news source (37 percent, for example, watch local television news). Remix videos circulate, alongside news clippings and blog posts, as one means among many for gaining insight into contemporary political debates, all of which provide springboards for discussion within shared friendship or interest-based networks.[12]

Whether or not political discourse enters into friendship-based networks, such as those characteristic of Facebook, for example, depends on the social dynamics of the peer culture: people of all ages often protect their most important support networks—close friends or family—from political disputes, avoiding political conversations where they know there are strong disagreements.[13] Youth seek to more actively mask their political commitments on social media for many of the same reasons[14] and there are anecdotal reports of people opting out of social media to avoid negative comments from those with whom they disagree as the 2016 campaign hit its lowest points. By contrast, interest-based communities often offer more supportive environments for political exchanges and the mechanisms encouraging cultural participation also foster greater civic engagement. YPP found that young people involved in interest-driven networks, such as fandom or gamer communities, are five times as likely as those who aren't involved to engage in participatory politics, and nearly four times as likely to participate in institutional politics.[15]

The Media, Activism, and Participatory Politics (MAPP) group at the University of Southern California has developed ethnographic case studies of groups, organizations, and networks that have been particularly effective at getting youth involved in the political process. MAPP interviewed more than 200 young activists for *By Any Media Necessary: The New Youth Activism*.[16] More recently, MAPP members have been collecting examples of political remix from a range of different online communities, trying to better understand the roles that practices of participatory politics have played in the 2016 campaign. For example, Samantha Close explored forms of political expression within crafting communities. She finds many crafters mix folk and digital techniques, for instance Photoshopping the faces of political candidates onto traditional prayer candles to demonstrate their affective investment in candidates. In a cynical political climate, such objects might at first seem camp or ironic. However, reading the crafters' words and considering the time-intensive labor, more often than not political crafts express earnest, deeply felt support that will last far beyond an election cycle.

As politics enters this participatory culture space, it often does so in terms defined by more everyday and recreational activities. If crafters are expressing their commitments as citizens, they may do so through the objects they knit or, in the case of the candles, mold. If fans are going to speak out politically, they do so in images and situations borrowed from their preferred media franchise. When MAPP interviewed young activists, they heard repeatedly that the rhetoric of American politics was broken—both because it was exclusive (in so far as one has to already know a lot about the existing discourse to be able to understand what is being said, and young people are not invited into the process) and repulsive (in so far as partisan rhetoric often overrides the search for consensus or "commonsense" solutions to shared problems). The use of remix as a means of political participation addresses both issues: political issues are reframed in languages that are already part of the shared culture of young participants and, while remixes may be as sharply partisan as other political speech, there is also a sense of playfulness that can allow emotional distance from their messages.

Humor certainly entertains, but it also challenges our perceptions, inviting us to reconsider our assumptions, bringing about cognitive dissonance. It does so without necessarily incurring our resistance, but rather clandestinely encouraging us to laugh at ourselves in the company of others. Trump's offensive remarks regarding immigrants and minorities inspired critiques from media pundits and comedians alike. However, most made fun of Trump's bullying and blustering postures without removing him from the presidential podium. As Yomna Elsayed has explored, "Your Drunk Neighbor: Donald Trump" juxtaposes Trump's statements over the image of a drunk middle-aged white man sitting at the front

FIGURE 20.2 Screenshot from "Drunk Trump 1: Your Drunk Neighbor: Donald Trump."

porch of his house, suggesting that his unsubstantiated statements are just as likely to come from your next door neighbor (Figure 20.2).[17] Through humor, what is taken for granted is scrutinized and defamiliarized. Humorous remix serves a double function, on the one hand breaking down the sanctity of our political figures, while exposing the public's own failure to see beyond the pomp and circumstances of official politics.

Mechanisms of Translation

Remix is an example of what Neta Kligler-Vilenchik has described as "mechanisms of translation"[18] as social connections, cultural capital, and media literacies acquired through involvement in a participatory culture community are deployed for civic discourse and political mobilization. Kligler-Vilenchik traces a process that goes from linking real-world concerns to fictional content worlds (often in the form of analogy or allegory), using those shared cultural references as inspiration for creative production, and deploying the resulting products as the basis for discussion within and beyond the interest-based community.

Some of these remixes make extensive use of knowledge and cultural references specific to a particular community, depending on forms of subcultural capital. Rogelio Lopez, for example, has looked at a practice known as "no-nosing", which according to the popular Internet meme wiki "Know Your Meme," is part of a meme tradition dating back to 2013.[19] "No-Nose" remixes edit out noses in popular media. The primary purpose of no-nosing has been "for the lulz," with the most notable examples commonly juxtaposing otherwise serious situations or scenes in creative works with the absurdity and oddity of a nose-less character. However, Trump's outlandish performance can often serve as self-parody, with no-nosing converting an already comical moment into one that reveals his alien presence in the political arena (Figure 20.3).

FIGURE 20.3 No-nosed Trump meme.

FIGURE 20.4 Screenshot of "Donald Trump in *Mean Girls*."

While the general public may not understand the reference, such materials may provoke an intense response from a particular invested viewership. Such shared cultural practices perform bonding functions, strengthening ties amongst those in the know, and in the process, strengthening the community's shared ideological commitments. By contrast, other remixes depend on only loose associations more widely shared across a generational cohort—for example, situating Trump within the teen comedy, *Mean Girls* (Figure 20.4).[20] As such videos are more likely to go viral, these practices serve bridging functions between multiple audiences.

Genres of Participation

Just as mechanisms of translation make it easier for participants to deploy what they know as fans to make sense of the political process, there are also mechanisms, or genres, of participation that provide simple templates that model that next step into civic participation. For Marie Dufrasne and Geoffroy Patriarche, genres of participation refer to "a type of communicative action recognized by a community . . . as appropriate to attain a specific objective."[21] Genres of participation delineate particular sets of actions (in this case, communicative practices) that can be performed by diverse participants. These genres provide those who join these actions with a sense of shared purpose and practice, increasing their collective civic agency.

Consider, for example, the Bernie or Hillary meme generated during the Democratic primary season, traced by Michelle C. Forelle. A baseball-card-like format is designed to contrast Bernie Sanders and Hillary Clinton (and, at other times, Donald Trump): Sanders is often depicted as deeply knowledgeable about popular culture and Clinton as disconnected and clueless. This meme is easily

FIGURE 20.5 Sample Bernie vs. Trump meme.

passed from one public to another because participants understand its underlying logic and the pattern is flexible enough to be adapted to different cultural references or extended to other candidates. For example, one popular card (Figure 20.5) uses *Lord of the Rings* as its basic frame, contrasting Bernie's imagined fannish response ("I love the rich imagery and fascinating characters. The thought put into the history of the world and details of the mythos is nothing short of brilliant!") and Trump's less cerebral reaction ("Too long. Too boring. Not enough guns!").[22] Anyone can play this game, and the demand on any given participant is relatively simple: add a few sentences to the mix.

From Culture Jamming to Cultural Acupuncture

A decade ago, we might have read such political remix practices as culture jamming, a grassroots movement to disrupt or destabilize corporate signs. Culture jamming recognizes the power of mass media to colonize the imagination and uses remix as a tool of critique. Certainly, some contemporary activists such as the Anonymous movement or Occupy Wall Street for example, keep culture jamming alive, but others observe a different logic, such as the Harry Potter Alliance's "cultural acupuncture."[23] At its most basic level, cultural acupuncturists tap cultural pressure points to reroute circulation. This model recognizes fan investments in popular narratives as resources for their own fantasies of social change and political empowerment. Here, the goal is to deploy rather than destroy mass culture symbols. Linking their causes to these cultural reference points means their activist efforts are more apt to be pulled into discussions around these trending topics and their videos more likely to be spread by those who share their passions and interests.

Engaging the Civic Imagination

MAPP also understands such remixes as part of the civic imagination.[24] Stephen Duncombe stresses that political movements need to go beyond a "just the facts" approach if they are going to "manufacture dissent" against the powerful;[25] remix practices often tap popular myths in order to generate a stronger affective relationship to the candidate or cause. Imagination plays an important role in the political process, helping participants to imagine a better world and the mechanisms through which it might be achieved, to see themselves as political agents capable of making a change in the world and as parts of larger imagined communities that can act collectively on behalf of shared interests, and to develop empathy for others whose experiences may be different from their own. Around the world, young activists deploy images from popular culture—for example, superhero iconography,[26] the Three-Finger Salute from *Hunger Games*,[27] the Guy Fawkes mask from *V for Vendetta*[28]—to spark civic imagination.

While political memes are often discussed in terms of their snarky or satirical dimensions, other memes and remixes construct political heroes. For example, filmmaker Tabitha Holbert cast young singers and actors in "Sanders," which takes its inspiration from Lin-Manuel Miranda's multicultural Broadway musical, *Hamilton*, bridging two phenomena popular with millennial youth in early 2016 (Figure 20.6).[29] This ironic remix used songs designed to tell the story of the man who established the American banking system to narrate the life of one of Wall Street's sharpest critics. In some cases, these remixes may also deploy fictional protagonists as champions for grassroots communities: in one meme, a Spanish-speaking Birdman (drawn from the Oscar-winning film of the same title) slaps Donald Trump for his anti-Mexican comments (Figure 20.7).[30]

Not surprisingly, as campaigns court millennial voters, they mimic political remix and fan activism in hopes that their official videos will also be circulated through social media. For example, a video aired at the Democratic National Convention plays on the popular perception that Donald Trump is a bully,

FIGURE 20.6 Screenshot of the title image from "Sanders (Bernie Sanders + Hamilton)."

juxtaposing footage of famous instances where the Republican nominee was abusive of women, people with disabilities, and minorities, with scenes depicting stereotypical bullies from 1980s movies, such as *Back to the Future*, *A Christmas Story*, *Weird Science*, and *Home Alone*. The culture jammer frame reads remix as a tactic of the powerless, the marginal, and the dispossessed, but these same techniques can be deployed as a strategy from a top-down persuasion model.

Remix as a Civic Literacy

As more people have acquired the capacity to produce and circulate media, communities have developed mechanisms for translating politics into pop culture content worlds and created templates for their members to insert their own content

FIGURE 20.7 Birdman slaps Trump.

into the meme stream. Thomas J Billard has written that memetic activities using graphic design represent a new form of citizen participation in political campaigns, citing the example of how such participation is enabled by the relative technological ease of typographic manipulation.[31] Consider the online response to the initial Trump/Pence campaign logo. This early logo design, first distributed in a fundraising email, depicted the letters T and P interlocked in such a way that the T appeared to "penetrate" the P.[32] This design feature was immediately critiqued and parodied. Congressman Alan Grayson, for example, tweeted, "This logo accurately represents what Trump Pence will do to America."[33] Matt Negrin of Bloomberg News pixelated the image, a comedic referenced to television censorship of nudity and sexual material (Figure 20.8).[34] Another Twitter user, known by the handle @darth, animated the logo to make the T truly penetrate the P, with motion.[35]

FIGURE 20.8 Censored Trump and Pence logo.

While these manipulations can be seen as juvenile humor, understanding the policy positions of the candidates adds depth to one's reading. Mike Pence, during his tenure as governor of Indiana, signed a controversial "religious freedom" bill that legalized discrimination against LGBT individuals. Thus, to make Pence the recipient of Trump's penetration in their readings and manipulations of the logo is to satirize Pence's homophobic policy position. Similar commentaries were made without sexual innuendo, and with more sophisticated design manipulation. For example, one submission to a design crowdsourcing website replaced the red and white stripes extending from the interlocked T and P with a rainbow flag and replaced the tagline "Make America Great Again!" with "Make America Great Sweetiepie!"[36] Yet other policy commentaries were made through design parody,

FIGURE 20.9 Trump/Putin logo.

for instance by redesigning the ticket to read "Trump/Putin" with the tagline "Make Russia Great Again!" (Figure 20.9).[37] As such, these graphic remixes critiqued both the professionalism (where quality graphic design indicates a professional campaign) and policy positions of the Trump/Pence collaboration, ultimately pushing the Trump campaign to redesign its logo without such easily parodied features.[38]

In such a context, activism will more likely take the form of groups working together to reframe political issues and generate new cultural symbols. Emilia Yang, for example, invited activists at the 2015 West Coast Organizing Conference to discuss Trump's anti-immigration rhetoric using what she calls a "participatory media art" methodology.[39] In this project, titled "To Trump Trump's Wall," she installed a mock-up wall and asked activists to respond to it by imagining the immigrant experience and using an animation booth to create and project live remixed messages they would like to inscribe on the wall. The media they remixed were a combination of newspapers, magazines, found objects, and other materials. For her, the collaborative and public creation of media activates new spaces for political debate and possibilities of expression, tapping into practices associated with participatory culture, tactical media, and adversarial design.[40]

Civic education may take the form of giving young people the tools and training to critically remix and recode political advertisements. For example, the New York-based Learning About Multimedia Project (LAMP) has developed a curriculum around its Mediabreaker toolkit, with which students and teachers were encouraged to disrupt and critique the advertisements produced by the candidates and their political action committees. Such educational efforts are intended to ensure that the power to participate in the process of remixing and recirculating political content is part of the repertoire of every young citizen, suggesting that political remix will become an even more central aspect of public debates in future election cycles.

Conclusion

In this chapter, we've drawn on examples of remixed media deployed in relation to the 2016 U.S. Presidential Campaign to illustrate the ways that new forms of civic expression have emerged from the realm of participatory culture and become increasingly central to political debates. Looking at an event like a presidential campaign that occurs every four years allows us to trace what's changed in remix culture and also what has shifted in our understanding of the nature of participatory culture. We conclude with a summary of what we understand now that was not clear eight years ago when Barack Obama was running for the presidency.

Remixes, which may take the form of video mashups, memes, even parodies of design choices and typefaces, are now being deployed at all levels from non-profit organizations and even the campaigns themselves to various subcultural communities, especially those organized around shared interests (fandoms, crafters, no-nosers), where these forms of political speech can be seen as extensions of their routine practices and subcultural capital. Political remixes in a campaign context constitute the point of contact between participatory and institutional modes of politics. Remix often represents a mechanism of translation as people bridge between the content worlds of popular culture and real-world concerns, and the use of this comic or playful set of references reflects a desire to revitalize the language of American politics to make it more inclusive and inviting. In some cases, these remix practices intensify bonds within subcultural communities by tapping what amount to inside jokes, but in other cases, the use of widely recognized references perform a bridging function as memes circulate across diverse contexts.

The practices of participatory politics have proven most effective when they offer clear templates for what a desired contribution might look like while also remaining open-ended enough for many different groups and individuals to insert their own voice in the process. Remixes that draw on popular culture for points of comparison also tap into the civic imagination, allowing movement participants to imagine alternatives to current conditions and provide empowering models for what it might mean to change the world. As appropriation and remixing have become important literacy skills in participatory culture, more and more people have used these new communication capacities to seek to insert their own voices into core political debates. To this end, various civic education efforts have taught remix processes as a core tactic for social change. In short, remix represents one of the primary mechanisms by which young people have been able to transition from involvement within participatory culture to engagement with participatory politics.

Notes

1. This chapter has been expanded from a collective blog post: Henry Jenkins et al., "Civic Paths Hotspot: Remixing the U.S. Presidential Campaign," *Confessions of an Aca-Fan*, May 10, 2016, http://henryjenkins.org/2016/05/civic-paths-hotspot-remixing-the-u-s-presidential-campaign.html.
2. "Winter is Trumping," YouTube video, 2:40, posted by "huw parkinson," February 20, 2016, www.youtube.com/watch?v=I0tE6T-ecmg.
3. The Red Wedding was a gruesome massacre as several beloved characters on *Game of Thrones* were ambushed by their enemies at the marital feast, resulting in one of the most discussed incidents in the series' history.
4. Henry Jenkins, with Katie Clinton, Ravi Purushotma, Alice J. Robinson, and Margaret Weigel, *Confronting the Challenges of Participatory Culture: Media Education for the 21st Century* (Cambridge, MA: MIT Press, 2007).
5. Henry Jenkins, *Convergence Culture: Where Old and New Media Collide* (New York: New York University Press, 2006), 219 20.
6. Henry Jenkins, "Why Mitt Romney Won't Debate a Snowman," in *Satire TV: Politics and Comedy in the Post-Network Era*, ed. Jonathan Gray, Jeffrey P. Jones, and Ethan Thompson (New York: New York University Press, 2009), 191.
7. Nico Carpentier, *Media and Participation: A Site of Ideological-Democratic Struggle* (Bristol: Intellect, 2011); Chris Kelty, Aaron Panofsky, Morgan Currie, Roderic Crooks, Seth Erickson, Patricia Garcia, Michael Wartenbe, and Stacy Wood, "Seven Dimensions of Contemporary Participation Disentangled," *Journal of the Association for Information Science and Technology* 66, no. 3 (2015).
8. Neta Kligler-Vilenchik, "Mechanisms of Translation: From Online Participatory Cultures to Participatory Politics," *Journal of Digital Media Literacy* (2016), www.jodml.org/2016/06/27/mechanisms-of-translation-from-online-participatory-cultures-to-participatory-politics/; Tracy Van Slyke, "Spoiler Alert: How Progressives Will Break Through With Popular Culture," *The Culture Lab*, 2014, http://spoileralert.report/.
9. Henry Jenkins, *Textual Poachers: Television Fans and Participatory Culture* (New York, NY: Routledge, 1992).
10. Cathy J. Cohen and Joseph Kahne, *Participatory Politics: New Media and Youth Action* (Oakland, CA: Youth and Participatory Politics Research Network, 2012), vi.
11. Amy Mitchell, Jeffrey Gottfried, and Katerina Eva Matsa, "Millennials and Political News," *Pew Center for Internet & American Life*, 2005, www.journalism.org/2015/06/01/millennials-political-news/.
12. Mizuko Ito, Sonia Baumer, Matteo Bittani, danah boyd, et al., *Hanging Out, Messing Around, and Geeking Out: Kids Living and Learning with New Media* (Cambridge, MA: MIT Press, 2013).
13. Nina Eliasoph, *Avoiding Politics: How Americans Produce Apathy in Everyday Life* (Cambridge: Cambridge University Press, 1998).
14. Emily C. Weinstein, Margaret Rundle, and Carrie James, "A Hush Falls Over the Crowd: Diminished Civic Participation Among Young Civic Actors," *International Journal of Communication* 9 (2015).
15. Cohen and Kahne, *Participatory Politics*, ix.
16. Henry Jenkins, Sangita Shresthova, Liana Gamber-Thompson, Neta Kligler-Vilenchik, and Arely Zimmerman, *By Any Media Necessary: The New Youth Activism* (New York: New York University Press, 2016).
17. "Drunk Trump 1: Your Drunk Neighbor: Donald Trump," YouTube video, 2:04, posted by "Friend Dog Studios," October 3, 2015, www.youtube.com/watch?v=cRIy-0wwl_g.
18. Kligler-Vilenchik, "Mechanisms of Translation."

19 "Noseless GIFs," *Know Your Meme*, April 2016, http://knowyourmeme.com/memes/noseless-gifs.
20 "Donald Trump in *Mean Girls*," YouTube video, 1:17, posted by "TheCrazyGorilla," April 3, 2016, www.youtube.com/watch?v=wgxzQVGkTHk.
21 Marie Dufrasne, and Geoffroy Patriarche, "Applying Genre Theory to Citizen Participation in Public Policy Making: Theoretical Perspectives on Participatory Genres," *Communication Management Quarterly* 21 (2011): 65.
22 "Bernie or Hillary? – Lord of the Rings," *Know Your Meme*, 2016, http://knowyourmeme.com/photos/1074763-bernie-or-hillary.
23 Henry Jenkins, "Cultural Acupuncture: Fan Activism and the Harry Potter Alliance," *Transformative Works and Cultures* 10 (2012).
24 Henry Jenkins, Sangita Shresthova, Liana Gamber-Thompson, and Neta Kligler-Vilenchik, "Superpowers to the People! How Young Activists Are Tapping the Civic Imagination," in *Civic Media: Technology/Design/Practice*, ed. Eric Gordon and Paul Mihailidis (Cambridge, MA: MIT Press, 2016).
25 Stephen Duncombe, *Dream: Re-Imagining Progressive Politics in an Age of Fantasy* (New York: New Press, 2007).
26 Jenkins et al., *By Any Media Necessary*.
27 Seth Mydans. "Thai Protestors Are Detained After Using 'Hunger Games' Salute," *New York Times*, November 20, 2014, www.nytimes.com/2014/11/21/world/asia/thailand-protesters-hunger-games-salute.html.
28 Edward Lovett, "How Did Guy Fawkes Become a Symbol of Occupy Wall Street?" *ABC News*, November 5, 2011, http://abcnews.go.com/blogs/headlines/2011/11/how-did-guy-fawkes-become-a-symbol-of-occupy-wall-street/.
29 "Sanders (Bernie Sanders + Hamilton)," Vimeo video, 3:56, posted by "Tabitha Holbert," April 2011, https://vimeo.com/163185665.
30 Amber Jamieson, "'Cállate, Imbécil': The Best Mexican Responses to Donald Trump's Visit," *The Guardian*, August 31, 2016, www.theguardian.com/world/2016/aug/31/donald-trump-mexico-memes-cartoons-pena-nieto.
31 Thomas J Billard, "Fonts of Potential: Areas for Typographic Research in Political Communication," *International Journal of Communication* 10 (2016).
32 Nick Gass, "Trump's Campaign Logo Mocked on Twitter," *Politico*, July 15, 2016, www.politico.com/story/2016/07/trump-vp-pick-mike-spence-logo-225612.
33 Alan Grayson (@AlanGrayson), Twitter post, July 15, 2016, 10:11 a.m., https://twitter.com/alangrayson/status/754000353025220608.
34 Matt Negrin (@MattNegrin), Twitter post, July 15, 2016, 9:56 a.m., https://twitter.com/mattnegrin/status/753996594119401472.
35 darthTM (@darth), Twitter post, July 15, 2016, 9:05 a.m., https://twitter.com/darth/status/753983871880790016.
36 Mercy Yang, "Donald Trump's Campaign Couldn't Come Up With A Decent Logo, So These Artists Did It For Them," *Huffington Post*, July 28, 2016, www.huffingtonpost.com/?icid=hjx004.
37 Donald 'geoffrey1986' Drumpf, "Trump/Putin Campaign's New Logo—Make Russia Great Again!" *Reddit*, August 2016, www.reddit.com/r/Drumpf/comments/4uwr6y/trumpputin_campaigns_new_logo_make_russia_great/.
38 Katie Reilly, "Donald Trump Campaign Unveils New Logo After Social Media Mockery," *Time*, July 16, 2016, http://time.com/4409431/donald-trump-new-campaign-logo/.
39 Emilia Yang, "By Any Media Necessary: To Trump Trump's Wall (and Hate)," *Confessions of an Aca-Fan*, April 14, 2016, http://henryjenkins.org/2016/04/by-any-media-necessary-part-six-to-trump-trumps-wall-and-hate.html.
40 Rita Raley, *Tactical Media* (Minneapolis: University of Minnesota Press, 2009); Carl DiSalvo *Adversarial Design* (Cambridge, MA: MIT Press, 2012).

21
REMIX

Eduardo Navas

Remix has become culturally relevant due to its function as a binder for the constant recycling and repurposing of material and immaterial things; it has helped develop an awareness of the constant exchange of ideas across specializations and cultural niches for different purposes. Why this is taking place could certainly be considered from various points of view, which is what makes accepting remix as a vital creative process difficult. Once an awareness of the relation of remixing to culture at large was developed, a critical and historical engagement became encapsulated under the terms "remix culture" and more recently "remix studies." What remix studies itself may be is difficult to define, as many of its participants engage with remixing as a field of research based on different paradigms, which, as part of remix itself, question each other.[1] One could also argue that trying to define remix might be a moot point because, while the most basic meaning of the word appears to remain constant, its connotation changes as it continues to be discussed, reflected upon, and (most importantly) put into practice by those who actually produce material that both challenges and redefines it.[2]

What can be productive, then, is to evaluate how remix has evolved from a creative action to a cultural practice and a field of study. In order to accomplish this, we can evaluate the various stages that remix has gone through as it gained common usage. In what follows, I go over the brief history of the word "remix" with the aim to reflect upon its elusive cultural role. I will not provide variations of its basic definition, because it has remained fairly constant since it became related to the general understanding of creative production. What is outlined is how the concept itself has been repositioned to evolve into a subject of research and practice. I begin with remix's basic definition, moving on to its common understanding in music. The impact of remix on broader cultural studies is then reviewed under the umbrella of remix culture, followed by its own reflective meta-stage of remix studies. I then consider the current stage of remix and how it could possibly change in the near future.

Remix Practice

One could actually argue that all things in life, from nature to culture, are remixes. In the cultural realm, this in fact is the argument by Kirby Ferguson who titled his online film series "Everything is a Remix."[3] But one should wonder how, even on a rhetorical level, everything could be considered a remix. And consequently question if remix as a concept, once it is applied to everything, may lead to a type of hegemonic view of the world—particularly if it is mainly defined by Western meta-narratives.

To begin, we must reflect on the basic meaning of remix; the term consists of two syllables, the prefix "re" and the root "mix." According to the New Oxford American Dictionary "mix" can be defined as a verb to "combine or put together to form one substance or mass." It can also be a noun describing something that has been mixed. The prefix "re" means "once more, afresh, anew." It can also mean "return to a previous state, restore, revert."

As a verb, remix is defined as to "mix (something) again. Produce a different version of (a musical recording) by altering the balance of the separate tracks." It is also defined as a noun, "a different version of a musical recording produced in such a way."[4] As we will learn, the fact that remix can be both a verb and a noun may be in part the reason why it is so difficult to define.

It can be noted thus far that the basic definition of remix is directly linked to music, not culture at large. It is remix's expansion as a cultural metonym for creative production as well as a practical means of communication that makes it elusive once it moves beyond the music realm. Note, however, that the term "mix" itself is not directly linked to music. This happens only after the prefix is added. This is in part due to the rise of "the remix" as a proper noun and verb during the time period when late mechanical reproduction took place in the form of digital technology.[5]

The term remix, in effect, is specific to the period in which media increasingly became part of daily life. The musical genres of Jamaican dub, disco, hip hop, trip hop, house, techno, drum 'n' bass, garage, grime, dubstep, and most recently trap, among others have all shaped remix and in turn have been reshaped by remix. This activity in music culture has become extended as a creative cultural form. The relation of music and culture is defined on material terms by the rise of mechanical reproduction, which evolved into electronic reproduction.[6] The foundation of remix, from a technical and technological point of view, starts with an innovation that made it possible to record the world. Photography made this possible in visual culture beginning in the 1820s. Yet, remix as a specific concept of sampling from recordings, became prevalent in music during the 1970s. In turn, it was extended to culture at large once the basic act of remixing became prevalent across culture and society. Computers made cut/copy and paste a basic principle of communication across networks, as well as a primary element for all types of creativity, from writing texts to creating the most complex multimedia works of art. As remix evolved, new ways of discussing creativity came about to explain what it means to produce things with pre-existing materials. This tendency was encapsulated in the term "remix culture," which was pivotal for Creative Commons.

Remix Culture

Lawrence Lessig noticed that established copyright laws were increasingly unfair to the creative practice of remix that was developing across the Internet, as people shared, copied, and uploaded new information. His initial writings, which arguably became popular and influential due to their accessibility for a general non-specialist audience, focused on the exchange of not just creative works, but all types of shared media, under the umbrella of "remix culture." This term turned out to be the backbone concept of Creative Commons, a non-profit organization whose mission is to promote the open sharing of information.[7] Lessig initially wrote about remix culture in terms of "free culture." His argument was initially linked to the free software movement. He writes, "we come from a tradition of 'free culture'—not 'free' as in 'free beer' (to borrow a phrase from the founder of the free-software movement), but 'free' as in 'free speech,' 'free markets,' 'free trade,' 'free enterprise,' 'free will,' and 'free elections.'"[8] He claims that any new work that is a result of borrowing from a previous work protected under copyright law should be allowed to be shared based on fair use, and the free exchange of ideas.

Lessig plays an important role in the history of remix. He helped deploy the concept across culture by popularizing it beyond the music realm in order to make a case for the fair and free flow of all types of creative works; albeit, his argument was primarily focused on digital works. Lessig's first book *Code and Other Laws of Cyberspace* was published in 2000—around the time that the concept of remixing began to move from the music realm to mainstream culture.[9] It is crucial to note that remix culture's popularity turned the act of remixing into a form of resistance against the implementation of copyright laws that deter creativity. Because of Lessig's interests, remix became understood as an important tool for critical practice. His contribution informs the assumption that if one is to practice remix, such an act is expected to function under the paradigm he helped establish—as a form of expression often critical of corporate interests; yet, remix does not only function as a form of resistance, but also can be implemented as an effective commercial tool. In other words, remixing can be used to do the opposite of what remix culture envisions. In fact, the first remixes were produced in part because they proved to be potentially profitable.[10] This not so apparent contradiction increases the complexity of the term.

Lessig was not alone in shifting the general understanding of remixing from music to culture at large. There were a number of other scholars who wrote about the potential of repurposing material. These include Lev Manovich, who in his book *The Language of New Media* (2001) considered the DJ, who remixes live for an audience, a key figure for understanding the emerging role of the new media producer. For Manovich it is the act of selecting from a set of information (music recordings) to create a new composition that makes the DJ a good example of a digital media producer.[11] Henry Jenkins, in his book *Convergence Culture* (2006), discusses his own term "participatory culture" to evaluate how content is recycled and transformed by fans across online communities. He discusses the economic and cultural tensions that such acts tend to develop in terms of authorship in relation to corporate interests.[12] Michael Veal, in his book *Dub* (2010), discusses the history of Jamaican versions, and at the end of his book proposes dub in terms of remix, specifically as part of global popular music. Veal's work is foundational in understanding the complex history of versioning as part of remix.[13] Paul D. Miller (aka DJ Spooky that Subliminal Kid) has been active as a DJ and music producer as well as an author on remixing since the 1990s. In his book *Rhythm Science* (2004), he discusses remix in terms of the flow of patterns across media and culture.[14] Miller also positions the DJ as a key figure for understanding creativity in times of ever-increasing recyclability.

> Paul D. Miller aka DJ Spooky is the author of Chapter 24, "Versioning," in this book.

There are many other major researchers who certainly laid the groundwork for remix studies. Some of them did not necessarily focus on remix specifically as a concept, but rather explored other elements such as sound, sampling, and repetition as foundational creative elements in the development of a global society. Tricia Rose's *Black Noise* (1994) is certainly one of these important contributions, whose focus on hip hop culture helps us better understand why the recontextualization of previously existing elements would become vital for the creative process once we developed an awareness of constant cultural recyclability.[15] Admittedly, Lawrence Lessig was and remains the most cited writer on remix culture between 2000 and 2010.[16]

Remix Studies

By 2009, scholars from various disciplines had written about remix from different points of view. Aram Sinnreich published *Mashed Up* in 2010, in which he discusses configurability to re-evaluate how creativity, primarily in music, changed once data exchange became a common activity.[17] In 2011, Kembrew McLeod and Peter DiCola published *Creative License*, in which they examine the act of sampling in music, and how it redefines our views on originals vis-à-vis copies.[18] In 2010, Vito Campanelli published *Web Aesthetics*, a book that reviews digital media in culture at large. Although only the fifth and final part of his book focuses on remix, there is a clear emphasis on remix principles throughout his argument. Campanelli's publication can be considered a predecessor to the broader interest in remixing that began to take effect around this time.[19] Carolyn Guertin published *Digital Prohibition* in 2012, a book that engages issues discussed by Sinnreich, McLeod and DiCola with a clear focus on creativity across culture.[20] The emphasis in these and similar written works published around this time, including peer-reviewed essays, emphasized the relation of the limitations on creativity by copyright law informed by Lawrence Lessig's arguments for fair use. Remix was broadened to other areas well beyond music in *Mashup Cultures* (2010), edited by Stefan Sonvilla-Weiss.[21] The book comprises essays by different authors on remix's role in media, culture, and pedagogy. My own book, *Remix Theory: The Aesthetics of Sampling* was published in 2012.[22] My goal was to trace the history of remixing as a cultural act that was not primarily related to copyright fairness, but rather as a type of discourse that permeated culture.

These books are the result of research that had been taking place for many years, and they form part of a collective body of work that continues to be produced by a growing number of scholars. There are certainly too many individuals to include here, but some that should be named include Margie Borschke, who questions Lessig's assumptions on the history of remix; Patricia Aufderheide who aims to clarify the misunderstandings that take place in fair use by creative individuals; Janneke Adema, who discusses remix in terms of the future of the book's ever-changing electronic forms; Katharina Freund and Francesca Coppa who research fan culture in relation to vidding and feminism; and Annette Markham, who discusses remix as a discourse for critical practice and ethically conscious production.[23]

Remix and the eventual development of remix studies are also informed by a great number of documentaries that cover the history of major genres, including disco, hip hop and house music, as well as the creative application of music sampling. Media companies in the United Kingdom, in particular, produced films such as *Pump Up the Volume: The History of House* (2001),[24] *Krautrock: The Rebirth of Germany* (2009),[25] and *The Joy of Disco* (2012).[26] Other documentaries focusing on remix, sampling, and turntablism include *The Hip Hop Years* (1999),[27] *Scratch* (2001),[28] and *Copyright Criminals* (2011).[29] An interest in the history of disco and hip hop has led to the production of fictional stories for Internet and TV viewers such as *The Get Down* (2016)[30] and documentaries such as *Hip Hop Evolution* (2016),[31] which attest to the ongoing interest in the history of music in relation to remix.

This consistent interest in the early days of extended remixes and sampling in disco and hip hop, is part of a reflexive moment in which material is being repurposed based on a growing awareness of recycling as a creative act. This, however, leads to a particularly formulaic approach to deliberately reuse pre-existing material. This is also sensed in social media. Facebook, in particular, at the time of writing, is reminding its members about their previous photo shares from at least three years ago. In effect, people not only recycle what they find online anew, but also recycle material that they have already shared. Simon Reynolds actually foresaw this moment in his book *Retromania*, in which he discusses an obsession with the recent past found in music during the past 40 years. It appears that such a tendency is now part of culture at large.[32] In effect, we have entered a third stage of remixing in which we are not only aware of how we recycle all things we encounter in one way or another, but how we recycle ourselves for our own amusement.

Remix studies, consequently, emerged as a diverse field of inquiry as researchers and practitioners developed a body of reflective work on the subject. *The Routledge Companion to Remix Studies*, published in 2015, can be considered a body of texts edited with the aim of capturing some of the diverging ideas on the ways remixing has been taking place, going back to the early days of rhetoric in Western history as a proper form of appropriation and repurposing.[33]

Remix, Remixability, Remixology

If remix studies makes anything evident it is our awareness that principles that have come to shape creativity have been with us since at least the time we developed the concept of culture. Different terms have been used to evaluate this issue. This is evident in the development of remix culture and remix studies outlined above. There are particular terms that have spun out in order to develop an emphasis on aspects relevant to a specific researcher's interests. In this regard, the keywords that comprise *Keywords in Remix Studies* include appropriation, collaborative, bricolage, cut-up, mashup, memes, sampling and versioning, to name just a few.[34] There are certainly many more terms that are also closely related to remix that were not included in this book, which only adds to the point that remix is a common practice that continues to promote and support social awareness of creativity as a collective process.

Some variations on the term remix are worth mentioning. Lev Manovich, for instance, discusses remix in terms of "deep remixability," which he sees informing a structure at play in direct relation to modularity and data.[35] Another term that should be mentioned is "remixology," which has been specifically used by three authors who have published books on the subject. *Remixology* is the title of a book by Paul Sullivan; he traces the influence of Jamaican dub in different music genres around the world.[36] The term is also used by Mark Amerika to describe his approach to remixing creative and theoretical material, which he publishes as hybrid fictional and theoretical works such as *Remixthebook*.[37] David J. Gunkel uses the term to encapsulate his philosophical reflections on remix studies, based on primary and secondary research, produced by many of the scholars previously mentioned. Gunkel makes a point of taking remix all the way back to the early days of the Greeks. He claims in his book, appropriately titled *Of Remixology*, that Plato's *Phaedrus* is a type of remix of the performed word.[38] It is in Gunkel's book where we can find a moment of meta-reflection, which may well show that remix is developing into a proper, yet sprawling field of study. For this reason, it is worth elaborating a bit more on his argument.

What is unique in Gunkel's argument is his claim that everyone, both those who see remix as a truly creative practice and those who see it as a lazy activity, have been approaching it in a limited fashion:

> both sides of the conflict value and endeavor to protect the same things. One side sees remix as providing new modes of original expression that require considerable effort and skill on the part of producers; the other argues that there is not much originality, innovation, or effort in merely sampling and remixing prerecorded material. [. . .] Consequently, if one wanted to summarize what follows [in the book] in a neat sound-bite package, it could be said that what I will argue is that the copyright gets the remix wrong but does so for the right reasons, while the copyleft gets the remix right but for the wrong reasons.[39]

Gunkel goes on to argue that we need to re-evaluate such normalized positions in order to reconsider Platonic thinking, which, according to him, has been the order that has defined representation of the world, including remixing, since the beginning of culture. Gunkel's answer to the usual approach to remix from both sides of the argument is to flip Platonic thinking. To achieve this, he applies to remix the philosophical ideas of Gilles Deleuze in terms of difference and repetition to propose a Nietzschean approach to representation as defined by Plato.

Gunkel argues that everyone who has written about remix thus far has done so based on what Deleuze sees as a first order of repetition, which presents copies in juxtaposition to originals. This is the Platonic model that, according to him, has defined how we view the world. Gunkel, based on Deleuze, proposes to view the world according to a second order of repetition, one that is defined not by differentiating copies from originals, but by viewing what normally would be called copies or originals as compositions consisting of pre-existing materials and ideas; from this standpoint, everything already is a copy of a copy, or copies. In other words, for Gunkel, following Deleuzian thinking, all things consist of already-existing elements that are brought together through the "difference of repetition."[40] This is quite evident for him in remix: "Remix does not consist in the technological preservation and reproduction of some original and prior live performance. It instead manufactures new originals from copies."[41] His main issue is that repetition in remix, as practiced under Platonism, is turned into a concept, which is not what Deleuze proposes in terms of difference and repetition.[42] In other words, once the relation of difference and repetition is turned into a concept, the terms, in effect, become subjects of representation under Platonism. Deleuze rather sees repetition and difference in relation to a constant *becoming*.

Gunkel's position is arguably polemical, due to the fact that he is calling out major figures in Western thought to be subjected to Platonic thinking. He argues that such individuals are unable to move past a specific type of worldview that is defined by a somewhat narrow type of repetition as a concept that is comfortably re-implemented by each generation as cultures evolve. His criticism sweeps over some of the most respected philosophers in history, such as Kant, Hegel, Adorno, and Heidegger, among many others, as well as just about all of the most relevant remix theorists and practitioners. It is with Deleuze, as noted above, and Žižek (in the last part of his book) that Gunkel finds some innovative approaches to remix that can help us, according to him, move in a different direction from the first form of Platonic repetition.

Conclusion: [Re]-mix-[ed]-[de]-terminations

Whether or not one agrees with a particular position in remix studies, from its early days, mainly as a practice, to a time of cultural acknowledgment as remix culture according to Lessig, on to remix studies, remixability and remixology as discussed by Manovich, Amerika, and Gunkel among many others, what must be noted is that such contributions to remix do provide much to reconsider. Based on this, after having surveyed the brief history of the word "remix" as a cultural variable, one can notice the complexity that has developed as it continues to play an important role in all aspects of cultural production. If anything, the term has entered an advanced meta-stage, which makes possible critical reflections that not only continue to re-evaluate remix itself, but the actual debate around it.

This brings us back to my previous point on the two syllables that comprise remix, the "re" and the "mix," and their relation to the word functioning as both production and action. To reiterate, remix is both a verb and a noun. This is the case with other words, but what is peculiar about remix is that what it describes and also is, is a specific cultural variable that is vital to just about all areas of cultural production. It describes the repurposing of something by being both action and object. This in itself may well be a constant process of becoming, but one that also is likely to push remix to remain on the margins of the mainstream. Paradoxically, this is what enables it to keep changing, because when a remix is produced, it is a thing that can be named, commodified and repurposed—only to begin that cycle afresh: such a thing is then taken and repurposed to become something different.

To conclude, if there is a possible consensus among the individuals who have written and continue to write about remix, it is that remix is a peculiar form of cultural production that points to constant change, defined by its very own process of constant becoming in terms of practice and criticism. And to this effect, paradoxically, to engage with remix critically also exposes its limitations. This may well be what becomes apparent in remix's meta-stage at the time of this writing. When we reconsider Gunkel's contribution, which, while asking us to turn Platonism on its head, is also inscribing inadvertently an abstract and open-ended yet "proper" way of both producing and writing about remix by using Deleuze's reflections on constant becoming as the way to engage with it critically, such a view remains defined by Western thought, unable to acknowledge the fact that remix itself is not solely informed by Western practices. An example of someone who has looked at representation and repetition from another point of view is Tricia Rose, who argues that repetition for hip hop does not function as outlined by Gunkel. Rose explains that repetition as defined by Western thought in the works of Adorno, Attali, and Jameson is presented as a tool of mass production—directly linked to capitalism, in contrast to its musical function in repetitive patterns found in African rhythms.[43] Rose views repetition not in terms of originals versus copies, or copies of copies, but rather as a circular process (a loop) marked by cuts that make possible the actual repetition that allows for something to be left and picked up as one comes around to it, thus falling outside of Western philosophy's ideological tendency to function in terms of progression towards some greater goal, based on an abstract concept of accumulation (contribution to knowledge, which finds an equivalent drive in mass culture as gain of capital). Considering Rose's position on repetition, which she directly connects to sampling and hip hop culture in order to discuss originality in rap music, what becomes evident in the critical writings of remix studies is not so much a blanket Platonic interpretation by everyone who participates, but rather a constant and fragmented renegotiation of "repetition" as a form of resistance to emerging forms of marginalization often found in capitalism. Ultimately, in order for remix studies to remain a critical field, it needs to stay alert against becoming a homogenized form itself; because remix, as a practice, by default, thrives on the margins of culture, and burgeons by remaining resistant to the very elements that make it possible.

Notes

1 For different approaches in remix studies see Eduardo Navas, Owen Gallagher, and xtine Burrough, eds., *The Routledge Companion to Remix Studies* (New York: Routledge, 2015).
2 In this sense remix is dialogical. See Martin Irvine, "Remix and the Dialogic Engine of Culture," *Remix Studies*, 15–42.
3 Kirby Ferguson, "Everything is a Remix," available on http://everythingisaremix.info.
4 For the definitions of mix and remix see *The New Oxford American Dictionary* (Oxford: Oxford University Press, 2015).
5 I explain this at length in Eduardo Navas "Remix[ing] Sampling," in *Remix Theory: The Aesthetics of Sampling* (New York: Springer, 2012), 9–31.
6 John Mowitt, "The Sound of Music in the Era of Its Electronic Reproducibility," *The Sound Studies Reader*, ed. Jonathan Sterne (New York: Routledge, 2012), 213–224.
7 Creative Commons remains an important organization in the debates of fair use: https://creativecommons.org.
8 Lawrence Lessig, *Free Culture: The Nature and Future of Creativity* (New York: Penguin, 2004), xiv.

9 For a set of charts that show this development, see Navas, "Remix[ing] Sampling."
10 This can be noted in the early stages of disco, when extended remixes were produced because there was a demand for them by the emergence of DJ pools and nightclubs, initially in NYC. An early and parallel example is the production of dub plates, (versions) in Jamaica because there was a demand by the local dancehalls. Both were countercultural movements reacting to different types of political repression, closely bound with a basic monetary incentive that led to the professional production of remixes for the gain of capital. These examples expose the complex relation of remix with for-profit interests in forms that cannot be aligned solely with an anti-corporate position.
11 Lev Manovich, "From Object to Signal," in *The Language of New Media* (Cambridge: MIT Press, 2001), 134–135.
12 Henry Jenkins, *Convergence Culture: Where Old and New Media Collide* (New York: New York University Press, 2006).
13 Michael Veal, "Coda: Electronica, Remix Culture, and Jamaica as a source of Transformative Strategies in Global Popular Music," in *Dub: Soundscapes and Shattered Songs in Jamaican Reggae* (Middletown, CT: Wesleyan University Press, 2007), 220–260.
14 Paul D. Miller, *Rhythm Science* (Cambridge, MA: MIT Press, 2004).
15 Tricia Rose, *Black Noise: Rap Music and Black Culture in Contemporary America* (Middletown: Wesleyan University Press, 1994).
16 Lessig's research, at the time of this writing, deals with the electoral politics in the United States.
17 Aram Sinnreich, *Mashed Up: Music, Technology and the Rise of Configurable Culture* (Amherst and Boston: University of Massachusetts Press, 2010).
18 Kembrew McLeod and Peter DiCola, *Creative License: The Law and Culture of Digital Sampling* (Durham and London: Duke University Press, 2011).
19 Vito Campanelli, *Web Aesthetics: How Digital Media Affect Culture and Society* (Amsterdam: Nai Publishers, 2010).
20 Carolyn Guertin, *Digital Prohibition: Piracy and Authorship in New Media* (London: Bloomsbury, 2012).
21 Stefan Sonvilla-Weiss, *Mashup Cultures* (New York: Springer, 2010).
22 Navas, *Remix Theory*.
23 There are many more individuals that cannot be listed. For some of them see other keyword contributions in this publication as well as *The Routledge Companion to Remix Studies*, also see the bibliography of this chapter.
24 Karl Hindmarch, director, *Pump Up the Volume: The History of House*, Flame Television, USA, 2001, www.imdb.com/title/tt0847411/.
25 Benjamin Walley, director, *Krautrock: The Rebirth of Germany*, BBC, UK, 2009, www.bbc.co.uk/programmes/b00nf10k.
26 Benjamin Walley, director, *The Joy of Disco*, BBC, UK, 2012, www.bbc.co.uk/programmes/b01cqt72.
27 David Upshal, director, *The Hip Hop Years*, Channel 4, UK, 1999, www.ovguide.com/tv/the_hip_hop_years.htm.
28 Doug Pray, director, *Scratch*, Firewalks Film, 2001, www.imdb.com/title/tt0143861/.
29 Benjamin Franzen and Kembrew McLeod, directors, *Copyright Criminals*, Changing Images, www.pbs.org/independentlens/copyright-criminals/.
30 Stephen Adly Guirgis and Baz Luhrmann, creators, *The Get Down*, Netflix, USA, 2016, www.netflix.com/title/80025601.
31 Darby Wheeler and Sam Dunn, *Hip Hop Evolution*, Netflix, US (2016), www.netflix.com/title/80141782.
32 Simon Reynolds, *Retromania: Pop Culture's Addiction to Its Own Past* (New York: Faber & Faber, 2011).
33 See the "History" section in *The Routledge Companion to Remix Studies*.
34 See the table of contents for other keywords.

35 Lev Manovich, "Deep Remixability," *Software Takes Command* (New York: Bloomsbury, 2013), 267–277.
36 Paul Sullivan, *Remixology: Tracing the Dub Diaspora* (London: Reaktion, 2014).
37 A book that encapsulates Amerika's long term practice and research is Mark Amerika, *Remixthebook* (Minneapolis and London: Minnesota Press, 2011).
38 David J. Gunkel, *Of Remixology: Ethics and Aesthetics after Remix* (Cambridge, MA: MIT Press, 2016), 33-58.
39 Ibid., xx.
40 Ibid., 111.
41 Ibid., 61.
42 Ibid., 97, 111.
43 Tricia Rose, *Black Noise*, 69–72

Bibliography

Remix

Attali, Jacques. *Noise: The Political Economy of Music*. Translated by B. Massumi. Minneapolis, MN: University of Minnesota Press, 1985.

Bennett, Andrew. *The Author*. New York: Routledge, 2005.

Burgess, Jean, and Joshua Green. *YouTube: Online Video and Participatory Culture*. Cambridge: Polity Press, 2009.

Boon, Marcus. *In Praise of Copying*. Cambridge, MA: Harvard University Press, 2010.

Bourriaud, Nicolas. *Postproduction: Culture as Screenplay: How Art Reprograms the World*, 2nd edition. New York: Lukas & Sternberg, 2005.

Brewster, Bill and Frank Broughton. *Last Night a DJ Saved My Life: The History of the Disc Jockey*. London: Headline, 2006.

Bryant, John. *The Fluid Text: A Theory of Revision and Editing for Book and Screen*. Ann Arbor, MI: University of Michigan Press, 2002.

Chang, Jeff. *Can't Stop Won't Stop: A History of the Hip Hop Generation*. New York: St. Martin's Press, 2005.

Cox, David. *Sign Wars: The Culture Jammers Strike Back*. Australia: LedaTape, 2005.

Evans, David, ed. *Appropriation*. London & Cambridge, MA: Whitechapel & MIT Press, 2009.

Eshun, Kodwo. *More Brilliant than the Sun: Adventures in Sonic Fiction*. London: Quartet Books, 1998.

Flusser, Vilém. *Into the Universe of Technical Images*. Minneapolis, MN: University of Minnesota Press, 2011.

Goldsmith, Kenneth. *Uncreative Writing*. New York: Colombia University Press, 2011.

Hyde, Lewis. *The Gift: How the Creative Spirit Transforms the World*. Edinburgh: Canongate, 2007.

Jameson, Fredric. *Postmodernism or, the Cultural Logic of Late Capitalism*. Durham, NC: Duke University Press, 1991.

Jenkins, Henry. *Fans, Blogger, and Gamers: Exploring Participatory Culture*. New York: New York University Press, 2006.

Katz, Mark. *Capturing Sound: How Technology Has Changed Music*. Berkeley, CA: University of California Press, 2004.

———. *Groove Music: The Art and Culture of the Hip-Hop DJ*. Oxford: Oxford University Press, 2012.

Lessig, Lawrence. *Code and Other Laws of Cyberspace*. New York: Penguin, 1999.
Manovich, Lev. *The Language of New Media*. Cambridge, MA: MIT Press, 2001.
———. *Software Takes Command*. New York: Bloomsbury, 2013.
Poschardt, Ulf. *DJ Culture*. Translated by Shaun Whiteside. London: Quartet Books Ltd., 1998.
Reynolds, Simon. *Retromania: Pop Culture's Addiction to Its Own Past*. New York: Farber & Farber, 2011.
Rose, Tricia. *Black Noise: Rap Music and Black Culture in Contemporary America*. Middletown: Wesleyan University Press, 1994.
Schäfer, Mirko Tobias. *Bastard Culture! How User Participation Transforms Cultural Production*. Amsterdam: Amsterdam University Press, 2008.
Shirky, Clay. *Here Comes Everybody: The Power of Organizing Without Organizations*. New York: Penguin Press, 2008.
Sterne, Jonathan. *The Audible Past: Cultural Origins of Sound Reproduction*. Durham, NC: Duke University Press, 2003.
———, ed. *The Sound Studies Reader*. New York: Routledge, 2012.
Tapscott, Don and Anthony D. Williams. *Wikinomics: How Mass Collaboration Changes Everything*. New York: Penguin, 2006.
Vaidhyanathan, Siva. *Copyrights and Copywrongs: The Rise of Intellectual Property and How It Threatens Creativity*. New York: New York University Press, 2001.

Remix Culture

Aufderheide, Patricia. *Reclaiming Fair Use: How to Put Balance Back in Copyright*. Chicago, IL: University of Chicago Press, 2011.
Berry, David M. *Copy, Rip, Burn: The Politics of Copyleft and Open Source*. London: Pluto Press, 2008.
Borschke, Margie. *Rethinking the Rhetoric of Remix: Copies and Material Culture in Digital Networks*. PhD dissertation, University of New South Wales, Sydney, 2012.
Boyle, James. *The Public Domain: Enclosing the Commons of the Mind*. New Haven, CT: Yale University Press, 2008.
Bruns, Axel. *Blogs, Wikipedia, Second Life, and Beyond: From Production to Produsage*. New York: Peter Lang, 2008.
Crews, Kenneth. "The Law of Fair Use and the Illusion of Fair-Use Guidelines." *Ohio State Law Journal* 62 (2001): 98.
Decherney, Peter. *Hollywood's Copyright Wars: From Edison to the Internet*. New York: Columbia University Press, 2012.
Evans, David. *Appropriation: Documents of Contemporary Art*. Cambridge, MA: MIT Press, 2009.
Jenkins, Henry. *Convergence Culture: Where Old and New Media Collide*. New York: New York University Press, 2006.
Lessig, Lawrence. *The Future of Ideas: The Fate of the Commons in a Connected World*. New York: Vintage, 2002.
———. *Free Culture: The Nature and Future of Creativity*. New York: Penguin, 2004.
———. *Remix: Making Art and Commerce Thrive in the Hybrid Economy*. New York: Penguin, 2008.
Mason, Matt. *The Pirate's Dilemma: How Youth Culture Is Reinventing Capitalism*. New York: Free Press, 2009.

McLeod, Kembrew. *Freedom of Expression®: Resistance and Repression in the Age of Intellectual Property*. Minneapolis, MN: University of Minnesota Press, 2007.
McLeod, Kembrew, and Peter DiCola. *Creative License: The Law and Culture of Digital Sampling*. Durham, NC: Duke University Press, 2011.
McLeod, Kembrew, and Rudolf Kuenzli, eds. *Cutting Across Media: Appropriation Art, Interventionist Collage, and Copyright Law*. Durham, NC: Duke University Press, 2011.
Miller, Paul D. *Rhythm Science*. Cambridge, MA: MIT Press, 2004.
———. *Sound Unbound*. Cambridge, MA: MIT Press, 2008.
Veal, Michael. *Dub: Soundscapes and Shattered Songs in Jamaican Reggae*. Middletown, CT: Wesleyan University Press, 2007.

Remix Studies

Amerika, Mark. *Remixthebook*. Minneapolis and London: Minnesota Press, 2011.
Aufderheide, Patricia, and Peter Jaszi. *Reclaiming Fair Use: How to Put Balance Back in Copyright*. Chicago, IL: University of Chicago Press, 2011.
Campanelli, Vito. *Web Aesthetics: How Digital Media Affect Culture and Society*. Amsterdam: Nai Publishers, 2010.
Guertin, Carolyn. *Digital Prohibition: Piracy and Authorship in New Media*. London: Bloomsbury, 2012.
Gunkel, David J. *Of Remixology: Ethics and Aesthetics after Remix*. Cambridge, Cambridge, MA: MIT Press, 2016.
Jenkins, Henry et al. (2013) *Spreadable Media: Creating Value and Meaning in a Networked Culture*. New York: NYU Press.
Laderman, David and Laurel Westrup. *Sampling Media*. Oxford: Oxford University Press, 2014.
Morales, Aaron. *American Mashup: A Popular Culture Reader*. London: Pearson, 2012.
Navas, Eduardo. *Theory: The Aesthetics of Sampling*. New York: Springer, 2012.
Navas, Eduardo, Owen Gallagher, and xtine burrough, eds, *The Routledge Companion to Remix Studies*. New York: Routledge, 2015.
Sinnreich, Aram. *Mashed Up: Music, Technology and the Rise of Configurable Culture*. Amherst and Boston: University of Massachusetts Press, 2010.
———. *The Piracy Crusade*. Amherst and Boston: University of Massachusetts Press, 2014.
Sonvilla-Weiss, Stefan. *Mashup Cultures*. New York: Springer, 2010.
Sullivan, Paul. *Remixology: Tracing the Dub Diaspora*. London: Reaktion, 2014.

22
SAMPLING

Owen Gallagher

> If we can quote text from Hemingway's *For Whom the Bell Tolls* in an essay, we can quote a section from Sam Wood's film of Hemingway's *For Whom the Bell Tolls* in a film. If we can quote lyrics from a Bob Dylan song in a piece about Vietnam, we can quote a recording of Bob Dylan singing those lyrics in a video about that war. The act is the same; only the source is different.
>
> Lawrence Lessig[1]

It is fitting to begin a chapter on sampling with a quote, and this particular quote from Lawrence Lessig's *Remix* (2008), demonstrates the tension that exists when attempting to conceptualize the idea of sampling in a multi-modal context. Sampling is one of the most fundamental terms to understand in relation to remix. It is also a term that has been interpreted differently by numerous authors,[2] as with the term remix itself, resulting in a plethora of semantic variations in the existing literature. This chapter considers a number of these interpretations and attempts to clarify and distil the core elements of sampling. In our media-saturated societies of the 2010s, the inconsistent ways we deal with sampling in different forms, whether legally, ethically or practically, does not always tally with the reality that the fundamental act of sampling is the same, whether one samples from a book, a picture, a film or a song. The historical context of how sampling developed throughout the twentieth century is considered, as well as its symbiotic relationship with recording technologies, and how sampling works differently across various forms of media from audio to video; text to image; software to interactive media.

Defining Sampling

My earliest personal memory of sampling is from my childhood—in 1980s Ireland, my brother and I would make our own news and weather broadcasts using an old Sanyo tape recorder. We would record our voices onto cassette using the built-in microphone and play back music from TV shows we had "taped," such as the themes from *The A-Team* and *MacGyver*,[3] which acted as intro and outro music for our fictional news segments. We used a JVC VCR to record the TV shows onto videotape (a process that came to be known as "time-shifting") and the speakers from our old wooden PYE television played back the music while we "broadcast" our news and weather segments. We were young kids having fun with the analog technologies available to us at the time and we didn't realize it until much later, but we were engaged in the practice of sampling. By capturing these snippets of well-known TV themes and repurposing them as intro music for our fictional news segments, we were remixing them.

Many authors who have considered sampling in their work acknowledge the fundamental stages of remix, which include: (1) the appropriation of an extant recorded artifact as source material; (2) the manipulation or editing of a sample from the source; and (3) the repurposing and recombining of the sampled element with other elements as part of a new remixed work.

According to the Oxford English Dictionary, a "sample" is "a representative part or single item from a larger whole or group."[4] Westrup and Laderman define sampling as "the process of taking already existent musical ingredients and recombining them in an original mix."[5] McLeod and DiCola, in their definition, also consider sampling to be specific to the realm of sound: "Fundamentally, sampling is a form of the fine arts practice of collage, but one that is done with audio tools rather than scissors and glue."[6]

Sonvilla-Weiss offers a more expansive and inclusive definition, choosing not to restrict sampling solely to music:

> Collage, montage, sampling or remix practices all use one or many materials, media either from other sources, art pieces (visual arts, film, music, video, literature etc.) or one's own artwork through alteration, re-combination, manipulation, copying etc. to create a whole new piece. In doing so, the sources of origin may still be identifiable yet not perceived as the original version.[7]

Navas goes further, beyond merely sampling from an existing recorded artifact, to include in his definition sampling from life itself:

> Sampling as an act is basically what takes place in any form of mechanical recording—whether one copies, by taking a photograph, or cuts, by taking part of an object or subject, such as cutting part of a leaf to study under a microscope.[8]

Such a range of definitions begs the questions, what is the nature of sampling? Where does it end and where does it begin? What may or may not be described as sampling? Is the term suitable for all forms of media? These questions are important because confusion can be caused when the terms "sampling" and "remixing" are used synonymously. Sampling plays a fundamental role in the creation of any remix; however, there are important distinctions between the two activities. Sampling is a precursor to remixing. It is an essential stage in the process towards producing a remix. As Gunkel observes, "Sampling has been distinguished from and situated as the antecedent to remixing, which is then characterized as the subsequent process of recombining these sampled fragments."[9] At the risk of stating the obvious, the samples are what is being remixed. If one were only to sample and stop there, it would be akin to physically cutting out a number of images from different magazines and leaving them in a pile on the floor. If one does nothing with the samples, then all you have done is selected, without composing, recombining or remixing them into a coherent whole.[10] The sampling stage is merely the compiling of an archive of elements that will subsequently be used to create something new. Once the magazine images have been pasted onto a piece of paper in some kind of order, we have the makings of a collage. When any sample is inserted or pasted into a new composition, the process of creating a remix has begun. 'Pasting' can occur in various digital ways, such as copying and pasting an image onto a new Photoshop canvas or importing a video or audio clip into Adobe Premiere's editing timeline, for example. As Navas notes: "Sampling is the key element that makes the act of remixing possible. In order for Remix to take effect, an originating source must be sampled in part or in whole. However, sampling favors fragmentation over the whole."[11]

Remix is the second, compositional stage that can only occur post-sampling. Remixing is post-production—deciding which samples to use, where to place them in the composition, creating juxtapositions of meaning by placing two different samples in temporal or spatial proximity, or recombining them in some way to produce something novel. The techniques and methods used to blend the samples together, i.e., mixing, fading, masking and transitions, bring the remix together into a single work of art, as opposed to merely selecting a disparate collection of random samples.

Historical Context

According to Westrup and Laderman:

> The history of sampling stretches as far back as the 1590s, where "to sample" was a term of comparison. In its original usage, one item or emotion could be sampled and matched to other such items or emotions. These connotations of comparison and matching persist in the discourse of sampling in

the sense that samples are always *placed* in a new context that warrants comparison between the old text and the new text.[12]

This comparison between the source material and the remixed version is a fundamental aspect of sampling. Sampled elements in a remixed work become explicitly identifiable to an audience once the source material has been seen, heard or read. For this reason, it is relatively difficult for a remixer to plagiarize a sample with the intention of passing it off as one's own work, especially in the age of the Internet, when one can easily search and compare texts, images, songs and videos online. In mainstream and academic discourse, the origins of sampling have frequently been situated within DJ culture and the development of hip hop in the underground music scene of 1970s New York.[13] DJs often sampled from obscure music tracks in the production of their remixes, but generally endeavored to acknowledge the sources from which they sampled. However, the practice of sampling also has origins much earlier than this outside of music culture, for example in Duchamp and Picasso's Dada and collage art in the 1910s, in Eisenstein's Soviet propaganda films of the 1920s, and of course the use of direct quotation in literature and notated music is arguably a form of sampling that has been in practice since the invention of the printing press in the 1400s. As Gunkel notes:

> Sampling [is connected] to the practice of citation, especially in music composition . . . But unlike the forms of borrowing deployed in classical music, for example, sampling does not just quote from another work; it makes an exact copy of the actual performance of that work.[14]

In this sense, sampling from literature may be considered a special case, slightly different in nature to sampling from images, music or film, as the act of retyping the quoted words into a new text document is technically different from materially copying and pasting part of an existing photograph, a drum break or a film clip into a new composition. As Sinnreich argues, the language used to describe sampling can sometimes be inadequate to describe the level of conceptual detail involved in the process:

> The act of sampling, in which a bit of recorded sound or video is copied, transformed, and redeployed in a new setting and context, is still so strange and new that even the experts in the field can't find appropriate language to describe it . . . Sampling isn't "taking," because the borrowed source material is still available, intact, in its original form. It's not "borrowing," because the sampler doesn't ever return the work, except in a holistic sense. It's not "quoting" because a) it's the mediated expression itself, not merely the ideas behind it that's being used, and b) the output often bears little or no resemblance to the input. Even the term "expression" . . . is something of a misnomer; etymologically, the word suggests the process of squeezing

out something internal. Instead, sampling would more appropriately be termed "respiration"—the absorption, alteration, and exhalation of something external and ubiquitous.[15]

This idea of sampling as respiration, whereby content is absorbed/appropriated, transformed/remixed and released/published in an altered form, is a relatively accurate way to understand the remix process as it generally occurs. There are also parallels with the ways in which we learn as human beings: first we absorb what we see and hear (input); then we attempt to imitate this input in our own unique way; finally we apply what speaks to us in our daily lives and activities. It is important to note that while the basic act of sampling is the same regardless of the medium in which it takes place, the language used and the effects produced can be quite different. For example, the term "sampling" is most often used in the context of music. In literature, the same act of cutting, copying and pasting is known as "quoting." In film, photography and art we have different terms such as using "found footage," creating a "photo-montage" or using an act of "appropriation" as a strategy to describe the same fundamental process.

The contemporary and familiar form of sampling images, sound and film has been technically possible since the invention of various mechanical recording technologies in the late nineteenth and early twentieth centuries. When the camera was invented, one could sample images by taking a photograph of a painting or part of another printed photograph, or by stacking or combining negatives in the dark room. With a movie camera, one could sample by recording another film displayed on a projector screen or by splicing together different sections of a film reel by physically cutting and pasting them together. When the phonograph was invented, one could sample sound by recording the playback of the audio from another phonograph record, or multiple sources simultaneously. These devices, which enabled the "copying" or reproduction of reality in image, sound or motion picture form, also enabled producers to copy the copies they had created, by using one device for playback and another to simultaneously record.

Throughout the twentieth century, there were sporadic examples of experimental sample-based remix in the fields of fine art, photography, film and music but it is widely believed that sampling and remix did not come of age until the 1970s, in the underground DJ scene, as artistically depicted in Baz Luhrmann's Netflix series, *The Get Down* (2016).[16] Influenced by Jamaican dub mixes, New York DJs such as Grandmaster Flash and DJ Kool Herc began to manipulate and recombine obscure samples in their live DJ sets, remixing drumbeats and music from different records using twin decks simultaneously and often inviting MCs to rap over the sampled music (Figure 22.1). Thus hip hop and rap were born from sampling.

Sampling also continued to develop in other media forms reliant on analog recording technologies such as the video art of Craig Baldwin, Dara Birnbaum and Nam June Paik, as well as the appropriation art of Sherrie Levine, Richard

FIGURE 22.1 Screenshot of "Be in the moment" scene from *The Get Down* (2016) featuring Grandmaster Flash teaching the fundamentals of turntablism to his followers (www.youtube.com/watch?v=fo2Hqz0vamU).

Prince, Jeff Koons and Barbara Kruger, among others. Analog recording technologies were relatively cumbersome and time-consuming, involving a number of expensive processes and equipment—for example, grooving LP records, developing film, and so on—however, technologies advanced during the twentieth century. LP records were gradually replaced by magnetic cassette tapes and film reels by Beta and VHS videotapes. These represented significant improvements in portability and convenience, yet it was not until the 1980s and 1990s when computers and digital technologies converged with the Internet that sampling and remix truly became ubiquitous. It became possible to contain music, images and video in compressed digital files, which could be stored and played back on computers (e.g., mp3s, JPGs, mp4s). Once all media formats were reducible to binary computer code, it was easier than ever before to sample and remix in ways that were hitherto difficult, time-consuming, and prohibitively expensive. Now anyone with a computer, the appropriate software and a library of media files could sample and create remixes. As Westrup and Laderman summarize:

> While both sampling and remix truly reach back throughout the history of art, literature, and even culture itself, they can perhaps most fruitfully be understood as recent incarnations of the notion of appropriation, a practice that characterizes so many 20th century art trends (Dada ready-mades, surrealism, pop art etc.). Though some have cogently argued that what we think of today as sampling and remix began in the video age of the 1980s, both terms, in their current usage, seemed to really take off during the blossoming of digital culture in the mid-1990s.[17]

This paved the way for the rise of electronic music in all its forms, as well as the emergence of many well-known digital video remixers such as Emergency

Broadcast Network (EBN), Gorilla Tapes, Negativland and Eclectic Method. Today sampling has become a pervasive online cultural practice, perpetuated by apps, Internet-connected mobile devices and social media. Most people sample and remix regularly, without necessarily being aware that they are doing so. Remix has become part of the language and toolset with which we communicate online in the twenty-first century. As Navas observes:

> Technically speaking, when considering the basic definition of sampling [. . .] early technology enabled people to sample from the world and eventually from sampled material. In current times the latter becomes a default state with the computer: to sample means to copy/cut & paste. Most importantly, this action is the same for image, sound and text. In this sense, the computer is a sampling machine: from a wide cultural point of view, the ultimate remixing tool.[18]

It is now easier, faster and more affordable than ever before to copy and paste a sample from an image, video or piece of music and make something new with it. Powerful computers combined with Internet access and media editing software such as Adobe Photoshop, Premiere, Audition and After Effects make it easy to select, isolate and manipulate individual smaller samples from a larger whole and then recombine or remix them into a new composition.

People use these and similar tools for myriad purposes, from creating amateur social media memes to producing feature length documentary films like Michael Moore's *Where to Invade Next*,[19] which features numerous samples and remix sequences to more effectively communicate persuasive arguments and propositions.

Recording vs. Sampling

In *Remix Theory*, Navas states that recording and sampling are essentially synonymous:

> Early recording, in essence, is a form of sampling from the world that may not appear as such to those used to the conventional terms in which the concepts of recording and sampling are understood. According to the basic definition of capturing material (which can then be re-sampled, re-recorded, dubbed and re-dubbed), sampling and recording are synonymous following their formal signification [. . .] Recording is a form of sampling because it derives from the concept of cutting a piece from a bigger whole.[20]

While this position may be valid from a purely conceptual perspective, in practice it is important to differentiate between sampling from reality and sampling from extant recordings, as to equate these distinct activities can lead to confusion in understanding the effects of sampling in different forms of media. To illustrate this difference, let us first consider the process of recording sound. In audio engineering, the term "sample" has a more specific technical meaning than the definitions we have considered thus far. Most often used in the context of "signal processing," that is, the recording and converting of analog sound waves into digital form, sampling in this context may be defined as "the reduction of a continuous-time signal to a discrete-time signal," such as the conversion of a sound wave (a continuous signal) to a sequence of samples (a discrete-time signal).[21] Essentially, the value of the signal (i.e., the sound) is measured at certain intervals in time. The more frequent the intervals, the higher the fidelity of the recorded artifact. Each of these interval measurements is known as a "sample" and the frequency of these intervals is referred to as the "sample rate."[22] As we can already see, this type of sampling is somewhat different from copying and pasting part of an image for reuse in a collage, or reusing a drum-break from another song in a new hip hop track. The former is primarily about reproducing analog signals from the real world as authentically as possible, while the latter is part of an artistic process to remix disparate elements from extant sources into new creative works.

When someone's voice is recorded with a microphone into an audio recording device, the sound is captured at a particular sample rate, which effectively means that some, but not all of the original sound is captured. The higher the sample rate (e.g., 44,100 kHz for CD quality), the higher the fidelity and the more accurately the recording represents the actual sound in reality. So when we record audio with a microphone, we are recording sound from real life, whereas when a DJ creates a remix, they are sampling from an existing recording. As with Plato's *Theory of Forms*,[23] where a distinction is drawn between forms and representations of forms, we must similarly differentiate between recording from life and recording from a recording.

The Art of Sampling

Remixing samples is an art. As with all creative arts, simply knowing how to do something does not necessarily mean one knows how to do it well. Contrary to the popular belief that any kid with a laptop in his bedroom can be a remixer,[24] sampling and remixing, like most creative arts, require talent, knowledge, experience, timing and skill. Perhaps the best way to better understand sampling is by considering how samples are used in a well-known example of multi-modal remix. Let us consider a musical remix video by MelodySheep, aka John Boswell, from his *Symphony of Science* series. The most viewed remix video in this series is *A Glorious Dawn* (10.6 million views, YouTube, 2017), featuring Carl Sagan and Stephen Hawking.[25] Almost all of the sampled video clips are appropriated from the PBS TV documentaries *Cosmos* (1980)[26] and *Universe* (1997),[27] presented by Sagan and Hawking respectively (Figure 22.2). Boswell has produced numerous music remix videos in this style, including his *Remixes for the Soul* series, as

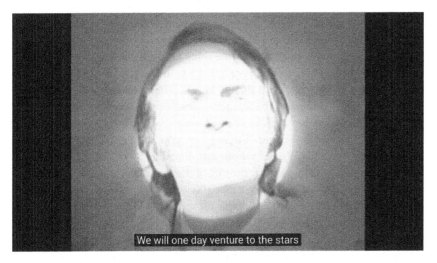

FIGURE 22.2 Screenshot from *A Glorious Dawn* (2009), with Carl Sagan "singing" about science (www.youtube.com/watch?v=zSgiXGELjbc).

well as a number of commercial remix projects for PBS, Old Spice, Lucky Charms and Disney Junior.[28] From a production perspective, Boswell's work is the polar opposite of hip hop, where rappers and singers perform new vocals over sampled and remixed music. In *A Glorious Dawn* and all of Boswell's subsequent work, new music is performed beneath sampled and remixed vocals. The dialogue is the primary sampled audio element, while the accompanying clips from the TV series comprise the sampled visuals. The well-known audio engineering process of "auto-tune" is utilized to full effect, along with other digital audio manipulation techniques, to create new melodies and rhythms from the recorded speech patterns of the video subjects' dialogue (Sagan and Hawking, in this case). Newly produced music, composed, performed and recorded by Boswell himself using a variety of instruments (frequently electronic drum beats, guitars, piano and orchestral keyboard/synthesizer tracks), is layered and seamlessly remixed with the auto-tuned vocal samples. The effect is surreal and arresting.

In *A Glorious Dawn*, the impact of hearing Professor Hawking's computerized voice "singing" auto-tuned about the vastness of the universe is truly memorable. Boswell's process for sampling and remixing follows the steps as described at the beginning of this chapter, that is, selection/manipulation/composition. In this case, the TV series *Cosmos* and *Universe* were the primary sources of material from which a number of specific samples were chosen to create a coherent lyrical composition. Certain phrases are elevated to the status of chorus or refrain through repetition in the song. It requires great insight and ability to select phrases that go well together poetically and fit rhythmically over the tempo of the music— Boswell is a master of this particular skill. This technique is one of the signature characteristics of his music and usually what one remembers after listening to his songs. Notable instances of this occur in *A Glorious Dawn* when Sagan "sings" the line "A still more glorious dawn awaits and not a sunrise but a galaxy rise, a morning filled with 400 billion suns—the rising of the Milky Way," and Hawking "sings" "For thousands of years people have wondered about the universe . . . did it stretch out forever or was there a limit?" The words are so evocative and visually stimulating, allowing the listener to imagine the enormity of the cosmos, assisted and illustrated by carefully selected visuals from the source material. The remix begins with Sagan stating "I'm not very good at singing songs, but here's a try," then proceeding to "sing" various auto-tuned "whoop" and "aww" sounds, which are gradually revealed to form part of the percussive elements of the song as it progresses and builds to a crescendo. Newly composed and recorded piano and bass elements blend seamlessly with the sampled material to produce a truly exceptional and masterful piece of remix music and video art. This blending of disparate elements highlights the distinction between samples and recordings discussed in the previous section. The musical parts are recordings from life, as Boswell played the parts live and recorded his performance, as musicians do when recording a song in a recording studio. The "singing" parts are samples, appropriated from pre-existing recordings (the documentary series), and significantly manipulated to blend musically with the rest of the track. Boswell is a relatively unusual remix artist, in that many of his remixes were authorized, or in some cases commissioned, by the copyright holders of the material he sampled (i.e., Disney, PBS). However *A Glorious Dawn* and other remixes from the *Symphony of Science* series were not authorized by the copyright holders—they were "passion projects" created by Boswell because he felt strongly about the material he sampled and wanted to share it with the world, albeit in remixed form.

Perhaps the most widely debated issue in relation to sampling stems from an ethical question: how much can one sample from a copyrighted work without permission, if any? The majority of sample-based works are unauthorized; that is, produced without the knowledge or permission of the copyright holder of the original work from which the samples were appropriated. This is a difficult and contentious issue, primarily due to the existence of outdated copyright laws, which encourage a culture of unwarranted litigation between copyright holders, unnecessary censorship and legal threats against ordinary citizens. However, the reality is that every day millions of people ignore copyright law in order to create and publish innovative sample-based remix art and will continue to do so as long as the necessary tools, technologies and platforms remain available to them. Sampling, particularly in popular music, has unfortunately attracted a significant degree of negative media attention in relation to legal and ethical issues over the past 50 years. As Gunkel notes:

> The term "sampling", in whatever mode it is operationalized, focuses attention on an act of cutting, extracting, citing, and/or recording. For this

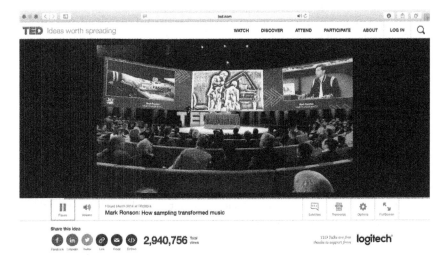

FIGURE 22.3 Screenshot from "How Sampling Transformed Music" (2014), depicting Mark Ronson remixing previous TED talks live in front of an audience.

reason, it is this word, more so than "collage", for example, that has become the privileged term in discussions and debates about intellectual property law and ethics, where such "borrowings" confront the limits of intellectual property law and the moral questions concerning plagiarism.[29]

DJ and music producer Mark Ronson, in his 2014 TED talk, "How Sampling Transformed Music," states with refreshing honesty, "In music we take something that we love and we build on it. I can't help it [. . .] there are these things that I love and I want to mess around with them"[30] (Figure 22.3). This is a very fitting synopsis of why remixers do what they do, in music, in film, in literature, in art and all media forms. Remix artists tend to feel strongly about the source material they sample from, whether they love it or hate it or whether they are saddened or angered by it, and they seek to somehow inject themselves into that particular cultural moment from which the sampled material is taken—to offer their own unique perspective. They wish to contribute in their own way to the ongoing global cultural conversation by sampling and remixing the dialogue.

Conclusion

In my own way, I have included many samples (appearing as quotes) in this chapter to outline the related processes of sampling and remixing and to differentiate them from one another as clearly as possible, while also highlighting the important distinctions between recording and sampling across various media. The fundamental act of sampling is the same in any media form; however, the language and effects produced by sampling in music, film, art and literature can be quite different. For many authors, sampling applies only to music. For others, sampling includes all forms of capturing media and even recording from life itself. The most accurate definition lies somewhere in-between these two extremes. In the past, medium specificity distinctions were more clear-cut because the technologies, platforms and formats were so different, and perhaps it made more sense to use alternate terms to describe appropriation in various forms. But now that all forms of media can be digitized, it makes sense that the term "sampling" can be applied to all forms of digital media, because the process of cutting, copying and pasting is essentially the same, albeit using different types of specialized software to sample text, image, audio and video.

Sampling should not extend its definition to include recording, however, because recording from life and sampling from an extant recorded artifact are fundamentally different activities that should not be confused with one another. The legal and ethical issues associated with sampling are discussed in detail elsewhere in this volume, however despite the current copyright problems associated with using sampled material in creative works, the production and consumption of remix art is more popular than ever and on the increase. The future looks bright for sampling and remix creativity. I will conclude with two of my favorite samples about sampling:

See Chapter 7, "Copyright/Fair Use," and Chapter 14, "Intellectual Property."

> You could say that all humans are sampling machines. We all learn by taking in what we hear and see and trying to imitate it, and output it again. That's how we learn to speak. That's how we learn to paint and make music as well.[31]

> [Sampling encourages] the kind of creativity that the technology has at its soul: the creativity, which you're going to see more of in music and film, the creativity of remixing other creativity.[32]

Notes

1 Lawrence Lessig, *Remix: Making Art and Commerce Thrive in the Hybrid Economy* (New York: Penguin, 2008), 53.
2 Authors who have defined "sampling" include Eduardo Navas; David Gunkel; Aram Sinnreich; Stefan Sonvilla-Weiss; David Laderman and Laurel Westrup; Kembrew McLeod and Peter Dicola.
3 *The A-Team* and *MacGyver* were both popular television shows produced by Universal and Paramount Television respectively, initially broadcast in the mid- to late 1980s, and subsequently aired regularly as reruns. They were famous for their instantly recognizable intro sequence theme music. Younger readers may be more familiar with the rebooted versions of the shows as a movie and TV series in 2010 and 2016 respectively.
4 OED via David Gunkel, *Of Remixology: Ethics and Aesthetics After Remix* (Cambridge, MA: MIT Press, 2016), 7.

5 Quoting Ad-Rock of the Beastie Boys, Laurel Westrup and David Laderman, *Sampling Media* (New York: Oxford University Press, 2014), 1.
6 Kembrew McLeod and Peter DiCola, *Creative Licence: The Law and Culture of Digital Sampling* (Durham, NC: Duke University Press, 2011), 36.
7 Stefan Sonvilla-Weiss, *Mashup Cultures* (Germany: Springer-Verlag, 2010), 9.
8 Eduardo Navas, *Remix Theory: The Aesthetics of Sampling* (New York: Springer-Verlag, 2012), 11–12.
9 David Gunkel, *Of Remixology: Ethics and Aesthetics After Remix* (Cambridge, MA: MIT Press, 2016), 9.
10 In relation to this point, consider such works as Sherrie LeVine's re-photographed series, "After Walker Evans" (1981) and Richard Prince's Instagram-inspired installation, "New Portraits" (2014). The difference in both of these cases, compared to what I refer to as the "sampling stage" of the remix process, is that they were both published—consciously presented to the public as works of art, even though there was no alteration or "composition" involved. In my analogy, sampling is akin to only selecting samples without doing anything with the selections (leaving them in a pile on the floor), i.e., not publishing them, not composing, recombining, remixing or even recontextualizing them. If one were to decide to publish the selections, even without altering them, then the act of presenting them as artworks would be, in my view, a second stage that takes place after the sampling process.
11 Eduardo Navas, *Remix Theory: The Aesthetics of Sampling* (New York: Springer-Verlag, 2012), 12.
12 Laurel Westrup and David Laderman, *Sampling Media* (New York: Oxford University Press, 2014), 3.
13 Eduardo Navas, *Remix Theory: The Aesthetics of Sampling* (New York: Springer-Verlag, 2012), 47–48.
14 David Gunkel, *Of Remixology: Ethics and Aesthetics After Remix* (Cambridge, MA: MIT Press, 2016), 8.
15 Aram Sinnreich, *Mashed Up: Music, Technology, and the Rise of Configurable Culture* (Boston: University of Massachusetts Press, 2010), 124.
16 Baz Luhrmann, writer/director, *The Get Down* (Bazmark Films and Sony Pictures Television, 2016).
17 Laurel Westrup and David Laderman, *Sampling Media* (New York: Oxford University Press, 2014), 4.
18 Eduardo Navas, *Remix Theory: The Aesthetics of Sampling* (New York: Springer-Verlag, 2012), 15.
19 Michael Moore, writer/director, *Where to Invade Next* (Dog Eat Dog Films and IMG Films, 2016).
20 Eduardo Navas, *Remix Theory: The Aesthetics of Sampling* (New York: Springer-Verlag, 2012), 11–12.
21 John G. Proakis and Dimitris K. Manolakis, *Digital Signal Processing: Principles, Algorithms and Applications*, 4th edition (New York: Pearson, 2006), 43.
22 Thomas Zawistowski and Paras Shah, *An Introduction to Sampling Theory* (Texas: University of Houston, 1992), www2.egr.uh.edu/~glover/applets/Sampling/Sampling.html.
23 Marc Cohen, *Theory of Forms* (Washington: University of Washington Philosophy Department, 2006), http://faculty.washington.edu/smcohen/320/thforms.htm.
24 An example of the perpetuation of this myth occurs in the opening sequence of Kirby Ferguson's 2010 mini-documentary, "Everything is a Remix," where he categorically states that "anybody can remix anything," "you don't even need skills," and "anybody can do it," https://vimeo.com/14912890.
25 John Boswell aka MelodySheep, *A Glorious Dawn* (YouTube.com, 2009), www.youtube.com/watch?v=zSgiXGELjbc.

26 Carl Sagan, *Cosmos: A Personal Voyage* (PBS, 1980), https://en.wikipedia.org/wiki/Cosmos:_A_Personal_Voyage.
27 Stephen Hawking, *Stephen Hawking's Universe* (PBS, 1997), https://en.wikipedia.org/wiki/Stephen_Hawking's_Universe.
28 John Boswell aka MelodySheep, *Symphony of Science*, www.symphonyofscience.com/about.html.
29 David Gunkel, *Of Remixology: Ethics and Aesthetics After Remix* (Cambridge, MA: MIT Press, 2016), 9.
30 Mark Ronson, "How Sampling Transformed Music" (TED.com, 2014), www.ted.com/talks/mark_ronson_how_sampling_transformed_music.
31 An Interview with Matt Black, founder of Coldcut via Kembrew McLeod and Peter DiCola, *Creative Licence: The Law and Culture of Digital Sampling* (Durham, NC: Duke University Press, 2011), 45.
32 Richard Koman, *Remixing Culture: An Interview with Lawrence Lessig* (OReilly.com, 2005), http://archive.oreilly.com/pub/a/policy/2005/02/24/lessig.html.

Bibliography

Boswell, John. *A Glorious Dawn*. 2009. www.youtube.com/watch?v=zSgiXGELjbc, accessed January 19, 2017.
Boswell, John. *Symphony of Science*. 2017. www.symphonyofscience.com, accessed January 19, 2017.
Cohen, Marc. *Theory of Forms*. Washington: University of Washington Philosophy Department, 2006, http://faculty.washington.edu/smcohen/320/thforms.htm, accessed January 19, 2017.
Gunkel, David. *Of Remixology: Ethics and Aesthetics After Remix*. Cambridge, MA: MIT Press, 2016.
Hawking, Stephen. *Stephen Hawking's Universe*. PBS, 1997.
Koman, Richard. *Remixing Culture: An Interview with Lawrence Lessig*. 2005. http://archive.oreilly.com/pub/a/policy/2005/02/24/lessig.html, accessed January 19, 2017.
Lessig, Lawrence. *Remix: Making Art and Commerce Thrive in the Hybrid Economy*. New York: Penguin, 2008.
Luhrmann, Baz. *The Get Down*. Bazmark Films and Sony Pictures Television, 2016.
McLeod, Kembrew and DiCola, Peter. *Creative Licence: The Law and Culture of Digital Sampling*. Durham, NC: Duke University Press, 2011.
Moore, Michael. *Where to Invade Next*. Dog Eat Dog Films and IMG Films, 2016.
Navas, Eduardo. *Remix Theory: The Aesthetics of Sampling*. New York: Springer-Verlag, 2012.
Proakis, John G. and Manolakis, Dimitris K. *Digital Signal Processing: Principles, Algorithms and Applications*, 4th edition. New York: Pearson, 2006.
Ronson, Mark. "How Sampling Transformed Music." TED.com, 2014. www.ted.com/talks/mark_ronson_how_sampling_transformed_music, accessed 19th January 19, 2017.
Sagan, Carl. *Cosmos: A Personal Voyage*. PBS, 1980.
Sinnreich, Aram. *Mashed Up: Music, Technology, and the Rise of Configurable Culture*. Boston: University of Massachusetts Press, 2010.
Sonvilla-Weiss, Stefan. *Mashup Cultures*. Germany: Springer-Verlag, 2010.
Westrup, Laurel and Laderman, David. *Sampling Media*. New York: Oxford University Press, 2014.
Zawistowski, Thomas and Shah, Paras. *An Introduction to Sampling Theory*. Texas: University of Houston, 1992. www2.egr.uh.edu/~glover/applets/Sampling/Sampling.html, accessed January 19, 2017.

23

TRANSFORMATIVE

Francesca Coppa and Rebecca Tushnet

The following chapter focuses on how transformative works in media fandom reflect and refigure the concept of "transformativeness" in copyright fair use law. We begin by framing the cultural context within which transformativeness began to mainstream as an idea, then move to a discussion of the legal concept, especially its focus on creating new meanings or messages. We then turn to how media fans creating fan fiction, fan video, and other fan works specifically deploy the concept, appropriating it for their own similar purposes but with a non-legal spin. The adoption of "transformative" as a label by the media fan community is itself an example of transformativeness in action.

"Transformative" in Context

In his recent book, *Thank You For Being Late* (2016), Thomas Friedman argues that we are currently living through "one of the great transformative moments in history."[1] He dates this era from 2007: the year of the first iPhone, the year Facebook and Twitter went global, the year Google bought YouTube, the year of the Kindle, the Android, Airbnb, and GitHub; the year "the cloud" was born and connectivity exploded. To this list we might add the 2007 founding of the Organization for Transformative Works (OTW), a nonprofit that has become a hub for the advocacy of fan works—fan fiction, art, video, film, crafts, etc.—as transformative fair uses.

In May of that year, a large group of fan work creators (including the both of us) came together to form a nonprofit corporation dedicated to providing access to and preserving the history of fan works and culture. After considering various alternatives (Fans for Fair Use, Coalition for Transformative Culture, Fandom Arts Network, etc.) the board decided to call the group the Organization for

Transformative Works, a name that was announced to the fandom community via LiveJournal on September 28, 2007 in a post called, "An Introduction to the Organization for Transformative Works." The response to the name was mixed at first, because the term *transformative* was new to some and off-putting or forbidding to others, with some fans claiming it was "an SAT word" that "just doesn't resonate with a fourteen year old or a sixteen year old";[2] that is, with the many younger fans who had come into fandom via the Internet.

That is not to say that the word was totally unfamiliar in fandom. In fact, *transformative* had begun to circulate in fannish "meta articles" (blog posts and essays written by fans about fandom itself) as fans began collectively to craft a defense of their creative activity in the face of fandom's greater, and rapidly growing, visibility. The idea of a *transformative use* had made its way into fan and remix studies from the *Campbell vs. Acuff-Rose* decision of 1994[3] in which the Supreme Court reversed a lower court's decision against 2 Live Crew's parody version of Roy Orbison's "Pretty Woman." The Supreme Court found the parody to be a transformative fair use: it was significantly altered in meaning and purpose. The idea of remix art and fan work as transformative work began to appear in legal works about fandom, to which we have also contributed Rebecca Tushnet's "Legal Fictions: Copyright, Fan Fiction, and a New Common Law" (1996) and Meredith McCardle's "Fanfiction, Fandom, and Fanfare: What's All the Fuss?" (2003). From there—or perhaps more accurately, from fans such as these who were also budding lawyers and interested in turning the tools of their profession on their fannish interests—the term began to trickle down into media fandom's own self-conception, and the term took on a kind of grassroots use.

Still, it took a while for the word to become mainstream, even among academics and lawyers. *Transformative* doesn't appear in Henry Jenkins's seminal work of fan studies, *Textual Poachers* (1992). In the introduction to the twentieth-anniversary edition of the book, however, Suzanne Scott claims that *Textual Poachers* is itself a transformative work, "much like the transformative fan texts at the center of Jenkins's study,"[4] even though Jenkins hadn't used the term. In 2008, the word transformative appears in Lawrence Lessig's *Remix* (2008), although only barely (twice, to be exact). Lessig uses the word only to distinguish between amateur appropriation for the purpose of remix (which he labels "transformative work") and amateur copying for the purpose of distribution. The word isn't central to his book, even as he advocates for an expansive concept of fair use.

Despite its absence from these semi-canonical texts, the word *transformative* was well on its way, working itself into and through various cultures of amateur creativity on the web. If opinion about the word was mixed in 2007, today the word is almost ubiquitous in fandom, even among the 14- and 16-year-olds who might be forgiven for finding legal jargon off-putting. Read through the notes sections beneath many YouTube fanvids and you'll see the disclaimers: "Transformative Work protected by Fair Use of copyrighted material," "A Peggy

Carter fanvid. (A transformative fan work.)," "[[this is a non-profit, transformative work as allowed under fair use]]."[5] Fans discuss their creations in terms of transformative work: "Don't ever let anyone tell you transformative work is a waste of time,"[6] and some offer their own transformative work statements, like this one on Fanfiction.net: "Anyone who wants to use my work as a basis for their own fanfic, fanart, podfic, translation, or other transformative work has my permission to do so."[7]

"Transformative" in Law

Under U.S. law, whether a fanwork or other instance of copying is fair use depends on four factors—(1) the purpose of the use, (2) the nature of the original work, (3) the amount of the original work used, and (4) the effect of the use on the market value of the original or its licensed derivatives. The concept of *transformativeness* comes from factor 1, the purpose of the use, which is often the most important. The more new meaning and message in the new work, or the more distinct the copier's purpose is from the purpose of the original, the more "transformative" it is likely to be declared, and fair use favors transformative uses. The Supreme Court has stated, "the goal of copyright, to promote science and the arts, is generally furthered by the creation of transformative works."[8]

Factor 1 also considers whether the use is commercial, but the more transformative the use, the less likely commerciality is to matter. Transformative works need not be free to be fair use, although fans whose primary experience of fandom is online sometimes believe this. Still, non-commerciality does help make the case, and a non-commercial fanwork will likely need less transformation than a commercial one to justify a fair use finding. Likewise, factor 2 considers whether the original work is highly factual or highly creative, but transformative uses often take highly creative works—such as science fiction TV shows and supernatural novels—as their jumping-off points, and thus factor 2 generally has less importance in a transformative use case. Moreover, courts consider whether a work has been previously published as part of factor 2, and a work that has inspired transformative uses is usually publicly available; the copyright owner has already had a chance to control publication and to receive a return for the work. It's very hard to argue, for example, that *Star Trek* hasn't had a decent bite at the apple, with five television series, 11 movies, and countless tie-in novels and other merchandise. In what conceivable way have transformative works hurt *Star Trek*'s bottom line?[9] Similarly, factor 3 asks whether the amount taken is reasonable in light of the purpose, and a transformative use may be justified in taking the "heart" of a work. Finally, factor 4 requires courts to understand and define the appropriate market for a work: one copyright owner's willingness to license critical reviews or parodies doesn't mean that reviews or parodies are within the market it has a right to control. In the current climate, content owners may try to control fandom by issuing "best practices" for fanworks or offering fans "a bill of rights," but it's not the IP holder who has the rights to offer or grant us. Fair use isn't their gift to us, and a highly transformative use is unlikely to interfere with the kinds of market opportunities to which the copyright owner has a right.

Transformativeness was a concept developed by a respected court of appeals judge, Pierre Leval, in an influential article in the *Harvard Law Review*, "Toward a Fair Use Standard."[10] It replaced earlier language in copyright fair use cases referring to "productive" use, generally referring to socially beneficial uses. Critics of "productive" use argued that copyright owners deserved to be paid even for socially beneficial uses, just as we would expect that owners of physical property should be compensated when it is used to benefit society, as a local government might condemn a patch of land to use as an airport. When a private party seeks to make a use that it thinks is socially beneficial—such as a shopping mall that might bring economic benefits to the area—we generally allow the current owner to decide whether or not they agree, and to demand their own price, even if would-be buyers think the price is too high. *Transformation* was an attempt to identify situations in which the copyright owner shouldn't, as a normative matter, have control. A key reason not to allow such control, Judge Leval argued, was that the defendant was making a *fundamentally different kind of use* than the plaintiff, and thus possessed a separate interest in presenting its own new speech to the world, without interfering with the incentives that led to the creation of the original work. Reviews and parodies, as well as some educational uses of works not created for use in schools, are classic examples of transformative uses.

It is within this context that legal scholars seized on transformativeness to describe the acts of fans. This concept sets up the authorial claims of people who are making transformative works as equal or not subordinate to the claims of other authors. If you are a fan and you write a new story about the adventures of Kirk and Spock, you are doing something that copyright law recognizes as worthwhile, even though you don't profit from the characters in the way Paramount Studios does. And if you write erotic fiction about Kirk and Spock, you are writing stories for a different purpose, and perhaps audience, than the original producers intended. There is no reason that they should control your work.

It is worth noting at this point that transformative is a concept that, in law, applies to the resulting works themselves, not to the process of remix or the effects of making remix on creators' own self-understandings, even though it's those things that often provide most of the value of remix in a non-legal sense. Copyright law looks at the work, not at the producer; 2 Live Crew could afford expensive lawyers and a fight all the way to the Supreme Court; Google has also won significant fair use cases, although it is more of a copyright Goliath than a David. Nonetheless, the concept of the "work" as an output of remix can also give dignity to fans who are making things, who are often culturally disadvantaged people, and who are regularly mocked for consuming the very things that mainstream culture has produced and asked them to like, from Star Trek to boy bands.

The current concept of transformativeness has been criticized by a number of copyright owners, and a few academics, for being too expansive. If current literary theory understandings of intertextuality are valid, after all, then perhaps every work should count as "transformative." Julia Kristeva remarks, "[a]ny text is constructed as a mosaic of quotations; any text is the absorption and transformation of another."[11] Fair use case law has struggled with this issue: where does cultural influence and intertextuality stop and transformativeness begin?

A recent court case found no transformativeness in one character's use of the classic comedy routine "Who's on First?" to entertain another character in a play; that use served the same entertainment purpose as the original. But a rewriting of the 1970s sitcom *Three's Company* to provide a much darker take on the stereotypical sitcom characters was transformative because of its skewed and jaded perspective, as was a staging of the screenplay for the cult classic Keanu Reeves film *Point Break* (1991) that featured randomly chosen audience members performing as Reeves, implicitly critiquing the acting in the original.

Courts have, perhaps surprisingly, had an easier time identifying a transformative purpose for exact copying—for example, the purpose of copying web pages to index them for a search engine is different than the original purpose of conveying whatever expression the pages were set up to transmit, so that kind of exact copying is fair use. This is why the courts ultimately found that the Google Books project, which scanned hundreds of thousands of books, was fair use. Transformation in content—changing the words, images, or video so that the audience has a different perceptual experience—will generally not be enough to count as "transformative" in fair use cases unless the use is somehow different in purpose or meaning. Courts are both uncomfortable playing at art criticism and inevitably drawn to it, given their general mission of interpreting texts (statutes, cases, and other written documents that make law).

See Chapter 7, "Copyright/Fair Use."

"Transformative" in Practice

Those of us interested in fair use as it pertains to creative work have paid close attention to legal cases featuring arguments about transformative works or uses. However, it's worth noting that in practice, most transformative works don't get near lawyers at all (except when those lawyers are themselves remixers or fans). Amateur transformative works are often left to circulate, especially if they're not for profit; many commercial transformative works are legally cleared and licensed, even though these professional creators also have a right to fair use.

Nonetheless, both amateur and professional works are sometimes involved in legal actions or chilled through cease and desist letters or algorithmic takedowns. Some of these cases are fought through online copyright dispute systems such as YouTube's or via the DMCA's counter-notification process. Other copyright disputes become lawsuits, although few lawsuits reach a decision: most are settled out of court. By examining a range of these cases and by focusing on particular examples, we can extrapolate the current state of transformative use: what's happening in practice, on the ground, legal theories notwithstanding.

Music and Transformativity

While *Acuff-Rose v. Campbell* put transformativeness on the map, much musical remix and sampling has been more or less forcibly brought into the market by means of licensing; in fact, 2 Live Crew had attempted to license the bit of "Pretty Woman" that they wanted to use but were rebuffed by Acuff-Rose. Professionals with deep pockets can afford to pay lawyers to clear samples regardless of the purpose of the use, but professional musicians who don't have money have had to more or less eschew sampling or beat-making as a practice, which many have argued has badly stifled musical innovation in hip hop. On the amateur side, YouTube's Content ID system now routinely scans the work of noncommercial or cottage industry artists, identifying and monetizing musical content used by grassroots creative types such as remix artists, amateur musicians, and fanvidders. This works well in many cases, and has effectively decriminalized a lot of popular musical creativity.

But just because a particular use was professionally cleared by lawyers or monetized on YouTube—or, for that matter, taken down by YouTube—doesn't mean that it was or wasn't a transformative use. Right now we have a system more based on the size of the deal and the power of the players than the justness of the claim. "Weird Al" Yankovic licenses the works he parodies, and Lin-Manuel Miranda cleared even tiny bits of music quoted in *Hamilton*, even though both are near-textbook transformative uses; presumably they didn't want the headache that comes with fighting for fair use. Seth MacFarlane had the deep pockets to assert his fair use rights via lawsuit—and win—when Disney refused him a license to parody "When You Wish Upon a Star" in *The Family Guy*. Yet the very phrase *license to parody* hurts us to type, and people who are not rich do not have the same options. Musical takedowns on YouTube or SoundCloud are more likely to be based on the whims and misunderstandings of IP holders than the merits of the fair use case, and while there continues to be a vibrant semi-underground scene of bootlegs, mashups, and user-generated music videos, some genuinely transformative uses of music are randomly suppressed or improperly monetized.

Remix Video and Vidding

But many fans, creators, and remix artists are aware of their fair use rights and willing to assert them when they make transformative works. Political remix vidder Jonathan McIntosh fought Lionsgate's 2013 attempt to monetize his "Buffy vs. Edward: Twilight Remixed" video.[12] McIntosh feels that the video, which critiques the gender politics of pop culture vampires by having Buffy the Vampire

Slayer dust Edward Cullen from *Twilight*, shouldn't be monetized with ads from Nordstrom's. In the end, even though McIntosh went through YouTube's elaborate copyright appeals process twice and made a strong case (including the fact that the video was shown at the U.S. Copyright office and name-checked in their 2012 DMCA exemptions for non-commercial remix) he still had to have lawyers from the nonprofit New Media Rights approach Lionsgate directly. Lionsgate's response was that they did not allow work they couldn't monetize, which not only goes against the law regarding transformative work but, as McIntosh notes, creates a world where "fair use will be ignored in favor of a monetizing model in which media corporations will 'allow' critical, educational and/or transformative works only if they can retain effective ownership and directly profit off them." In other words, a world in which we need a license to critique and dissent as well as parody, and in which satirists and critics shouldn't be able to earn a living from their work. McIntosh had to begin what can be, for amateurs, a daunting DMCA counter-notification process before YouTube restored his video online and de-monetized it.

Fanvidders have had similar problems keeping their work online, even when they agree to have it monetized, and even when, like McIntosh, they make work that has been explicitly recognized in various ways as transformative. In 2012, the OTW put up a Test Suite of Fair Use Vids in order to explain the various transformative aspects of vids. Vids are fan-made music videos created from the rhythmic editing of mass media footage to music. They are transformative in form, distilling hours (and sometimes days) of movies or television shows into three or four minute music videos; they are transformative in genre, typically substituting lyrical and poetic values for action-packed spectacle and plot; they are transformative in terms of content, proposing alternative readings and realities of the source material, many of which are critical or political either directly or by implication. Today's digital vidders tend to literally, materially transform the footage they work with: speeding it up, slowing it down, changing its color, cropping, zooming, and applying effects. These digital effects are often used to significantly change the emphasis of the footage, bringing background characters to the fore, isolating individual moments and altering their meaning. Thus, small elements such as the face of Captain America's childhood friend Bucky, at the edge of the frame in one scene in the original movie, become central to a vidder's interpretation of the bond between the two.

But even the vidders featured in the Test Suite, whose work has been celebrated and appreciated as fair use, have had trouble with takedowns of obviously transformative work. Some content matching systems stop people from uploading their videos based on the very fact of there being matching footage or audio, and the computer can't judge whether the use is transformative or not, and doesn't ask. Lim, a noted vidder whose work has appeared in shows on music video, mashup, and remix culture at venues such as the California Museum of Photography, the Museum of the Moving Image, and the Vancouver Art Gallery, wrote an essay on Content ID's effect on vidding aesthetics. She claims that "Content ID is an invisible hand, basically, promoting some kinds of vids and pruning others," and notes that technological factors are now guiding artistic decisions: "Winners: fast cuts, dissolves, FX, overlays, voiceovers, multis. Losers: long shots, hard cuts, no FX or soundwork." She concludes: "So you can see how, cumulatively, across a whole site and across a whole artistic community, this shapes the landscape. It controls what is seen, and what is not seen, and that changes vidding."[13]

Fanfiction and Textual Remix

There have been some interesting legal cases featuring literary remixes and transformative works. In terms of fictional retellings, Alice Randall's *The Wind Done Gone* (2001),[14] a rewriting of *Gone with the Wind* from the perspective of an invented mulatto sister of Scarlett O'Hara, was found to be a transformative use. Pia Pera, the author of *Lo's Diary* (1999),[15] a novel which retells *Lolita* from Lolita's point of view against a 1950s characterized not by kitsch but by the Cold War and the atom bomb, published her book after settling with the Nabokov estate for a 50/50 split of the profits; *60 Years Later: Coming Through the Rye* (2009),[16] a self-proclaimed "unauthorized sequel" to *Catcher in the Rye*, was published in the UK but banned in the U.S. The novel, which picks up the story of J.D. Salinger's Holden Caulfield (here dubbed "Mr. C") and sends him to confront J.D. Salinger himself, was hoist on the petard of having called itself a sequel, with a judge ruling that its most transformative element—the confrontation between character and author—was more a comment on Salinger's personal idiosyncrasies than on his novel or its most famous character.

We can see from these professional literary cases that the degree of transformativeness in textual remix matters a great deal, which bodes well for the great majority of fanfiction, a genre written primarily by women, which often makes radical transformations of the text. These include slash and other forms of queering, the gender and race-swapping of characters, the insertion of supernatural elements such as vampires, soul-bonds, and magic into texts where they don't originally appear, a gendered preoccupation with details of domesticity, caregiving and other emotional work (including pregnancy and even male pregnancy), and a drawing out of themes of sex and power. In *The Fanfiction Reader: Folk Tales for the Digital Age* (2017), Francesca Coppa has curated a selection of transformative tales in a range of fandoms. These stories showcase many of fandom's most transformative moves. For example, in "Lunch and Other Obscenities,"[17] fan author Rheanna imagines Uhura's first days at Starfleet Academy and gives her the female friends and classmates she never had in *Star Trek*; in Astolat's "Queen of Spades,"[18] Judi Dench's M both seduces and mentors James Bond; in "The Vacation,"[19] Kaneko imagines the members of boyband NSYNC having an existential crisis when they are replaced by humanoid performing robots. These literary moves both enrich and critique the original source material.

Conclusion

Despite critiques of the expansiveness of transformativeness offered by courts and commentators, fans still need and use the concept to understand themselves and their works. Actual practice can inform our ideas of what constitutes a transformative change in meaning, message, or purpose. Concepts change as they drift from one field to another, and from experts to laypeople; transformativeness is no exception to this process of transformation. When Suzanne Scott claims that reading Henry Jenkins's *Textual Poachers* was "a transformative professional moment"[20] for her personally, we see the legal term begin to blend with its use in the literature of education and social justice, where a transformative work is one that brings about a revolution in society or the self: enlightenment, change, or social justice. Fandom's use of transformativeness may have always had that seed of meaning inside of it, where to transform a text is to make space for new ways of seeing and new ways of reading, and in that way, to transform the self and the world.

Notes

1 Thomas Friedman, *Thank You for Being Late* (New York: Farrar, Strauss, and Giroux, 2016), 29.
2 Partly bouncy, comment to the otw_news Livejournal post, September 29, 2007.
3 Campbell v. Acuff-Rose Music, Inc., 510 U.S. 569, 579 [1994].
4 Suzanne Scott, "Textual Poachers, Twenty Years Later," in *Textual Poachers* by Henry Jenkins (New York: Routledge: 2013), vii.
5 See the notes for "Kiss With A Fist," www.youtube.com/watch?v=sDNXrXbrSRE, "Peggy Carter: Secret Agent," www.youtube.com/watch?v=6YrzKBgMncw and "Geronimo" www.youtube.com/watch?v=ozROaURH24Q, accessed February 21, 2017.
6 See "Live Magically," http://cursed-druid-girl.tumblr.com/post/146684436494/dont-ever-let-anyone-tell-you-transformative-work, accessed February 21, 2017.
7 See the profile for Fox in the Stars on Fanfiction.net, www.fanfiction.net/u/131343/Fox-in-the-Stars, accessed February 21, 2017.
8 Campbell, 510 U.S. at 579.
9 However, a recent court ruling found that a Kickstarter-funded fan film, dedicated to being as canonically accurate as possible, was not fair use, in part because of its commerciality, in part because it continued the Star Trek story in a standard way rather than commenting on it, and in part because the high visual quality made it possible that the fan film would substitute for authorized versions.
10 Pierre Leval, "Toward a Fair Use Standard," 103 *Harvard Law Review* 1105 (1990).
11 Julia Kristeva, "Word, Dialog and Novel" in *The Kristeva Reader*, ed. Toril Moi (New York: Columbia University Press, 1986), 37.
12 www.youtube.com/watch?v=RZwM3GvaTRM.
13 Lim, "Notes Toward ContentID's Effects on Vidding: fx, cut-styles, technique, genre," https://limblogs.tumblr.com/post/145865736496/notes-towards-contentids-effects-on-vidding-fx, accessed February 21, 2017; post locked to tumblr users only.

14 Alice Randall, *The Wind Done Gone* (New York: Houghton Mifflin Harcourt, 2001).
15 Pia Pera, *Lo's Diary* (New York: Foxrock Books, 1999)
16 John David California, aka Fredrik Colting, *60 Years Later: Coming Through the Rye* (Windupbird Publishing, 2009).
17 Rheanna, "Lunch and Other Obscenities," in *The Fanfiction Reader: Folk Tales for the Digital Age*, edited by Francesca Coppa (Ann Arbor: University of Michigan Press, 2017), 23–46.
18 Astolat, "Queen of Spades," in *The Fanfiction Reader*, 126–134.
19 Kaneko, "The Vacation," in *The Fanfiction Reader*, 105–119.
20 Suzanne Scott, "Textual Poachers, Twenty Years Later," viii.

Bibliography

Coppa, Francesca. *The Fanfiction Reader: Folk Tales for the Digital Age*. Ann Arbor: University of Michigan Press, 2017.

Fox in the Stars. Profile. Fanfiction.net., www.fanfiction.net/u/131343/Fox-in-the-Stars. Accessed February 21, 2017.

Friedman, Thomas. *Thank You For Being Late*. New York: Farrar, Straus and Giroux, 2016.

Jenkins, Henry. *Textual Poachers: Television Fans and Participatory Culture*. New York: Routledge, 1992 and 2013.

Kristeva, Julia. "Word, Dialog and Novel" in *The Kristeva Reader*, ed. Toril Moi. New York: Columbia University Press, 1986, 34–61.

Lessig, Lawrence, *Remix: Making Art and Commerce Thrive in the Hybrid Economy*. New York: Penguin, 2008.

Leval, Pierre. "Toward a Fair Use Standard," 103 *Harvard Law Review* 1105, 1990.

McCardle, Meredith. "Fanfiction, Fandom, and Fanfare: What's All the Fuss?" *Boston University Journal of Science Technology & Law* 9(2), 2003.

McIntosh, Jonathan. "'Buffy vs. Edward' Remix Unfairly Removed by Lionsgate." *Ars Technica*, January 9, 2013. https://arstechnica.com/tech-policy/2013/01/buffy-vs-edward-remix-unfairly-removed-by-lionsgate/. Accessed February 21, 2017.

Newton, Matthew. "Is Sampling Dying?" *Spin*, November 21, 2008. www.spin.com/2008/11/sampling-dying/. Accessed February 21, 2017.

otw_news. "Introducing the Organization for Transformative Works." *LiveJournal*, September 28, 2007. http://otw-news.livejournal.com/9256.html. Accessed February 21, 2017.

Tushnet, Rebecca. "Legal Fictions: Copyright, Fan Fiction, and a New Common Law," 17 *Loyola of Los Angeles Entertainment Law Journal* 651, 1996.

24
VERSIONING

*Paul D. Miller aka DJ Spooky
with Eduardo Navas*

This chapter is an exercise in versioning. It is different from other chapters in that it is not an academic text that focuses on delineating the history of a particular term. Instead, it is a *versioned* reflection on how basic elements that inform remix are at play across music culture and the politics of race and ethnicity. This contribution punctuates the social, technological, and cultural dimensions of this book on keywords in remix studies at the time of publication. It consists of two parts that focus on how sampling, remixing, and versioning are at play in both music and politics. The first part is a version of a reflection by Paul D. Miller juxtaposing Melania Trump's 2016 plagiarism of Michelle Obama's 2008 Democratic Convention speech with a May 31, 2016 court ruling against Kraftwerk, who sued for unauthorized sampling of one of their music compositions.[1] The second part is the transcript of a conversation, that took place between Paul D. Miller and Eduardo Navas on January 11, 2017. In Part 2, Miller discusses with Navas the complexities of remixing, sampling, and versioning in relation to the issues raised in Part 1.

Part 1: The Politics of Appropriation and Plagiarism

The main issue I want to highlight here is that public speech/public expression in the political domain is of the national discourse around originality, authenticity, and what it means to use other people's words and creative expression in the public domain. To make a point on this, I first focus on Michelle Obama's 2008 speech, which was plagiarized by Melania Trump in 2016 to discuss how remixing, sampling, and versioning are part of an unprecedented knowledge-based economy.

What's the difference between Melania Trump's speech at the Republican National Convention in summer 2016 and Michelle Obama's speech from the Democratic Convention in late summer 2008? The answer: almost nothing. The eerie situation in our postmodern info-overloaded culture is that within minutes of Melania Trump's plagiarism airing live on every possible media outlet, there was a direct confrontation with the fact that her speech contained material directly copied from Michelle Obama's speech. The basic premise was a critique of plagiarism from people all over the world using the web. That's a good thing.

We live in a knowledge-based economy that is unprecedented in human history. Knowledge requires sharing. There is no question that the copyright industries have been blocking and undermining pro-user reforms for decades. The Internet is built modularly, and it grows rapidly because people with all levels of knowledge copy code and share resources. Digital music, in terms of versioning and remixing, is made in the same manner. Imagine this: on a fundamental level, as packets of data are sent through the fiber optic cables and satellite transmissions that hold the modern world together, they are copied from one ISP to another and by the time they reach the "end-user" the data has been replicated many times. This is how we use the Internet: Users constantly send copies over the network, whether partial fragments, edits, or entire pieces. This is a "problem" only if copyright is viewed as a form of fixed property ownership that gives content creators the power to prevent copies from being made and transmitted. Amusingly enough, this simply means that everyone, every day, is breaking the various laws of copyright, as an informal aspect of everyday culture.

But what makes lifting entire parts of a speech and presenting them as one's own justifiable, given that there is much discussion about everything being made of pre-existing elements? And how is this different from basic information sharing? To make a point on this, it is worth evaluating a court case that took place just a few months before Melania Trump's plagiarism.

First, the basics. In Germany and all over the world, Kraftwerk is one of the leading forerunners of electronic music and hip hop. From Afrika Bambaataa's "Planet Rock" on over to the scratch routines and computer-influenced sounds of almost any song in twenty-first-century music, their impact is undeniable. After more than ten years, the Bundesverfassungsgericht (the Supreme German Constitutional Court) overturned a lower court's ban on a song that used a two second sample of a Kraftwerk recording.[2] In 1997, Moses Pelham used a clip from Kraftwerk's 1977 song "Metall auf Metall" in a song he produced entitled "Nur Mir" (Only Mine) that was sung by Sabrina Setlur. Ralf Huetter, the lead singer for Kraftwerk sued Pelham and in 2012, he won a case for copyright infringement in Germany's Bundesgerichtshof (Federal Court of Justice). He won damages and a block on further distribution of "Nur Mir." Pelham and his team appealed the decision. After years of being batted around the German legal system, on May 31, 2016, eight judges of the First Senate of the Federal Constitutional

Court decided that the lower court did not consider if the impact of the sample on Kraftwerk might be "negligible."

What makes the ruling consequential, in the European Union and beyond, is the basic premise that all music is iterative and involves building on previous songs, lyrics, and rhythm patterns. *To me, everything is connected.* All stories are worth sharing. All ideas are part of the collective base of humanity's quest to better understand the world. That means any creative artist can and should be able to look at the commonly held ideas of "artistic freedom" as a series of building blocks.

All innovation is built on previous innovations: the way we live now and the way laws are written have parted ways. Why? Because copyright was conceived 300 years ago in an analog world where objects were scarce and copies were easy to detect and police. Imagine trying to hide a printing press! In the twenty-first century, creativity has been democratized and it's no longer under the control of specialists.

Creativity now is a reflection of the messages we send, the videos we upload and the comments made on articles, published online and across social media—a version itself of an earlier reflection on politics and music. What makes the Kraftwerk versus Pelham copyright dispute interesting for this context is that Pelham took a short sample, and looped it, without much editing and without engaging Kraftwerk. Appropriation is as old as language itself. It does not ask permission and it never gives permission. It is basically creativity as a verb—not as an adjective. It is continuous and unrelenting; and it often leads to versions of all types. A sample is a collision between context and content. It is a fragment taken out of context and juxtaposed wherever the artist wants to put it. Imagine if you had to clear the rights for every piece of a collage? So, too, with remixing, versioning, and sampling online in the twenty-first century, we must consider the impact of rights management. In a world of copies, an "original" is an atavistic throwback to a time when the fiction of individual creativity was a norm. We've moved from "genius" to "scenius," as Brian Eno once said.[3]

What happened between Kraftwerk and Pelham is more than a simple copyright infringement issue. It was a collision between value systems based on whether people can think of music simply as music, or music as an information system, which, in terms of our focus here, can be repurposed as versions and remixes. Norbert Wiener, the mathematician who coined the term "cybernetics," made a fitting observation at the dawn of the information age after World War II, that, "Progress imposes not only new possibilities for the future, but new restrictions."[4] His insight was meant to show that information requires structure and redundancy, and that innovation requires rules. The issue with these terms is the question of how we define content and form, which in terms of media also implies context.

Marshall McLuhan theorized in *Understanding Media: The Extensions of Man* that a light bulb was a great example of the collision between content and context. In comparison to digital media production, a light bulb doesn't have content in the way a magazine has articles or a television has programs; but it is a medium with a social effect, a light bulb allows people to create dimensionality. It creates spaces out of darkness. McLuhan thought of the light bulb as a medium without content: "a light bulb creates an environment by its mere presence."[5] When a sample is implemented, it also creates an environment, and that environment is often a version of one that came before. Is a record a document that can generate other documents (recordings and versions) or a static dead space in the culture where it was made?

So, where does the lawsuit between Kraftwerk and Pelham end? Not in the courtrooms of the government, but in the hearts and minds of people who use digital media every day in every aspect of our information and data driven society. The algorithms that drive all aspects of Internet culture are just as much a part of a larger collision between code and culture as the computer systems and hardware that are the backbone of the twenty-first century information society. Where the judges of the Bundesverfassungsgericht observed "artistic freedom" as an aspect of the ability to sample previously made "found sound," one could argue that the merits of being able to look freely through the collective archive of digital society is just as much a part of that essence of freedom.

Perhaps Nietzsche was on to something when he wrote a manifesto looking at some of the same ideas about freedom and restraint in his 1881 opus *Morgenröthe—Gedanken über die moralischen* that "the real world is much smaller than the imaginary."[6] To me this means that sampling, collage and the infinite possibilities of remix culture in terms of versions outweigh the original objects, songs, and artworks in the archive of digital media. They, in turn, are all reflections of the infinite possibilities that are available to us if we can update our vision of copyright law. That is the new freedom, perhaps, implied by the judges of the Supreme German Constitutional Court.

Part 2: Sampling, Versioning, and the Hip Hop Component

Eduardo Navas (EN): In your essay, you discuss Melania Trump's speech at the Republican National Convention in 2016 in relation to Michelle Obama's speech at the Democratic Convention of 2008. You frame their situation in terms of a well-established postmodern awareness to explain that there was almost nothing different in parts of the speech by Mrs. Trump. Basically, she was accused of plagiarizing by diverse communities across the Internet, yet while you make this argument directly in your essay, this is not the issue you emphasize but rather use it to point to the cultural conflicts that arise when repurposing content with emerging technology, due to our understanding of originality and copies. Based on this, could Melania Trump's speech be a type of "versioning"?

Paul D. Miller (PM): Let's clarify a couple of situations here. First Melania Trump absolutely appropriated Michelle Obama. And we have to be careful about language here when we discuss appropriation, plagiarism, and versioning. Versioning usually implies a sort of homage to an already established song or what they call track. And what happened with Melania Trump versus Michelle Obama is if it wasn't homage, it was a full-scale appropriation. The key issue at hand, and the key frame—I'm using the term "frame" in that it was a deeply cultural negative dialectic—was that what Melania Trump, as Donald Trump's wife, did was perform publicly according to the Trump platform. That is, to denigrate people of color to create a dynamic about Asians, Mexicans, African Americans, and other non-white ethnic groups. I think most people who have followed politics in the past few years would agree that Michele Obama is an incredible speaker, which only would demand of anyone considering her as a possible source for a speech of their own to acknowledge her work. This is quite important in contemporary politics because appropriation without respect or homage has been part of American culture over the centuries. Those in power have incorporated African American culture on so many levels that at this point they might as well call it the American subconscious. So I think that is something with a very clear relationship to power and the ability to appropriate within a broader dynamic of intellectual exchange, what Jean-Paul Sartre would call bad faith, in French *Mauvaise foi*.

So to me, at least, when Melania Trump does that, she points out the deep hypocrisy of white "appropriation" of African American culture. At the same time, her performance was a deeply important political moment because appropriation in that context is extremely inappropriate, when we consider that Donald Trump's platform was anti-immigration, disrespectful of people of color's contribution to society and, above all, racist. What Melania Trump's speech exposes is America's longstanding history of cultural appropriation in the form of plagiarism.

It shows a deep degree of intellectual poverty on the part of Melania Trump. Now, that being said, I also think that this notion of intellectual poverty is really fascinating because I'm someone whose entire practice is based on sampling, so it's difficult for me to condemn someone for "plagiarism"; but what I can do— and am doing—is pointing out the cultural dynamic of a situation in which someone appropriates someone else's work without any cultural engagement at all. There is no respect; there is no sense of homage or kind of looking at those sources of inspiration and giving them new life. It's just an act of taking. And that, to me, is an impoverished use of sampling.

EN: You also write about appropriation in relation to respect. So in a way you see appropriation as you explain now, and as you also mention in your essay, as an almost subversive act to some degree. Basically what you are saying now is that within appropriation there is an element of resistance that may lead to critical commentary, but based on what you are saying now about Melania Trump, this is not what is going on at all with her because she is just taking Michelle Obama's speech and pretending that it was hers, right?

PM: Right, and so in terms of art, for instance, I'm a big fan of Andy Warhol; I'm a big fan of Jeff Koons; so, I understand appropriation in a fine arts context. But the specific political context of appropriation, of specifically African American culture in the United States, from Elvis to the Beastie Boys to Melania Trump, is that there are important differences to point out. For instance, the difference between Elvis and the Beastie Boys is that the Beastie Boys would at least pay respect or homage to their sources. And I think that's what makes an archive a living document. If you look at Wikipedia, it's a living document that is changing everyday as people add new information and edit; the editing is an art form in itself. But with someone like Melania Trump, what is very different from the Rolling Stones, to give another example, or even Elvis—he would acknowledge that his music came from African American culture. And here we are talking about music, and literature; we're also talking about political, economic and social dynamics in the society at large.

EN: So you see plagiarism and appropriation intricately connected in a way but it has to do with this difference of acknowledging how you are appropriating something to create something new or in a new context maybe as homage as you're saying, yes?

PM: I believe so. And don't forget that I appropriate every day, all of the time. I sample. I'm no hypocrite here. I want to be clear about that!

EN: In relation to this, you do mention in your essay how even language is a form of appropriation. We're taking words and repurposing them to make our own sentences.

PM: But that does not give someone like Melania Trump a free pass.

EN: In relation to this, you mention the German court case ruling against Kraftwerk as an example of sampling and its eventual relation to versions at the end of your essay. Interestingly enough the court ruled that the sample followed fair use practice. So in a way these issues we are discussing are defined in large part by the copyright industry, and it appears that basically what you are saying is that plagiarism would be an issue regardless of how copyright is written. Do you think that the way we understand intellectual property is at play, working against our understanding of the plagiarizing that Melania did? Do you think this would be seen differently if we had different copyright laws; these issues of lifting Mrs. Obama's speech?

PM: Let's put it this way, imagine if the appropriation had been in a different direction. If Michelle Obama had "appropriated" from Melania Trump— the Republicans within that power dynamic would have gone insane. You would hear all types of negative recourse. Everybody would go crazy, they would say, "she's intellectually lazy," or, "African Americans don't study." They would make every possible hypocritical statement they could. But I also think that in the case of Kraftwerk, specifically, you have to remember that they have a legacy, they have a long history of influential music at every level in the global electronic culture overall. So taking from that, let's look at this idea of the commons. If someone has become part of the basic fabric of society and the way that we think about electronic music, it's the equivalent of folk culture, which is much more about open sharing and everyone using that as a building block to forge a better, stronger culture. And I'm OK with that. I do feel that the Kraftwerk case really brought home the fact that these people who had been so innovative actually don't know the legacy they created, which is kind of funny.

EN: The other thing that you mention in relation to Kraftwerk is the idea of genius to scenius. One thing that contemporary discussions about remixing, versioning, sampling, mashups, and so on, often expose is that we do borrow from previous things that are flowing in culture. So, if we begin to use the term that Eno proposes, how would you say we would view individual work in relation to collectivity? The issue of authorship and versioning is implicated here as well.

PM: First, the West has a pathological relationship to authenticity and truth. Truth is a kind of reactionary definition here because whoever has enough power to create a political and economic structure and enforce it has "truth." So as an example, with Donald Trump in this last election, the whole relation to authenticity went out the window, and I'm really intrigued how that set the tone for the entire election cycle. On the other side of the spectrum you have to remember, truth creates this idea of a scarce resource. It's actually much harder to create truth or authenticity than to fake it. Fakeness is kind of open-ended: anybody can do anything, no problem, but then how do you create criteria for judgment? How do you decide what is good and what is bad? Those are all issues that I think are metaphysically tied to our current moment, which is that we don't have criteria for judgment, and perhaps we should politically, socially, and economically accept that there is no one way anymore. And what this means is that intellectual property and creative issues are tied to power, finance, and the ability to enforce the law versus the actual way we live, which is about sharing and appropriation. It's about all these issues, which expose that whoever has enough power and money can set the tone. If I have a huge navy and a huge army then I'm an emperor. But if I don't have a huge navy and I'm just kind of a guy running around taking stuff, then I'm a pirate.

EN: Those are interesting points. In terms of all this you also mention that there is a clash of value systems at play in how sampling is perceived. In terms of versioning, this was already seen in the early dub compositions that were coming out of Jamaica in the 1970s. Along these lines, I was wondering if you could elaborate on the relationship of value systems. In your essay you mention Wiener to argue that we should see music not as it is commonly understood and consumed but as a system of information. At the same time, how do we balance the clash of cultural values when we start to see content or what we share or consider our own as information, or a system of information because when we do that, as you know Claude Shannon for example, was not focused on content itself when he was trying to isolate noise from moving packets from one end to the other, which you also mention in your essay; he was not concerned about what was being passed, in terms of the content, but he just wanted the content to get moved from point A to B effectively. So if we take your evaluation of the clash of values and we start looking at music, or any content for that matter, on such terms as well as how that is a system of value information as you state, how can we balance the complexities of race and plagiarism at the beginning of your essay? I think that is a conundrum that can be played up by those who do not want to admit that what Melania Trump did was illicit.

PM: Let's look at this from the point of view of economics. You have to remember that economics is the glue that holds our global society together. I really think that if we are honest with ourselves, we moved deeply into an information-based economy and information is now part of the currency of how we think about what we think is authentic, what is valid. If you look at the whole issue of fake news, for example, versus an authentic song or an inauthentic song all of it is propaganda. All of it is fake, where do we draw the line? And who draws the line? Those are all things that we should be clear and careful about as we move further into the twenty-first century. So what previous eras would have described as propaganda, or would have set as a kind of scenario where they had defined the king's law, or this or that, is really because they had enough power to enforce that. That's it.

And so I think right now we are realizing as we move into the twenty-first century is that truth, I mean there is a very semiotic Roland Barthes approach here. But I also want to call out the Frankfurt School here, in particular Max Horkheimer's essay titled *The Eclipse of Reason*.[7] It's about this idea of post-rational aesthetics. How do we really engage with the idea, with the notion of rationality and subjectivity that is tied to the nation-state; that's a really big deal. I think that as we move further and further into the twenty-first century, we must ask who has the ability to determine truth and authenticity? Is it Digital Rights Management (DRM) of the mind? And that is going to be much more a play on people like Antonio Gramsci's ideas of power and communication. Gramsci is one of my favorite theoreticians precisely because he really understood early semiotics. And if you ever think about his critique of the state, it's a very powerful idea right now; the state is a component of media—not like the media is the component of the state.[8] But it's actually turned upside down. And media and music are part of that dynamic today.

EN: These issues you have raised in terms of value systems as you just explained, reminds me of Trump's slogan in relation to versioning, specifically in terms of testing sounds on the people at the dancehall. As we know, versioning functions just like remix, anybody can implement them for any agenda, and in a way, Trump's slogan, or campaign byline if you prefer to call it that, was "Make America great." Then, he literally versions it with the word "again," to present a nostalgic, misplaced, throwback of "Make America Great Again." And for me it's very interesting how basically he has taken all of these elements that are celebrated in remix culture and repurposes them into a type of demagoguery in order to combine sound bites that he was able to reposition without substance. In a way, he is really, truly unoriginal. And he's really versioning, sampling sound bites from things that people heard which are familiar that then those listening at rallies react to, and may say or think, "Oh yeah, that sounds familiar. I'll go with that." So it flips the testing of sounds from the dancehall to political rallies the other way.

PM: There is a hip hop component to the way Donald Trump speaks. And kind of intriguing if you think about the development of memes and the way someone like Richard Dawkins would talk about repetition and the idea of mimetic processes unfolding in a social context.[9] Trump is a perfect example of the use of public space. And you talk about versioning; what he normally does is he tries out phrases on an audience and sees what works and then he starts repeating them enough so that they become a modular component. These phrases function like building blocks that become core components, repeated throughout a building. So he is not what we would consider a lyrical person, but what he does works to an extent for people in a particular dynamic—for his specific demographic, it works. I tend to be very skeptical of anything that is a broad indictment on any subject because, guess what? Everyone is hyper-relative. And I'm a big fan of relativism as a core component of the twenty-first century. I mean, letting go of this idea of totalizing frameworks is the best thing and healthiest thing we can do right now. There is no central narrative, and any idea that claims one is grounded in a twentieth century mentality. Now that might be a controversial statement, but I'm OK with that.

Notes

1 An earlier version of the essay that is Part 1 appeared on Monopol on September 28, 2016, www.monopol-magazin.de/random-variable-generator. The current version has been edited with a focus on versioning itself.
2 "Kraftwerk Lose Legal Battle Over Their Music Being Sampled," *The Guardian Online*, May 31, 2016, www.theguardian.com/music/2016/may/31/kraftwerk-lose-legal-battle-over-their-music-being-sampled.
3 A contextualization of this process is found in Kevin Kelly "Scenius or Communal Genius," *Wired*, June 2008, www.wired.com/2008/06/scenius-or-comm.

4   Norbert Wiener *The Human Use of Human Being* (London: Free Association Books, 1989), 46–47.
5   Marshall McLuhan, *Understanding Media: The Extensions of Man* (Cambridge, MA: MIT Press, 1964), 2.
6   Friedrich Nietzsche, *Daybreak: Thoughts on the Prejudices of Morality* (Cambridge: Cambridge University Press, 2003), 12.
7   Mark Horkheimer, *The Eclipse of Reason* (Eastford, CT: Martino Fine Books, 2013).
8   For Gramsci's major ideas see Antonio Gramsci, *Selections from the Prison Notebooks* (New York: International Publishers, 1971).
9   Richard Dawkins, *The Selfish Gene* (Oxford and New York: Oxford University Press, 2006).

INDEX

Figures are shown by a reference in *italics*.

Actor Network Theory (ANT) 36, 37, 184, 262
Adorno, Theodor 126, 253, 254
Agamben, Giorgio 70
Albers, Josef 16
amateur production: consumer/producer inequalities 129–30; DIY culture as 125–7, 128, 137; as participatory democracy 125–7, 222; self-production via social media 130–1; *see also* fan culture; fan edits
Amerika, Mark 109–10, 251
Amoy, Sian 148
Andrejevic, Mark 129
appropriation: and authorship 15–16, 21; creation of a third meaning 16–17, 20; cultural appropriation 15, 20; defined 15; digital archives and 21–2, 27–8; as empowerment 14–15; fan edits 19; historical practices 58; intergenerational 19; Kraftwerk lawsuit 284–5, 288–9; of mass culture 126; Melania Trump's appropriation of Michelle Obama's speech 284, 286–8; and originality 18; vs. plagiarism 20–1, 283–4, 287–8; play and creation 17–18; in a political context 287, 288; practice of 16–17; recontextualization of referents 17–18
Arcangel, Cory 95–6, *96*

archives: appropriation and digital archives 21–2, 27–8; definition 23, 25; functions 24; historiography and 30–1; online access 28–9; physicality of 25; remixed museum exhibitions 26; social memory and 24–5, 30; wunderkammern as 25–6
Aristotle 36
art: amateur production 57; collaboration vs. solo creation 58–9; commodification of creative expression 56–8; *see also* pop art
audiences: commodification of 129; convergence culture and 129–30
Aufderheide, Patricia 163
authorship: and appropriation 15–16, 21; Aristolian 36; artistic authority debates 141; authorcentric copyright laws 160; authority of 37–8; body writing 48; collaboration vs. solo creation 58–9; concepts of 33; copyright laws 59–60; cut-up techniques (Beat movement) 105; Enlightenment era 36–7; Homeric notions of 34–5; originality 37–8; ownership of works 36; Plato's theory of mimesis 35–6; post-authorial concepts 37–9, 61; and remix 33, 39; Romantic era 37, 60; on social media platforms 64

Bakhtin, Mikhail 99, 217–18, 220
Barbie Liberation Organization (BLO) 150
Barthes, Roland 37–8, 39, 59, 61, 105–6, 197–8
Benjamin, Walter 39, 57, 70, 121
Bennett, Andrew 34, 35, 37–8
Bhabha, Homi 180–1, 185
Born, Georgina 184, 185
Boswell, John (MelodySheep) 266–8, *267*
Bourriaud, Nicholas 70, 72–3
Breitz, Candice 126, *127*, 136–7
bricolage: as action 47–9, 51; adaptation by women 48–9; definition 43–4; as epistemology 45–7; hypertexts 50; within ideological constructs 48; as product 49–50; and remix 50–2
Burgess, Jean 125
Burroughs, William 105, 107, 110–11

capitalism: cultural production within 20, 30; DIY culture as counterculture 127; industrialization of creative process 56–7; visual pollution of 70
Clinton, Hillary 220, *221*, 236–7
collaboration: etymology 60; prevalence of term *61*
collaborative: collaboration vs. solo creation 58–9, 61–2; and cooperativism 64–5; etymology 56, 58, 60–1; and the industrialization of creativity 56–7, 61; prevalence of the term *61*; and remix culture 62–3; on social media platforms 64
commonplace books 106–7
concrete music 93–4
consumerism: brands and remix 75–9; brands as religion 70–1, 75; consumer manipulation 72; global-scale advertising 68; hyper-consumerism 70–1, 76; pop art and brand iconography 67, 68–70, *68*; production-consumption nexus in digital culture 62; recycled design 72–5
container concept 181–2
convergence culture 129–30
Coppa, Francesca 280
copyright: American copyright laws 60, 85, 86, 159; as authorcentric 160; concept of solo creation 59–60; and concept of transformativeness 276–8; Content ID systems 89, 278, 280; copyright policies 84; corporate monopolies 84–5; and creativity 87–8, 90–1; cultural conflicts and 284–6; digital copying 284; Digital Millennium Copyright Act (DMCA) 88, 90, 140, 160, 277; fair use 86, 162–4, 248; fair use and transformative works 86–7, 275–8; fair use risk assessments 87–8; fan edits 139; Kraftwerk lawsuit 284–5, 286, 288–9; lawsuits 277–8; licenses to parody 278; mashups 193; monetization and fair use 279; origins of 285; overriding clauses 84; overview of 83; within remix culture 85–6, 88, 248; and sampling 268–9, 270; takedown policies 88–9, 90, 140, 277, 278; Test Suite of Fair Use Vids 279; user rights 84, 86, 90–1; *see also* intellectual property
copyright trolls 161
crafting communities 233–4
Creative Commons 3, 29, 85–6, 164, 248
creativity: abstract compositional practices 94–5; authenticity and power structures 289, 290; code bridging through remix 101–2; commodification of creative expression 56–8; and copyright laws 87–8, 90–1; in the digital era 285–6; extended remixes 96–7, *97*; fan edits and artistic authority debates 141; as modern-day problem solving 92–3; reflexive remixes 98–101, *100*, 102; relational activities 95–6, *96*; selective remixes 98–9, *99*, 102; and transformative works 93–4, 96–7, *97*, 274–5; using heterogenous samples 95; using homogeneous samples 95, 97, 99; vernacular creativity 125–6
culture: container concept and 181–2; cultural acupuncture 238; cultural appropriation 15, 20; cultural hybridity 180–1; essentialist theories 181; fandom and cultural consumption vs production 136–7; within industrial capitalist societies 20; location of 178; place-bound cultural identities 180–1, 182; as practice 184; *see also* mass culture; participatory culture
culture jamming 237–8
cut-up: commonplace books 106–7; computer/algorithm generated texts 108; cut-copy-paste functions 107, 109, 248; cut-up method (Beat movement) 105; cut-up techniques 104–5;

détournement 220; dialogic parody 218; and human subjectivity 110–11; intertextuality 105–6; patch-writing 109–10; as performative act 110–11; permutation poems 105, 108; political commentary 222; and remix theory 108–9; technological developments and 107–8; vidding 110
cyberfeminism 150–1
cyborg remixes 149

Danger Mouse (DJ) 116, 121, 192–3, *192*
Dawkins, Richard 69, 202, 291
Debord, Guy 220
deconstruction: binary opposition in 118; conceptual emergence 119–20; double science of 119; *The Grey Album* (Danger Mouse) 116, 121, 192–3, *192*; practice of 117–20; remix as 120–2; and remix theory 115–16; term 115, 117, 119–20
Deeb, Hadi Nicholas 36
deep remixability 251
Deleuze, Gilles 252, 254
democracy: amateur production as participatory democracy 125–7; political remix parody 222
Derrida, Jacques 44, 115, 117–18, 121, 122
Dery, Mark 118
digital culture: consumer/producer inequalities 62, 129–30; convergence culture and 129–30; data transmission 284; emergence of 62; labor and corporate exploitation 63; and location 180; mashups 193–4; sampling in 264–5; transformative era (2007) 273
DIY culture: as amateur production 125–7, 128, 137; as appropriation of mass culture 126; consumer/producer inequalities 129–30; as a counterculture 127; feminism within 127–8; hierarchies of power within 128; mashups 193–4; punk movement 127; self-production via social media 130–1
DJ culture: *The Get Down* (Luhrmann) 263, *264*; and remix culture 179; sampling 262, 263; use of the turntable 170
DJ Spooky (Paul D. Miller) 109, 120, 249, 286–91
Driscoll, Catherine 127–8
Dyer, Richard 225

Eclectic Method 194, *195*
Electronic Dance Music (EDM) 224, 225
Elsayed, Yomna 234–5, *234*
Emerson, Ralph Waldo 120–1
Eno, Brian 285, 289
essentialism 181
ethics 2–3, 64

fan culture: cultural consumption vs cultural production 136–7; Organization for Transformative Works (OTW) 273–4; vids 279; *see also* amateur production
fan edits: appropriation and 19; artistic authority debates 141; *Batman v Superman* 135–6, *135*, 215, *215*; cinema remixes 137–9; copyright and fair use 139; distribution channels 140–1; Imminent Ned meme 215, *215*; Internet Fanedit Database (IFDb) 139–40; *Mad Max: Black & Chrome* (nuxwarboy) 140–1; online communities 139, 140; *The Phantom Edit* (Nichols) 137–8, *138*, 139; production technologies 139; *Raising Cain: Re-cut* (Gelderblom) 141–2; *Star Wars: Fall of the Jedi* (Monaghan) 142–3; video editing project file sharing 142–3
feminism: avatars 153; Barbie Liberation Organization (BLO) 150; cinema and the male gaze 153; counter-narratives 151–2; cyberfeminism 150–1; cyborgian feminist theory 150; *Distaff [Ain't I Redux]* (Amoy) 148; embodiment 153; feminist remix 147–8; feminist remix nodes 154–5; femmage (collage) 149; "GashGirl/ Doll Yoko" (da Rimini) 151; interactive applications 152–3; intersectionality analysis 151; mass culture vs. subculture girl bands 127–8; net art 150, 152, *152*; ORLAN 150; photomontage and female bodies 149–50; *Project Everyone* (remix) 147, 149, 154; vidding 152; video game remixes 153–4
film: fan edits 135–6, *135*, 137–8; location and remix in 180; and mainstream culture 128; the male gaze 153; movie trailer parodies 218–19; *The Phantom Edit* (Nichols) 137–8, *138*, 139
Fisher, Carrie 202–3, *203*

Foucault, Michel 38–9, 59, 61
Friedman, Thomas 273

Gelderblom, Peet 141–2
globalization: consumer advertising 68; copyright monopolies 84–5; global intellectual property order 161–2
Google 87, 163, 276, 277
Gordon, Douglas 96–7
Grace, Topher 141
Gramsci, Antonio 290
Graw, Isabelle 14
The Gregory Brothers 194–5
The Grey Album (Danger Mouse) 116, 121, 192–3, *192*
Gunkel, David J. 39, 251–4, 261, 262, 268–9
Gysin, Brion 105

Haraway, Donna 149, 150
Herbert, Matthew 185
hip hop 161
Höch, Hannah 149
Homer 34–5
Horkheimer, Max 126, 290
hyper-consumerism 70
hypertexts 50

Instagram 164
intellectual property: concepts of 158–60; ethical considerations 164–5; global intellectual property 161–2; individual vs corporate interests 160–1; and information commodification 159–60; remixed music and 2–3; in the US Constitution 159; US court rulings on 162–3; World Intellectual Property Organization (WIPO) 161–2; *see also* copyright
intersectionality theory 151

Jamaican music 189–90, 247, 263
Jameson, Fredric 225
Jaszi, Peter 59, 88
jazz culture: academic jazz culture 172; Amazing Slow Downer (ASD) 169, 174; the Berklee sound 173–4; improvisation from record listening 169–70; looping and tempo alteration method 168–9, 170; non-mechanical playing 171, 172; Play-A-Long records 169, 172–3; quoting 171–2; reflexive performances 173; regressive practices 173; remix technologies 174–5; repetition in 170–1, 173; Stretch Music app 169, 174–5; the turntable as a tool 168, 169–70; "two-five, lick, insert" technique 171
JazzAdvice.com 170
Jenkins, Henry 129, 136–7, 222, 230–1, 249, 281
Jensen, Peter Kragh 218

Kearney, Mary 128
Kember, Sarah 110
Kincheloe, Joe L. 46, 50
Kligler-Vilenchik, Neta 235
knowledge-based economies 284
Koons, Jeff 19, 288
Kraftwerk 284–5, 286, 288–9
Kreisinger, Elisa 147–8
Kristeva, Julia 105, 198, 277
Kruger, Barbara 149–50

labor: collaborative 58; creative expression as 56–7; cultural production within remix culture 63; intellectual property as ideological instrument 160–1
Laderman, David 261–2, 264
Land, Chris 105, 107, 110–11
Lawrence, Jennifer 214, *214*
Lenhart, Laura 37
Lenz, Stephanie *88*, 89–90, 162
Lessig, Lawrence 3, 19, 87–8, 126, 137, 248, 259, 274
Leval, Pierre 87, 276
Lévi-Strauss, Claude 43–4, 47, 49
Lim 279–80
Lipovetsky, Gilles 70, 72
location: container concept 181–2; and hybridity 180–1, 185, 186; place naming 182–3; of remix culture 178, 179, 180, 183–4, 185–6; schizophonia 180, 186; of sound 179–80; the Third Space 181, 185
Locke, John 36
Lord, Albert 34–5
Lozano-Hemmer, Rafael 27–8
Luhrmann, Baz 263, *264*

MacFarlane, Seth 278
MacKay, Megan 99–101, *100*, 102
Mandiberg, Michael 17
Manovich, Lev 249, 251
Martín Lucas, María Belén 48, 50
mash down 190, *190*

mashup memes 194–5
mashups: copyright and 193; definition 188–9; digital technologies and 116, 193–4; and DIY culture 193–4; "Donald Duck Meets Glenn Beck in Right Wing Radio Duck" (McIntosh) 98–9, *99*, 198–9, 221; *The Grey Album* (Danger Mouse) 116, 121, 192–3, *192*; in Jamaican culture 189–90; musical mashups 191–3; significance in 198; software mashups 195–7; term 188–90, *189*; as third meaning 197–8; "U2" (Negativland) 191–2, *191*
mass culture: cultural commodification and DIY culture 125–7; as non-participatory 232
McCoy, Kate 45
McIntosh, Jonathan 98–9, *99*, 102, 198–9, 278–9
McLuhan, Marshall 285–6
Media, Activism, and Participatory Politics (MAPP) 233
mediation theory 184–5
MelodySheep (John Boswell) 266–8, *267*
memes: Bernie or Hillary meme 236–7; Bernie vs. Trump meme 237, *237*; *Civil War* meme 206, *207*; definition 202; *Downfall* parodies 195, 210–11, *211*; *Drei Klavierstücke op.11* (Arcangel) 95–6, *96*; *Dumb and Dumber* 211, *211*; graphic design memes 240–2, *241*, *242*; The Gregory Brothers 194–5; Imminent Ned 215, *215*; insider memes 213–15; Jennifer Lawrence as representation of identity 214, *214*; Koi Dance (Love Dance) 204–6; *La Carta Postal* 206–7, *208*; La Paz, Bolivia zebra 206, *206*; mashup memes 194–5; no-nosing 235; *Øystein og jeg* 210, *210*; as parody 210–11; political memes 202–6, 238; *The Princess Bride* 207–9, *209*; Princess Leia and the Women's Marches 202–3, *203*; the pussyhat 203, *204*; re-popularization of culture 212–13; to rewrite culture 206–9; rickrolling 212–13, *213*; *The Treachery of Images* (Magritte) 213–14, *213*; "Vaping in the gender neutral bathroom" 205, *205*; *You on Kazoo* 212, *212*
memory 24–5, 30

Metz, Christian 101
Miller, Paul D. (DJ Spooky) 109, 120, 249, 286–91
mimesis 35–6
Monaghan, Scott 143
museums: as archives 24–5; museological methods 26; online databases 28–9; open museums 29; remixed exhibitions 26
music: copyright trolls 161; genre documentaries 250; hip hop litigations 161; as information system 285, 290; Jamaican music 189–90, 247, 263; music mashups 191–3; punk movement 127; recycling 250; Riot Grrrl bands 127–8; sampling 262; Spice Girls 127–8; *see also* jazz culture; remixed music

Navas, Eduardo 39, 107, 109, 178, 260, 265
Negativland 191–2, *191*
net art 150, 152, *152*
Nichols, Mike J. 137
nuxwarboy 140–1

Obama, Barack 219–20, 223
Obama, Michelle 284, 286–8
open museums 29
open-source culture: in museums 29; video editing project file sharing 142–3
Organization for Transformative Works (OTW) 88, 273–4, 279
ORLAN 150

parody: dialogic quality 99, 217–18; parody/pastiche differences 225–7; *see also* remix parody
participatory culture: defined 230; fandom within 232, 249; political practices in 230–2; traditional folk culture 232
participatory politics: amateur production and 125–7, 222; Birdman slaps Trump 238, *240*; civic engagement 238, 242–3; within crafting communities 233–4; cultural acupuncture 238; culture jamming 237–8; emergence of 231–2; "Game of Trump" 230; genres of participation 236–7; graphic design memes 240–2, *241*, *242*; group activism 242; humorous remixes 234–5, *234*; Learning About

Multimedia Project (LAMP) 242;
Media, Activism, and Participatory
Politics (MAPP) 233, 234, 238;
methodology of and top-down
persuasion tactics 238–9; within a
participatory culture 230–2; political
memes 202–6; political remix parody
219–25; practices of 243; remix and
243; role of shared cultural capital
235–6; "Sanders" 238, *239*; "Your
Drunk Neighbor: Donald Trump"
234–5, *234*; Youth and Participatory
Politics (YPP) 232–3; youth
participation in 232–3, 234, 242–3
pastiche remix 225–7
patch-writing 109–10
Pelham, Moses 284–5, 286, 288–9
Pence, Mike 240–2, *241*
photomontage 149
plagiarism 20–1, 262, 283–4, 287–8
platform cooperativism 64
Plato 35, 120
political culture: appropriation in a
political context 287, 288;
Melania Tump's appropriation of
Michelle Obama's speech 284,
286–8; *see also* participatory politics
pop art: brand iconography 68–70, *68*,
76–8; images of consumerism 67
post-colonialism: bricolage of the Other
48, 49; place-bound cultural identities
180–1
posthumanism 151
postmodernism: and the collaborative 61;
concepts of authorship 37–9, 61;
intertextuality (cut-up method)
105–6
Potolsky, Matthew 35
Prince, Richard 163, 164
printing press 36, 37, 57, 262
production: consumer/producer
inequalities in DIY culture 129–30,
160–1; production-consumption nexus
in digital culture 62

recordings: jazz improvisation from
169–70; and the location of sound 180
Redman, Joshua 171, 172
reflexive remixes: and creativity *100*, 102,
173; in jazz culture 173
religion (brands as) 70–1, 75
remix: alternative terms 251–2; and
authorship 33, 39; brands and
consumerism 75–9; and bricolage 50–2;
and cultural change 11; cultural
relevance of 246; definition 33, 34, 83,
115–16; and Platonic repetition 251–4;
relationship with sampling 261; term
247, 253
remix culture: as aggregation of multiple
mediations 184–5; and the collaborative
62–3; copyright within 85–6, 88, 248;
corporate takedown policies and
copyright 88–9, 140; current condition
of 162; emergence of 2, 248–9; and the
free sharing of ideas 3–4; open-source
culture 29; term 179
remix parody: "Candidate Obama
Debates President Obama on
Government Surveillance." 219–20,
223; "China All the Time" (Bombs
Away) 222–5, *224*; citation recognition
and pastiche 225; dialogic quality 218;
"Donald Duck Meets Glenn Beck in
Right Wing Radio Duck" (McIntosh)
98–9, *99*, 198–9, 221; "Donald Trump
Says 'China'" 223; "I Have a Scream"
remixes 222–3; within the larger media
ecology 223–5, 226–7; licenses to
parody 278; movie trailer parodies
218–19; political commentary 219–25;
"Pretty Woman" (2 Live Crew) 274,
278; "Shining" trailer (Ryang) 218–19,
219; Trump/Pence campaign logo
240–2, *241*; "Vote Different" remix
220, *221*
remix studies: documentaries 250;
emergence of 2, 246; scholarship
249–50
remix videos: "Buffy vs. Edward: *Twilight*
Remixed" (McIntosh) 198, 278–9;
"Donald Trump in *Mean Girls*."
236, *236*; feminist 99–101, *100*, 152,
153–4, 155; *Feminist Frequency* (website)
154; *A Glorious Dawn* (MelodySheep)
266–8, *267*; monetization and fair
use 279; political 98–9; "Ray Rice
Inspired Makeup Tutorial" (MacKay)
99–101, *100*, 102; sampling in 264–5;
Too Many Dicks in Video Games
(Sarkeesian) 154; video editing
project file sharing 142–3; *see also*
participatory politics; remix parody;
vidding
remixed music: abstract compositional
practices 94–5; concrete music 93–4;

Electronic Dance Music (EDM) 224, 225; evolution of 2; heterogenous samples 95; homogeneous samples 95; intellectual property rights 2–3; mediation and agency in 184–5; *Project Everyone* (remix) 147, 149, 154; remix culture and 179; rise of 247; sound objects 93–4; vaporwave 225–6, *226*; *see also* mashups
remixology 251–2
remixstudies.com 3–4
repetition: in jazz culture 170–1, 173; remix and Platonic repetition 251–4
Riot Grrrl bands 127–8
Rojas, Peter 138
Rollins, Sonny 171, 172
Ronson, Mark 269, *269*
the Roots 190, *190*
Rose, Tricia 249, 254
Ryang, Robert 218–19, *219*

sampling: as an art 266–8; as citation 262; and copyright 268–9, 270; definition 260–1, 270; DJ culture 262, 263, *264*; historical practices of 261–5; impoverished (Melania Trump) 284, 286–8; Kraftwerk lawsuit 284–5, *286*, 288; in literature 262; recording vs. sampling 265–6; as respiration 262–3; as synonymous with remix 261; and technological developments 263–5; in video remixes 264–5
Sarkeesian, Anita 154
Schaeffer, Pierre 93
Schafer, Murray R. 180, 186
Scholz, Trebor 64
Scott, Christian 174–5
Scott, Suzanne 281
Serroy, Jean 70
Shannon, Claude 290
Simpsonwave 225–6, *226*
simulationism 68, 69
Sinnreich, Aram 83, 249, 262–3
Smits, Helmut 75, *76*
Smyth, Adam 106–7
social media: female users 129, 148; individual authorship 64; recycling 249–50; self-production and DIY culture 130–1; software mashups 197; youth participatory politics 233
Soderbergh, Steven 141
software mashups 195–7
Sonvilla-Weiss, Stefan 260

sound: recording 265–6; schizophonia 180
Spice Girls 127–8, 147, 154

technologies: and cut-up methods 107–8; Digital Millennium Copyright Act (DMCA) 88, 90, 140, 160, 277; and evolution of remix 247–8; for fan edit production 139; jazz remix technologies 174–5; mashup digital technologies 116, 193–4; printing presses 36, 37, 57, 262; and sampling 263–5; the turntable in jazz 168–70
textual remixes 280–1
transformation, creative 93–4, 96–7, *97*
transformative: creative works as 274–5; fair use and copyright 86–7, 275–8; fanvidders and fair use 278–80; literary remixes 280–1; Organization for Transformative Works (OTW) 273–4, 279; term 274
transformativeness 275, 276–7
Trump, Donald: Birdman slaps Trump 238, *240*; "China All the Time" (Bombs Away) 223–5, *224*; "Donald Trump in *Mean Girls*" 236, *236*; "Donald Trump Says 'China'" 223–5, *224*; election debate parody videos 231–2; no-nosing meme 235, *235*; "To Trump Trump's Wall" 242; Trump/Pence campaign logo 240–2, *241*; Trump/Putin logo *242*; versioning of campaign slogan 291; "Winter is Trumping" 230, *231*; "Your Drunk Neighbour: Donald Trump" (Elsayed) 234–5, *234*
Trump, Melania 284, 286–8
2 Live Crew 274, 278
Tzara, Tristan 104, 105, 106

United States of America: concept of intellectual property, US Constitution 159; copyright laws 60, 85, 86, 159

vaporwave 225–6, *226*
Veal, Michael 249
Vellis, Phil de 220, *221*
versioning 287, 291
vidding: cut-up method 110; defined 279; fanvidders and fair use 278–80; feminist practices and 152; Test Suite of Fair Use Vids 279; *see also* fan edits; remix videos

video mashups *see* remix videos
Vimeo 140–1

Warhol, Andy 26, 288
Weick, Karl 47, 49–50
Westrup, Laurel 261–2, 264
Wiener, Norbert 285
Wilf, Eitan 172, 173–4
Wilson, Fred 26
Wolman, Gil 220
women: amateur production within DIY culture 128; bricolage activities 48–9; commonplacing activities 106; Princess Leia and the Women's Marches 202–3, *203*; *see also* feminism
Woodmansee, Martha 37, 59
Woolf, Virginia 48

World Intellectual Property Organization (WIPO) 161–2
wunderkammern 25–6

Yang, Emilia 242
Young, Lester 168, 169
Youth and Participatory Politics (YPP) 232–3
YouTube: Content ID systems 89, 278, 280; fan edits 140; female self-production on 131; makeup video tutorial formula subversion 99–101, *100*, 102; takedowns (Digital Millennium Copyright Act (DMCA)) 88, 90, 140

Žižek, Slavoj 67, 71, 72
Zylinska, Joanna 110